Teaching Music
in the Secondary Schools
Second Edition

THE WADSWORTH MUSIC SERIES

MUSIC LITERATURE

English Folk Song, Fourth Edition by Cecil J. Sharp
The Musical Experience, Second Edition by John Gillespie
The Musical Experience Record Album by John Gillespie
Scored for the Understanding of Music — Supplemented Edition by Charles R. Hoffer and Marjorie Latham Hoffer
Scored for the Understanding of Music Record Album by Charles R. Hoffer
Talking about Symphonies by Antony Hopkins
The Search for Musical Understanding by Robert W. Buggert and Charles B. Fowler
The Understanding of Music, Second Edition by Charles R. Hoffer
The Understanding of Music Enrichment Record Album by Charles R. Hoffer

MUSIC FOUNDATIONS

Basic Concepts in Music by Gary M. Martin
Basic Resources for Learning Music, Second Edition by Alice Snyder Knuth and William E. Knuth
Foundations in Music Theory, Second Edition with Programed Exercises by Leon Dallin
Introduction to Musical Understanding and Musicianship by Ethel G. Adams
Music Essentials by Robert Pace

MUSIC SKILLS

Advanced Music Reading by William Thomson
Basic Piano for Adults by Helene Robinson
Intermediate Piano for Adults, Volume I by Helene Robinson
Intermediate Piano for Adults, Volume II by Helene Robinson
Introduction to Ear Training by William Thomson and Richard P. DeLone
Introduction to Music Reading by William Thomson
Keyboard Harmony: A Comprehensive Approach to Musicianship by Isabel Lehmer
Keyboard Skills: Sight Reading, Transposition, Harmonization, Improvisation by Winifred K. Chastek
Master Themes for Sight Singing and Dictation by Winifred K. Chastek
Music Dictation: A Stereo-Taped Series by Robert G. Olson
Music Literature for Analysis and Study by Charles W. Walton
Steps to Singing for Voice Classes by Royal Stanton

MUSIC THEORY

Harmony and Melody, Volume I: The Diatonic Style by Elie Siegmeister
Harmony and Melody, Volume II: Modulation; Chromatic and Modern Styles by Elie Siegmeister
A Workbook for Harmony and Melody, Volume I by Elie Siegmeister
A Workbook for Harmony and Melody, Volume II by Elie Siegmeister

MUSIC EDUCATION

A Concise Introduction to Teaching Elementary School Music by William O. Hughes
Exploring Music with Children by Robert E. Nye and Vernice T. Nye
Music in the Education of Children, Third Edition by Bessie R. Swanson
Singing with Children, Second Edition by Robert E. Nye, Vernice T. Nye, Neva Aubin, and George Kyme
Teaching Music in the Secondary Schools, Second Edition by Charles R. Hoffer

Teaching Music
in the Secondary Schools
Second Edition

Charles R. Hoffer
Indiana University

Wadsworth Publishing Company, Inc.
Belmont, California

Designer: Gary A. Head

Editor: Victoria Pasternack

Photo on page 124 courtesy of Joel Mathias, Bloomington
High School South, Bloomington, Indiana.

ISBN 0-534-00230-7

L. C. Cat. Card No. 72-96823

Printed in the United States of America

1 2 3 4 5 6 7 8 9 10—77 76 75 74 73

to my mother and father

Preface

This book is written for those who plan to teach or are now teaching music in the secondary schools. It seeks to cover in a practical, thorough, and comprehensive way the things that a music teacher needs to know and do in order to be effective. It is designed to help the prospective teacher explore and understand the challenges of what sometimes deceptively appears to be the simple job of teaching music. In addition, this book may stimulate experienced teachers to compare and try different ways of teaching, and to take a new look at some old problems.

In several respects the second edition of *Teaching Music in the Secondary Schools* differs significantly from the first edition. The arrangement of chapters has been revised to answer more directly the essential questions involved in teaching: Why teach music? What should be taught in music classes and rehearsals? Who is being taught? How can the content best be presented? How does a teacher assess the results of his work? This grouping provides a clearer idea of the various aspects of teaching. The opening chapter lays a foundation for the book, the second chapter deals with the personality and training of the music teacher, and the final chapter discusses the profession of music education.

The second edition delves into a number of areas that have become increasing concerns of the profession since the first edition was published nine years ago. Now an entire chapter is devoted to curriculum, and another to the evaluation of learning in music. New topics include teaching musicianship in the rehearsal, developing fine arts and humanities courses, and encouraging positive attitudes toward music in the students. Changes in the contemporary school scene have necessitated updating, especially in the discussions of teacher education, teenage behavior, learning principles, creativity, public performances, and resources for teaching musical styles and interpretation.

Several features of the first edition have been retained in the second. There is an emphasis on practical suggestions and realistic situations, as well as an attempt to make the writing clear and alive, reproducing as much as possible the "feel" of actual teaching. Theoretical and practical considerations are fused whenever possible, because each aspect is valuable and each influences the teaching of music.

I am grateful to the many people who encouraged and enlightened me in my efforts to be a teacher and writer. Citing a few names here would not be fair to the greater number who would not be mentioned. I can only thank them as a group, therefore, and hope that this is adequate. Specific recognition is due Indiana University for the use of its libraries. I also wish to acknowledge the following persons for their reviews of the first edition and/or the manuscript of the second edition: Charles H. Benner of the University of Cincinnati, Clifton A. Burmeister of Northwestern University, Mary E. English of State University College at Potsdam, Robert E. Nye of the University of Oregon, Mrs. Rodney Witte of Concordia College, and Wolfgang Kuhn of Stanford University.

Finally, I thank my wife, Marjorie, for her valuable suggestions and excellent editorial work.

Charles R. Hoffer

Contents

1   So You're Going to Teach Music 1

2   The Complete Music Teacher 9

Section One   Why Teach Music? 31

3   The Reasons For Music in the Secondary Schools 33

Section Two   What: The Subject Matter of Music 51

4   The Music Curriculum 53

5   Managing The Music Curriculum 81

Section Three   With What Result: Feedback 105

6   Evaluating the Results of Instruction 107

Section Four   To Whom: The Students 125

7   Teenagers: Their Manner and Motivation 127

8   Guiding Student Behavior 151

Section Five   How: The Methods of Teaching
                           Music   175

 9   Guidelines for Teaching Music   177
10   The General Music Class   199
11   Teaching Music in the Rehearsal   243
12   Teaching Musical Style and Interpretation   293
13   Achieving Correct Intonation   319
14   Singing and Teenage Voices   337
15   Teaching Instrumental Music   369
16   Music Appreciation, Fine Arts, and Theory
                           Courses   403
17   School Music Performances   429
18   The Profession and Progress   459

Appendix A   Code of Ethics with Professional Musicians   469
Appendix B   Ohio Code of Ethics with Music Merchants   473
Appendix C   From "Some Remarks on Value and Greatness
                           in Music" by Leonard B. Meyer   475
Appendix D   Teacher Rating Form   481
Appendix E   Adjudication Forms   487
Index   491

Teaching Music
in the Secondary Schools
Second Edition

1

So You're
Going to Teach Music

A person who chooses to teach music in the schools has selected a profession that is interesting, worthy, and challenging. Certainly few would maintain that the subject of music lacks variety or interest. Nor would anyone say that the modern American adolescent is a dull type of *homo sapiens*. Music, and especially teaching music to young people, is to be esteemed, for it involves transmitting a significant part of Western culture to younger generations. The prominence of music in contemporary society and the need for music instruction in the schools make music education an area deserving a teacher's best efforts, and a field meriting the respect of society and educators in general.

Teaching music in the schools is challenging because it requires a wide spectrum of abilities. A successful music teacher needs more than innate musicianship, more than "a way with youngsters," more than good training for the work he undertakes. He needs all three—plus the imagination and intelligence to apply his talents creatively to his particular teaching situation. Music teaching is not for the prosaic, the lazy, or the faint of heart.

What Is Music?

A simple question. Or is it? Can a cruel dissonance be music? What about the crash of a cymbal or an eerie sound from a tape recorder? Why is the boom of a bass drum considered musical, while a sonic boom from a jet airplane is regarded as noise? The difference depends on whether the sounds are organized. *Music is organized sound.* If a boom from any source is part of an organized sequence of sounds, then it qualifies as music. Otherwise it is random noise.

Music is a human activity created for people who perceive organized sounds as interesting and psychologically valuable. Music is not ordained by cosmic laws, so a search for the perfect chord or melody is bound to be a fruitless venture. Instead people create sounds that seem orderly and satisfying *to them.* Because people vary, music varies from time to time and place to place.

This human creation known as music is immense and complex. Not only does the world of music include all the music that man has created — folk, symphonic, instrumental, vocal, dance, electronic, opera, chamber, rock, and much more — but it also encompasses all associated activities such as music reading, performance, listening, theory study, composition, improvisation, musical criticism, and so on.

The vastness of the world of music forces every teacher to make choices about what to teach and how to teach it. The definition of music as organized sound provides a clue to the most important responsibility of the music teacher. Students in music classes should learn to perceive, contemplate, and appreciate organized sound. This learning often involves active manipulation of the sounds themselves, either through performing existing music or creating new music.

Sometimes teachers emphasize one aspect of music so much that other aspects are virtually ignored. For example, some teachers stress almost exclusively the techniques of performing. Their students play or sing but have little understanding of what they are doing. In other cases experiencing sound has been slighted because the teacher is more interested in presenting facts about music. Factual information has its place, but without some relation to musical sounds, facts are as useless as leaves fallen from a tree.

In this book you will be urged to make your teaching musical and to preserve the validity of the subject matter. This admonition does not mean that you should sing instructions to your classes (although in some respects that is not a bad idea). Rather, it means that your teaching should relate factual learning and technical skills to musical sound. For example, it is unmusical to ask a student to practice triple tonguing on the B flat major scale, or to figure out key signatures without also helping him to apply these achievements to actual music.[1]

The nature of music determines how it should be taught. Defining music as organized sound is not a philosophical gambit; it is a basic, practical consideration in the teaching effort.

What Is Teaching?

Essentially a teacher is a person who organizes and presents a subject in such a way that students learn it. He executes a process — the transmission

---

[1]The tradition of unmusical drill apparently dies hard, especially in eastern Europe. The author once observed a Bulgarian youth choir practice solfège exercises for nearly an hour without singing one phrase from a musical work! Occasionally similar emphasis on drill has been observed in this country, but fortunately never to that degree.

to the students of some skill or knowledge that they did not have prior to the class. Teaching produces changes in the students; it results in new meanings, knowledge, and skills.

Teaching is *not* just dispensing facts; the process is not complete unless learning takes place. A teacher cannot be like a letter carrier, who fulfills his job simply by delivering mail to the correct address. The letter carrier does not care whether or not the bill he delivers is paid. The teacher, in contrast, must follow through until the desired learning occurs. Teaching effectiveness, then, is defined primarily by the students' learning, rather than the actions of the teacher. A person may exhibit charm and good looks, lecture brilliantly, manage the classroom well, and use the latest teaching methods, but if no learning takes place in his students he has not succeeded as a teacher. A teacher is known by what he *does* (he brings students new and greater understanding) and not by what he *is* (a musician or a charming personality).

The teacher's job involves some duties other than teaching — checking out instruments, taking attendance, keeping order in the classroom. Many of these duties are important and necessary, but they are not really part of the process of teaching. One can be tops as a classroom manager and attendance taker and still not be a successful teacher.

The Ingredients of Music Teaching

Remembering the definitions of music and teaching, let's examine the "ingredients" that go into the process of teaching. They can be listed in five simple questions: (1) Why? (2) What? (3) To whom? (4) How? (5) With what result? Because these questions cover the essential elements of the teaching process, they form the basic outline of this book. Each will be developed briefly in this chapter.

Why?

The answer to this question is the basis for all subsequent thinking about teaching. A teacher's goals and reasons for teaching are like the rudder of a ship — they set the direction and provide guidance. Without answering the question "Why teach music in the schools?" little progress can be made in answering the subsequent questions of "What," "How," "To whom," and "With what result."

Different answers to the question "Why?" lead to different actions. A teacher who views school music primarily as a source of entertainment for the public will teach quite differently from one who tries to give his students a rich understanding of the subject. The two teachers will select different types of music, teach different skills and information, and evaluate the students differently.

Fortunately, it is unnecessary to return to this question in thinking about each class or rehearsal. If one's purpose can be articulated with a reasonable degree of confidence, it will give direction and consistency to one's teaching efforts. The teacher who feels strongly that he is primarily a provider of free entertainment for the community need not review his decision with each class he teaches. But it is a good idea for every teacher to rethink from time to time his fundamental purpose for teaching music. Maturity, experience, and changed circumstances often call for a reevaluation of one's views. The question is too important to be answered once and for all at the age of 20. This is not to say that a prospective teacher shouldn't develop his own answer to the question "Why?" As Chapter 3 will point out, an answer must be formulated. The important thing is not to "chisel your beliefs in stone."

What?

This question gets down to the specific content the teacher transmits to the students—pieces of music, facts, fingerings, patterns of sound and rhythm, and interpretation. It includes all types of information and under-standing, skills, and attitudes. It also involves lighting a spark of creativity and developing individual thought within the students. In short, it refers to all the course content and the experiences that take place in the classroom.

Deciding what to teach is an enormously complex matter. As pointed out previously, the world of music is huge. That fact alone makes choices difficult. But other factors also contribute to the complexity—practical considerations such as the musical sophistication of the students, the availability of time and materials, the community tradition, and the size of the class.

This book is written on the premise that music teachers do have something of value to give to teenagers—namely, a far greater understanding of music than can be gained without a teacher. But students do not learn only in a classroom or under a teacher's guidance. After all, the student spends only about 1,000 of his 8,736 hours each year in school, so it is not reasonable to credit or blame the school for all that he knows and is. But the fact remains that there are a number of things that will not normally be learned without organized, competent instruction.

Unlike the question "Why?" the question "What?" should be considered and spelled out specifically for each teaching endeavor. So that classes and groups do not merely "put in time" the teacher must know precisely what he wants his students to learn. A goal such as teaching Beethoven's Fifth Symphony is too general. The objective should be articulated in distinct state-

ments, such as "Recognize by sight and sound the motive in the first movement of Beethoven's Fifth Symphony," or "Learn to play the Beethoven
sforzandi correctly."

To Whom?

The capabilities and motivation of the students are essential considerations in thinking about teaching. Not only must the teacher consider such
obvious matters as range of voices and previous musical knowledge, but he
should also be aware of the probable use the students will make of what they
learn. A seventh grade general music class and a high school orchestra may
both study a Bach fugue, but each will approach the work in a different way
and with a different degree of technical information.

In recent years much attention has been focused on the educational
needs of non-middle class children. Students from a low socioeconomic background may not learn effectively with approaches devised for the more
privileged students in society. And so the "to whom" consideration requires
the teacher to put himself in the place of his students to recognize better
their varied interests, needs, and backgrounds. He must see the subject
through the eyes of the pupil. He needs this ability not only to know how
to adapt methods and materials, but also to establish a teacher-class relationship that will encourage a positive attitude in the students. Teenagers are
sometimes slow to distinguish between their feelings toward the teacher
and their feelings toward the subject. And in an art such as music, in which
so much depends on sensitivity of feeling and perception, the students'
attitudes are crucial. When the students realize that a teacher is sensitive to
their interests, the relationship between pupils and teacher is greatly improved, and more learning ensues.

The suggestions in this book are geared to what is loosely called the
"typical" school situation. But there are almost no truly typical schools, and
certainly each student is unique. The ideas presented apply to perhaps 80 or
90 percent of all teaching situations. They may be valid under more unusual
circumstances as well, depending on the particular conditions. Much as one
might like to, it is impossible to offer specific ideas about how to teach music
in each of the 25,000 secondary schools in the United States.

The wide variance among teaching situations makes it impossible to
name specific teaching procedures that will be universally valid. This lack
of prescribed steps is not characteristic of several other professions, including medicine. Since everyone's appendix is in approximately the same
place in the body, surgeons can be taught a specific surgical procedure for
its removal. But human behavior is far less consistent than human physi-
ology. Not all students have the same interests, musical background, and

academic ability. So, identical teaching procedures sometimes produce exactly the opposite results in different classrooms. This situation makes teaching interesting and sometimes frustrating. Suggestions about educational methods must necessarily be somewhat general or tailored to a particular set of circumstances. It is the teacher, finally, who must observe his own students and make educational judgments about how they can best be reached.

How?

This question focuses on the way in which subject matter is taught. It involves organizing and structuring the lesson, and deciding on a manner of presentation. Some people assume that teaching is a job in which one merely stands up in front of the students and talks. If that were the case, teaching would be easy indeed!

Determining which methods are appropriate for teaching specific material to a specific group of students is one of the challenges of teaching. An example from the elementary school will illustrate the point. Suppose a teacher wishes to teach a second grade class to sing a song with pleasing tone and accurate pitch. Because the song is simple it presents the teacher with no technical obstacles. The children themselves are enjoyable to work with and tractable, offering the teacher little challenge in guiding the class. The excitement comes from presenting the art of music so that it becomes meaningful to the seven-year-old youngsters. How can the design of the melodic line be impressed on children who scarcely know what the word "design" means? How does one make second graders conscious of pitch and exact in its rendition? Certainly not by telling them "Watch your intonation!" Does a gentle sweep of the arm really aid a child in feeling the shape of the phrase, or doesn't it? Are there other means that would be more effective?

A significant body of knowledge exists about learning and its conditions, but much remains unknown. Ideas on methodology change as new evidence becomes available from research and practical experience. For example, it was once believed that language reading should be introduced by teaching the letters of the alphabet first, since words are made up of letters. When the words were learned they were put into phrases and finally into sentences. This method seems sensible, but it simply was not effective. Today teachers know that words are comprehended as a whole. Without this knowledge and without training in how to use it, teachers would waste much time and introduce habits that would have to be broken later. A fluent reading ability and a gracious way with children are not sufficient qualifications for teaching reading. The same is true of teaching music.

The greater share of this book is devoted to methods of teaching music.

The discussion does not claim to offer the only way to teach. So many variables are involved that no one can make the "correct" judgment for any and all situations. Although you can't expect a book to offer complete and final answers in an area as complex as teaching music, you do have the right to expect some valid suggestions.

With What Result?

Earlier in this chapter, teaching was defined as a process in which information or skills are so organized that the students learn them. The process is incomplete if the students do not learn. Therefore, the fifth ingredient in the teaching "mixture" is outcome: What are the results of the teaching? What do the students know or what are they able to do after the lesson that they could not do before? Every teacher must look at the results of his teaching with a cold, clear eye and answer the question "What did the students accomplish?"

This last question offers the clue to the proper evaluation of teaching results. A teacher cannot determine the amount of learning by trusting luck or by watching the students' facial expressions. Evaluation demands concrete evidence of what the students can do as a result of the learning experience. The currently popular term "observable behaviors" does not refer to classroom deportment, although there is some relationship between the quality of teaching and classroom conduct. Instead it refers to specific understandings revealed through the student's ability to answer questions, to signal when a theme returns, to sing or play the third of a triad when asked, and so on.

Finding out whether students are learning is a complex task. It calls for an understanding of what to look for as well as imagination in planning how to elicit such evidence of learning.

Why? What? To whom? How? With what results? The answers to these questions are the essential ingredients of the compound called teaching. Without thinking through each one of these questions a teacher runs a risk of creating an educational failure marked by wasted time and lost opportunities for learning. Teaching is similar to getting an airplane off the ground. If any important part is missing or not working—engine, tail, wing—the plane will not take off. Because educational failures are less dramatic and less immediately visible, some teachers are able to get by without including all the ingredients. Only their students are the losers! Sometimes the material is too difficult, too easy, or meaningless; sometimes the hours spent in music classes add up to little additional knowledge or skills for the students; sometimes the good ideas of the teacher do not get over to the students; sometimes teachers and classes wander rudderlessly, not knowing what they are trying to learn, or if they have learned anything. When any of these situations occurs the result can properly be called an "educational failure."

Note that the five questions have been discussed in an intentional sequence. That is, a teacher should know the purpose of music instruction in the schools before he makes decisions about the content of a particular class. And the decision of what will be taught should precede the consideration of method. Sometimes music teachers put the cart before the horse by declaring allegiance to a particular method or system of music teaching without having a clear idea of what they want to teach.

There are also some interrelationships between "How?" and "To whom?" Because one affects the other, they must be considered together. Ideally the observation of results should be coordinated with method.

The five questions provide an outline for thinking about teaching, and they focus ideas that would otherwise be a formless blob in one's mind. Analyzing the teaching process is one long step toward becoming a good teacher.

2

The Complete Music Teacher

About three hundred years ago a celebrated Englishman named Izaak Walton compiled a treatise on what was required of a person to be a good fisherman.[1] His work was logically entitled *The Compleat Angler*. If Walton's words about fishing are true, there is more to being a complete angler than throwing an appropriately baited hook into the water. Likewise, there is more to being a good music teacher than merely leading a class through a song or conducting the band in a march. A person who plans to teach needs to become aware of what goes into the making of a "complete" music teacher.

Personal Aspects

While it is true that a teacher's main concern should be his educational impact on the students, it is also true that most successful teachers possess certain attributes that contribute to the process of education. For example, if some aspect of a teacher's personality or character causes his students to reject or ignore his teaching efforts, he will fail in those efforts, no matter how good his techniques or how valuable the subject matter.

Personality

Many people regard personality as God-given, intangible, incapable of being changed. They fatalistically believe that one is either "born" with an

---

[1]I use the word "compiled" because scholarly investigations indicate that Walton, as was customary in his day, plagiarized large portions of the work. See H. J. Oliver, "The Composition and Revisions of 'The Compleat Angler,'" *Modern Language Review*, XLII, 3 (July 1947), 295–313.

attractive nature or he is not, and that's that. Personality *is* important, but to feel that it is all-important is to overrate it. Some persons do seem to be more naturally inclined toward teaching than others, but essentially teachers are made, not born. For students to learn music, much more is necessary than merely exposing them to a "personality."

The research and writings on the question of the personality of a good teacher have tended to reaffirm what nearly everyone already knows: warm, friendly, understanding teachers are more effective than those who aren't; businesslike and organized teachers are more effective than teachers who are careless and disorganized; and imaginative and enthusiastic teachers surpass in effectiveness those who are routine and dull.[2] One writer finally concluded that a good teacher is "held to embody most human virtues along with a great many qualities more frequently attributed to divinity."[3]

A few points can be stated with confidence, however, about the personality of a successful music teacher. He should be an adult in the fullest sense of the word. He must be conscious of the needs and feelings of others. The whims and idiosyncrasies of an "artistic temperament" have no place in public education. Nor has education a place for the teacher who uses students as a means to build his ego. Adolescents cannot respect (although they may tolerate) a person who is not sincere and honest with them; neither can they respect erratic, impetuous leadership. Sincerity, stability, and good sense, then, form the basis for the effective teaching personality.

The grooming and appearance of a teacher is a subject that has occasionally produced heated debate, but it probably has little effect on the educational process *as long as it does not distract from or interfere with the respect and confidence the students have in the teacher.* It is your right as a citizen to wear any hairdo or clothing style you wish. But if your appearance causes the students to look upon you as a freak or egoist, it is simply not worth the loss of learning that will result. Whether or not some aspect of appearance interferes with the educational process will vary according to the cultural background of the students. In one instance some student teachers thought they would relate better to children in a poor inner-city school if they wore old, battered jeans and shirts. The students weren't one bit impressed; that type of dress was what they were trying to get away from. Common sense is the most reliable guide to personal appearance.

A teacher's speaking voice should be pleasing, and more important, it should carry a quality of decisiveness. During student teaching the complaint is sometimes leveled at the young teacher by his supervisors that his voice cannot be heard in the back of the room. This problem usually disappears as

---

[2]D. G. Ryans, *Characteristics of Teachers* (Washington, D.C.: American Council on Education, 1960). See also W. W. Lutz, "Personality Characteristics of High School Music Teachers," unpublished doctoral dissertation, University of Illinois, 1963.

[3]J. M. Stephens, "Traits of Successful Teachers: Men or Angels?", *Theory into Practice*, II, 2 (April 1963).

the young teacher gains confidence and experience and makes efforts to improve in this area.

Facial expressiveness is of more value than glamour or good looks. In a performing class the teacher's facial expressions can be especially effective in communicating with the musicians. Close-up views of outstanding conductors show that facial expressions are as expressive as hand and arm movements. Some beginning teachers are so serious and intent about their work that they look doleful while directing a group. A smile of encouragement at a good performance of a passage can do much for the morale of a young musician.

> A teacher was serving as guest conductor of a fine church choir. The choir sang the anthem extremely well. After the service one of the singers asked the director, "How did we do?" "Fine!" was the reply. "Oh," she said, "I was a little concerned because you looked so serious all through the number; I thought maybe something had gone wrong."

When all is said and done, there is something beyond personality, grooming, voice, and facial expressiveness. David Ausubel, the noted educational psychologist, has written, ". . . perhaps the most important personality characteristic of a teacher . . . [is] . . . the extent of the teacher's personal commitment to the intellectual development of students. . . . It determines in large measure whether he will expend the necessary effort to teach for real gains in the intellectual growth of pupils, or will merely go through the formal motions of teaching."[4] Myron Brenton makes this point very succinctly: "the best teachers wear a large invisible button that reads, 'I give a damn.' "[5]

The Importance of Being Yourself

Many young teachers who study under a dynamic, extroverted individual, or observe such a person in full swing at a workshop or festival wonder, "Is it necessary for me to have that kind of extroverted personality to be successful?" A young teacher may find that when he stands before a performing group it is all he can do to give the necessary directions and go through the conventional conducting gestures. No matter how hard he tries he cannot seem to break out of his "shell." Is he a poor teacher? Is he in the wrong line of work?

First, extroversion does not guarantee a teacher's ability to convey ideas

---

[4]David Ausubel, *Educational Psychology* (New York: Holt, Rinehart & Winston, 1968), p. 412.

[5]Myron Brenton, *What's Happened To Teacher?* (New York: Avon Books, 1970), p. 40.

to the students and to draw from them their best efforts. Suppose a choral director dons a red sweat shirt for rehearsals and conducts his choir in the manner of a cheerleader. His colorful behavior may be effective for a few rehearsals, but what about the fiftieth or the hundredth rehearsal? What was once inspiring can become annoying. Further, if the students become accustomed to such vigor from the teacher, there is little left for him to do when he wants still more emphasis.

Many people are not extroverts and would only look silly if they tried to be. Fortunately extroversion is not necessary for success. The many non-extroverts who are excellent teachers offer living proof that the important thing is to be yourself.

Extroversion should not be confused with the quality of decisiveness that is so necessary in an effective teacher. A teacher must be able to get his feelings and ideas over to the students with conviction and cogency. A "mousy" person cannot do this. How the teacher achieves this quality depends on his unique personality, but *he must achieve it.* This often takes time and effort. He can develop it by coming to terms with the experiences in his own life, by growing in his knowledge and love of music, and by working with young people.

A teacher becomes unique not by imitating others but by developing himself in his own way so that he can command the respect of his students and bring forth their best efforts. Every teacher has strong and weak points, and must learn to make full use of his strong points for maximum effectiveness with his students. For example, one band director plays the trumpet very well and uses it frequently to show the group how the music should sound. The students often ask him to play an entire solo, which he does occasionally. Another teacher has a most winning personality. Because of their fondness for this teacher the students let nothing prevent them from fulfilling his requests. A third teacher is a somewhat scholarly sort, with a deep knowledge and love of music. At first the students were slightly baffled by his approach, but now they realize that he has something significant to offer them. Three different people meeting a common objective in three different ways—each using the means most natural and effective for him.

Human Qualities and Professional Competence

It is all very well to say that a teacher should be intelligent, sensitive, mature, fair, forceful, and imaginative. But how do these attributes relate to his ability to work with people, an ability that is so crucial to the teaching process? How important are the "human" aspects of teaching? The Teacher Education Commission of the Music Educators National Conference (MENC) presented the following thoughts on the subject in its 1970 Interim Report.[6]

---

[6]*Music Educators Journal* (October 1970), Vol. 57, No. 2, pp. 33–48.

Like all teachers, music educators need to be first and foremost "live and growing" human beings. The fact that they have elected music as their particular discipline places certain special requirements on them but in no way relieves them of their need to be outstanding persons.

Music educators must:

Inspire others. They must demonstrate qualities of leadership that will enable them to excite the imagination of students. They must be able to communicate their enthusiasm for music.

Continue to learn in their own and in other fields. They must develop an attitude of intellectual curiosity that will assist them to find answers not provided in their preservice education.

Relate to individuals and society. They must develop empathy with students and colleagues of varying backgrounds, and restore positive attitudes and commitments toward children of all cultural backgrounds to effect the common goals of mankind. The strengths and qualities valued by cultural minorities must be incorporated to alter, temper, or strengthen traditional goals for the ultimate benefit of a humane and effective society.

Relate to other disciplines and arts. They must be familiar with the scientific method and its application to the physical and social sciences, and know the similarities and differences between their own and other arts. They must seek relationships between music and other disciplines.

Identify and evaluate new ideas. They must develop an attitude that enables them to seek and evaluate new ideas. They need to welcome and utilize technological, experimental, and exploratory developments in musical composition, teaching procedures and aids, and sound-generating devices.

Use their imaginations. They must learn to be creative not only with musical materials but also in the way they approach learning problems and their dealings with colleagues.

Understand the role of a teacher. They must understand that many attitudes and values that are common and appropriate among college music students need to mature substantially for effective music teaching. The desired maturity in attitude must be initiated during prospective teacher training. For example, the ego-satisfaction of the music student in college is often gained through personal performance whereas that of the music educator is gained largely from creating opportunities for students' musical expression.

Most importantly, music educators must demonstrate their understanding that the level of performance and the literature performed must be appropriate to the needs of a specific group of learners. They must also understand that the nature of performance reinforces the teacher-dominant classroom and that the music educator needs to give special attention to overcoming this tendency.

Professional Preparation

Colleges and states vary greatly in their requirements for certification in music. Some programs call for professional preparation in applied music and performance proficiencies, including a solo recital; other programs require a minimum of music study, sometimes omitting courses in conducting, aural theory, and vocal or instrumental techniques. Most state minimum requirements for music study and music method courses are low. Many states specify a large number of hours in courses other than music or education.

From time to time committees of the MENC and the National Association of Schools of Music (NASM) have made suggestions about the allocation of priorities in the undergraduate curriculum. One MENC committee in the 1950s suggested that one-third of the program be allocated for "general culture," another third for applied music and conducting, and another third for basic musicianship and professional education. In recent years there has been a trend away from suggesting specific courses or allocations. In 1970 the Teacher Education Commission of the MENC published a report emphasizing the characteristics and quality of instruction within each area instead of the amount of time allotted to each. The Commission has developed a list of musical and professional competences to which the undergraduate curriculum should lead. The competences portion of the Interim Report states:[7]

Skills in Producing Sounds (Performance)

All music educators must be able to:
Perform with musical understanding and technical proficiency. Their performance ability on an instrument or with their voice must be sufficient to enable them to interpret representative works of past and present. They must be able to improvise rather than be limited only to performance through reading music. Their performance opportunities during their education should have included solo, small ensemble, and large ensemble experience.

Play accompaniments. They must be able to perform simple accompaniments on the piano and on instruments such as the guitar or accordion, and be able to employ these instruments as teaching tools.

Sing. Music educators must have a basic understanding of the human voice as a musical instrument and be able to use their own voices effectively. Not everyone possesses a solo voice, but all music teachers must be able to sing passages for illustrative purposes and lead singing.

Conduct. They must demonstrate conducting techniques that will enable them to elicit from ensembles musical performances appropriate to the compositions being performed.

Supervise and evaluate the performance of others. Music educators must be able to instruct others in developing performance skills. They must have a broad knowledge of repertoire in many areas of music performance, and must develop a knowledge of ethnic instruments and materials suitable for

---

[7] *Ibid.*

instructional activities in music of other cultures. Those who plan to teach instrumental music must develop sufficient technique to demonstrate and supervise beginning students on all kinds of instruments, including electronically amplified equipment. They should be familiar with current devices for sound modification and be equipped to explore new developments as they appear.

Skills in Describing Sounds (Analysis)

All music educators must be able to:

Identify and explicate compositional devices as they are employed in all musics. They must be able to apply their knowledge of music to diatonic and nondiatonic Western and non-Western art, dance, and folk music, to such popular idioms as rock, soul, jazz, and country-and-western music, and to traditionally nonmusical sounds.

Discuss the affective results of compositional devices. They must know the ways in which composers in various cultures combine the elements of music to elicit particular responses in the listener.

Describe the means by which the sounds used in music are created. Music educators should be familiar with the tone-production capabilities of conventional instruments, instruments of other cultures, and electronically amplified instruments, electronically controlled tone-altering devices, and electronic sound synthesizers. They must be equipped to explore new developments as those appear.

Professional Qualities

The ability to communicate with students is essential for teachers. Therefore music educators must be able to:

Express their philosophy of music and education. They must establish a commitment to music as an art and a component of education. They should be able to communicate this commitment not only verbally and in written form, but also through their professional attitudes and activities.

Demonstrate a familiarity with contemporary educational thought. They must know how people learn and be able to apply this knowledge in teaching music. They must be familiar with the latest media of instruction and various schemes of educational organization.

Apply a broad knowledge of musical repertory to the learning problems of music students. Familiarity with comprehensive musical resources permits the teacher to respond imaginatively and significantly to the diverse situations and demands that arise in the classroom.

Demonstrate, by example, the concept of a comprehensive musician dedicated to teaching. Musical expertise and inspiration are essential leadership qualities that can command of students their most dedicated efforts.

Preparation in both vocal and instrumental music is an important part of music teacher training. Not only is this requirement musically and philosophically desirable, it is a practical necessity for many teachers. Although precise figures are not available, several surveys have indicated that at least one-fourth of all music teachers have responsibilities in areas other than their primary area. In other words, instrumental teachers teach some general music, and vocal teachers sometimes have responsibility for instrumental groups. Beginning teachers most often have a dual responsibility because they are likely to work in school systems too small to warrant hiring specialists within the various areas of music.

There is another reason for the instrumental music major to know something about choral and general music, and for the latter to understand the former's course of study. Each teacher is responsible not only for his own classes, but also to some extent for the entire music program at a school. It is not unusual for an entire music faculty to develop a curriculum or to explain budget and personnel needs to school administrators. To do this a music teacher needs a broader viewpoint than the particular area of music that he teaches. Furthermore, assignments change throughout one's career. More than one teacher who planned on directing a band or choir has moved into a supervisory position in which he is responsible for all aspects of the music education program.

Two abilities not cited in the MENC report should be mentioned. It is important that a teacher be able to hear pitch accurately and pick individual parts out of a maze of sound. When something goes wrong with the performance of a group, the director has to diagnose the trouble immediately. If the basses are flatting a certain interval, thereby losing their pitch, he must be able to hear this and correct the basses. Anyone who cannot do this is unlikely to succeed as a teacher of school music.

A new teacher may be discouraged by his first experience in this area. When he begins his student teaching and directs a group for the first few times, the newness of the sound and of the situation may so consume his attention that he will feel at a loss to pick out the various parts. He should not become alarmed; this is a natural reaction. With each attempt he should notice a gradual improvement in his ability to identify individual parts aurally. If he cannot do this by the end of his supervised teaching experience, some serious reevaluation of his choice of teaching area is called for.

In addition to good aural discrimination, he must be able to read music fluently. A person who teaches five or more periods a day is developing a current music repertoire of considerable size. Unless he spends many hours each week reviewing and memorizing the music, it is impossible for him to recall every phrase accurately. Music reading—the use of the printed page to refresh the memory on the sound of the music—is essential.

Four years is too short a time in which to prepare adequately for everything a music teacher may be requested to do. Every teacher, therefore, should be engaged throughout his career in strengthening his knowledge and preparing for future situations.

Skill in Teaching Techniques

The "complete" music teacher must know how to teach whatever he wants his students to learn. For example, if he knows that the band should play a passage in a staccato style, how does he get the idea of staccato over to the players so that they can execute it effectively? Without a knowledge of effective teaching methods he must resort to pleading, "Now, make those notes *short!*" This is all right as a beginning, but an experienced teacher knows that words alone are insufficient to ensure staccato playing, except for that which might occur by trial and error.

He needs to have in mind numerous examples, analogies, and explanations for use in teaching. He cannot stop the class, run to his desk and thumb through a book to find this technique or that bit of information. Whenever possible he should anticipate the problems that will be encountered in a certain piece. If a work demands staccato playing, then he can review various ideas on the performance of staccato prior to presenting the piece to the group.

The teacher of a performing group should teach more than executing the printed music symbols and following the conductor's gestures. Such skills can become mechanical responses, so that the student makes music in a parrotlike fashion without understanding what he is doing. Playing and singing are fine, but they constitute only a partial music education. The student should also be taught about the style, harmony, form, rhythmic structure, and composer of the more "meaty" works the group performs. Specific techniques and publications that aid in doing this are presented in Chapter 11.

The Student Teaching Experience

Almost every teacher training institution requires a practical, supervised teaching experience variously called "student," "apprentice," or "cadet" teaching. To get the most from this experience, the student must understand the reason for it and know what is expected of him.

Student teaching has three purposes. First, it provides the student with the opportunity to observe an established, successful teacher. The basic educational steps taken by the teacher are what should be looked for in the observation. For example, the teacher is introducing a new piece of music in 6/8 meter. How does he present the rhythm? How does this teaching relate to what has been previously taught about 6/8 meter? How do the students react? What other methods might the teacher have considered? This is the type of significant pedagogical procedure that should occupy the observer's attention.

The second purpose of student teaching is to provide guided teaching experience. The student moves step by step in a situation structured by the supervising teacher; consequently he is not pushed into a job in which he must either sink or swim. Student teaching cannot, of course, completely simulate teaching as it will be encountered in regular employment. The pupils are not the permanent pupils of the student teacher, and they know it. The amount of teaching is usually a half day for one semester or a full day for half a semester. While limited time may hamper the student teacher, it is good that he is not suddenly overwhelmed with the work required by a new, full-time assignment.

The third purpose of student teaching is to establish the fact that the student teacher can teach. A prospective employer wants to know, "How did this candidate do when he actually stood before a class?" A good college record and good character recommendations are fine, but there is no better test of a teacher than teaching.

The student teacher's attitude largely determines what he will gain from the experience. He must *look for* opportunities to contribute to the supervising teacher's classes, even in such menial chores as handing out music, adjusting window shades, or moving music stands. He should not sit around waiting to see what will happen. Most supervisors welcome signs of initiative on the part of the student teacher.

Because of the delicate relationship involved, the attitude of the student teacher toward his supervisor is important. In most cases the supervisor accepts student teachers for reasons of professional interest. There is little or no monetary benefit, and in most situations a student teacher means *more*, not less, work for the supervisor. Therefore the student teacher should be grateful for the interest and efforts of his supervising teacher. He need not agree with all the procedures of the supervisor, but he should realize that there is much he can learn from a person who does some things differently. Finally, he should accept criticism and suggestions in the constructive spirit in which they are given, and not as personal affronts.

The student teacher should know what is expected of him. If he must be absent, whom should he notify? Who is responsible for his grade and for the report of his student teaching experience? When he is teaching is he in full charge of the class and responsible for discipline? Who decides the interpretation of a particular piece of music? If a vacation day occurs at the college but not at the school in which he is student teaching, is he expected to report to school that day? Much misunderstanding can be avoided if the answers to such questions are clearly understood. If he has a question on any matter it is his responsibility to ask until he gets an authoritative answer.

For the student teacher who demonstrates initiative, optimism, and a willingness to learn, the apprentice experience will be worthwhile.

Personal Efficiency

Proper planning requires personal efficiency and organization. Unless the teacher has these qualities both he and his students are apt to find themselves in a state of confusion. Music teachers have been known to forget to order chairs or risers for a performance, to lose their own music, to fail to keep track of uniform and instrument numbers, and to wait until the last moment to prepare a program for a concert. What excitement these foibles create! But when confusion reigns, educational results are cut down. Musicians, along with almost everyone else, may dislike "administrivia," but trivial or not, details must not be neglected.

A help to the music teacher in handling business details efficiently is the *Business Handbook of Music Education* published by the Music Industry Council, an auxiliary of the MENC. This free booklet is especially useful in ordering music, materials, and equipment.

Relations with Professional Colleagues

In some instances a music program is hampered because of a poor relationship between the music teacher and the people with whom he works. For example, if the teacher is personally disagreeable the school guidance counselor may be hesitant to encourage students to enroll in a music course. Some instrumental music teachers consider themselves in competition with choral music teachers, and vice versa. Not only do the two factions fail to work together, but occasionally the efforts of one group are deprecated in an attempt to build up the other. Such friction undermines the total music program of the school. Music teachers sometimes overlook the school clerical and janitorial staff. A successful concert, for example, depends on the assistance of these people. But too often a thoughtless teacher takes this help for granted and fails to acknowledge it in any way.

The music teacher must take an active interest in school affairs. He cannot say on the one hand that music is an integral part of the curriculum, and then shy away from serving on a schoolwide curriculum committee because he feels that music is a "special" area. Nor should he display no interest in the fate of the football team or the winter play, especially if he wants the support of the physical education and drama departments for his music.

The Music Teacher and the Community

A school music program is affected by the other music activities and interests in the community. A community with an active music life helps the school music teacher, and in turn, an effective school music program contributes to the level of culture within the community. Cities that have lost their professional orchestras know what this means to the school music program. Good private teachers leave the city in search of other employment, and professional musicians are not available for performances such as chamber music and educational concerts. But worst of all, the absence of an active music life tacitly says, "Music is not important here." School music finds it hard to flourish in a cultural wasteland.

The school music teacher, then, has a stake in the status of the professional performer. He needs to support the local orchestra and other musical groups in the larger metropolitan centers; in the smaller communities he can work toward bringing in good music through live performances or radio and television. The high school assembly is an excellent occasion for presenting good music. There are talented artists, mainly young performers gaining experience, who tour smaller communities. Outstanding ensembles such as those associated with Young Audiences, Inc.[8] are also becoming increasingly available.

Not only should the music teacher support good performers and ensembles, he should work with them whenever possible. An educational concert should be planned jointly by teacher and performers. The professional musician usually knows that the way to raise the musical level of a community is through educating the young people. He is generally willing to work with the music educator to make the performance as effective as possible. Sometimes music teachers and performing organizations show little interest in each other's educational efforts, to the detriment of both.[9]

Attempts have been made to define those areas in which either professional musicians or school groups should take precedence. In 1947 the MENC, the American Association of School Administrators, and the American Federation of Musicians drew up a comprehensive Code of Ethics, delineating which activities are properly in the domain of the music educator and which are in the domain of the professional musician. Music teachers should be familiar with the provisions of the Code and abide by them. The Code is duplicated in Appendix A.

The dealings between music teacher and music merchant must also be conducted ethically. Because he is employed by the public, a teacher should not accept personal favors from merchants. The choice of merchant and subsequent purchases should be made solely on the basis of the quality of goods

---

[8] Young Audiences, Inc. (645 Madison Ave., New York, N.Y. 10022). This organization has chapters throughout the United States. Under its auspices professional musicians give performances of chamber music oriented toward school audiences.

[9] Charles R. Hoffer, "Common Efforts of the Community Orchestra and the School Music Program in Providing Listening Experiences for School Students," *Journal of Research in Music Education*, VI, 1 (Spring 1958), 39–40.

and service in relation to the cost.[10] When purchases amount to $25 or more, it is wise for the teacher to secure bids, if the school system does not already have a person to handle such matters. Competitive bidding encourages the best price from the merchants and provides tangible proof that business transactions are handled fairly and openly. The Ohio Music Education Association and the Music Merchants Association of Ohio have drawn up a Code of Ethics which can serve as a reasonable guide for the music educator. (See Appendix B.)

Finally, the school music teacher should work cooperatively with the private music teacher for their mutual benefit. The school music teacher must never deprecate the work of a private instructor, although he should not recommend an incompetent teacher either. Whenever possible he should supply interested parents with the names of more than one competent teacher. The level of the school music program can be advanced considerably by the efforts of a few good private music teachers. This is especially important in the case of instrumental students who have progressed beyond intermediate levels. Because few instrumental teachers know the advanced techniques on more than one or two instruments, the progress of the school band or orchestra depends in part on the availability of good private instruction.

In some cities an attempt has been made to ally all the arts under one central board which oversees artistic endeavor in the city and undertakes a common fund raising effort for community activities in the arts. Such projects are well worth the music teacher's attention.

Other community organizations, such as service clubs, should not be ignored either. They sometimes provide scholarship money to enable worthy music students to study at summer camp, and occasionally they are willing to finance a modest tour for an entire performing group. In addition to the financial benefits that may accrue to the music program, these community organizations provide the music teacher with a means of disseminating information to the public, a task of major importance.

The teacher has another valuable community contact in the parents of his students. Information can be sent to parents at regular intervals. An attractive booklet can be compiled explaining the music program. The booklet will have special appeal if it includes pictures of students and teachers at work. In some school systems a set of color slides has been prepared to educate the public about the music program. A good color picture of a group of youngsters playing instruments or singing is sure to draw a favorable reaction. Parent organizations such as "Band Boosters" also provide the teacher with a means of contact with the community.

Students and parents look to the music teacher for guidance when their

---

[10]*Business Handbook of Music Education* (8th Ed.). Music Industry Council, an auxiliary of MENC, 1959.

teenager is contemplating a career in music. The school guidance counselor should also be involved in such a case, but his knowledge of specific demands in music is usually not as great as that of the music educator. To assist students who are considering music teaching as a career, the MENC has prepared publications and a film strip which can be secured for little or no charge.[11]

For many teenagers the public library is the best and only source of good recordings. Librarians usually welcome suggestions from music teachers regarding the purchase of books and recordings.

Inner-City Community

No two communities are alike, of course. Each has its unique combination of problems and opportunities. For a number of reasons inner-city areas present different problems from suburban areas. One factor is the sheer quantity of people crowded into a small area. It's hard to feel that teachers know and care about you when there are 4,000 or more students in the school. Furthermore, inner-city families move more frequently than the average, which is about one family in five moving each year. Or the school boundaries may be changed, and the student required to change schools. So inner-city families often feel that they have never "put down roots" any place. Then there is often a high incidence of broken homes, inadequate housing, youth gangs, drugs, and a sense of hopelessness in the people. Generally those families who are more successful have moved out, taking with them their leadership, which is needed in the community. Adequate financial support for the schools is often lacking. For example, one inner-city school system had no funds in the budget for the purchase of such basic supplies as writing paper.

These conditions mean that relationships with the students and community are more difficult and more important than in other schools. The teacher must in some way establish a personal contact with the student and his family to get across a simple message—"I care. I care about you as a person, and I care about your learning something." This is what the Teacher Education Commission is talking about when it says the teacher should "relate to individuals." And in relating it is important for the teacher not to give the slightest impression of a condescending or patronizing attitude, a suggestion that applies to relationships in all schools. Often individual contact with the student is best made in an after-school program. In some

---

[11]*A Career in Music Education* (Washington, D.C.: Music Educators National Conference, 1965). See also *Careers in Music,* 1970, and *Music: A Teaching Career,* a 17 minute filmstrip (Music Education National Conference, 1969).

cities the school system supports a wide variety of after-school activities. In some cases a home visit is the most effective way to make contact.

The conventional avenues of communication in a typical middle class community — service clubs, PTA, and so on — are often ineffective in the inner-city. Inner-city residents seldom belong to Rotary or Lions Club, and many times are reluctant to come to school for meetings. Contacts with the adult community may be through advisory committees, which may or may not be associated with the PTA. In recent years many city school systems have delegated some control over the educational program to the population of a district in an effort to involve all elements of the community in the school program.

The students in the inner-city are discussed further in Chapter 7.

Continued Growth and Self-Evaluation

Continued professional development is a necessity for several reasons. If one graduates from college at the age of 22, he has 43 years remaining before he reaches 65, the most common mandatory retirement age for school teachers. Think of it, 43 years! This is a long time to remain fresh, vital, and interesting. Without continued professional growth the teacher is likely to repeat one year's experience 43 times, rather than to improve with each year of experience. Second, many women teach for a few years after they marry, then withdraw from teaching to raise a family. Perhaps ten or fifteen years later, when their children are old enough, they return to teaching. Some refresher education is obviously needed after such an extended absence from the field.

What can the teacher do to achieve continued professional growth? The most obvious method, and one required in most states before permanent certification can be attained, is to continue study at the college level during the summer or in the evenings.

Another means of growth is membership in professional organizations such as the MENC and the many state and local music education associations. These organizations keep the teacher informed of current happenings in the field through their publications and meetings. Most colleges and universities have student MENC chapters in which the prospective music teacher should take an active part.

Keeping informed about pertinent research in music education also improves a teacher's professional capabilities. The teacher should be familiar with the results of new attempts to improve music teaching, especially those studies of direct value to his teaching assignment. He should also seek to unearth the reasons for various practices in music education, many of which have never been subjected to rigorous intellectual examination. The music teacher must ask not only "Does a certain teaching procedure work?" but also "Would another procedure work better?" Being satisfied with a teaching technique just because it appears to work is like being content to spend a lifetime hopping about on one leg. Undoubtedly, hopping "works," but there is a more efficient way to move oneself about.

Even after availing himself of every professional resource the beginning teacher should realize that he still must teach himself how to teach. No course, no professor, no book, no college can impart enough information about the particular school, its students, and the unique problems he will face, to train him fully for his job. There comes a point at which he must succeed or fail on his own. He must undergo the sometimes excruciating process of looking at himself critically and improving on his own teaching.

Sometimes a teacher feels that other music educators are the best judges of his teaching ability. For instance he may place inordinate value on the comments and ratings he receives from judges at festivals, regarding the adjudication form as an evaluation of his success in teaching. Some teachers even send favorable rating sheets along with their credentials when applying for a better job. Such reliance upon the evaluations of others is based on shaky assumptions. Although outside evaluations are usually objective, they are necessarily made with incomplete information. The adjudications made at festivals are formed on the basis of one segment of the entire music program — the performance of one group on one particular day. The adjudicators know nothing of the total situation and must necessarily ignore all the factors that make schools and groups different. If the evaluation is made in the teaching situation itself, it is often done by a school principal, who is seldom a musician. In most cases the only outside evaluation that carries much validity is that of a music supervisor, who is a musician and is informed about the situation and the group.

When a teacher makes his objective the attainment of favorable evaluations by other persons, he is demonstrating his own lack of conviction by following an aimless, pointless pattern in which he is buffeted from place to place by comments from other people. He will inevitably receive conflicting evaluations and be forced either to flounder in a state of hopeless confusion or to begin evaluating for himself the statements of his critics.

Although self-evaluation has the obvious disadvantage of being subjective, it is the only practical means open to the teacher. For one thing, self-evaluation is a continuous process. It is not something that occurs once or twice a year, but rather it can go on in one form or another during every moment of every class. Furthermore, the teacher alone is thoroughly familiar with his teaching situation.

Self-evaluation is more valid and useful when directly related to teaching objectives and observed results. The teacher's responses to the questions "Why?" and "With what result?" are important for his continued professional growth and development.

Teacher Rating Forms

In addition to self-examination there are specific techniques that can be helpful in assessing the teacher's growth. One means is a teacher rating form to be filled out by the students. It is easy to be cynical about such forms and to assume that there is an automatic formula for success: easy tests + high grades + lots of jokes = a favorable rating. Teachers may also fear that adverse ratings will be seen by their superiors and used as a basis for critical judgment. But this is not the purpose of the teacher rating form. The device is an aid to self-evaluation to be used by the teacher alone with only one thought in mind: the improvement of his own teaching.

To contribute to the validity of a teacher rating form:

(1) Keep the wording of the questions simple so the students can understand what is being asked of them.

(2) Write questions requiring a variety of responses so that the form cannot be filled out mechanically. If the responses require placing an X on a continuum, vary the placement of the positive and negative extremes from one side of the page to the other.

(3) Present the form to the students on an "average" day, a day as far removed as possible from trips, tests, report cards, and concerts.

(4) Eliminate forms that students have filled out in a haphazard manner. Thoughtless answers can be detected by checking items for obvious inconsistencies. For example, a form may indicate that this year the teacher was too easy in managing the classroom, and yet the next item may state that the teacher should be easier next year. Several comparable items should be included in the form to check against careless and insincere responses.

Appendix D contains a form created by a choral director for his high school glee club. By changing a few words the teacher can adapt it for use with instrumental groups as well.

When considering the results of such a form, several points should be kept in mind. (1) Some items are more significant than others. For instance, the students' attitude toward the teacher's manner of dress is not as important as their ability to understand his conducting. (2) Students with limited musical background cannot accurately judge the musicianship of the teacher. For this reason questions relating only to musicianship need not be included in the sample form. (3) When the results are tabulated the median evaluation is more valid than the mean evaluation. Sometime 50 students will rate a teacher high on an item, and five dissident students will rate him low on the same item. The five low ratings will pull down the mean to a lower level than is warranted.

Space should be provided on the form so that the students can make any comments that seem relevant to them. Unless a particular point is mentioned several times, these remarks need not be taken too seriously. The "open end" type of question demonstrates the sincerity of the teacher in wanting the students to express any significant feelings and serves as a guide in formulating items that can be included in a new teacher rating form.

Rehearsal Playback

Another specific means of self-evaluation is the use of videotape or tape recorder. Some directors make a tape recording of every rehearsal. Before each group practice they listen to the preceding rehearsal. The recordings serve two purposes: they allow a more leisurely and thoughtful study of what the group has done, and they enable the teacher to evaluate his own efforts in leading the rehearsal. In studying a tape for self-evaluation purposes a director should ask himself these questions:

(1) Were there unnecessary delays and wasted time?

(2) Were the points on which I corrected the group really those points that needed the most attention?

(3) Did my suggestions to the group actually result in improvement?

(4) Were my statements clear and decisive?

(5) Did I repeat certain words and phrases — such as "O.K.?" "you know," "right" — so frequently that they became annoying?

(6) Did I stay long enough or too long with one number or musical passage?

(7) Were there relaxing breaks in the rehearsal routine, a little humor, or music performed just for the pleasure of it?

(8) Specifically, what was accomplished at the rehearsal?

(9) Did I encourage the students to discover and learn some points for themselves, or did I direct every action?

Supplementary Employment

Some teachers undermine their effectiveness by assuming a herculean work load in addition to their regular teaching schedule. Many teachers are hard-pressed financially and outside work such as teaching piano or directing a church choir may be a necessity. But teaching is a full-time job, and the beginning teacher will find that the duties connected with it consume all of his time and energy. He must consider the ethical and practical questions of how much outside work he should do. One of the pioneers in music education used to schedule one night a week which he spent at home reading, practicing, or in some way improving himself professionally. His example might well be emulated. Every teacher needs time not only to rest himself physically, but also to redirect himself so that his goals become better clarified and his efforts more productive.

No one has ever achieved the status of "complete music teacher." Teachers are human. But each teacher's unique strengths and weaknesses give him his own distinctive way of teaching. Such individuality is desirable and can be consciously developed along with the requisites of sensitive musicianship and personal maturity. The music teacher should seek to relate his educational efforts to the efforts of other professionals in music and education, and to involve the community in the educational process. Finally, he must look objectively at himself and his work if he is to achieve his full potential as a teacher of music.

Questions

1. Think of two good school music teachers you have had, and of two that you felt were not as good. What in their personality and work made them successful or unsuccessful in your eyes?

2. Being as objective as you can be, do some self-examination of your personality and how it relates to teaching music. What are your strong points? What needs your special attention so that it can be improved?

3. Think of a community that you know well. Is there a coordinated effort to promote music between the music teachers and the professional musicians? What is the relationship between the private music teachers and the school music teachers? between music teachers and music merchants? Are there educational concerts by the local orchestra? How and by whom are these organized?

4. Suppose that you are responsible for planning a set of slides to explain the music program to parent groups. How many pictures would you use? What would they depict? What would you say to accompany the pictures?

5. Suppose that you wish to study current research on one phase of music teaching. Where would you find pertinent magazine articles? graduate studies? references from books?

6. Examine the adjudication forms in Appendix E. Are these forms set up as teacher evaluation forms? How adequately do they indicate to a teacher how well he is doing his job?

7. Suppose that the parents of a boy with above average musical ability and achievement wish to discuss with you a possible vocation for him in music. What would you ask them about their son's interests and ambitions? What could you tell them about the various vocational possibilities in music?

8. Suppose you begin teaching in a town of 5,000 with a high school that receives some of its students from the rural areas around the town. The level of musical interest is not high. What steps could you take over a period of two years to stimulate and raise the community's musical interests and activities?

9. During your first year in a new job you take your musical instrument to a local music store for repair. As you pick it up the merchant says, "Forget the bill. It's on the house." Should you accept this favor?

Projects

1. Visit a secondary school rehearsal. Seat yourself where you can hear the group well. With score in hand attempt to focus your ear on one particular part and follow it as the number is sung or played.

2. Make a tape recording of yourself teaching a class during a methods class or student teaching experience. If this cannot be done now, tape-record yourself teaching a lesson to a fellow student on your major instrument or in singing. Evaluate the effectiveness of what you said, the amount of talking you did, the pertinence of your comments about the student's work, and the general pace of your teaching.

3. Compute the allocation of course hours in your collegiate training according to the categories listed in this chapter. Compare your training with that recommended. Discuss with other members of your class what phases of your training might have been stressed more.

4. Visit two identical classes (high school bands, seventh grade general music classes, etc.) in two different schools. Make some evaluation of the comparative musical maturity of the students, their innate ability, equipment available for music, schedule, and other factors. Make a list of the areas in which the two classes differ.

Suggested Readings

Brenton, Myron, *What's Happened to Teacher?* New York: Avon Books, 1970.

Earhart, Will, *Teacher, Philosopher, Humanitarian.* Washington, D.C.: Music Educators National Conference, 1962.

Interim Report: Teachers Education Commission. Washington, D.C.: Music Educators National Conference, 1970.

Lutz, Frank W. (Ed.), *Toward Improved Urban Education.* Worthington, Ohio: Charles A. Jones Publishing Co., 1970.

Section One
Why Teach Music?

The first major question to answer before preparing to teach is, "Why should students learn music?" The answer to it is the foundation on which successful teaching rests. No one should assume the role of teacher without a carefully considered and logical answer to the question. Because it is fundamental, the question "Why?" is the first "ingredient" of music teaching discussed in some depth in this book.

3

The Reasons for Music in the Secondary Schools

Sometimes music teachers are reluctant to think through fundamental questions about what they are teaching and why. Can't they just go ahead and do a good job of teaching, leaving philosophical explorations to college professors? No, the consideration of basic questions cannot successfully be left to someone else. There are at least four reasons that compel every music teacher to think through such matters for himself.

Reasons for Considering Basic Objectives

First of all, a teacher cannot avoid taking a position on fundamental, philosophical questions. He may not often state his position verbally, but his decisions and actions are necessarily based on his beliefs about music education.

> John Marsh believes that the main value of music is social and psychological. His music classes are first of all enjoyable. He selects easy, popular songs and seldom requires the students to learn them thoroughly. His chorus members are given little understanding of how musical sounds are organized, the meaning of the song texts, the literature of music, or performing skills. Grades are based on attendance and class participation, with no written or performance tests.

By his actions John Marsh has provided a clear statement of his beliefs about the purpose of music in the schools. The rightness or wrongness of his beliefs is not the point here. What is significant is that through his actions he has revealed a philosophy—a set of beliefs—about music education.

Second, there is still a need to "sell" music in the secondary schools. Many times the problem is not one of coping with obvious and deliberate doubts about the value of music in the curriculum. Rather the teacher has to do some "convincing" so that he can work out schedule conflicts, upgrade course credit, secure an adequate budget, and handle other problems.

> Sandra Green, teacher of general music at South Middle School, has discovered that the curriculum contemplated for the more academically able seventh grade students contains no music requirement. Furthermore it allows for only one elective class, which will meet for only one period every other day, and the elective field includes five courses in addition to music.
>
> Sandra finds that she has to convince the school administration of the need for music for all seventh grade students, including the able, and then establish the fact that music is sufficiently important to warrant an adjustment in the curriculum to allow room for it.

The job of promoting music education rests primarily on the music teacher. He needs enthusiasm and conviction in what he does and says. How can he convince someone else if he is not sure himself? He must remember that *he* is music to the students and faculty; he is the leader, the spokesman, the promulgator of music.

Third, for the teacher's sake he needs to be clear on what he is trying to do.

> Marian Knowles is tired. It's been a hard day; nothing has gone right. The classes have been talkative, their singing dull and often flat. As an added disappointment she has just realized that she has used up most of the budget, with none of the music for the spring program purchased yet.
>
> As she drops into a chair in the teachers' lounge after school a veteran teacher notices her dejected air and says, "Don't worry so much, Marian. Why work so hard? After all, who wants to be the best teacher in the graveyard?" Marian wonders, "Is it really worth all the work and worry?"

A teacher must be able to answer these questions, if for no other reason than to clarify his own perspective and objectives.

A teacher needs to be clear on his basic objectives in order to be consistent.

> Last fall, because it was Neal Groton's first year as band director at St. Mark's High School, he was anxious to have his football marching band make a big impression. Accordingly he enrolled anyone interested enough to join the band, even students with substandard training. By doing this he was able to field a large organization. Its sound was not good, but he was pleased to have so many students involved in instrumental music.
>
> At the end of marching season, he realized that he should eliminate about half the players so that the concert band could study and play music

at a level appropriate for a high school group. Because students could not be dismissed in the middle of the course, Neal made rigorous demands for extra rehearsals and made caustic remarks to the less able players in the hope that the unwanted students would quit. At the end of the semester several players did drop band, but among them was the first clarinet and second chair trombone. The remaining band members resented the affronts to fellow students and became indifferent to learning.

In March, prodded by his conscience and some conversations with the principal, Neal changed to a more good-humored approach and took greater interest in the welfare of the students. But the time was late. The students did not easily forget the experience of the past months. His more relaxed handling of the band initially brought forth more talking and fooling around. After a month the behavior improved and the band made an effort to prepare for the spring concert. As the year finishes, Neal wonders what he will do next fall when he again wants a big group to march. He feels torn between a desire to look good in the public eye and a desire to teach his students music.

Neal Groton's vacillating sense of direction is making him miserable. He needs to realize that the band cannot be and do everything. In short, he must make the best choice of goals he can and then stick consistently to them, so that the action he takes in December will not tear down what he sought to do in November.

For these reasons, then, all music teachers must understand the basic purposes of their job. One: A teacher cannot avoid acting on fundamental beliefs, even if he can avoid talking about them. Two: There is a need to convince others of the importance of an adequate music program. Three: A teacher needs clarity of purpose so that he can do his job and evaluate it accurately. Four: He must know his purposes in order to be consistent.

The Value of Music and the Fine Arts

In one sense, listening to a song or looking at a piece of sculpture is a rather silly thing to do. Such activities don't accomplish anything practical; they don't provide nourishment or shelter from the weather, nor do they help a person fight off a cold or earn money. Why are the fine arts important? Because they enhance the quality of human life.

Mankind seeks more than mere survival; people want to be more than animals grubbing their way through existence. After all, wasn't man created "in God's image"? When someone attempts to define the extra dimension that makes man different from the lower animals, the fine arts are nearly always cited. Both humans and animals have basic biological needs such as nourishment and sex. But as far as can be determined, animals have no symphonies, sonnets, or sculpture. These are human creations, human achievements. They are among the activities that mark the difference between *living* and merely *existing*.

The physical scientist Lecomte du Noüy, in his fascinating and profound book *Human Destiny*, discusses the ultimate meaning of man's evolution. Of Cro-Magnon man and his significance in the history of the human race, du Noüy says:

> . . . the Cro-Magnon was above all a great artist. The paintings which adorn his caverns are often admirable. His sculptures, his engravings on bone and ivory are wonderfully realistic, his tools and his weapons are superbly decorated, his jewels and ornaments are remarkably ingenious and graceful . . . These *useless* manifestations — the word is taken in the sense of "not absolutely necessary to maintain or defend life" — mark the most important date in all the history of mankind. They are the proof of the progress of the human spirit in the direction of evolution, that is, in the direction leading away from the animal. The primitive "useless" gestures of man are in reality the only ones that count.[1]

Du Noüy's statement regarding the importance of artistic activity in the development of the human race has been substantiated by other scholars: music and other artistic experiences are necessary if man is to reach his full stature. Man is not fully human without them. Not fully human without the arts and music — an untenable proposition? Not when it is closely examined. An idea of great importance? To the music educator it is the foundation of his work.

Philosophers disagree about why the arts are significant to the quality of human life. Some, perhaps best represented by John Dewey and Susanne Langer, hold that in the arts man reexperiences in a symbolic way the feelings associated with life, and through them gains insight into subjective reality. Others, such as the nineteenth-century philosopher Schopenhauer, maintain that music is "transfigured Nature" transcending the world and revealing the realm of the ultimate Will (God). And there are other points of view. Fortunately this disagreement does not alter the fact that the arts provide a fundamental and important contribution to the quality of human life.

Aesthetic or Anesthetic?

The fine arts involve a type of human experience called "aesthetic," a word that is often heard and seen in music education. For about a decade

---

[1]Lecomte du Noüy, *Human Destiny* (New York: Longmans, Green & Co., 1947), pp. 125–26. Courtesy of David McKay Company, Inc.

now music teachers have been urged to emphasize the aesthetic qualities of music, to make youngsters aesthetically sensitive, and to involve themselves in aesthetic education. Fine. But what does the word "aesthetic" mean?

First of all, an aesthetic experience is valued not for its practical benefits, but rather for the insight, satisfaction, and enjoyment it provides. A person normally hangs a painting on the wall not for its usefulness — to cover a safe or a crack in the plaster — but because the painting in and of itself is interesting and pleasurable to look at. An aesthetic experience is terminal in that it is complete, an end in itself.

A second characteristic of an aesthetic experience is that both intellect and emotion are involved. When a person looks at a painting aesthetically, he is contemplating and considering thoughtfully the shapes, lines, and colors he sees. At the same time he is reacting to what he sees; he has feelings about the painting. Usually these feelings are not so strong that he weeps, laughs, or emotes in some fashion, but he does react. In short, the viewer is involved both emotionally and intellectually with what he is observing.

Because intellect is involved, recreational activities such as playing tennis and purely physical sensations such as standing under a cold shower or riding a roller coaster are not considered aesthetic experiences. Purely intellectual undertakings such as working multiplication problems are not aesthetic either, since little emotional reaction or feeling is involved.

A third characteristic is the importance and value of experiencing, of studying the lines and colors in a painting, or of hearing the progression of sounds in a musical work. Because an aesthetic experience has no practical value, it has no final solution or "answer." In statistics, on the other hand, one can look up the answer to a problem. Unless one enjoys computing t tests and such things, he will miss nothing by accepting the answer from a book or a computer. In contrast, anyone who listens only to the final ten bars of a symphony will miss the aesthetic impact of the work. Any ten measures have value only as part of an experience of the total art object.

Aesthetic experiences are more than the contemplation of beauty. Some art works are fascinating without being pleasant or beautiful in the usual sense. They qualify as art because they are skillfully executed and have a compelling, magnetic quality that causes one to return to them again and again. Innocuous works may be "pretty," but if they lack the requisite skill and magnetism, they possess little aesthetic value.

The opposite of "aesthetic" is not "ugly" or "unpleasant," but "anesthetic" — no feeling, no life, nothing. A person who is insensitive to aesthetic experience is confined to a drab existence. Conversely, the person who experiences things aesthetically lives more richly and fully; he gets more out of life. Some years ago there was a hair coloring advertisement that proclaimed, "Blondes have more fun." The validity of that statement has never been established, although it has inspired some interesting speculation. With one slight change, the statement becomes true: "Aesthetically sensitive people have more fun" — they get more out of life.

Aesthetic experiences vary in degree or intensity, depending on the quality of the object and the reaction of the observer. Almost anything can be viewed aesthetically—pencils, paintings, comic strips, even trash cans. But not all objects offer an equal aesthetic reward. One can look aesthetically at the line, shape, and color of a refrigerator (not at all an unsightly object), but one would probably derive more satisfaction from viewing a painting or etching by Rembrandt.

The inclination and perception of the individual have a definite bearing on his aesthetic experience. Sometimes a person appreciates a work more than at other times; sometimes he is tired or distracted and consequently less perceptive than he is on other occasions. Furthermore, two people can react differently to the same thing. One person is "turned on" by what he sees, while the other doesn't seem to notice anything. Some people just seem more naturally disposed to think and react artistically. It may be their background, their environment, their intelligence, their personality, or a combination of these factors.

Aesthetic experiences seldom reach out and grab a person, so mere exposure to aesthetic objects is insufficient to ensure a response. The observer must put forth some effort—and this is where education steps in. One of the teacher's main tasks is to encourage his students to be more aesthetically inclined, more aesthetically sensitive. And in most cases education is necessary to develop a person's aesthetic capacities.

Aesthetic experiences are not the exclusive property of any class of persons. They are not confined to people of a certain age, educational level, or social or ethnic group. Nor can aesthetic experiences occur only in the rarified atmosphere of a museum or university. They can be part of everyone's everyday life. Although young persons do not usually experience aesthetically to the same degree as adults, or express their feelings with equal clarity, they do notice and respond. And in a democratic society each student is entitled to the guidance of a sensitive teacher and an equal access to the arts. Only in this way can every student develop his full aesthetic potential.

Teaching aesthetic inclination or sensitivity is no easy matter. The teacher achieves little by telling a student to "Be sensitive!" That is about as ineffective as telling him to "Grow up!" Aesthetic attitudes and inclinations are probably more "caught" by indirect teaching efforts than taught by direct frontal assault. Certainly an aesthetic attitude cannot be learned in a few class periods; the development of aesthetic sensitivity is something that needs to be encouraged day after day, year after year, throughout the entire school music program.

How can this be done? First, the teacher must present music in such a way that its aesthetic properties can be grasped. Students should be taught to be sensitive to the qualities of the sounds, the rising and falling intensity in the harmony and melody, and the organizing force of the rhythm, because these and similar characteristics give music its aesthetic appeal. Furthermore the students' attention must be specifically focused on these qualities.

Students must learn that the essence of musical feeling goes beyond merely counting and fingering the notes. It is possible for a student to play in the choir, band, or orchestra throughout high school without noticing what is happening musically.

> At a meeting of music educators, one teacher commented that so many high school second trombonists, when they play, ignore the rest of the band and are conscious only of the first and third trombone parts. A colleague answered, "I disagree. They aren't even aware of the first and third trombone parts!"

Second, knowledge in music derives meaning from its association with the qualities found in music. This principle applies equally to concepts such as melody, harmony, and rhythm, as well as to facts such as the pitches sounded in the dominant seventh chord in the key of G. And third, if students are to become alert to aesthetic qualities, good music must be selected. It's hard to teach artistic values from compositions that are trite or superficial.

Other implications of aesthetics will be developed in succeeding chapters.

Nonmusical Reasons for Teaching Music

Traditionally music has been included in the schools for reasons of citizenship, character development, team spirit, health benefits, and so on. Such justifications for music have a long history. Plato in his *Republic* cites the need for music in the education of every citizen. His reasons were consistent with the ancient Greek idea of *ethos*—the belief that each mode has an ethical character. A man could be made or ruined by the proper combination of notes! Music was also more broadly conceived in his day, because it included aspects of poetry and physical education. Since music was closely allied with mathematics during the Middle Ages, music was taught in the medieval university partly because scholars were fascinated with the acoustical ratios of musical sounds. During other periods of history music was included in the curriculum primarily because a knowledge of music was a mark of an educated gentleman or gentle lady. In 1837, when Lowell Mason was given permission to institute music in the Boston schools, the subject was justified because it contributed to reading and speech and provided "a recreation, yet not a dissipation of the mind—a respite, yet not a relaxation,—its office would thus be to restore the jaded energies, and send back the scholars with invigorated powers to other more laborious duties."[2] The utilitarian con-

---

[2]Edward Bailey Birge, *History of Public School Music in the United States* (Washington, D.C.: Music Educators National Conference, 1966), p. 43.

tributions of music were still being stressed through the era of the Seven Cardinal Principles of Education and the progressive education movement during the first half of the twentieth century. As late as 1941 such eminent music educators as Peter Dykema and Karl Gehrkens were emphasizing nonmusical outcomes with their philosophy that "the teacher teaches children through the medium of music."[3] The clear implication was that music exists to achieve some goal greater than itself.

Not until the late 1950s did music educators begin publicly to question the validity of statements about music's ability to promote nonmusical goals. Their doubts had three sources. One was the inability of research to demonstrate that music classes cause students to become better citizens or healthier individuals. Granted, music does not encourage poor citizenship, loose morals, or failing health. But claims that stress "absence of harm" are inadequate grounds on which to justify music in the curriculum.

A second factor that weakened the traditional utilitarian claims for music was the realization that other curricular and extracurricular activities can do the job better. Courses in history and government are more pertinent to citizenship than music courses are, and physical education is more beneficial than music for bodily well-being. If a school administrator wishes to strengthen these areas of personal development, it is highly unlikely that he will expand the music program to do so.

A third reason for the change was the emerging awareness that music and the fine arts are significant and valuable in themselves. Just as chemistry and history teachers do not claim to teach something "through the medium of chemistry or history," music educators began to realize that their subject is also valid in its own right. Music should be in the school curriculum because it is culturally significant. Music educators realized that to advocate music for unsupportable utilitarian reasons made them look weak, illogical, and uncertain. Beginning with the publication of *Basic Concepts in Music Education*[4] in 1958, many music educators "turned the corner" in thinking about their profession. Most music educators today do agree that music is a worthy subject in itself, equal in value to other academic curricular disciplines.

Because nonmusical benefits are still espoused today, and because there is some truth in a number of these claims, they merit closer examination. Happily, music can often be two things at the same time. It can be great art replete with aesthetic merit and insight, and it can serve as leisure-time diversion, emotional outlet, and social activity. These peripheral, nonmusical outcomes can be valuable too.

---

[3]Peter W. Dykema and Karl Gehrkens, *The Teaching of High School Music* (Evanston, Illinois: Summy-Birchard Publishing Company, 1941), pp. 380–81.

[4]Henry B. Nelson (Ed.), *Basic Concepts in Music Education.* Fifty-seventh yearbook of National Society for the Study of Education (Chicago: University of Chicago Press, 1958).

Personal Development of the Student

Music contributes to a student's personal and social growth in several ways. For example, being able to perform creditably in front of an audience has inestimable value for increasing self-confidence. Do the students in music organizations feel the need for public approval? They most certainly do!

> Roger was a senior. He had little academic success and liked to be considered "rough and tough." He took choir because he needed the credit and because he had heard that choir could be enjoyable. When asked what day he remembered most clearly in his choral experience, his answer ran something like this: "The day we sang for assembly on Veteran's Day. It was the first time I ever did anything in front of anyone. I sure was scared. But our first song went real good and I felt a lot better after that."

Whether he realized it or not, Roger had succeeded at something besides getting into trouble. Now he had a good feeling about music, which started him in the right direction in other areas. Of course music cannot be advocated mainly as therapy for problem students, but it can help change the outlook of many young people.

A student's self-image is also enhanced through the recognition awarded to members of a successful music organization. The choir gave Roger an opportunity to be recognized for his positive, rather than his negative, accomplishments. As an avenue for gaining recognition, music has an advantage usually enjoyed only by the extracurricular activities that the school offers. Music, especially vocal music, is probably used as a means of achieving recognition more often by girls than by boys, because boys have opportunities for athletic recognition that are not always open to girls.

Several studies have shown a positive correlation between participation in music and student leadership and acceptability. In one study students in the top 25 percent on a social acceptability scale were compared with students in the bottom 25 percent on the scale.[5] The students rated themselves in singing ability. The testing procedure involved subjective evaluations and thus reduced the validity of the musical judgments. But it did reveal the correlation between social acceptability and confidence in an area of musical endeavor. The results showed that most students with the lowest scores did not sing at all, while two-thirds of the boys and seven-eighths of the girls with the highest scores were average or better in singing.

Correlation should not be confused with causation; the fact that two events are related does not necessarily mean that one causes the other. In

---

[5]Raymond G. Kuhlen, *The Psychology of Adolescent Development* (New York: Harper Bros., 1952), pp. 340–41.

these studies it is not clear whether the good students select music, or music makes good students. But there is clearly some relationship.

The social aspects of music can be far-reaching. For example, music provides rapport among students from different schools. They can meet at festivals and concerts, under circumstances in which success does not depend on directly competing with the other fellow. This is an aspect of social interchange that athletic events seldom provide.

Psychological Factors

The problem of mental health is becoming increasingly important in our society and our schools. Authorities on mental health estimate that one child in twelve born today will at some time in his life be confined to a mental institution. An extensive survey in New York City revealed that 81 percent of the population in Manhattan could be classified as being "emotionally disturbed," 23 percent severely so.[6] Such facts suggest that the psychological and personal adjustment of the student must receive the attention of educators.

Music can play a significant role in helping students emotionally. Music not only *expresses* emotion, but also *releases* emotion. When children are asked about their feelings toward music, their responses indicate that youngsters like music not because it is culturally good for them, or because it improves them personally, but rather because it makes them "feel good." They offer comments such as "I can't describe how I feel when I play — it's wonderful, that's all." And, "When I get moody and down, I get away from the family and listen to my record player. . . ."

These remarks are significant because they are made by normal children. The need for emotional catharsis is common to everyone, and this is especially true of young people who are going through many rapid changes. The problems of the teenager may seem simple to an adult, but they often cause more frustrations, fears, and repressed feelings than adult problems cause for a mature person. The secondary school student needs some means of emotional release other than racing an automobile or using narcotics. Admittedly, mere release of feelings does not solve a person's basic emotional difficulty, but it can help to prevent the intensification of these problems and take some of the "sting" out of them.

In many communities music has been promoted with slogans such as, "The boy who blows a horn will never blow a safe." Although guiding adolescent behavior is far more complex than the statement indicates, it does suggest that there are psychological benefits for the student who studies music.

---

[6]L. Srole et al., *Mental Health in the Metropolis* (New York: McGraw-Hill Book Co., 1962), p. 138.

Although music does not always have the power to "soothe the savage breast" it sometimes works wonders with emotionally and physically handicapped people. The professional field of music therapy has become established in the last few decades. Universities have instituted research and training programs in using music as an aid in curing mental illness.

Avocational Value

Much has been said recently about the worthy use of leisure time. While life expectancy is increasing, the average work week is decreasing, and these factors create more leisure. This situation affects not only wage-earners and retired people, but young people as well. Teenagers need to use their energies in one manner or another, and music is an excellent, constructive outlet.

Music is one of America's more common and more desirable avocations, for it involves participation — playing in a community orchestra, singing in a church choir, or playing chamber music. But far greater than the number of people who take part in musical groups is the number of people who listen to music. Because of mass communication and the availability of recordings, practically everyone listens to music. It follows that training for intelligent listening is a pressing challenge for music educators.

There is little a teacher can do directly to make these psychological and avocational benefits happen. The student's self-image, his social and psychological needs, and his choice of what to do in his leisure time — all are influenced by circumstances over which the teacher has little control. He cannot through some teaching procedure assure positive results, although good teaching can help bring them about.

The Student or the Subject?

Realizing that a student can learn the subject of music while gaining its personal and social benefits should lay to rest the long-standing dilemma: Should a teacher teach the subject or the student? He teaches both; the two are inseparable if learning is to take place. There is no need to consider the subject matter and the student as an either/or proposition. The student is not helped if he is left ignorant about what he should learn in a course. If he fails to learn chemistry in the chemistry course or French in the French class, he has been cheated, no matter what his particular social or psychological problems may be. On the other hand, the teacher must be more than an "information peddler" who cares little about the individuals to whom he dispenses skills and information. The teacher must be flexible and sensitive to his students' needs so that he can do the best possible job of communicating the subject matter to them.

The Teacher and Educational Objectives

The teacher's role in determining goals in public education is ambiguous, presenting both limitations and opportunities. A teacher in the public schools of the United States must accept the broad objectives endorsed by the educational system. No teacher can go contrary to these goals without harming to some degree the total effectiveness of the educational effort. For instance, no teacher can ignore the many for the benefit of the few, or teach the violent overthrow of the government, without detracting from the accomplishments of the schools. Such practices are contrary to the tenets of American society.

The objectives of education apply to all areas of the school, including music. Sometimes directors of performing groups feel that since music is a specialized activity, there is no need to be concerned with what the rest of the school is trying to do. Music *is* a specialized study, but it operates within the framework of the school. Everyone wants to have student music organizations perform well, but not at the expense of everything else the school seeks to accomplish.

The educational mandates that guide the individual teacher are broad and general. The process is analogous to the directions a passenger gives to a taxi driver: the passenger tells him the destination (sets the general objective), but decisions about the best way to get there are the driver's, since he is the expert. The taxi driver, like the teacher, makes the detailed decisions about the process of reaching the goal and implements them as intelligently and efficiently as possible.

The forces that operate in developing a curriculum are diverse and often conflicting. Teachers sometimes wonder where they fit into the picture. Is the teacher the one to determine what should be taught in music, or is he simply to teach what he is told? Who finally decides such matters: teachers, administrators, school boards, state offices of education, or the public? Unlike European countries the United States government has no agency which possesses authority over what the schools shall teach. This matter is left to the states and local school boards. School board members are elected by the people or appointed by elected officials. Basically the curriculum derives its authorization indirectly from the public at large.

But the matter does not rest there, because the public in turn looks for guidance from professional educators. The views of educators nationally are articulated by professional associations, professional writings in books and journals, and by teachers and administrators in the local community. The interaction between the public and the teachers is active and dynamic, with each influencing the other. In this relationship the teacher gives the public the benefit of his professional judgment.

The teacher can also influence decisions within the school system. The superintendent of schools is employed by the board of education to administer the total educational effort of the school district according to the policies established by the board. He must consider not only the curricular problems of music, but also the effect of the program on the finances of the school district, the building space available, and the support and interest of the public. Because the superintendent cannot know all and do all, he must delegate much of his responsibility. He must depend on the music staff for recommendations concerning the music program. In light of the other educational demands on the school system, he will render a judgment on how completely the suggestions of the music faculty can be followed. Unless he is informed about what the music teacher feels is necessary, he will assume that the present situation is satisfactory.

Educating the school administration and community about the needs and work of the music department is a difficult matter, because few citizens or educators outside the fine arts are informed about the purpose of school music instruction. First the music educator himself must understand aesthetics and the manner in which music and the arts meet people's fundamental psychological needs. Next he must try to educate nonmusicians in the merits and complexities of aesthetic experiences—not the kind of thing that can be summed up in a catchy slogan or described with a few phrases. So what should the music educator do? Should he attempt to impress people with long discourses on aesthetics, or make glib statements about the intent of school music instruction, or inspire competitiveness by saying, "Other schools have this or that, and we don't want to look bad by comparison . . ."?

No single rationale works with all people, of course. But a great many parents and school administrators do sense—correctly—that there is something good about having youngsters involved with music. Although their reasons may be unarticulated, they want young people to know and appreciate the arts. In one community the most successful fund-raiser for the local arts fund is a businessman who calls on other executives and says, "Look, you and I don't know much about the arts. But do you want the young people of this community to grow up as ignorant about art and music as we are?" His approach is perhaps a bit blunt, but it works. Most citizens, and especially parents, do not want young people to miss out on one of life's lasting and meaningful pleasures.

In addition to the "Let's-not-cheat-the-kids" approach, it ought to be pointed out that some formal education is necessary for more than a superficial understanding of the arts, a fact that is true of almost all school subjects. And to warrant a place for music in the curriculum, there must be commitment to the idea that music is an academic subject, not merely a pleasant promotional device for the school. Ironically music's essential appeal has been the main factor blurring this distinction. Communities appreciate good entertainment, especially when it's free; service clubs are delighted to have luncheon entertainment provided by the schools, and football fans are happy to be treated to a band show at half-time. Attractive as these prospects may be (they're fun for the students and an ego-builder for the teacher), the public must be educated to the fact that music is first of all an academic subject seeking to teach the students something of substance.

It is better to do the right thing for the right reason than for the wrong reason. School music has often been "sold" to the public and school administration on the basis of its public relations value. Music, along with physical education, is especially susceptible to this use (or misuse). Too often superintendents are urged to buy a sousaphone because the band needs it to look good on the football field or to win a higher rating in the festival, not because the sousaphone is necessary for a better instrumentation by which the students can learn more adequately how the music should sound. The fact that a neighboring school band, orchestra, or chorus might "show us up" has been used more than once to sway the thinking of a superintendent, who because of his public relations responsibilities is sensitive to public opinion. The attempt to achieve the right ends by the wrong means has come back to haunt some teachers. When the music program becomes a servant to public relations, the emphasis changes from education to entertainment. The tendency is to concentrate on the most talented young persons and to bypass the others, who will eventually become the public that elects school boards, who in turn hire superintendents.

How can a music teacher educate the school administration and the community about the music program? He can offer comments at public performances, and speak to the PTA, Rotary, and other groups. He can present information through publications prepared by the school district and sent to all local households. Perhaps he could prepare a statement about the purposes of the program, its present status, and goals for the future. Sometimes such a document is requested as an annual year-end report, but it can be submitted even if unsolicited. Most administrators are willing and even glad to consider ideas from the professional staff of the school.

Such publicity techniques as newspaper stories, radio spots, and videotaping are usually well worth the effort. The details of a press release will not claim every reader's attention, but many people notice and remember that *something* appeared in the newspaper about the school music department. (And at least a few persons will read the story!) Especially effective is a photograph in which every music student can be individually identified.

Strong, articulate teacher guidance is vital in establishing an effective music curriculum. The music teacher must know why music is needed in the schools and what course content will fill this need best. Then he must educate the school administration and the public in the merits of the music program.

Questions

1. Is John Marsh's devotion to entertainment justifiable philosophically? Why, or why not?

2. Suppose that you are Sandra Green. How would you justify the inclusion of music in the curriculum for all seventh grade students? Would the reasons differ significantly from those used for including music in the senior high school?

3. This chapter stressed that the primary reason for teaching music in the schools is to give students an understanding of its aesthetic qualities. Is this also the primary function of art? of English literature? of typing and home economics? of mathematics? of extracurricular activities such as scouting and interscholastic athletics? If the reasons are not the same, in what ways are they different?

4. Assume that an instrumental music teacher believes that one of the major purposes of his job is to develop self-confidence and poise in his students. In what way will his teaching differ from that of the teacher primarily interested in developing a knowledge about and sensitivity to music? What, if anything, can a music teacher do specifically to develop character or provide emotional catharsis for students in his classes?

5. Suppose that you are teaching in a school whose music budget is very inadequate, especially in relation to the financial support given other areas of the curriculum. The members of the music faculty decide to go to the superintendent to present their case for increased financial support. What arguments would you use for the increase? Would comparisons with the amount spent in other schools for the music curriculum be a valid technique? Suppose that the average size of the general music classes is 70. What arguments could be made for reducing the size?

6. Assume that you are asked to give a 15-minute talk to a local service club on the local school music curriculum. How would you explain in simple, practical terms the goal of aesthetic sensitivity? Or would you just ignore the subject and talk about the more obvious features of the program?

7. How consistent with the objectives of education in the United States are the following statements by music teachers?

(a) "You can't make a silk purse out of a sow's ear. No use straining yourself over a kid who just doesn't have it."

(b) "I've one of the best positions in the state. Three fine junior highs feeding in well trained players, and I use the best of these."

(c) "I know that not many youngsters take choral music. But if the few I have get a good music education — not just the milktoast so many teachers hand out today — it will be worth it."

(d) "I don't care how poor they are, or what color their skins happen to be. I'm determined to teach them as much as I can about music and what makes it tick."

Suggested Readings

Gaines, Joan, *Approaches to Public Relations for the Music Educator.* Washington, D.C.: Music Educators National Conference, 1968.

Leonhard, Charles, and Robert W. House, *Foundation and Principles of Music Education* (2nd Ed.) New York: McGraw-Hill Book Company, 1972.

Meyer, Leonard B., *Emotion and Meaning in Music.* Chicago: University of Chicago Press, 1956.

————, *Music, the Arts, and Ideas.* Chicago: University of Chicago Press, 1967.

Reimer, Bennett, *A Philosophy of Music Education.* Englewood Cliffs, New Jersey: Prentice-Hall, 1970.

Toward an Aesthetic Education. Washington, D.C.: Music Educators National Conference, 1971.

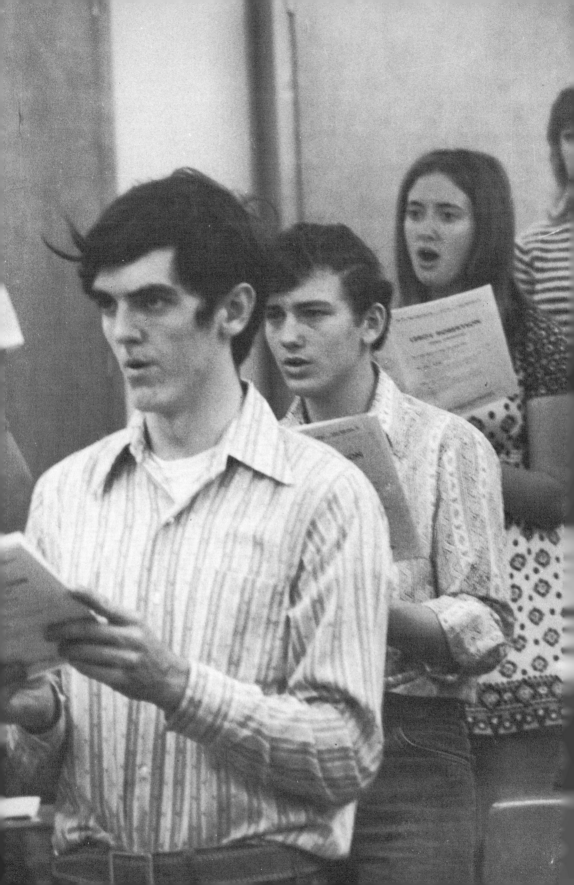

Section Two
What: The Subject Matter of Music

What should students learn about music? Are some areas of music more important than others? On what basis are decisions about the subject matter of music classes made? Should there be a common content for all students? These questions are part of the major ingredient of the teaching process — the concern for what is taught and learned in music classes and rehearsals.

Unless course content is thought through carefully the teacher can waste much of the limited time available for music in the schools. The students can wind up with a superficial acquaintance with music and never gain an understanding of what it's all about. Or they come away with a lopsided, distorted idea of music.

Most teachers are also involved in managing the music curriculum. They counsel students about music courses and lessons, work for better schedules, and make budget requests. In addition they sometimes deal with parents' organizations, set up systems of filing music, and offer advice about the music rooms when a new building is constructed. These and related topics are discussed in Chapter 5.

4

The Music Curriculum

All music teachers are responsible for the content of music classes. It's not a matter only for supervisors and curriculum specialists. In most school situations there is no district-wide plan that the music teacher is expected to follow, and when such plans do exist, they are the products of a committee that has included a number of music teachers.[1] Furthermore most state and school district guides are not specific, a fact that gives the teacher considerable latitude and decision making responsibility.

When one starts to explore the topic of curriculum and course content, he may feel like the sorcerer's apprentice, who, desperately trying to stop the broom from carrying buckets of water, grabs an ax and chops the broom into pieces, only to see each new segment begin to carry still another bucket. When curricular issues are examined each idea and its ramifications seem to multiply, and before long the topic is involuted with questions about ends and means, goals, content, methods, skills, concepts, maturation, and countless interrelated factors. Unlike the apprentice, a music teacher can't count on the sorcerer to return and straighten things out; he has to work out the problem by himself. Because this chapter is confined to the question of subject matter content, perhaps the discussion can be held to manageable proportions. What is being discussed here are *ends* (content and curriculum), not *means* (methods). This distinction must be kept in mind to avoid confusion: curricular questions are *ends* and are discussed in this chapter; instructional questions are *means* and are discussed in Section Five.

Learning in Music

What should students learn in music classes? At least five things:
(1) Organized patterns of sound — the syntax of music.
(2) The song or composition as a musical work.

---

[1]Philip T. McClintock, "An Examination of Curriculum Guides in Music with Reference to Principles of Curriculum Planning," unpublished doctoral dissertation, Indiana University, 1970.

(3) Intellectual understandings about musical processes and organization.

(4) Skills in making music and listening.

(5) Attitudes about the particular piece and music in general.

To discover how each of these five outcomes fits into the total picture, let's look at each one separately.

Musical Syntax

An essential characteristic of music is that its sounds are organized into an orderly pattern. A sense of syntax is necessary for music to be more than a mere jumble of sound. When learning language a child finds out that "runs big slowly dog black the" isn't a meaningful pattern. He needs similar learning in music. For the most part, an awareness of syntax in music is developed in the same way as in language: through experience and familiarity. A child enters first grade with about four years of experience in speaking the language, and he understands about 24,000 words.[2] He has all this practice and competence before he is shown visual symbols for the word-sounds he already knows.

Research indicates that the fundamental language skills, including a feeling for syntax, develop early in a child's life. By the age of ten the ability for such learning begins to slow down.[3] This is one important reason for providing a quality program of music experiences, comparable to language development programs, in the primary grades.

Developing an awareness of musical syntax is not a verbal process. People can sense the logic of music familiar to them, although they may not be able to describe why it seems "right." Like the early jazz musician, many an untutored person has a keen intuitive feel for musical patterns. This sense serves him well — to a point. Unless he has further training his appreciation is usually limited to short, relatively unsophisticated musical works.

The problem of musical syntax is complex and has many more implications for teaching music than can be discussed here. For example, how should the teacher approach such syntactical systems as tonal harmony, serial music, or Balinese music? Should he present music in some sequence of syntactical complexity? How much attention should he focus directly on syntax?

---

[2] Ruth G. Strickland, *The Language Arts in the Elementary School*, 2nd Ed. (Boston: D. C. Heath and Co., 1957), p. 230.

[3] Wilder Penfield, "A Consideration of the Neuro-Physiological Mechanisms of Speech and Some Educational Consequences," *Bulletin of American Academy of Arts and Sciences*, Vol. VI.

Music Literature

The term "music literature" sometimes calls forth memories of a dull, unmusical class in which opus numbers, keys, and themes had to be memorized. The term is *not* used here in that sense. Instead, it means all the music and types of music that have been created—folk, art, popular, improvised or composed, recorded or written down.

A knowledge of specific musical works and a sense of musical patterns are closely related. For example, to recognize a certain type of music as being "romantic," a person must have ideas about style, rhythm, timbre, and so on, used in a certain way. In fact, a knowledge of music and a strong sense of its syntax complement each other.

The problem for the music teacher is mainly one of selection. No one, not even the most ardent concertgoer or musicologist, will in an entire lifetime learn about or hear all the music in the world. The literature of music is too vast for that. Not only does it include all combinations of instruments and voices; it involves the entire history of music in all its geographical locations and at its varying levels of sophistication.

The dimensions of music literature can be illustrated graphically with a cube, as in Figure 1. The cube has one plane representing an ascending level of sophistication, extending from the more crudely organized sounds to the most intricate and artistically created musical works. The other two planes are not hierarchical. Renaissance music is simply different from contemporary music, not inferior or less sophisticated; instrumental and vocal music are different media—neither is superior to the other.

The sheer quantity of the music represented by the cube is almost incomprehensible. The nearly six feet of shelf space occupied by the *Bach Gesellschaft* is impressive, but Bach was only one of many prolific Baroque composers. Vivaldi wrote about 450 concertos and 49 operas, Alessandro Scarlatti more than 600 cantatas, and Telemann about 3800 pieces. About 1660 trouvère and troubadour melodies of the Gothic period have been preserved. Mozart's catalog lists 626 works, and years ago the contemporary composer Darius Milhaud's opus numbers passed 300. Many lesser known composers have been just as prolific. The amount of folk music is staggering. Bartók collected over 2000 folk songs in just Hungary and Roumania. More than 2000 musicals have opened on Broadway in the last century. Hundreds of popular songs are published each year in the United States. And the body of music literature is growing rapidly.

Several facts should be pointed out about the cube. The cubelets are not discrete; one merges into the next, especially on the complexity and historical planes. Many of the cubelets can be subdivided further. Modern music, for example, can be divided into neoclassical, serial or tone row, primitivism-barbarism, and so on. The cubelets are not of equal size; some contain more music than others. The amount of music varies from cubelet to

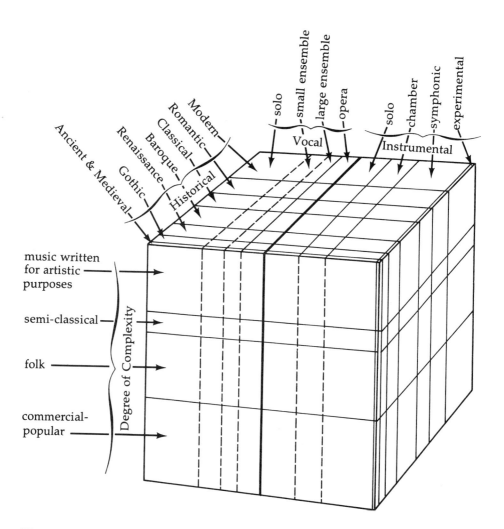

Figure 1

cubelet on the same plane. For example, choral music represents a greater proportion of music during the Renaissance than it does during the Romantic period.

Not all cubelets are of equal educational importance. Of the 224 possible cubelets, some, such as opera before the Baroque, are virtually empty. Selecting one work from each category does not by any means ensure good course content. Renaissance lute music would seem less significant for the average school student than the Renaissance madrigal or motet. The popular ballad of the Gay Nineties isn't as likely to be worthy of study as a song of Brahms. Not only must the choral teacher make judgments about which twentieth-century choral work to study; he must also evaluate the aesthetic and academic importance of this type of work in relation to a rondeau of the Gothic period. For purposes of music teaching, each category or cubelet must be evaluated in relation to all other classifications of music.

Intellectual Understandings

Intellectual understandings of music involve a way of thinking, the formation of concepts about music, and some knowledge of the processes of creating music.

Ways of Thinking.   Every discipline has its mode of thinking, its way of looking at the world. A physicist, for example, is interested in the physical properties of sound; the social scientist is interested in the effect of sound on human behavior; the musician is interested in how sound is manipulated and the tonal effects and compositions that can be created using sounds. A student should learn to think as a scientist in science class, as a sociologist in a sociology class, and as a musician in a music course. Appropriate thinking is as much a part of the subject as the factual information associated with it.

Concepts.   If a student is to think like a musician, he must have the means for doing so. This is where concepts come in, a term sometimes used loosely by music educators. A concept is "the resultant of a generalizing mental operation: a generic mental image abstracted from percepts."[4] Concepts vary in scope—some are broad and general; others are more concise. "Music" is itself a concept, which in turn involves more specific concepts such as melody, harmony, form, rhythm, expression, and timbre. Under each of these terms there are still more specific concepts. Under melody there are *contour, theme, motive, phrasing, expression,* and *range,* in addition to the previously mentioned concepts. There are concepts of melody associated with nearly every cubelet in Figure 1. The hierarchy of comprehensiveness of concepts is similar to the classification system employed in biology—from general to more specific.

Concepts facilitate a person's ability to think about music. The fact that words are mental tools as well as a means of communication is well estab-

---

[4]*Webster's Third International Dictionary* (Springfield, Massachusetts: G. & C. Merriam Company, 1965), p. 469.

lished.[5] A student who has no concept of melody is seriously impaired in his ability to think about, understand, and appreciate melody. He needs a concept of melody in order to be musically educated.

Considered alone a musical concept is not very useful, simply because concepts do not stand alone in actual music. Melody, for example, always involves rhythm because it occurs within a span of time. Since it is sounded by some medium it has timbre. Often it has other sounds occurring with it, thereby involving harmony and/or counterpoint. It is almost always preceded and followed by other music, so form is involved. And all melodies are sounded at some dynamic level. This integration and interplay of elements is part of the structure of music essential for the student to understand. When he can answer such questions as "What effect do the accompanying chords have on the melody?" he is well on the way to being educated in music.

Concepts and words are necessary for the student to be analytical about music, another characteristic of musician-like thinking. Being analytical also heightens one's awareness of the qualities in a particular musical work. The student should be able to answer the question "What's happening in the music now?" as he listens or performs. And he should apply the analytical approach to all music—past, present, and future. In this way he will best be able to cope with the music of A.D. 2000—music for which no one at present can teach the syntax or literature.

Because a concept represents a generalization about many experiences, one never reaches a point of final and complete understanding. Each new melody contributes to one's concept of melody. The process is cyclical. If an idea such as melody is truly basic to the subject, it will be encountered again and again, and with each appearance the concept is further developed for the student. (Other educational applications of concepts will be discussed in Chapter 9.)

Creative Process.   Musical learning should not be confined to the re-creation of what others have done. At a level consistent with their musical sophistication, students should engage in creating music through composition or improvisation, or both. Creative activity is valuable because it requires the student to think about how sounds are manipulated, which is a central feature in thinking as a musician. It also educates students about the process of creating music, including its mental trial and error, and just plain, hard work. In addition, creative activity allows a student to explore his own musical potential, and in that sense to know himself better.

---

[5]Tamotsu Shibutani, *Society and Personality* (Englewood Cliffs, New Jersey: Prentice-Hall, 1961), pp. 187–191.

Skills and Activities

The place of such skills as reading or developing good violin vibrato, and activities such as singing or playing an instrument, should be carefully defined. First, they are *not* subject matter content. A list of activities carried on in class is not a summary of the understandings that the children acquire. The activities themselves are no more the content of musical education than chiseling constitutes the study of sculpture.

But skills and activities are valuable as a *means* of effecting learning. Other things being equal, a student who sings a Schubert song is more likely to understand and appreciate it than one who just listens to it, especially if students have not had much musical experience. When an English teacher wants his students to understand drama, he has them read it and discuss the purposes, literature, and the technical production of a drama. To increase the students' understanding of a certain point, he might have them act out a portion of the play in the classroom. Such active engagement with the subject is a way of promoting learning.

To regard skills and activities as a means of learning the subject does not diminish the merits of performing or giving public programs. Far from it. Making music motivates students, fulfills the need for recognition and group participation, educates the public about the music curriculum, and brings the subject of music to life. (Other reasons for public performance are discussed in Chapter 17.) To re-create and resurrect music from the printed page to actual sound is vital to the art of music. Furthermore students who can read notation and perform reasonably well are more likely to maintain a continuing interest in music because they are not handicapped by a lack of skill. The significant point is that skills and activities, both creative and re-creative, do have a place in educating students in music. But the goal is not just to make music. It is to make music with comprehension and technical excellence to develop further understanding. The purpose of performance in the school music program differs from the goal of professional performing musicians, who quite properly see performance as an end in itself.

Attitudes

How one feels about what he knows is also important. This is probably more true for music than for the more traditional academic subjects in school. We use our ability to read and write daily, regardless of whether we enjoy reading or writing. We balance checkbooks and compute income taxes regardless of how we felt about arithmetic in school. Not so with music. If we don't like music we can refrain from buying recordings and attending concerts; if forced to listen to music in the supermarket, we can psychologically "tune it out." Much of the ultimate success of a music course depends on how the students feel about the subject after the course is over. And students acquire attitudes about the subject whether or not the instructor realizes it. Young people react to nearly everything they encounter in life, including music classes and teachers. The question is not *will* the students develop feelings about music, but rather *what* feelings will they develop?

Attitudes and knowledge are complementary. People cannot have intelligent reactions to something they don't know. If asked, "Do you like aardvarks?" they will likely answer, "I don't know." So the instructor's first task is to remedy ignorance so that at the least there can be *intelligent* dislike, and at the best there can be what the educator–philosopher Harry Broudy refers to as "enlightened cherishing."[6] Few people enjoy all types of music equally well. Being educated about something does not mean that one necessarily likes it. Education offers the opportunity to make intelligent choices.

Just as it is human nature to dislike and reject the unknown, it is also human nature to appreciate new insights about something not previously known. Most students, whether they admit it or not, do not want to be left out of any aspect of life, including music and the arts. This initial spark of interest or curiosity can be the basis for the student's later open-minded study of the subject.

Nonmusical Outcomes

Nonmusical benefits also occur from the study of music. For instance, a student may derive emotional release from singing. Whether or not this happens depends primarily on the inclinations of the particular individual, and not from any direct action of the teacher, as discussed in the preceding chapter. As long as the classroom atmosphere is not repressive, emotional release and other nonmusical outcomes will occur as a by-product of the class. Incidentally, the psychological satisfactions from music participation are as great, if not greater, when performing Bach and Bartók as when performing music of lesser quality. In any case, the teacher does not need to make emotional release, worthy use of leisure time, or improved self-esteem a part of his curricular planning.

Interrelationship of Outcomes

The five outcomes of music teaching—syntax, literature, understandings, skills, and attitudes—are interrelated. For example, the syntax of a style is

---

[6]"The Tanglewood Symposium: Music in American Society," *Music Educators Journal*, LIV, No. 3 (Nov. 1967).

presented in its musical works. Intellectual understandings take on meaning when they are associated with musical works and sound patterns. Skills aid in learning about music, but unless they are applied to musical works, skills are pointless. Understanding a musical work usually contributes to liking it, and in turn, positive attitudes motivate students to learn a subject better.

Outcomes usually follow a sequence. A syntactical sense and a knowledge of musical works must precede lasting concepts. Some people learn to play or sing very well but have little musical understanding. Such instances are the exception rather than the rule. Skills usually develop in conjunction with or after understandings. A teacher may decide on the skills and concepts to be learned, and then select the music to fit his plans. Or he may do the opposite: decide on the music, and then teach the skills and concepts that are clearly present in that music. For example, a Bach chorale lends itself well to the study of harmony, but would not be appropriate for studying meter. Either approach—concepts to music or music to concepts—can be effective.

Deciding What to Teach

From the vast world of music what should the teacher select to teach? There are no easy, clear-cut answers; schools and students differ too greatly for that to be possible. Some general guidelines can be stated, however. These broad considerations may help the teacher to make decisions about the content of a particular course.

Educational.   The first guideline is that the student should gain understandings, skills, or attitudes that he did not have prior to the course, and would probably not learn without some organized instruction. This idea is as basic to education as the law of gravity is to the operation of our planet. Without this basic "law," formal education has little point, except perhaps as babysitting or recreation. To deny this principle in word and deed means: (1) an abdication of the teacher's contractual and moral obligations to educate students, as well as a denial of the role of schools in general, (2) a limitation on the student's potential by restricting him to his present knowledge and skills.

In recent years, the charge has been made that schools and subject matter are not relevant to non-middle class students. Should there be different music curricula for different students? Should the college-bound, intellectually able student be given one course of study and the potential school drop-out another? To an extent, yes. Certainly the approach should be different for the two types of students. But the course content should be similar. Why? Because in a democratic society each person deserves the same opportunity for a good education. No one should be discriminated against in what he has the chance to learn. Some well-meaning persons have advocated programs with sparse and unchallenging subject matter for disadvantaged students. Such an approach keeps the youngster in his present deprived status by restricting his education to what he already knows. One of the clearest statements regarding this indirect discrimination was made by Raymond Lopez, a consultant in the Los Angeles Public Schools:[7]

> As soon as you can establish rapport, then you can introduce Brahms and Wagner. You don't have to stoop to "all they can sing is pop." In one school, all they were doing was drivel, in any old way. There was no attempt to organize it. The kids could just as well have been walking down the street—and maybe that's what we're preparing them for. We say that we are preparing the student for the world of reality. But shouldn't we always be struggling for enrichment? Why not acquaint the kids with those in the stream of time who have created outstanding music? I have heard a teacher say, "Why give them that stuff (a great composer's music)? They've never heard it. They'll never know it, and it won't make any difference to them." If I had had teachers like that maybe today I wouldn't know the difference. My teachers exposed me to the greats in music and that enriched my life. I'm better off for those teachers.

A practical approach to the question of being educational is to ask yourself what music the students would learn if they had no instruction in the subject in school. Is there some music which, like riding a bicycle, will probably be learned easily without skilled instruction? What music and skills demand the help of a teacher?

Subject Matter Validity.   Music is an established discipline, a recognized branch of knowledge and study. The teacher must ask himself, "Is this course content a legitimate representation of the field of music? Would most trained musicians (performers, musicologists, teachers) recognize and accept what I teach as a part of the discipline?" For example, a few teachers of string instruments to young children promote a kind of notation in which notes are identified not by pitch but by string name and fingering: A1, D3, and so on. The system is inadequate for depicting highness and lowness, note values, and differentiation of sharps, flats, and naturals that may be played by a single finger. It must be unlearned as the student progresses. No music theorists, symphony musicians, or musicologists use the system in studying or playing music. So it can hardly be considered valid in the music discipline.

The call for validity is a logical one: why teach something under the name of music that is not really part of the field of music? It is neither logical nor

---

[7]*Music Educators Journal,* LVI, 5 (January 1970), p. 96.

honest to adulterate a subject, even in the name of facilitating learning. The fact that some school subjects were being altered into a form not recognizable by professionals in the respective fields led to the "curriculum reform movement" in the late 1950s and 1960s. This movement stressed the subject matter validity of learning at all levels by inviting scholars from the various disciplines to help design curricula and develop teaching materials. Greater emphasis was placed on the subject matter preparation of teachers, and on teaching the fundamental ideas of each discipline.

Fundamental Knowledge.   Closely related to validity of content is the belief that students should learn the basic ideas of the subject, not just factual minutiae. Knowing the keys of all the solo piano works of Franz Liszt is not as useful as understanding his technique of theme transformation or his use of programmatic associations. When facts are associated with a larger idea they are important, but memorizing insignificant information is not good education. Fundamental ideas—tonality, motive, the 2:1 ratio in rhythmic notation, and the unity of words and music in art songs, to cite a few examples—are valuable because they are comprehensive and have wide application to a large amount of music.

Representative Selection.   The cube on page 56 shows the wide diversity of music. If a curriculum is valid it cannot be limited to only a few types of music. Such a situation is comparable to a foreigner who visits one city and announces that he has seen America. What a pity! He is missing so much without realizing it.

The crucial job for the teacher is to teach a representative selection of educationally worthwhile music, and to teach it as fully as time and the students' abilities permit. Overemphasis on any one type of music is detrimental to an education in music. The band director who has his band play one march after another and the choir director who gives his singers a heavy diet of Renaissance motets are both guilty of cheating their students, because both are passing over many other significant areas of music. Most serious of all is neglecting music written to stand on its own artistic merits—music that represents a sophisticated handling of sound. Many students go through school thinking of music only as something for whistling, dancing, or entertaining audiences. They are never introduced to the idea that organized sounds can be a fascinating and satisfying form of human thought.

Contemporary Content.   There should be an element of currency in what is taught. Obviously the material for study should not be restricted to recently composed music, but neither should contemporary music be omitted or ignored. If a teacher fails to cover any music written since Debussy, he is failing to educate his students adequately. Teachers must be more than curators of the past.

Relevance.   The word "relevant" has been used in several ways in recent years. To some people it means those things vital for survival and living; to others it means topics that one happens to like or in which one is interested; and to others it means the relationship between a person and a given subject. It is in the third sense that the word is used here. As mentioned in Chapter 3, there is an almost time-honored conflict between the integrity of the subject—the need for validity—and the needs, interests, and backgrounds of the students—relevance. The pendulum has swung back and forth between these extremes several times in the rather short history of music education in America. Proponents of the curriculum reform movement ask, "What good is a subject that has lost its integrity and character?" and the advocates of relevance answer, "What good is a subject that seems meaningless and worthless to the student?" Both views have a just claim for the attention of teachers, and the two positions need not be mutually exclusive.

Relevance is probably affected more by method than by course content. Topics and subjects have little inherent relevance; a topic that is important and interesting to one person couldn't matter less to another. Relevance results when a subject is given meaning through the teacher's knowledge and attitude. His role is to teach in such a way that the real content of the subject of music becomes relevant to the students. This is quite an assignment, but as the first sentence in this book says, the job of teaching music is not an easy one.

Learnable.   The curriculum must be learnable by the students. It is useless to teach something for which they are not adequately prepared. The students' background and interests should be considered. However, these are not the only criteria. Learnability must be considered in relation to the other guidelines, as well as to a host of practical matters such as amount of class time, books and materials, and performance obligations. A good teacher can build on interests the students already have without abandoning his subject. If the students seem uninterested he tries different approaches, perhaps modifying the level of knowledge and accomplishment he expects.

When one works with students from city ghettos, rural areas, or suburbs, it becomes evident that each teaching situation is unique, and each individual has his own abilities and ambitions. Such statements as: "inner-city children like . . ." or "kids from the country want . . ." contain nearly as much error as truth. Generalizations and stereotypes about people are best laid aside in making curricular decisions. The teacher must make the subject valid, meaningful, and learnable for the specific students he is teaching, not for a psychological or sociological abstraction.

Some of the guidelines presented here may appear to be contradictory. For example, the need to offer substantive instruction seems to work against the idea of relevancy, and contemporary content appears to be at odds with a representative sample of the subject. In the case of education v. relevancy the solution lies in good teaching methods. In other cases the teacher must strike a balance between conflicting needs. None of the guidelines is absolute and overriding. This situation means that the teacher must account for some divergent factors in planning a course. Difficult? Definitely.

Evaluating Music

It is nearly impossible to talk about the content of music classes without touching on the sometimes emotional and beclouded question of musical quality. Is there a difference in the quality of musical works, or is it simply a matter of what one happens to like? Because music is a human creation done in a particular cultural context, there are no absolute, universal rules for evaluating musical works. It is impossible and perhaps foolish to claim that a particular Japanese work is superior or inferior to a particular Mozart piano sonata. Each must be considered within its cultural context. The Mozart piano sonata does not conform to classical Japanese criteria, and Japanese music does not meet the standards of Western music.

Because teachers make judgments in selecting music, they should be aware of the basis on which the cultural evaluations are made. First, the purpose for which the music was created is one factor to consider. Some music is not intended to be heard as concert music (motion picture sound track music, most popular songs, hymns), and should not be evaluated in those terms. And the opposite is true; music written primarily for listening should not be judged by its suitability for social dancing or a film's sound track. Not all music studied or performed by school groups need be profound or serious. Some variety in this regard is desirable.

Second, evaluating musical works usually does not involve simple either/ or decisions. It is possible to make defensible judgments, but they tend to follow a continuum rather than fall into neatly defined categories.

Third, judgments can seldom be made only on the basis of the technical aspects of the music—the presence or absence of syncopation, range of melody, structure of chords, and so on. Most attempts at defining technical characteristics with specific selections end up excluding a number of works generally considered to be of high quality. Perhaps present analytical techniques are inadequate for making accurate evaluations about technical quality.

Four, evaluations can be made in terms of what the culture has deemed musical. *Not all works of music are of the same quality.* Music teachers should avoid simplistic thinking on this matter. The rationale and method of making evaluations are not simple matters, but they should be understood by every music teacher. For this reason a portion of Leonard Meyer's "Some Remarks on Value and Greatness in Music" is included in Appendix C. Meyer and like-minded aestheticians essentially agree that music of more value provides greater challenge and interest for the listener as it progresses in ways generally expected of music in the culture; less significant music is less challenging and intriguing, and more trite.

Five, the teacher should seriously consider (but not follow slavishly) how musical "authorities" — conductors, composers, and qualified musicians both past and present — of the culture have judged a musical work. If it is not possible for one to know all music, it is even more impossible to evaluate adequately every musical work. So it is only sensible to be familiar with the findings and efforts of other musicians. For example, in the 1870s the popularly recognized composer in Paris was Charles Gounod, and few paid much attention to a humble church organist at Sainte-Clotilde named César Franck. His *Symphony in D Minor* was coolly received at its first performance, and Charles Gounod himself called it "the affirmation of impotency carried to the point of dogma."[8] But through the intervening years musicians and listeners have found artistic quality in Franck and have weeded out much of Gounod's music. Because of its ability to fascinate and attract, Franck's symphony is still performed, while lesser composers and lesser works by Franck have been almost forgotten. Clearly there is room for a teacher's judgments. Sometimes he must consider a work about which no opinions of others are available, as in the case of many new compositions, or he may have a strong opinion about a work. As the old prospector said, "Gold is where you find it, not where it's supposed to be." The "musical authorities" may have overlooked a good work here and there.

Unity of Music Curriculum

Because music requires specialized abilities and training, music teachers often confine their attention to a limited area of the total program — band, strings, high school choral music, middle school general music. It is natural for each teacher to think of his specialty first and to be less concerned about the rest of the music program. But it is equally reasonable to expect each teacher to sympathize with and support the other aspects of the music curriculum.

---

[8] *The International Cyclopedia of Music and Musicians,* Robert Sabin (Ed.) (New York: Dodd, Mead and Company, 9th Ed., 1964), p. 739.

Although the level of student sophistication and the mode of instruction may vary among classes, essentially the same subject is being taught. Furthermore, nonmusic educators tend quite reasonably to look at the total program when they evaluate the effectiveness of the faculty and the curriculum. Unity of effort among the music specialties generally strengthens each area. For example, a good general music course helps to develop an audience that appreciates and understands the music the performing organizations present at concerts.

In some school situations students have been caught in a tug of war between two music teachers, each of whom wanted the student's talents for his group. In other cases there was no organized program for students to follow if they wished to prepare for majoring in music in college; the "course of study" was a particular teacher and his performing organization. Factionalism or a myopic view of the field doesn't help music teachers either.

Organizing the Material

For a number of reasons there can be no single, right curricular plan for a course. The abilities and interests of students and teachers vary too widely to create a uniform course of study. Also, class size, time, and materials and equipment differ from school to school. A uniform state or national course of study in band or general music would be too easy for some classes, too hard for others, not well taught by some teachers, and not attuned to local needs and interests. A more consistent music curriculum throughout the nation would be beneficial in some respects, but the prospects for any such effort are at the time of this writing virtually nil.

When planning a curriculum it is helpful to refer to any materials, guides, or courses of study that have been developed for an entire school system or for a state. This helps prevent unnecessary duplication or gaps in coverage, and these materials can be a source of new ideas.

Long-range course planning is not as common among music teachers, especially directors of performing organizations, as among teachers in other fields. One study discovered that only about one band director in a hundred prepares a written long-range course of study.[9] Often the teacher relies on a "first-aid" technique, consisting of placing a piece of music before the group, and then patching up the wrong notes, incorrect entrances, and faulty balance until the piece is ready for public performance. Rehearsing does call for on-the-spot judgments; but when a director does little more than fix up

[9]James Carlson, "The Status of Subject Matter Content of High School Band Rehearsals in Public Schools of the United States," unpublished doctoral dissertation, Indiana University, 1972. See also: R. Jack Mercer, "Is the Curriculum the Score—or More?," *Music Educators Journal*, LVIII, No. 6 (February 1972), p. 52.

music for performances, he deprives the students of much that can be accomplished in a performing organization. There should be more to a teacher's plans than setting of concert dates. And with most people the plans will be better organized and followed if they are written down.

What should a teacher's long-range plans include? Basically they should contain *specific* statements about the information and skills to be learned that year, as well as titles of the music for study. Such planning may seem burdensome at first. But just as a pilot does not start to fly an airplane across the continent without knowing where he is headed, a teacher should not try to guide a year's study of music without knowing what he wants to accomplish. The students and the community reasonably expect the teacher to know what he is about.

To organize specific plans, the teacher can sit down with a blank piece of paper before him and draw two vertical lines to divide the page into thirds. One column can be labeled "Music," another "Information," and a third "Skills." When the columns are filled out and the items are arranged in logical order, the names of months can be added to the left side to indicate approximately when the goals should be accomplished.

The teacher's daily lesson plan should contain specific statements about the material he will teach, as well as other reminders and cues for the lesson. It is often prepared only one day ahead of presentation and almost never more than five days in advance. Some suggestions on the preparation of lesson plans are given in Chapter 10.

It is wise to note what is actually covered during the year. The original general plan, plus the daily log of what was accomplished, can serve as the basis for next year's outline. When considering future plans the teacher should check his ideas against the guidelines presented earlier in this chapter.

Courses in the Music Curriculum

Music courses traditionally have been classified as either "performing groups" (band, orchestra, and chorus) or "classes" (theory, music appreciation, and general music). The distinction has some justification since the two types of courses normally approach music differently — one by performing and the other with textbooks, tests, and discussions. Fortunately each type of course can take on a few of the characteristics of the other.

Balanced Offerings.   Nonperforming classes have both suffered and profited from a lack of public attention. Because their achievements are seldom displayed the teacher feels freer to have his students study whatever he considers most worthwhile. But for the same reason these classes have been somewhat neglected in music education. Andrews and Cockerille describe the problem imaginatively:

> . . . we find a situation such as that in Albert School District, where the marching band dominates the music program—a marching band of seventy members and eighty flag wavers, majorettes, and rifle twirlers. Yes, they look mighty good marching down the field on a bright October afternoon.
>
> Trouble is, while they represent only eight percent of the school population, they receive approximately fifty percent of all the money that is expended on the school music program. This town doesn't know what the other children are missing. And frankly, there is little appreciative value to be had in listening to this band. It takes so long to teach marching and formations every September that there isn't much time left to spend on the music. The spectators applaud a show, not music. Here is a music director who has given up music education and gone into show business.[10]

The effort in music education should be spread evenly throughout the levels of the school system and among the various music courses. While the balance among courses is affected by the distribution of money, more important is the teacher's attention and effort. Sometimes the choral director will prepare ever so carefully for the choir period, but just before general music he will run into his office and grab at random some records to play for the class. Music teachers must not slight the nonperformers just because no one knows or seems to care about the quality of teaching in these classes.

Nonperforming Classes

There are several types of nonperforming music classes in the secondary schools. A general music course usually offers a wide variety of activities and topics and is usually populated by students not in a performing group. It is usually required of all sixth and seventh grade students except those in instrumental music. After eighth grade, general music is an elective, if offered at all. General music is discussed in Chapter 10.

A few high schools offer a music theory course, while more offer either music appreciation or a combined fine arts course, neither of which requires previous musical experience. These are further discussed in Chapter 16.

As school schedules become more flexible another type of music experience is becoming available: the individual study project. A student meets with a teacher periodically to seek direction on an independent study or

---

[10] Frances M. Andrews and Clara E. Cockerille, *Your School Music Program, A Guide to Effective Curriculum Development* (Englewood Cliffs, New Jersey: Prentice-Hall, 1958), p. 103.

creative project. To date, the chances for music teachers to work with students during school time under a tutorial arrangement have been very limited. Flexible scheduling offers more opportunity for individualized programs.

The nonperforming class has one advantage over the performing group. Because it has no public performance obligations it can cover specific phases of music more broadly and comprehensively than a performing group. It is not tempted to relegate musical learning to second place because of an impending concert. A teacher would be highly unusual if he neglected a performance, which the public will observe, to stress musical learning that the public will not see and hear.

Just as performing groups can benefit from a more academic study of music, nonperforming classes can also engage in making music and can even appear publicly. For example, as an outcome of the theory class some of the better student compositions can be performed in a laboratory-seminar situation or before the public. The music appreciation course should include singing themes and should teach the skills necessary for being a good listener. In short, no music class can afford to be detached from music or to be dull.

Performing Groups

The performing group has almost completely dominated the musical scene at the high school level, and to a degree in the junior high/middle school. The most recent statistics show that in grades 9 through 12 of public schools about 1,000,000 students were enrolled in band, 1,500,000 in choral music, and 163,000 in orchestra. These teenagers constituted 23.6 percent of all high school students.[11] By contrast only 42,000 were enrolled in theory and 107,000 in music appreciation. (Because of semantic problems with the word "appreciation" the authors of the study admit that the latter course actually may have been general music.)

To explain why secondary school music has become so performance-oriented, some historical background may be useful. The big step forward in secondary school music occurred with the expansion of the secondary school itself in the decades between 1910 and 1940. During that period the chances of a child's attending high school increased from one in ten to three in four.[12] This increase caused curricular changes because now the schools

---

[11] *Subject Offerings and Enrollments in Public Secondary Schools.* U.S. Department of Health, Education and Welfare—Office of Education (Washington, D.C.: U.S. Government Printing Office, 1965).

[12] *Digest of Educational Statistics,* Department of Health, Education, and Welfare (Washington, D.C.: U.S. Government Printing Office, 1970), p. 49.

had to serve many students who were not planning to go to college. In addition, a more enlightened view of what was worthwhile for teenagers brought music into the secondary school curriculum with new vigor. Because school music at the secondary level expanded so rapidly, there were few teachers trained for school music instruction. The secondary schools often turned to professional musicians, a trend that was accelerated with the unemployment caused by the advent of the talking motion picture and the depression of the early 1930s. Because so many former professional musicians were employed to teach music in the schools, their influence on music education was profound. These men naturally worked with their groups in much the same manner as the director of a professional organization. The period when the band or choir met was a "rehearsal," and the purpose of the band or choir was to present polished and perfected performances. Any teaching technique that contributed to a top-flight performance was a "good" technique. The teacher was called the "director," a term more familiar to professional musicians.

Many of the professional musicians who entered the teaching field made valuable contributions to music education. Even today the paucity of other professional employment for the musician has turned many performers toward teaching in the schools. Common interests bind the professional musician and the music educator together, and the teaching profession needs capable and sensitive musicians. What must be realized, however, is that whatever is good for a professional organization is not necessarily good for the performing group in the school. Because the two groups exist for different purposes, they should be approached in different ways.

For many years there was little question about the educational value of the professionals' approach. Beginning in the late 1950s, though, there was a reexamination of all education. Since that time people have looked at performing groups with new objectivity, and wondered how much music the students are learning in such classes. An accurate and comprehensive answer has not always been given with assurance. It has even been suggested that performing groups be replaced—not merely supplemented—by a more academic type of class.

A performing group has several features that justify including it in the curriculum. As the pragmatists point out, people learn by doing, by experiencing. A student who goes through the work of learning his part and rehearsing with the group knows the music in a way that someone who only listens can never know it. He has seen the music dissected and put together again; he has heard its thematic material over and over until it is part of him. Many a teenager has had an initial dislike for a difficult and profound piece. But as the weeks went by he gradually began to comprehend its meaning and beauty. Without the intensive work required to perform the music, he would have been left with little understanding of it.

Performing groups are well suited to meeting teenage needs for recognition, for activity; and students at this age want things to happen. The thought of passively studying about music is not as appealing as playing or singing for most of them. Preparing music for public performance motivates students. Such reasons as these do not negate what was said in Chapter 3 about the reasons for music in the curriculum. On the contrary, a performing group can take advantage of adolescent characteristics so that the students learn music more effectively.

A third point in favor of the performing group is its established existence. While not a compelling reason, it must be considered. Teachers are already trained in the instruction of performing groups, materials have been prepared, and the inclusion of performing groups in the curriculum is largely secured. Before discarding such achievements, something must be found as replacement. What is needed is not revolution, but rather evolution toward more educationally valid performing groups.

Enriching the Rehearsal.   What then is the educational weakness of the performing organization? Its efforts are devoted almost entirely to learning performance skills. This is fine — to a point. But there is more to being musically educated than fingering notes and following the conductor. Many students make sounds with little musical or intellectual understanding of what they are playing or singing. As a result they receive a lopsided education in music. For example, a young man who had been a first-chair player in an outstanding high school band was once asked what he remembered most clearly from his three years in the group. His response was, "Man, you'd better not make a mistake!" After years of training and academic credits, the worry about an imperfect performance had impressed him most.

Many teachers of performing groups do try to teach more than the correct execution of notes. Sometimes, however, their supplementary efforts are not presented with enough consistency or depth to be meaningful to the students. Offhand remarks about historical settings or theoretical features of a work are fine for educated musicians, but most students do not have the musical background to learn from a scattershot approach. It's easy for a director to believe that because he once told the group about the continuo in Baroque music, and that Haydn (not Handel) was a composer of the classical period, the students now understand the significance of the information. A short quiz on such items will usually dispel a teacher's optimistic assumptions about the students' level of retention.

For a performing group to achieve its educational potential, it should study some music in addition to what it performs. Otherwise the students' musical education will be limited to the small number of pieces they can play or sing. For most students, a performing class is their only formal music study. In addition the modest level of technical proficiency in many organizations may limit students to performing only the easier works in the literature. How many high school orchestras can perform Stravinsky's *The Rite of Spring,* for example? If a group studies only the music it can perform, not only are advanced works precluded but music for other media is eliminated as well. Band members study no choral music; neither band nor chorus studies keyboard or chamber works. Generally, even the choral students do little with art songs or opera. How limited their contact with music is!

How can a teacher give his performing groups an education beyond mere technical skills? He can set aside a *small* amount of time to enrich and supplement the regular rehearsal. Because the members of the group already know something about music and are interested in it, and can also perform *and* study the music, a small effort by the teacher can reap large educational dividends. If there seems to be no time for anything except learning to perform the music, then perhaps the group has too many performance commitments or the music is too difficult or is being over-rehearsed. In any case, studies have indicated that some rehearsal time can be taken for learning about music without adversely affecting the performance ability of the group.[13]

Two alternatives are available for the director who wants to enrich the rehearsal period. He can develop his own program of study, which should be varied and may include programed theory materials, reading and listening in the library, oral and written reports, a limited amount of lecturing, and student discussions. The most effective program of study should center on the music the group is performing. If the selection of music is properly representative of styles and types, the study program will be more valuable and easier to develop.

An easier course of action is to purchase materials especially prepared for rehearsal enrichment. Currently only one such series is available: *Performing Music with Understanding,* which comes in two nonsequential books, *Orange* and *Green.*[14] The books are in a programed, self-instruction format to save rehearsal time, and are of equal benefit to band, orchestra, and choral students. The material integrates the study of literature and theory through musical works in a variety of styles. The following aids are available for each book: a Teacher's Edition containing specific teaching suggestions and graded music lists, a record album containing all the music examples cited in the book, and a series of quizzes.

The director should make plans for a two or even three year period. Music is virtually the only subject in the curriculum in which students at different levels of training are in the same group. Although this contributes to the quality of performance it creates difficulties in organizing music study.

---

[13]Larry Gebhardt, "The Development and Testing of an Integrated Course of Study Providing for the Acquisition of Musical Knowledge and Skills by Students in a Junior High School Band," unpublished doctoral dissertation, Indiana University, 1973; E. L. Coleman, "Some Effects of Teaching Musical Knowledge in a Performance Class," unpublished Master of Arts thesis, University of Kansas, 1966.

[14]Hoffer, Charles R. and Donald K. Anderson, *Performing Music with Understanding,* Orange and Green editions (Belmont, California: Wadsworth Publishing Company, 1970, 1971).

The director runs the risk of boring the second year students by covering previously learned material, or of bewildering the first year students by omitting necessary background material. Basic information should probably be reviewed each year. But if the majority of the material is nonrepetitive, as in *Performing Music with Understanding,* it doesn't matter in which year a student enters the cycle of study—he will still receive the comprehensive coverage made possible by the long-term nature of the course.

In making plans for enriching the rehearsal the director should select music to suit educational as well as performance needs. Some pieces should be chosen for public performance, some for just reading through, and some selected so that the students can perform or listen to a work of a particular type or one containing a particular technical feature. The planning should also include books, film strips, and recordings. Such items are as important to music education as instruments, uniforms, and music.

What is the students' reaction to enriching the rehearsal period? For years students have been given the idea that all one does in a performing class is play or sing. At first they may seem uninterested in additional musical learnings, although this has *not* been the observation of teachers who have made significant efforts to enrich their courses. An unenthusiastic reaction from the students may have several causes: (1) The students may not understand the relationship between what they are studying and what they are performing in class. (2) It seems easier to play or sing through a music class than it does to read, think, and learn. It's only human to prefer the easier possibility. (3) Students are usually shrewd enough to realize that such study will involve homework and tests, neither of which they particularly like. However, if performing groups are to be curricular subjects on an equal academic footing with other courses, a comparable effort is required from the students.

Naturally, if the program is poorly taught, it will not succeed. Dull 20-minute lectures on hemiola and rote memorization of the intervals in the Phrygian mode are likely to alienate all except the most ardent scholars.

Need for Variety of Performing Groups

Not all students can profit equally from music instruction. Students want and need music that is suited to their ability and interest. When enrollment permits, groups at different levels of ability should be offered. There can be a choir for the more interested and talented young persons, and glee clubs for the less gifted. The same arrangement can be set up in instrumental music. Such a practice is consistent with the democratic philosophy of equal opportunity. The teacher must guard against slighting the less talented group, however. The education given students in a glee club is just as important as the education given in a choir; only the level at which the learning takes place is different.

The Need for Orchestras.   For a variety of reasons, including the growth of the band and the shortage of teachers during World War II, the number of school orchestras shrank considerably between 1930 and 1950. Since 1950 there has been a slow but steady growth in the number of school orchestras. The dearth of school orchestras is still a serious matter. First, in instrumental music the orchestral literature is vastly richer than the literature for band. And as was pointed out earlier in this chapter, literature is one of the important aspects of music. While the band can perform transcriptions of many fine works, the aesthetic qualities of string music frequently do not transfer well to winds—something is usually lost in a transcription. The band is acquiring a fine contemporary literature of its own, and possibly in 50 years the problem of literature will no longer be a serious one.

Second, the experience available to the interested amateur after graduation from high school lies largely in orchestras, which use only a limited number of winds and many strings. There are over 1,000 nonprofessional orchestras in the United States today, and almost all of them want additional string players.

Many band directors give three candid reasons for not offering string instrument instruction. One: students who study strings often represent a loss from the band, and hence a lowering of its quality. The end result may be two mediocre groups instead of one good organization. Two: there is no one competent to teach strings—the band director plays a wind instrument. Three: there is no time in the current teaching schedule. As for the first objection, in school systems of less than 1,000 enrollment in grades 7 to 12 there is some reason for concern. If the orchestra has only four violins and one cello, it cannot perform much of the good music available to it. However, some smaller school systems have both a creditable band and an orchestra, so two worthwhile groups can be developed if conditions are right. The plea of incompetency is seldom valid, at least at the beginning level. Most colleges require study on string instruments as part of the training for an instrumental music teacher, and most instrumental music teachers who majored in a brass instrument, for example, do not avoid teaching woodwinds.

The matter of teacher time and additional expense to the school must be faced. No school can expect to get something for nothing, and if it wants to offer a well-rounded curriculum in music, it must realize that an increase in teacher time will be required. Fortunately string instruments are no more expensive than band instruments, and their maintenance costs are usually lower. The amount of teacher time needed in addition to an already existing wind instrument program amounts to about a third of the existing instrumental teacher load. The time allotted to an instrumental music curriculum that includes strings is roughly one-third each to woodwinds, brasses, and strings, with the percussion worked into either the woodwind or brass classes, depending on which are smaller.

The Marching Band.   The marching band has commendable features. It is good public relations for the music department. Since many people see the band only at the football game, the band is their only contact with the school music program. Students achieve recognition, school spirit is bettered, and good feelings are generated all around as the colorful group parades by. To criticize the marching band is something like criticizing Santa Claus. What could anyone have against something that gives so many people harmless enjoyment and impresses them favorably with the school music program?

The objection is that the marching activity of bands, especially at the half-time of football games, has in some cases dominated the music education curriculum. Just as Santa Claus may draw people's attention away from the real religious meaning of Christmas, the marching band may divert music teachers, students, and the public from the real purpose of music in the schools. That purpose is to teach music. But consider the music that is played on the football field. When the band makes a formation of a four-leaf clover it plays "I'm Looking Over a Four-Leaf Clover"; Beethoven is not appropriate here. Not only has the marching season robbed the band of time it could have spent working on good music, it has encouraged bad playing, because the heat and cold, dust and dirt, plus trying to play on a bobbing instrument take their toll. How often instrumentalists talk about "getting my lip back in shape" to play well after the marching season is over. The half-time show is fun, but it is largely valueless for the students as far as getting an education in music is concerned. Unless school music is regarded primarily as an activity that gives youngsters a chance to gain recognition and a sense of teamwork, things which scouting and athletics also provide, then marching does not contribute to their musical education.

Now, what should the music educator do about it? To begin with, he can treat the problem honestly. If the appearance of the band at half-time shows is necessary for public relations, then let everyone admit it, rather than trying to pretend that the students are gaining a valuable educational experience. In most American communities today the marching band at football games is so much a part of life that it is unrealistic to suggest that it be discontinued, and perhaps because of its public relations value discontinuing the band would not be desirable in some communities even if it were possible.

In addition to facing the situation honestly, the instrumental teacher, by himself, or better yet in conjunction with band directors from neighboring schools, can reduce the effort expended for the half-time show. One way to do this is to cut down on the number of games at which the band marches.

Out-of-town games and the first game in the fall are most easily eliminated. (The band may still play at the games; this is quite a different matter from marching.) The other way to cut down on the time spent in marching is to simplify the band show. With a minimum of strain, a band can form the school letters in block style and march up and down the field. Considerable effort is required, on the other hand, for the band to spell out words in script and make automobiles, airplanes, and merry-go-rounds. What makes some of the effort spent on intricate formations rather pathetic is the fact that the low bleachers available at many high school fields prevent most of the on-lookers from seeing what the formation is.

In most schools the band director is also responsible for training the non-musicians (flag carriers, pompon girls, baton twirlers) — students who frequently are not members of the band. Although such participation is good for the students because it provides them with recognition and helps develop confidence, their activities are only distantly related to music. If possible the director should secure the cooperation of the physical education department to assist in or take over the training of these students.

The Complete Music Curriculum

There is some question whether groups that study a limited repertoire — stage band, swing choir, madrigal singers — should be included in the school curriculum on the same basis as band, orchestra, choir, and general music. Certainly such groups should be offered when possible, but in most cases they are better operated as adjuncts to the more basic courses in the music curriculum. That is, stage band membership might be available only to members of the band, or choir membership might be a condition for joining the madrigal singers, and so on. Otherwise the student's musical experience is likely to be limited by his prematurely choosing a specialized area before investigating broader forms and media.

The complete music curriculum consists not so much of drafting a list of course titles as it does of providing a quality education in music. Deciding what to teach requires thoughtful attention to subject matter validity, relevance, and the process of selection necessary for the vast body of music to be properly explored. Most important, the music teacher should realize that he is teaching a legitimate subject, and that in his classes students should learn about music, both as an academic discipline and as an art.

Questions

1. Should a performing group hear and study musical works in addition to those it performs? Why, or why not?

2. What are some features of musician-like thinking?

3. Are performance skills the main goal of music education? Are other outcomes equally important? What are the values of performing skills in the school situation?

4. What relationship exists between the attitude one has toward a subject and his understanding of that subject?

5. What does the term "subject matter validity" mean? What does the term "relevance" mean?

6. On what basis do Meyer and some other scholars make value judgments about musical works?

7. Why is a planned course of study or curriculum needed for music classes, including performing groups such as band and choir?

8. What are some ways in which the director can increase what the members of a performing group learn?

9. Why is it especially important that strings and orchestra be part of the curricular offering of medium-sized and large high schools?

10. What does the word "syntax" refer to? Why is it important that students recognize it?

11. What are the strengths and weaknesses of the concept of music literature as represented by the cube in Figure 1?

12. Why is creative activity important in music education?

Projects

1. Select three musical works that might be included in the repertoire of a performing group. Decide what you could teach the students about music as the group learns each work.

2. Select a book designed for use in a general music class and evaluate it according to the curricular guidelines suggested in this chapter.

3. Select three songs or other musical works and evaluate them for their musical quality.

4. Secure a curriculum guide or course of study for a music course and evaluate it in terms of the suggested curricular guidelines.

5. Using your main performance medium (band, orchestra, choir) plan an eight week course of study. Indicate the music you plan to use and what you specifically plan to teach.

Suggested Readings

Bechner, Weldon, and Joe D. Cornett, *The Secondary School Curriculum: Content and Structure.* Scranton, Pennsylvania: Intext Educational Publishers, 1972.

Berman, Louise M., *New Priorities in the Curriculum.* Columbus, Ohio: Charles E. Merrill, 1968. Ch. 11.

Broudy, Harry S., "The Nature of Knowledge and the Uses of Schooling," Lecture I (monograph). Wash., D.C.: National Education Association, 1969.

Facing the Music in Urban Education. Washington, D.C.: Music Educators National Conference, 1970.

King, Arthur R., and John A. Brownell, *The Curriculum and the Disciplines of Knowledge.* New York: John Wiley & Sons, 1966.

Klotman, Robert H., *The School Music Administrator and Supervisor: Catalysts for Change in Music Education.* Englewood Cliffs, New Jersey: Prentice-Hall, 1973. Ch. 4.

Madeja, Stanley S., and Harry T. Kelly, "The Process of Curriculum Development for Aesthetic Education" in *Toward an Aesthetic Education.* Washington, D.C.: Music Educators National Conference, 1971.

Music in General Education. Karl D. Ernst and Charles L. Gary (Eds.). Washington, D.C.: Music Educators National Conference, 1965.

Reimer, Bennett, *A Philosophy of Music Education.* Englewood Cliffs, New Jersey: Prentice-Hall, 1970. Chs. 8 and 9.

5

Managing the Music Curriculum

Every music teacher is to some degree a manager of the music curriculum, and has a legitimate concern for the amount of money available and the classrooms and equipment in his teaching situation. In small school systems, the music teacher administers the entire music program because he is the only teacher of the subject. Even in large school systems, teachers exert influence on administrative matters through their membership on district-wide committees and through their requests regarding equipment and schedules. Because it consumes large amounts of money, its product is displayed publicly, and its course offerings are varied and not firmly established by tradition, the music curriculum requires considerable management.

Counseling Students in Music

The specialized nature of music often makes guidance counselors hesitant to advise students in the subject. The music teacher's judgment is necessary for placing students in musical organizations, recommending outside-of-school music activities, advising families on the purchase of an instrument, or suggesting private lessons. Guidance skills are necessary for a music teacher at the secondary level.

The advising and placement of students in music is a serious responsibility. At stake are the student's self-confidence and self-image, as well as large investments of time and money on the part of the student, his family, and the school. Purchasing a quality instrument, taking years of private instruction, and investing hundreds of hours of rehearsal and individual practice should not be taken lightly. Encouraging or discouraging a student in music should never be a casual judgment made without solid information.

Placing each student in the course that is best for him does not mean admitting everyone to the orchestra or to the select choir regardless of his talent. A student is no more helped by being in a class too advanced for him than he is by being placed in a group too elementary for him. Jim, with his limited musical sensitivity, intelligence, and aural acuity, would be frustrated in a group that sings Renaissance polyphony. If Susie's out-of-tune violin playing significantly damages the efforts of the second violin section, she should not be allowed to limit what the other students can learn. If she has been given adequate instruction and opportunity, there may come a time when she should be guided into other areas that represent a better use of her abilities. Fortunately, students are usually aware of their deficiencies: Susie decides to try an art course; Jim is not interested in the select choir because it doesn't sing music he likes anyway, so he decides to stay in glee club.

To ensure that each student receives full benefit from the music program, the faculty must act on the basis of as much information as possible. Music teachers of early secondary classes might fill out a form recording the musical status of each student. (A sample is shown below.) The student fills in the front side of the form with information about his musical background. The other side contains space for music grades and comments from each of his music teachers pertaining to the student's growth in music and his level of achievement in the class. The sheet can be a cumulative record of the student's progress through school. It would be valuable to keep more complete records and collect more information, but most music teachers see so many different students each week that this is not a practical possibility.

Pupil's Music Record Card

Name _____ Date _____

Address _____ Phone _____

Have you ever taken private music lessons? If so, what and where? _____

_____

What musical instruments are owned by your family? _____

Do other members of your family play musical instruments? _____

Do you have a piano at home? _____

Do you have a good record player at home? _____

How many records does your family own? _____

Are most of them popular music or classical music? _____

Have you sung in any glee clubs or choirs after school hours? _____

If so, when and where? _____

What is your favorite kind of music, and what is your favorite piece? _____

_____

Do you listen to music programs on the radio or on television? If so, which ones? _____

What do you like best about music classes—listening to records, singing, playing instruments? _____

_____

_____

Report of Elementary Music Teacher

_____

_____

_____

_____

Musical aptitude test scores _____

Musical Aptitude Tests

A musical aptitude test attempts to measure inborn ability. Before administering such a test, the teacher should understand its purpose and be able to interpret the results. There are some things an aptitude test *cannot* do. One: it cannot infallibly predict success in music. No agreement has yet been reached among psychologists and musicians about what music talent is nor what sort of test would measure it most accurately. Even if there were some acceptable and valid indicator of talent, there are still variables such as intelligence, perseverance, and willingness to work. Furthermore, there is considerable specialization among musicians. Some compose, some sing and act, some play in symphony orchestras, some conduct, some accompany on the piano, and so on. The abilities required for each job differ, making it nearly impossible to devise a single test that will assess each talent accurately.

Two: a test cannot prove that a person lacks talent. Sometimes students are bothered by the strangeness of a testing situation, by a temporary physical condition such as a cold, or by inadequate understanding of the directions. On a machine-scored test, a student might omit a response and proceed to mark the rest of the responses out of proper order, thus making the test results worthless. Musical ability is an elusive thing and is likely to be misjudged for a number of reasons.

What *can* an aptitude test do? It can indicate that a person does have musical ability, and this fact makes the test worth giving. The laws of chance for all practical purposes preclude an accidental high score. As long as the results are not regarded as final or infallible, the aptitude test can provide information which, when combined with other observations about the pupil, permits better guidance. The teacher should use the test as a doctor uses his observations in making a diagnosis: a physician would never prescribe treatment solely on the basis of the patient's temperature, although he does want to know the temperature and will consider it in deciding what to do for treatment.

Aptitude test scores are especially valuable if the test is given twice in a student's school experience, once in fourth or fifth grade and again in seventh or eighth grade. Two tests greatly reduce the effect of chance, and the second provides up-to-date information that can be valuable for guidance when commitments to high school music organizations are requested of the students.

When the first aptitude test appeared after World War I, its purpose was to measure native endowment with such accuracy that the probability of success could be determined before music study. The test would serve as a screening device for large numbers of youngsters, showing quickly which ones possessed natural musical ability. Such a test would prevent spending limited teacher time and equipment on the unmusical student.[1] In school systems with limited resources, the aptitude test was thus used *as an expedient.* Today, music educators know that the aptitude test is worth giving because it provides useful information. But they also know that it is far from perfect, and that it is capable of providing only clues to talent. The aptitude test is for guidance purposes, not for determining whether a student should study music. The difference between the two functions is significant.

The pioneer work in musical aptitude testing was done by Carl E. Seashore, whose work is available today as *The Seashore Measures of Musical Talents* (revised edition by Seashore, Don Lewis, and Joseph G. Saetveit).[2] The test consists of six elements — pitch, time, rhythm, timbre, tonal memory, and loudness. It may be administered to students from grade four up. The student marks an answer sheet as he hears the sounds played on a record. The results of each of the six sections are given in percentiles according to the level attained by the student on the test. Seashore did not want the results of the six parts combined to form a composite score, although this is frequently done. The reliability of the various parts (the consistency of scores when the test is repeated) is about .75, and the reliability of the pitch test is .79 to .88.[3] This degree of reliability is satisfactory.

The validity of a test is the degree to which it measures what it claims to measure. Seashore said that "by definition" his tests were valid. For example, pitch is usually a factor in music, and it can be established with analytical acoustical instruments that the Seashore Measures do test pitch. Re-

---

[1] Peter W. Dykema and Karl W. Gehrkens, *The Teaching and Administration of High School Music* (Evanston, Ill.: Summy-Birchard Publishing Company, 1941), p. 373.

[2] Available from Psychological Corporation, 304 East 45th St., New York, N.Y. 10017.

[3] Oscar Krisen Buros (Ed.), *The Third Mental Measurements Yearbook* (New Brunswick, N.J.: Rutgers University Press, 1949), p. 177.

searchers have attempted to correlate the scores of the Seashore Measures with some aspect of success in music, and have achieved varying results.[4] The correlation coefficients are generally satisfactory in the areas in which one would logically expect some relationship.

The validity of the Seashore Measures has been challenged on the basis that the test is not musical. But the critics have missed the point. Suppose that a test is devised to select safe drivers before they actually climb behind the wheel of a car. The test consists of carrying a glass full of water across the room, with the safe driver spilling almost none of the water and the accident-prone driver spilling much. The fact that carrying water is not like driving a car is irrelevant, as long as the water carrying test really differentiates between the good and bad drivers. The weakness of the revised edition of the Seashore Measures is that the number of items in each part has been reduced by one half. A chance error in the raw score, therefore, has an inordinate effect on a percentile rank.[5] This can be remedied by giving the pitch test twice, since most teachers consider it the most important measure. The loudness test can be eliminated, and in its place the students can mark their responses to the second pitch test. Of course, the scorer must be informed of the change.

Edwin Gordon's *Musical Aptitude Profile* tests three areas — tonal imagery, rhythm, and musical sensitivity — through seven subtests.[6] The recordings are of high quality. Strings perform all the musical examples. The subtests usually consist of 40 original, short musical phrases. The student is asked to decide which selection he thinks is more musical on a particular subtest, or to determine if the phrases are alike or different. As with the Seashore tests, the scores can be interpreted in percentiles. Reliability is high at .95, and correlations with other measures of success in music range from .12 to .97, but are generally good.[7] The Gordon Profile is probably the most carefully designed aptitude test. It enjoys the benefit of being able to build on the efforts of its predecessors. Its drawbacks are length and cost. The total time required to administer all seven parts is about an hour and a half; Gordon recommends that the time be divided into two sessions. A number of the subtests correlate highly with the composite test score, so it isn't necessary to give all seven parts to secure adequate information.

Another major attempt in aptitude testing is the *Wing Standardized Test of Musical Intelligence* (revised edition).[8] H. D. Wing was critical of the unmusical, "atomistic" approach of Seashore, and set about to devise a more musical test based on a single or "omnibus" theory that music talent is not

---

[4]Robert W. Lundin, *An Objective Psychology of Music*, 2nd Ed. (New York: The Ronald Press Company, 1967), p. 242.

[5]Buros, *The Third Mental Measurements Yearbook*, p. 177.

[6]Edwin Gordon, *Musical Aptitude Profile Manual* (Boston: Houghton Mifflin Co., 1965).

[7]Gordon, pp. 4–5, 60–61.

[8]Available from National Foundation for Educational Research in England and Wales, 79 Wimpole Street, London W. 1.

fragmented.[9] Working carefully over a period of years, Wing constructed an aptitude test more musical in nature, in which the results are more affected by musical training than Seashore's raw talents. Its reliability is .91. Its validity has not been tested as thoroughly as the Seashore or Gordon tests. Although Wing built his test on a premise different from Seashore's, the students who score high on one also do well on the other.[10] Wing's test is not as easily obtained as the Gordon or Seashore, and the quality of its recording is inferior to the other two.

The *Test of Musicality, Fourth Edition,* by E. Thayer Gaston, is about half the length of the Seashore.[11] The student is asked to respond to examples played on a recording, and to give information about his musical background. The reliability of the test is .88 to .90, and its validity is good, although probably more influenced by musical training than the Seashore test.[12]

Some aptitude tests are intended to be given by the examiner at the piano, but this testing method has two serious drawbacks. First, when the human element figures so prominently in administering a test, the likelihood of error and variation on the part of the examiner eliminates the possibility of comparative norms, and considerably reduces the worth of the results. Second, the piano is inadequate for checking pitch discrimination because it cannot indicate intervals smaller than a semitone, a pitch difference too wide to be of much value.

Other tests are available from musical instrument manufacturers. Most of these do not make a valid assessment of ability because they lack sufficient items — sometimes there are as few as ten for pitch discrimination. On tests provided by instrument makers, it isn't surprising that a vast majority of the students are evaluated as good prospects for music study.

Administering Courses

The Student's Course Load

Sometimes a school's course requirements make it difficult for students, especially those preparing for college, to find time for music. This pressure is reflected in the number of students enrolled in music, and the size of en-

---

[9] Oscar Krisen Buros (Ed.), *The Fourth Mental Measurements Yearbook* (Highland Park, N.J.: The Gryphon Press, 1953), p. 230.

[10] Buros, *The Fourth Mental Measurements Yearbook*, p. 230.

[11] Available from O'Dell Instrument Service, 925 Massachusetts Ave., Lawrence, Kansas.

[12] Oscar Krisen Buros (Ed.), *The Fifth Mental Measurements Yearbook* (Highland Park, N.J.: The Gryphon Press, 1959), pp. 252–53.

rollment affects in turn the quality of learning that can be carried on. It is almost always *possible* for the student to enroll in music, but sometimes he must give up something else of such importance that it is not *reasonable* for him to choose music. For example, the student believes (often wrongly) that by taking music instead of an academic subject, he may forfeit his chances for admission to a good college. Naturally, a student cannot always take every course he wants; choices must sometimes be made. But the choices offered students should be reasonable ones, such as between art and music or between practical arts and fine arts for the college-bound student.

Several avenues of action for improving the situation are open to the music teacher. He might work with the counselor to arrange a student's program so that he can continue in music. Some courses can be taken a year earlier, a year later, or in summer school. The music teacher should not assume, unless there is conclusive evidence, that the counselor is "against" music. The problem is seldom his fault, and creating hard feelings may actually encourage him to advise students not to take music.

Sometimes students give a half-true reason for not continuing in music: "I don't have time." The real reason, which the student is either too polite or lacking in courage to admit, is a loss of interest in the subject. The teacher needs to be discerning of a student's underlying reasons before he goes to the counselor or principal to try to change a schedule.

Finally, the music teacher can work to install an additional period in the school day. A majority of schools still operate on a six-period day, in which the student is expected to take four subjects required for graduation. A fifth period is for physical education (in many states required by law), and the sixth period is for study hall or an elective such as music. The addition of a seventh period greatly increases the likelihood that the student will be able to take music. In fact, unless another period is added, the increasing requirements in other curricular areas will make it more difficult to keep music in the school day.

Course Scheduling

Setting up a schedule for classes within the school day, with the exception of small instrumental or vocal classes, is usually the responsibility of the school principal. When the teacher must work in more than one building, the principal schedules in cooperation with a music supervisor and other principals. The music teacher may indicate preferred periods, but with the many demands for special classes and groupings, making a schedule is a difficult task.

Since most general music classes in junior high school do not meet daily, the music teacher in conjunction with other teachers in "special" areas may have some choice in the scheduling. Music classes can alternate days with physical education, art, or practical arts. Some schools have blocked out the year so that a class has music daily during a quarter of the year, then art daily for a quarter of a year, and so on.

The past decade has seen several valiant attempts on the part of some school administrators to introduce more flexibility into scheduling. For example, classes have been rotated so that a student attends a particular class four days out of five, or in other cases six days out of seven. The following diagram illustrates a four-out-of-five rotation that allows for six subjects.

Class Period

Days of the Week

	M	T	W	Th	F
1	A	B	B	B	B
2	C	A	C	C	C
3	D	D	A	D	D
4	E	E	E	A	E
5	F	F	F	F	Free

As an alternative, five shorter class periods are held on Monday, Wednesday, and Friday, while four longer periods are held on Tuesday and Thursday. In this way, the student can take nine subjects. With the aid of a computer, it is possible to combine short units or "modules" of time (usually about 20 minutes) to schedule short and long periods as they are needed. In a few schools the schedule for each day is semi-improvised during a 30-minute homeroom period. A valuable guide to scheduling is the MENC publication *Scheduling Music Classes.*[13]

The recent years of experimentation with scheduling have demonstrated what could probably have been predicted—a new schedule does not save an otherwise weak educational program. When handled properly, flexible modular scheduling *can* provide a better use of the school day, but such a benefit will not happen without careful planning and sensible administrative attention.

The music teacher faces special problems. One is the need for having the best winds in both band and orchestra. There are several ways to meet this need. Moving from the least desirable to the most desirable they are:

---

[13]Robert H. Klotman (Ed.), *Scheduling Music Classes* (Washington, D.C.: Music Educators National Conference, 1968).

Sample modular schedule for the music teacher

	Monday	Tuesday	Wednesday	Thursday	Friday
8:00 H.R.			Homeroom		
1 / 2	Choral A	Preparation	Student Activities	Choral A	Choral A
3 / 4	Choral B	Choral B	(Madrigal)	Choral B	Choral B
5 / 6	Student Conference	Student Conference	student	Student Conference	student Conference
7 / 8	Choral C	Choral C	Conference	Choral C	Choral C
9 / 10	Preparation	student Conference		Music	Music
11 / 12		Choral A	Preparation	Theory (lab)	Theory (lab)
13	Lunch			Preparation	Preparation
14	Music Theory	Lunch	Lunch	Lunch	Lunch
15 / 16		Music Theory			
17	Preparation		Preparation	Preparation	Preparation
18 / 19 / 20 / 21	Choral Large Group (A,B,C*)	Staff Planning	Choral Large Group (A,B,C)	Choral Large Group (A,B,C)	Choral Large Group (A,B,C)
22 / 23	Preparation	Student Conference	Preparation	Preparation	Preparation
24 / 25	Voice Coaching	Voice Coaching	Voice Coaching	Voice Coaching	Voice Coaching

*Choral A, B, C is a combined group formed of smaller sections.

(1) Have band and orchestra meet on alternate days. In the fall the band can meet three times a week, and in the spring the orchestra can meet three times a week.

(2) Schedule one of the orchestra practices each week during out-of-school hours and bring the winds in at that time.

(3) If room and teachers are available, have both band and orchestra meet during the same period. The best winds can move twice a week to orchestra, while the remaining winds get more practice on the band music and further ensemble experience.

(4) Schedule the best winds into a study period that meets during orchestra time. Two or three times a week they can work with the orchestra.

Teachers of large performing organizations find it hard to give students individual instruction or to arrange small ensemble experience. Furthermore, some directors are reluctant to work with anything less than the full group. In a large organization the talented students, who can perform most of the music at sight, are bored and learn little they don't already know. To remedy this problem, the more able students might occasionally be excused from group rehearsal to practice alone, read about music, teach younger students, or work in small ensembles. Studies indicate that such a procedure does not hurt the quality of a performing group; in fact, it provides for a better music education.[14] With a little planning (and luck) a small ensemble can be arranged during out-of-school hours. Some directors organize ensembles by study periods. While this does not always mean that players of comparable ability are together, it does provide ensemble experience, which is valuable for all music students. Flexible scheduling makes it easier to arrange special instruction during times other than rehearsal periods.

Credit and Graduation Requirements

If music is to be a curricular course, music classes should meet during the school day. If they are forced to meet outside the regular school hours, they are not curricular.

In the high school, credit should be offered for music study *on the same basis as all other subjects in the curriculum.* This means one full unit of credit per year for all music courses meeting five days a week and requiring homework, outside obligations, and practice at home. Half credit simply means that music is half as good as other courses and is only half as valuable to the student. Two excuses are given for allowing only half credit (or less) for music. One is that no textbook or homework is involved. The music teacher can answer this argument by suggesting the need for individual practice in performing groups, and the homework required in nonperforming classes. The *Performing Music with Understanding* books provide a two-year course of music study and furnish tangible evidence that performing groups are expected to cover academic subject matter in music. When the performing group is made a more educational undertaking, a good case can be established for offering full credit in music.

---

[14]Jay D. Zorn, "The Effectiveness of Chamber Music Ensemble Experience for Members of a Ninth Grade Band in Learning Certain Aspects of Music and Musical Performance," unpublished doctoral dissertation, Indiana University, 1969.

Another reason given for lower credit is this: since students from several grades are included in the same class, and since a student in a performing group takes the same course for several years, no new learning takes place after the first or second year. Although this statement indicates an ignorance of how music is learned, on the surface it appears to be a logical conclusion and should be answered thoughtfully. It is obvious that students over the years assume positions of leadership in a group. As a sophomore Joe Green may have played Beethoven's *Egmont Overture* as a hesitant second violinist; in his senior year he is concertmaster and is responsible for leading the section. In his sophomore year Joe got some of the musical idea of the Beethoven work, but as a senior he comprehends more fully the phrasing and the manner in which the thematic elements are combined. As Chapter 9 points out, music education is the increasing awareness of musical concepts such as tone and phrasing, and concepts are not learned quickly.

Most students do not need music credits to graduate from high school. The students currently in music courses would probably have enrolled no matter how little credit was offered. The concern here is for equality and prestige for both student and teacher. The teacher's claim that music is important is weakened if the school supports that subject only halfway. And when the students study hard and improve in skills and understanding, they can hardly be blamed for resenting the implication that so little is thought of their efforts. Because music is one of the fine arts which are so vital to the quality of human life it deserves equal credit with other academic courses.

Below is a typical listing of requirements for graduation:

> 4 units in English
> 2 units in history and social science
> 2 units in mathematics
> 1 unit in science
> 2 units in foreign language
> 5 units of electives
>
> A minimum of two years of physical education, including passing a swimming test

total: 16 units

Eleven of the sixteen requirements are in the traditional academic areas. There is a physical education requirement, and sufficient allowance for electives. What's missing? Any mention of the fine arts. The requirements tacitly say: "The fine arts are not an essential part of a high school graduate's education. We have plenty of requirements in other areas, including swimming." A fine arts stipulation would probably not have a dramatic effect on the enrollment in music courses. Most students enroll in one fine arts course during high school anyway. But such a requirement would place the fine arts on an equal footing with other studies, and draw attention to the rightful place of the arts in education.

Credit is a two-sided affair. If the school fulfills its obligation by granting credit to music, then music must fulfill its obligation by providing a course worthy of credit. For this reason, general music classes and beginning instrumental classes are not recommended at the senior high school level, when courses are expected to have more depth and to be less exploratory in nature. If a student in high school wishes to increase his musical understanding or gain instrumental experience and receive legitimate credit for it, he should involve himself in the more intensive study of a music appreciation course or take private lessons.

Credit for Private Study

Although private study is not supervised by members of the faculty, some school systems arrange for credit to be given for it. Again, the credit is seldom needed by the student for graduation, but it does give music study the respect it merits, and places such study on the student's record for all to see, including college admissions officers.

To ensure its validity, credit earned for private study should be carefully administered as to choice of teacher, enrollment, and method of grading. The private teacher may be approved by the state department of education, the school music teacher, or a local college or university.[15] A panel of two or three uninvolved music teachers should audition the student for grading at the end of the year. The course of study and standards must be made explicit before study is begun. This may be done by a panel of private teachers for each particular instrument, by the state department of education, or by music education organizations.

Advanced Placement Program

The Advanced Placement Program provides college level courses in high school. The student takes a nationally developed examination, which many colleges sanction by granting college credit to students who demonstrate a certain level of competence. Operated by the College Entrance Examination Board, the examinations are available in 11 subject matter areas, including art and music. The music examination emphasizes analytical listening, but

---

[15]See *Missouri Applied Music Plan,* Missouri State Department of Education, Jefferson City, Missouri.

also requires a knowledge of styles, cultural context, and some technical information. The examination calls for training in both theory and literature, but not performance. Some larger high schools offer a class designed to prepare students for the Advanced Placement examination. In many schools, however, students must acquire such information through their performing organization or through guided independent study.

Summer Music Study

Summer study helps maintain performance skills and interest, which can wane if the student engages in no musical activity for nearly three months. Music teachers need to become informed about and involved in programs of summer study, and teachers in schools that do not have summer music study should consider the possibility of promoting it.

Many school systems sponsor summer instruction supported by tax funds. In some cases it is included in the budget of the school board, while in others it is supported by a special tax levy, often as part of a recreation program. Sometimes participants in the programs are asked to pay a small fee. In the great majority of summer programs the emphasis has been entirely on instrumental music, probably as a carry-over from the traditional summer band concerts in the park. The program, however, can very well include vocal as well as instrumental music. In most summer programs, instruction consists of small classes and ensemble playing, but a large group rehearsal may be held once or twice each week. High school students usually do not participate in large numbers, because many find jobs or attend camps, and the classes are generally for less advanced players.

A second idea has been tried successfully in a few communities. A tuition supported summer music program meets in one school building but enrolls students from many nearby school districts and employs a faculty from several different schools. The advantage of such a program is that the student can study with an instructor who is a specialist in his particular field—woodwind, brass, or string. A second advantage lies in the fact that enough students can be brought together to make a high caliber performing group and allow greater variety of instruction, including some theory and literature.

A third type of summer study is offered at music camps and on the campuses of colleges and universities. Many school systems arrange financial assistance for worthy students by appealing to service clubs or by using the proceeds of concerts. A scholarship gives encouragement and incentive to the student, and stimulates in others a desire for summer study. Financial assistance should seldom cover the entire cost of the summer study, though, because a teenager frequently gains more from an undertaking when he has helped to pay for it. The procedure for selecting scholarship recipients must be carefully explained to parents and students, and a full accounting of the funds should be given to the school administration.

Finance and Budget

Public school systems are financed by tax monies from local, state, and federal sources, and the detailed budgeting is handled in various ways. Differences in the minutiae of budgeting are so numerous that it is difficult to discuss the matter in a general way. Besides, finance and budget eventually rest in the hands of the school administration, which prescribes how the money spent for music purposes shall be managed.

If a philosophy of equality among curricular areas is operative, then the music department should be treated as any other school department—no better, no worse. If possible, the budget should be set up according to the recommendations of the U.S. Office of Education on the basis of function, regardless of which department uses the money.[16] For instance, the repair of equipment should be placed under one heading whether the repair is for typewriters, scientific equipment, or musical instruments. It can then be broken down further into musical instruments, piano tuning, or typewriters, if this is desired.

Music is a subject area that requires large expenditures for supplies and equipment. If a school has fallen badly behind in its purchasing for music, the school's finances might not allow the fulfillment of these needs in one or two years. The music teacher, in cooperation with the administration and the school board, should plan a program of buying that spans perhaps five years. In this way, music needs can be met over a period to time without disrupting the school's financial situation.

The basis for financial requests should be the educational needs of the particular school system. It is useless to compare one school system's expenditures with another's, since one may be well supplied, while the other lacks essential equipment. The teacher should work out a list of necessary equipment and supplies, being restrained in requests for luxury items that are not essential to the educational program. Each request should be explained and supported by the music teacher or by the music faculty. Justification for the music program and its needs must be logical, reasonable, consistent, and educationally valid. "Consistent" is an important word because too often an unfulfilled request seems to be forgotten a year later

---

[16] *Financial Accounting for Local and State School Systems,* U.S. Department of Health, Education, and Welfare Bulletin No. 4 (Washington, D.C.: U.S. Government Printing Office, 1957).

when budget time comes around again. The administrators logically wonder what happened to the need of the year before, and may conclude that the request wasn't really necessary after all. Sometimes specific needs might be explained in terms a nonmusician could understand: "A baseball team needs a third baseman. It's much the same in music. It's hard to have a successful band without an oboe."

Sources for Funds

By training, desire, and contractual agreement, members of the music staff are teachers, not fund raisers. To involve them to any extent in bake sales, tag days, and card parties is a misuse of their time and talents. Besides, fund raising puts the music teacher in the awkward position of seemingly raising money to support and enhance his job.

Yet the financial situation in some schools is poor. A parents' organization may be one answer, and other sources can provide additional funds. A rental fee could be charged on instruments or a small tuition asked for instrumental lessons. There may be profits from the sale of tickets to public performances or special concerts by visiting musicians. Advertising space can be sold in the concert program. If a share of the music budget supports a marching band, it is only fair that a portion of the receipts from the sale of tickets to football games be allocated to the music department. Finally, if the school has a stage band, the income it derives from playing at school dances should revert to the music department.

Parents' Organizations

Many school districts have parents' organizations to meet equipment needs that cannot be covered by the school budget. The parents' group has much to recommend it: it provides solid support for music activity, financial aid, and offers assistance in such activities as chaperoning students on out-of-town trips. This, however, is not the entire picture. In some cases, after the initial equipment goals are met, the parents' organization turns into a pressure group. Besides harassing the superintendent with persistent demands (a procedure that at first glance might appeal to an inexperienced music teacher), the group begins to apply pressure on the teacher for more elaborate concerts, better festival ratings, more community performances. Then the teacher becomes burdened with providing new and interesting programs for every meeting of the parents' organization. Finally, if the son or daughter of the president of the group does not receive a privilege that the parent thinks is deserved, the teacher can be placed in a most uncomfortable position.

Before organizing a parents' group, these suggestions should be considered:

(1) Be certain that the organization is approved by the school administration, and that the administrators understand the purposes of the group. If possible, get administrative approval in writing.

(2) Form a parents' group only if the need for support cannot be fulfilled through the regular school budget. Probably at least two years should elapse before a teacher is assured that needs will not be met in the regular manner.

(3) If possible, integrate the needs of the choral and instrumental music departments. It should be Music Boosters or Music Patrons—not Band Mothers or Choral Parents' Club. Even inadvertently music teachers must not appear to pit one type of music against another.

(4) Avoid the possibility of a future pressure group by organizing only on a temporary, one-project basis. When the project is done, the group can disband. In this way, no nonfunctional remains will cause embarrassment or discord.

(5) Devise ways to meet and work with parents other than through a permanent, formal organization. The parents' night suggested in Chapter 17 is an excellent way to establish rapport with the students' families.

Managing Equipment

The Music Library

If the music library is disorganized or inadequate, the new teacher will have to establish a system for filing the music. Although some variation in the system is possible, certain basic considerations are important. Music not in use should be housed in cupboards or filing cabinets. All copies of a single work should be placed in manila paper envelopes or folders with index tabs for easy identification. (Several types of inexpensive commercially printed envelopes are available.) Filing in this way is swift and sure, and the music does not receive excessive handling. Filing alphabetically by title is recommended if most of the music is derived from folk music or has been adapted by arrangers. Otherwise, alphabetical listing by composer is a quick and accurate way to file. To accommodate music of various sizes—a situation encountered particularly among band publications—it is advisable to store all music of the same size together for more efficient use of space.

Each file drawer is assigned a number, which can be written on the file card and on the envelope of each work. Alphabetization is preferable to consecutive numbering within the drawer because new music can be inserted without disrupting the system.

Individual 3 × 5 cards should be made up for each selection in the library and placed in alphabetical order in a card filing box for reference. Information on the card should include the following:

> Title of composition
> Composer or arranger
> Instrumentation or voice classification
> Number of copies
> Publisher
> Dates and places of performance

To help the teacher in his planning, duplicate cards of different colors can serve as cross references. In addition to filing by title, there can be a filing by composer, and a third classification by the type of music—march, choral, overture, sacred polyphonic, or whatever categories the teacher finds useful.

As soon as a music library is established, it can normally be maintained by student assistants, with a minimum of supervision from the teacher. Before filing music, the librarians should check the copies for needed repairs and erasures. The inventory of copies and available parts should be kept up to date so that the teacher is spared the turmoil of passing out music in class only to discover that the supply is insufficient.

The music should be issued to each student in a music folder of heavy cardboard, with inside pockets that prevent the music from spilling out when the folder is moved. Inside should be a sign-out card, which the student leaves with the librarian when he takes his music home to practice. The card should include the folder number, date, and student's name. For ease of administration, the student should check out the entire folder, and not remove individual pieces from it.

Uniforms and Robes

Uniforms and robes should be kept in a dark, dry room or closet. Light has an adverse affect on some fabrics, and the better they are protected from moths, mildew, and dirt, the longer they last and the better they look. Uniforms and robes should be checked in and out by a student committee with each use. When students have free run of a rack of clothing, a few of them cannot resist the temptation to grab the first robe or belt they come upon, resulting in massive confusion.

Robes and uniforms are no longer considered a requisite for public performance. In a day that stresses and sometimes reveres informality, uniforms have lost some of their appeal. They are also expensive, and rapid changes in skirt length and clothing styles make it impossible for uniforms to remain fashionable. Furthermore, a group can look attractive without an expensive uniform, and the money saved can be spent on educational equipment and supplies. A band looks fine in inexpensive blazers, and a choral group can dress in any manner that is consistent and visually appealing.

Lending or Renting Equipment

A considerable sum of money is invested in the uniforms, instruments, and music that a music department loans or rents to its students. It is therefore necessary for the teacher to keep an accurate accounting of all equipment. Information about instruments should include type of instrument, manufacturer, serial number, school number, date of purchase, value, and accessories. Uniforms should be described by school number, size, date of purchase, and cost. No teacher wants to accuse a student falsely of losing a clarinet, nor does he wish to be responsible for the loss of a pair of band uniform trousers or a cello bow. Every item of significant value that is loaned or rented should be signed for by the parent on a bond, which obligates him in case of loss or damage. If the bond is printed on a 3 × 5 card, it will be more durable and easier to file.

Instrument Loan Contract

I, _____ , accept full
responsibility in the event of loss or damage to _____ ,
serial number _____ . I will present it for
inspection promptly when called for and return it on or before _____ .
I understand that the approximate value of the instrument at the time of its
assignment is $_____ . I agree to keep the instrument in good
playing condition and to pay for any repairs made necessary by misuse,
negligence, or carelessness. Accessories listed here are understood to be included under the terms of this contract:

_____ .

Date assigned _____   Student's signature _____

.   Parent's signature   _____

Date returned _____   Teacher's signature _____

Care of Equipment

Instruments should be cleaned and checked at the end of the school year. If repair is needed, the instrument should be sent out during the summer months so that it will not be out of service when it is most needed. The teacher or an instrument repairman should examine each instrument in June to check its condition and make needed repairs. Pianos should be tuned at least twice a year. Audiovisual equipment used in music classes should also be checked regularly, although in many schools this servicing will be under the supervision of the school's audiovisual specialist.

Insurance

Depending on the particular policy, the normal comprehensive insurance carried by the school district on its building will cover some of the music equipment. For other equipment, floater policies are available. Bids should be let, to obtain the lowest price. Some schools offer insurance on a group basis to families for privately owned instruments used in school. This incidentally helps to keep the insurance cost down. The insurance policies normally cover not only theft and fire, but also accidental damage—a far more frequent occurrence. The basic exclusions are intentional damage and normal wear and tear. The values of coverage are more than financial. The relationship between school and parent is reinforced when parents, whose son's trumpet was stolen at school, are told that despite the bond, in this case insurance will cover the loss.

Functional Music Rooms

Because of the variety in school size, educational needs, and construction materials, it is nearly impossible to summarize the information that might be useful in planning for building expansion. The MENC has published a helpful booklet on this subject, *Music Buildings, Rooms, and Equipment*, which should be consulted when new facilities are planned.[17]

A good architectural firm should consult with specialists in sound engineering to ensure adequate soundproofing and acoustical conditions in the rooms. The music teacher should ask specifically about acoustics for the new building.

---

[17] Charles L. Gary (Ed.), *Music Buildings, Rooms and Equipment* (Washington, D.C.: Music Educators National Conference, 1966).

New music rooms should consider the space and equipment requirements of an enriched program. For instance, room-darkening shades will be needed so that various kinds of projectors can be used. Storage space and properly placed electrical outlets should be specified so that listening equipment can be used.

Especially valuable are visits to the music facilities of recently completed schools. The tour should include a discussion with the music teachers who work there. These people can comment with authority on the adequacy of their new quarters.

Many existing rooms are not suitable for good music teaching. A few are too "dead"; that is, they soak up too much sound. Deadness is most often caused by too much acoustical tile and draperies. A room constructed for band rehearsal is usually too dead for choral groups. Such a condition is difficult to correct. The problem can be alleviated somewhat by placing large pieces of hard fiberboard over some of the acoustical tile on the walls, and on the ceiling if necessary. Both instrumental and vocal teachers will have to approve any acoustical changes, of course. Dead classrooms have one important advantage: if the students perform in another location, the place of performance will seem "live" in comparison to the regular room, and this can give the performers a psychological lift.

More common than dead rehearsal rooms are those that are too "live." It is easier to correct this condition caused by too much echo. Sound absorbing materials such as draperies, acoustical tile, or porous insulating board can be positioned around the room. Draperies can be made rather cheaply and easily, perhaps by students or parents.

The successful teacher is wise in his use of materials—equipment, money, and, most important, the limited time of his students. When matters of finance, curriculum, credit, and equipment are handled efficiently, the learning climate is improved and music teaching is more effective.

Questions

1. Suppose a principal asks you if you would mind meeting your performing group entirely after regular school hours. What points could you make for performing groups being curricular subjects?

2. Why should aptitude tests and other evaluations *not* be used to select those students who will be allowed to begin instrumental music study?

3. If a performing group is a curricular subject on an equal basis with English or biology, should the music organization have student officers and give service awards for contributions to it? Why, or why not?

4. If the school district is not in a financially fortunate position, should

tuition be charged for instrumental music study and a fee charged for the use of school instruments? Why, or why not?

5. What do the terms "validity," "percentile," and "reliability" mean in relation to tests?

6. What is the Advanced Placement Program? How does it benefit students?

7. Suppose that you are a band director. The first-chair flutist studies flute and piano privately, has attended a summer course at a college, reads correctly at sight almost all the band music, and is an able academic student. Should this student always be present in rehearsal? What other musically educational activities might he or she engage in during some rehearsals?

8. Is it more or less important than it once was for bands and choirs to have robes and uniforms? How necessary are robes and uniforms?

Projects

1. Find out about the opportunities for summer music study in your state. Compile a list of them, indicating the length of session, age level, expense, scholarship opportunities, and educational activities.

2. Test yourself with two of the musical aptitude tests that are available.

3. Interview two high school band directors:

(a) Inquire whether their schools have a parents' organization for the promotion of music. If so, ask their opinion of the idea and their experiences with it.

(b) Find out how budget requests are handled in their schools — when they are submitted and in what form, and who decides the amount of money to be allotted to the music department.

(c) Request permission to see the music library system that is used, and the instrument and uniform inventory and check-out forms.

Suggested Readings

Andrews, Frances M. and Clara E. Cockerille, *Your School Music Program, A Guide to Effective Curriculum Development.* Englewood Cliffs, New Jersey: Prentice-Hall, 1968.

Bessom, Malcolm E., *Supervising the Successful School Music Program.* West Nyack, New York: Parker Publishing Company, 1969.

Gary, Charles L. (Ed.), *Music Buildings, Rooms and Equipment.* Washington, D.C.: Music Educators National Conference, 1966.

Klotman, Robert H. (Ed.), *Scheduling Music Classes.* Washington, D.C.: Music Educators National Conference, 1968.

Klotman, Robert H., *The School Music Administrator and Supervisor: Catalysts for Change in Music Education.* Englewood Cliffs, New Jersey: Prentice-Hall, 1973, Chapters 8, 9, and 10.

Lehman, Paul R., *Tests and Measurements in Music.* Englewood Cliffs, New Jersey: Prentice-Hall, 1968.

Snyder, Keith D., *School Music Administration and Supervision,* 2nd Ed. Boston: Allyn and Bacon, 1965.

Whybrew, William E., *Measurement and Evaluation in Music,* 2nd Ed. Dubuque, Iowa: William C. Brown, 1971.

Section Three

With What Result: Feedback

I shot an arrow into the air,
It fell to earth, I knew not where.

These lines from Longfellow describe in a figurative way what many teachers do: they conduct an activity designed to teach the students something, but they never determine the results of their effort. In a sense, they carry on a one way conversation not knowing what impact, if any, their words have on the listeners. If teaching is more than just dispensing information—and it is—then evaluating the results of teaching is essential. Unlike the poet, a teacher must know where his "arrows" land. Feedback is a necessary part of the teaching mixture described in Chapter 1, and it is the topic of Chapter 6.

6

Evaluating the Results of Instruction

"What did the students learn?" has become a prominent question, for two reasons. First, teachers have grown increasingly aware that they need to have evidence on how well students are learning. Without such evidence the teacher has no firm basis on which to make educational decisions. Second, federal, state, and local school agencies have become more concerned about the results of education. To put it bluntly, the taxpayers want to know what they're getting for their money. Attention to the concrete, immediate results of learning may seem simplistic, but it is justifiable.

The need for evidence of learning has caused many educators to become interested in "observable behaviors," in having clear evidence that students have learned. Nearly everything learned must somehow be observable, they believe; otherwise, the existence of learning is questionable. But even the most enthusiastic proponent of "observable behaviors" knows that not everything learned can be seen. Just as one cannot observe love directly, one cannot see all aspects of an understanding of music. But one can make inferences about love and musical understanding from overt actions. Despite the fact that they are sometimes misinterpreted, observed behaviors are usually more valid than hunches and intuitions. When a man loves his wife, he does not (usually) beat her, cheat on her, insult her, or ignore her. If he commits many of these actions, we naturally assume he doesn't love her, no matter how loudly he professes his deep affection. Although actions speak louder than words, before making a judgment it is better to observe several actions and discern a pattern to reduce the possibility of error. A husband may forget his wife's birthday once without being considered unloving.

It is surprising how carefully some teachers prepare for a class and how careless they are about finding out what is actually learned in that class. Perhaps the casual attitude toward what the students learn is a carry-over from the lecture tradition of the European university. Maybe it results from the assumption that if a student doesn't learn, it's his fault. Possibly music teachers are unsure of how or what to evaluate, or maybe they fear an evaluation will indicate that they aren't teaching as much as they think they are.

Whatever the reason for neglecting evaluation, it should be clear that both preparation and follow-up are essential to the teaching process.

Most teachers truly believe that their class is learning what is presented. A band director, when confronted with the fact that his group is not playing the dotted-eighth and sixteenth-note figure correctly, responded, "But I've told them how to do it right!" He had overlooked the possibility that what he was trying to teach had simply not gotten across. Probably both he and the students share responsibility for the failure. Nevertheless, the director should be aware that the rhythmic figure is not being played correctly so that he can take steps to remedy the problem.

Securing Feedback

Securing *feedback*—evidence about the results of teaching—is necessary because it helps the teacher plan subsequent learning. The director cited earlier, whose band still hasn't learned to play the dotted-eighth and six-teenth-note figure correctly, should acknowledge the problem and try different methods to teach this skill. At the very least he should try his original approach again, perhaps more thoroughly than before. Unless past results are confronted and evaluated, planning for the future becomes an exercise in guesswork.

Securing feedback is also essential for the growth of the teacher because it tells him what was effective and what wasn't. Used properly, feedback applies to specific portions of one's teaching, enabling one to make small specific changes, while a major alteration in teaching method is a difficult accomplishment. For example, a teacher can try a different method of teaching the harmony in rock music without the unhappy feeling that so much of his past work was of doubtful quality.

Most important, a concern for results puts a teacher's attention where it belongs: on the students' learning. It is easy for a teacher to lull himself into the notion that things are going along satisfactorily. Most students like music, and probably enjoy music classes more than other classes. A well-received concert rightfully gives a sense of accomplishment to students and teacher. But there also must be concern for what the students are learning in their three or five periods each week, apart from what the public sees. Careful, thorough evaluation helps keep learning the prime objective of music instruction.

Assessing the effectiveness of a lesson does not mean giving one test after another. It isn't necessary to involve all the members of the class in every checking situation. A sample of four or five students selected at random to answer questions or in other ways indicate what they are learning is usually sufficient to provide a good idea of how much learning is taking place.

Here are some ways in which this can be done:

George Edwards is teaching his seventh grade general music class about major triads. His goal is to have the students recognize the chord aurally. He asks them to hear and sing major triads, and to play them on the piano and other melody instruments in the room. A few days later when he presents Dvořák's *Symphony No. 4* he plays the first few measures of the fourth movement, lifts the arm from the recording, and asks several students if they heard a particular type of chord outlined in the melody.

Aaron Feldman wants his band members to learn the difference between homophony and polyphony. After they play the trio of "*Colonel Bogie March*" he stops the band and asks several players whether the music is polyphonic or homophonic.

Janice Peters is teaching her high school humanities class about the main features of romanticism. At the end of the period she assigns this work to be completed by the next class: Read William Henley's "Invictus" and write down specific statements from the poem that make it a romantic work.

In each of the preceding cases, the process of securing feedback is short and simple, yet adequate to let the teacher know how well his students are learning. Although not every student is examined, these techniques are useful, quick spot-checks of learning.

Statements of behavioral objectives (as shown in Figure 2) should include: (1) how the students can indicate they have learned (words such as

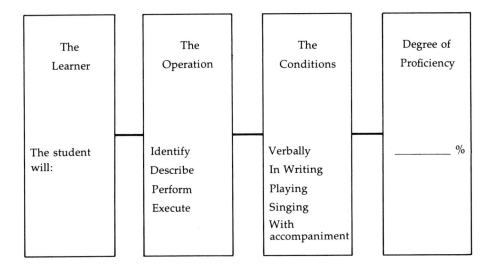

The Learner	The Operation	The Conditions	Degree of Proficiency
The student will:	Identify Describe Perform Execute	Verbally In Writing Playing Singing With accompaniment	_____ %

Figure 2   Components of a behavioral objective

"understand" or "appreciate" are not useful here because they are too vague); (2) the conditions under which the student's action will be performed (period of time, with accompaniment, tempo); and (3) a "criterion level," degree of proficiency or standard of what is passable (seven out of ten questions answered correctly or notes played accurately). Let's return to the three situations presented earlier, and state a behavioral objective to accompany each situation.

> George Edwards: "The students will indicate by answering questions after a triad has been played or by raising their hands during the playing that they aurally recognize the major triad seven out of ten times when it is present in melodies of musical compositions."
>
> Aaron Feldman: "Nine out of ten band members will be able to answer correctly in rehearsal whether the music they are playing at the moment is basically homophonic or polyphonic."
>
> Janice Peters: "Given a short romantic poem not previously studied in class, within five minutes 80 percent of the students will be able to locate and list in writing the particular romantic characteristics present in that poem."

There is a close relationship between lesson planning and evaluating learning from feedback. Only if the teacher has clearly specified his objectives will he be able to evaluate how well he has succeeded. Goals and assessing the attainment of those goals are obviously two sides of the same coin.

Tests and Testing

Since grading is involved in most courses, and since school administrators, boards of education, and state and national educational agencies often require formal data on student achievement, a teacher usually needs to construct and give tests. His informal observations of student learning are valuable for his own use, but inadequate for purposes of grading. So a more formal evaluation is needed, in addition to feedback.

What is being discussed here is the evaluation of achievement—what the students have learned—and not aptitude, which was discussed in Chapter 5. Admittedly there is a rather close relationship between the two types of tests—achievement and aptitude—but the correlation is not so high that the two can be used interchangeably.

Evaluation specialists have classified learning into three broad areas. One is the *cognitive* area or domain. It deals with facts, concepts, and information. It is the area one thinks of first when the word "testing" is mentioned, and it is the easiest one to evaluate.

A second area is the *psychomotor* domain. It includes physical skills — playing an instrument, hitting a tennis ball, hearing the root of a chord, or singing a song at sight.

A third area is the *affective* domain. It includes attitudes, beliefs, and commitments. In music it is probably as important as the cognitive area, but is much more difficult to evaluate, for reasons that will become apparent shortly.

Cognitive Tests

One type of cognitive test is the essay examination. It gives the student latitude in organizing his responses and expressing his ideas fully. But different graders vary in their evaluation of the answers, and even the same grader will vary from one time to another. Also, the verbally adept student has an advantage over the less articulate student on this type of examination. For many instructors, the essay examination is simply not feasible because the grading can be unduly time-consuming when large numbers of students are involved.

The true-false examination is generally unsatisfactory. The 50 percent chance of guessing the correct response requires that many items be written to cancel the effects of chance and achieve significant results. Furthermore, it is difficult to write true-false questions that probe an area in depth.

The completion question requires the student to fill in the correct word. For example, "The stick held by the conductor is called a _____." Completion questions are satisfactory when a precise term is called for. The question should be worded so that there is no ambiguity about the correct answer. For example, "A feature of Baroque music is _____." This question could be answered by the words "continuo," "harpsichord," "metrical rhythm," or a number of other terms. Such a question should be avoided.

The multiple-choice question has several advantages. It can be scored easily either by hand or by machine, so a large number of tests can be graded quickly. Its chance factor is usually one in four or five — much lower than the true-false item. With imagination and planning, a teacher can write multiple-choice questions to test general understanding as well as specific facts. A correct response does not depend on the student's ability to verbalize an answer.

A multiple-choice question consists of two parts. One is called the "stem," the statement that applies to all the choices. Example: "In sonata form the first large section is called . . ." The stem must be relatively short. The choices to complete the stem are called "foils." If an instructor has trouble inventing enough logical foils for four or five choices, he can write foils such as "None of the above," "All of the above," "True of both (a) and (b)," and so on. In preparing such a test, there is a tendency to put a disproportionately large number of the correct choices in the last foil, which causes an undesirable overbalance on it. Apparently there is a subconscious desire to withhold the right answer until the student has read the other choices. In addition, the correct choice often contains the most words because it must be accurate; the wording of the incorrect foils seldom matters. A statement or question employing a negative in the stem is useful when one can't think up enough logical foils. Example:

Brahms did *not* compose
(a) concertos
(b) operas
(c) chamber works
(d) art songs
(e) symphonies

The difficulty of an item can be varied by adjusting the specificity of the question. For example:

Brahms was born in
(a) 1831
(b) 1833
(c) 1835
(d) 1837
(e) 1839

is a much more demanding question than

Brahms was born after
(a) Bach
(b) Stravinsky
(c) R. Strauss
(d) Bartók
(e) Debussy

An in-depth examination of an area can be accomplished through a series of multiple-choice questions. Sometimes several questions can be built to refer back to a single descriptive paragraph or musical example.

The most important criterion of a test is whether it is valid — whether it tests the students on the real content of the course. If the general music class spends most of its time singing, and the band spends most of its time getting ready for public appearances, it is hardly fair to test the students on the keys of Beethoven's symphonies, since this information is not a logical outgrowth of their experiences in the course.

Levels of Questions.   No matter which tests are favored, the teacher should include questions that involve varying degrees of complexity and comprehensiveness. There is a big difference between these two questions: "What does the word *accelerando* mean?" and "Which of the two musical examples is most representative of the Renaissance polyphonic style?" The first question is confined to a specific musical fact, one that can be learned by rote without much understanding. The second requires pulling together knowledge, experiences, and comparative judgment for evaluating the intricacies of actual music. The first type of question is certainly acceptable; factual knowledge has its place in any subject. But the rudimentary level of comprehension should not be the only one tested.

The best recognized attempt to classify levels of comprehensiveness in cognitive learning appears in *Taxonomy of Educational Goals, Handbook I: The Cognitive Domain.*[1] The term "taxonomy" means "classification." Although the particulars of any taxonomy may be questioned, the basic notion of a hierarchy of increasing complexity and comprehensiveness is well founded. Briefly, the first level consists of knowledge of specifics — terms, methods, theories, and so on. The second level calls for comprehension, which is demonstrated by the translation, interpretation, or extrapolation of knowledge. The third level demands the application of knowledge. A sample question at this level would be: "Listen to this melody as it is played on the piano. Then decide which instrument it is best suited for." The fourth level is analysis. The fifth level is synthesis. Designing a plan to teach figured bass is an example of synthesis. The sixth level is evaluation, involved, for example, in deciding which of two musical examples is most representative of Renaissance polyphonic style.

Achievement Tests.   The most notable published tests of this type are the *Music Achievement Test* by Richard Colwell[2] and the *Achievement Tests in Music* by William Knuth.[3] Both use a recording and both are designed for evaluating students in upper elementary grades and junior high school. The Music Achievement Test includes subtests on pitch, interval, major/minor, and meter discrimination, auditory-visual discrimination, feeling for tonal center, tonal memory, melody, pitch, and instrument recognition,

[1] Benjamin Bloom, et al (New York: David McKay Co., 1956).
[2] Follett Educational Corporation, 1010 West Washington Blvd., Chicago, Ill., 1968–69.
[3] Creative Research Associates, Monmouth, Oregon. Revised 1967.

and identification of style, texture, and chords. Its reliability is high, and its validity has been established by correlations with other tests, by performance ratings of students made one year after taking the test, and a variety of teacher ratings of students. The norms were developed from a carefully selected sample of 9,600 students, a far greater number than used in standardizing any other music test.

Knuth's *Achievement Tests in Music* is neither as comprehensive nor as well standardized as Colwell's. It consists mainly of detecting errors in notation from hearing the phrase played. Its reliability is satisfactory, and its validity has been established by analyzing the content of basal music series, inviting the judgment of six authorities in music education, and correlating it with success in school music classes. The norms provided in the test manual are not as complete as most teachers would desire.

Psychomotor Tests

Music teachers are often concerned with the development of skills. Administering ear training examinations, adjudicating at contests and festivals, and deciding who will be first-chair clarinet are three examples of situations that require the teacher to evaluate technical skills. Often this area is not handled in as sophisticated a manner as cognitive achievement.

The problem in assessing skills fairly is apparent in the contest situation. The adjudicator must rely solely on his impressions of one performance. Even when an evaluation form is available, such as the MENC-NIMAC (National Interscholastic Music Activities Commission) forms presented in Appendix E, it calls for general observations about various aspects of the performance — tone quality, technical ability, and so on.

Most of the rating forms currently used list general categories of technical skills required in performance, and this encourages more consistent reporting. They do include some space for the adjudicator's comments and criticisms. Merely listing grades for each category is not very informative. For example, what does a grade of "B" on technique mean? That the group was not together? Some notes were missed? Some rhythmic figures were not executed properly? Some articulations were incorrect or sloppy? The tempo slowed down in the difficult places? The teacher and students can assume that "B" is better than "C" but not as good as "A," and that's all. In some respects, the adjudicator might have given a more useful report had he been provided a blank sheet of paper on which to make comments.

Sometimes adjudicators vary widely in their assessment of a performance. In one festival the same band received a first division rating from one judge, a third division from another, and a fifth (the lowest possible rating) from the third judge. Some states allow judges to confer about their ratings so that such embarrassing disagreements may be avoided. Differing opinions are not confined to contest adjudicators. Varying evaluations of performing ability occur regularly among juries of experts who hear individual performances of college music majors.

The probable cause for widely varying evaluations by teachers and adjudicators is not that they are incompetent but that they are each listening and looking for different things. For evaluations to be useful, they must be made on specific points that are agreed on by the panel or jury, and should be specifically stated, preferably in writing.

Within the class or rehearsal room, evaluation should also consider specific aspects—the more specific, the better. How can this be accomplished? One method is to tape-record a performance and replay the example enough times to hear everything thoroughly. This long and involved procedure is used in research studies, but it is too time-consuming for most teachers to undertake. The answer to the dilemma between the need for accurate evaluation and the restriction of limited time is to select a sample of the music and aspects of performance.

Suppose that in the "Hallelujah Chorus" from Handel's *Messiah*, the teacher decides to test the basses by concentrating on three phrases from the bass part. (The students may sing more than the three phrases. They need not know the exact places selected for evaluation.) One of the phrases is:

And He   shall   reign   for - ev - er   and   ev - er

From this phrase the teacher might choose three places for precise evaluation: (1) The tone quality and pitch of the high D. (2) The accuracy and evenness of the two eighth notes. (3) The diction and tone quality of the last note of the phrase. Other aspects can be chosen, of course, but these three present some solid evidence for assessment. Since these three places occur several beats apart, thereby allowing the teacher time to think, it is possible for their quality to be assessed during a live performance.

A published test employing some of the ideas advocated in this chapter is available for specific instruments: the *Watkins-Farnum Performance Scale* by John Watkins and Stephen Farnum.[4] The test consists of 16 graded levels of achievement. Reliability is .87 for seventh graders and .94 for high school students. Validation was made by correlating an overall ranking with the test scores. The correlations are high, from .86 on some brass instruments to .68 on drums. The test is carefully developed and provides norms. The most common complaint of teachers who have used this test is the complicated scoring process. Actually, the teacher can pursue the idea of specific, precise

---

[4]Hal Leonard Music, Inc., Winona, Minnesota, 1954. String edition, 1969.

evaluation without using this particular test by carefully developing his own performance examination.

A word of caution needs to be said about employing tape recordings to evaluate students, especially when large groups are involved. Even the finest equipment under the best conditions cannot reproduce exactly what the human ear hears. In some cases the recording is "juicier," which is of course a distortion of the actual sound. School recording equipment and recording conditions are usually not the best, and they do not faithfully reproduce some aspects of the music, especially timbre and overall balance. Ideally, one should evaluate those aspects during live performance and then use the tape recording to check for wrong notes, phrasing, and so on.

The tape recorder can be a valuable aid in hearing students individually without consuming a large amount of rehearsal time. The recorder can be set up in another room, with its volume, tone setting, microphone placement properly adjusted before the auditions begin. When his turn comes, each student goes into the room, pushes the "record" button, announces his name, plays or sings the assigned music, then stops the recording and returns to the rehearsal. The teacher can listen to the audition tape at his convenience.

How should a test of skill development be scored? The rating system used in some state contests assigns a specific number of points to the grade given in each category. The points are totaled to determine the overall rating. The practical result in some states is that as long as the student or group shows up and performs, it is impossible for that entrant to receive the lowest overall rating. This fact may reduce anxiety for the participants but it undermines the integrity of the ratings. A more serious flaw in assigning points is that they tend to blur valid distinctions among performers. For example, if a group does well on almost everything, but has terrible intonation, it can still be placed in the highest rating. In actual practice, adjudicators shave points in other areas so that this doesn't happen. But shaving points to achieve the correct overall rating is evidence of the weakness of such a point system. Another weakness is that each piece of music is different: in one work the tone quality and expression may be most important, while in another it is the execution of the notes. If points are assigned to areas of performance, they need to be adjusted for each musical work in order to be valid.

The best answer is to assign points to the specific places selected. Returning to the phrase from the "Hallelujah Chorus" cited earlier in this chapter, the teacher/adjudicator should determine how many points can be earned by the best possible execution of the three places selected. Then he should assign the points—so many for the timbre on the high D, so many for the accuracy of its intonation, so many for not sustaining the "r" sound on the final note, and so on. As in all testing, subjective judgment is involved in assigning points. However, by evaluating skills in an organized manner and as objectively as possible, the teacher can assess performance as accurately and fairly as he does cognitive learning.

Affective Evaluation

Evaluating attitudes presents obstacles that are not present in evaluating factual learning or skills. First, is it possible to test attitudes? A student either knows what a diminished seventh chord is, or he doesn't. But if asked, "Do you enjoy the sound of a diminished seventh chord?" the student can give the answer he thinks the teacher wants him to give. Furthermore, words are not good indications of true belief and practice. A person may blithely profess honesty, but cheat on his golf score and income tax.

Second, there also remains the question of whether beliefs and values *should* be assessed, a point mentioned in Chapter 4.

Evaluating attitudes should be separate from other types of evaluation; certainly it should have nothing to do with grading. Freeing evaluation of attitudes from grades prevents the undemocratic practice of forcing beliefs on the students, and encourages them to respond honestly by removing the influence of rewards or penalties from their answers. To assure the students that they may express their attitudes freely, the teacher can suggest that written responses to questions of attitude be anonymous.

Evaluating students' attitudes properly requires skill both in gathering information and in interpreting it. Although music teachers are not expert researchers, they still can gain insight into how students' attitudes are being affected by observing the choices students make regarding musical activities. Do they go to concerts voluntarily? Do they listen to music, or just daydream? Did more students attend concerts this year than last? What records do they check out of the library? Has there been a significant change during the year? What songs do students ask to sing? Do they read about musical events in newspapers and magazines?

Questioning students directly can also provide information. Questioning should be subtle: asking, "Do you like Benjamin Britten's music?" is too transparent an approach. The teacher will find out more by asking, "Would you like to hear Britten's *Ceremony of Carols* again?" or "Would you like to hear other music by Benjamin Britten?" or "'This Little Babe' from Britten's *Ceremony of Carols* is: (a) a sissy piece (b) weird and dull (c) okay, but not as good as many other pieces I know (d) different, but interesting to hear." Another way to ask questions about choices is: "Suppose you've won the lucky number drawing at the music store. You can have *free* any five records of your choice. Which would you choose?" Many variations of this question are possible: "Which composer would you most like to meet?

Why?" "Is 'This Little Babe' from Britten's *Ceremony of Carols* a piece that people will listen to a hundred years from now? Why, or why not?"

A somewhat different type of questioning asks the student to register his feelings on a scale from *strongly disagree, disagree, neutral, agree,* to *strongly agree.* The question might be stated: "Benjamin Britten's *Ceremony of Carols* is fascinating music." In this variety of question, the wording of the statements should vary. The student circles his choice from the five possible responses.

The projective question is another testing technique: "'This Little Babe' from Britten's *Ceremony of Carols* makes me feel _____
_____." The problem with this type of question is the interpretation required of the answer, especially in the case of students who are not articulate. Playing pairs of musical examples and then asking the students which of the two they prefer can also be used to assess musical attitudes. Several unpublished tests are based on this technique.[5] Unless a teacher can devote considerable time to developing such a test, he probably should not attempt to create one himself.

Finally, a test that can be used with older, verbally adept students is the adjective circle (Figure 3), consisting of ten categories of adjectives expressing a mood. A composition is played, and the student selects the category that describes the music best for him. The adjective circle has high reliability. Determining what the responses mean is a real challenge for anyone.

None of the techniques described here can provide conclusive information about students' attitudes, but they can indicate whether the students are becoming more receptive and interested in music.

Grading Students

Music teachers often consider grading a necessary nuisance, and feel justifiably that any grading system is inadequate to reflect what the student is accomplishing in music class. Therefore, the teacher sometimes tends to consider grading a rather insignificant, routine duty. The students look at grades with interest and concern, even though, paradoxically, grades as such are not a primary motivation for most teenagers. Because young people are sensitive about grades, and because learnings in music class are less often subjected to concrete examination in written form, it is important that

---

[5]Newell H. Long, "A Revision of the University of Oregon Music Discrimination Test" (unpublished doctoral dissertation, Indiana University, 1965). Long's revision is based on the work of Kate Hevner (Mueller), "Appreciation of Music and Tests for the Appreciation of Music," *Studies in Appreciation of Art* (University of Oregon Publication), IV, 6 (1934), 83–151; George Kyme, "The Value of Aesthetic Judgments in the Assessment of Musical Capacity" (unpublished doctoral dissertation, University of California, 1954).

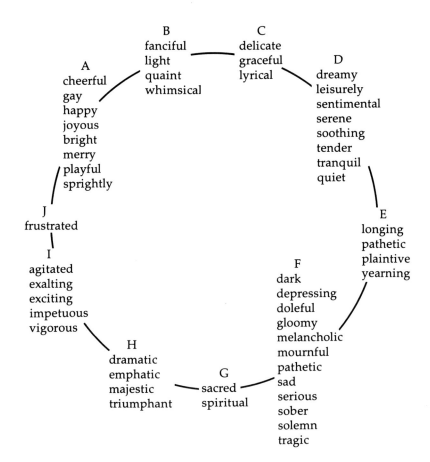

Figure 3

the manner of grading indicate to the students that the teacher is fair and understanding. If grading is handled brusquely or carelessly, it can hinder the establishment of a good relationship between students and teacher.

The teacher needs to establish clear-cut criteria for grading, consistent with the overall evaluation procedures of the school. To eliminate later misunderstanding, these standards can be written down and given to each student. The criteria may or may not carry definite point or percentage values. Assigning a certain number of points for effort, for deportment, for technique and the like, gives students a sense of concreteness, but the objectivity is more apparent than real.

The teacher should make clear to the student that the considerations forming a grade are interrelated; that effort is usually related to accomplishment, for example. Here are some criteria for a performing organization. Both effort and ability are considered.

Grade of A

(1) Has shown much improvement.

(2) Has shown outstanding willingness to assume responsibility, to cooperate, and to better the organization.

(3) Has shown outstanding ability to perform a part with accuracy and a good sense of ensemble.

(4) Has shown exceptional ability to perform with a properly produced, pleasant tone quality.

(5) Has shown exceptional understanding of the music performed by the organization.

(6) Has learned all assigned music.

(7) Has shown outstanding initiative by individual practice and study outside of school time, and by participation in community music activities.

For a "B" grade the words "good" or "above average" can be substituted for "outstanding" and "exceptional." The "C" grade can use "average" or "some" as modifiers, and the "D" grade can use "below average" and "little." Attendance is not cited in the criteria because it is assumed that the school has a policy concerning unexcused absences and makeup work.

The purpose of grading, of course, is to provide parents, students, and teacher with an accurate picture of the student's work. A single grade is insufficient to do this. If the report card allows for only a single grade, which is often the case, the music teacher should give the student and parent a clearer understanding of the evaluation by providing supplementary information. A narrative paragraph is often helpful. Another possibility is a form on which the teacher checks comments about singing, completion of assignments, progress during the marking period, concert attendance, aspects of playing, or whatever is significant for the class. The supplementary sheets should be mailed to the home if the teacher wants to be sure they're received; students are unreliable couriers, even of favorable reports.

Music teachers face two dilemmas in grading: one between pupil growth and a fixed standard, and the other between musical accomplishment and class deportment. Marks can be determined in relation to some standard fixed by the teacher, with an "A" or 100 representing perfection in this system, or they can be decided in relation to the progress and effort that the student has shown. Both methods are valid when applied to the right situations. In college work a grade should represent fulfilling some standard. In the lower grade levels, however, the concept of rigid standards becomes less appropriate. It is somewhat unfair to grade a child with many musical advantages by the same standard as another child with an impoverished musical background. Still, by the time a student reaches high school, one cannot ignore the existence of some objective standard of achievement.

A report on the student's musical achievement and his contribution to the entire group is especially pertinent in performing organizations. A boy may be the best tenor in the choir, but if his behavior impedes the progress of the group, determining his proper grade is difficult. If the school does not have a dual marking system—one for academic achievement and one for citizenship—his overall grade should reflect his lack of understanding of appropriate behavior.

A student's attitude toward music talent can have a considerable effect on what he does in music, and on his understanding of the grading system. Many persons believe that either you have talent or you haven't. If a person has talent he need hardly lift a finger—music will just pour from him; if a person does not have talent, then no amount of effort will matter. Of course such a concept is very much in error. The teacher should make sure that his students are set straight on this matter. Effort is especially important for musical achievement. Many students do not realize that plain hard work is required to excel in music. It is also advisable to stress that average and normal people can enjoy music and perform it creditably.

The merit of the curve as a basis for establishing music grades is dubious, especially for performing groups. First, one cannot precisely measure the amount and quality of music learning. (The same is true of learnings in almost all other subjects.) It is possible to measure the speed of someone's typewriting, but not his understanding of a musical phrase. Second, grading rigidly on the curve automatically sentences a certain number of students to failure or a low grade, and they see this as grossly unfair. Third, in high school performing groups that have achieved a fairly high level of advancement, students of lower ability have already been eliminated (especially in instrumental music) by the normal vicissitudes of study over the years, or they have been placed in less advanced groups. If students are learning well, they deserve to earn reasonably high grades, regardless of any overbalance at the upper end of an arbitrary grading scale. Although the curve can be considered in determining marks it should not be slavishly followed.

Some music teachers set up what is commonly called a "point system." Under this system a student receives a specified number of points for each rehearsal attended, each solo appearance, every hour of practice, each private lesson, and so on. When enough points have been earned, the student receives a specified grade or award. Point systems are based solely on quantity of work, and therefore lack validity for purposes of grading, although they are appropriate for determining awards based on service. The number of points earned may be considered in determining a grade if the teacher also evaluates quality, as well as quantity.

Many teachers have students in performing groups audition as a part of classwork and the grading process. These auditions can be held privately, apart from the rehearsal period, or during rehearsal by using a tape recorder outside the classroom. Some teachers prefer to have the students become accustomed to performing publicly, and so the young people perform by twos or threes, or singly, in front of the others. The teacher can easily distinguish individual performance in small groups and grade accordingly. The student is often stimulated to better efforts by the knowledge that he will have to perform in front of his peers.

Some teachers successfully promote self-evaluation by the students. Young people are surprisingly objective in rating their efforts, and often are more critical of themselves than the teacher would be. The exact wording of the points on which they are asked to evaluate themselves will vary with the age and development of the group. The students can be asked about the amount of effort they put forth and their achievement in musical areas. Educationally speaking, there is a strong case for self-evaluation: it helps the student acquire the ability to judge his own work. Whether self-evaluation should become involved with grades given by the teacher is another matter. Such involvement might undermine the success of self-evaluation. However, if students and teacher understand and accept this technique as a valid part of the grading process, it can be useful. The teacher should remember that the Bill of Rights protects all citizens from being forced to testify against themselves; self-evaluation should not force the students to do this either.

Questions

1. Which of the following statements are specific objectives stated in behavioral terms?

(a) The students will not throw paper in class.

(b) The students will learn the song "Chester" by Billings.

(c) Each singer will be able to sing his part in "Chester" in tune, with a clear tone, and at tempo, while the piano fills in the remaining parts.

(d) The students will learn the Baroque style.

(e) The students will be able to describe verbally the pattern of the exposition of a typical fugue.

2. Why are educational objectives and evaluation so closely related?

3. Name two music achievement tests, and describe how they evaluate learning in music.

4. What are the advantages and disadvantages of essay examination questions? of true-false? of multiple-choice?

5. Give an example of cognitive learning in music; of psychomotor learning; of affective behavior.

6. Describe some ways of evaluating students' attitudes and feelings.

7. How would you grade each of these students? (The school requires that you do so; therefore, you can't avoid it.)

(a) Herb — very talented; first-chair trumpet for past two years; loud-mouth; makes cutting remarks about other students' playing; written work average.

(b) Barbara — quiet seventh grader; can hardly be heard when she sings; written work below average but passable; shows little reaction to general music class.

(c) B. J. — tries very hard in chorus and is improving, but singing barely passable; written work passable; manager of group and takes care of risers, chairs, etc. Little aptitude for music, but loves it.

Projects

1. Administer the *Watkins-Farnum Performance Scale* to an instrumentalist friend.

2. Think up a question about music for each of the cognitive levels described on page 113.

3. Write objectives in behavioral terms for this chapter.

4. Examine and evaluate tests given you in this and other courses in terms of validity and reliability.

Suggested Readings

Colwell, Richard, *The Evaluation of Music Teaching and Learning*. Englewood Cliffs, New Jersey: Prentice-Hall, 1970.

Hughes, William, *Planning For Junior High General Music*. Belmont, California: Wadsworth Publishing Company, Inc., 1965.

Klotman, Robert H., *The School Music Administrator and Supervisor: Catalysts For Change in Music Education*. Englewood Cliffs, New Jersey: Prentice-Hall, 1973. Chapters 9 and 10.

Lehman, Paul R., *Tests and Measurements in Music*. Englewood Cliffs, New Jersey: Prentice-Hall, 1968.

Mager, Robert F., *Goal Analysis*. Belmont, California: Fearon Publishers, 1972.

Mager, Robert F., *Preparing Instructional Objectives*. Belmont, California: Fearon Publishers, 1962.

Popham, W. James, and Eva L. Baker, *Establishing Instructional Goals*. Englewood Cliffs, New Jersey: Prentice-Hall, 1970.

Section Four

To Whom: The Students

So far in this book the questions "why," "what," and "with what results" have each been the topic of one or more chapters. A fourth essential question in the teaching process is, "Who is being taught?" The special interest of this book is the student in secondary school—the teenager. The "to whom" question has two main aspects. One involves what the students know and feel about music. This aspect is discussed somewhat in Chapter 6, which deals with observing student learnings, and in Chapter 9, which will discuss adjusting methods to suit the different levels of student musical development.

"To whom" also concerns teenagers and their characteristics, the subject of Chapter 7. Closely related to the matter of understanding adolescents is managing classes of adolescents. Chapter 8 suggests methods for doing this.

7

Teenagers: Their Manner and Motivation

The problems of today's youth have not suffered from lack of news coverage. In fact, the problems have often been blown up out of proportion to their prevalence, a situation of little benefit except to the commercial interests of the media.[1] Teachers and parents often find discussions about youth contradictory, inconclusive, or not applicable to the specific questions they encounter.

What does a music teacher need to understand about adolescents, their motivation, their interests, and their physical and social development?

Teenage Problem Areas

The main area of difficulty for the teenager is the *transition from childhood to adulthood*. This "betwixt and between" situation is a trying time because the adolescent is unsure where he stands in relation to these two stages of life, and adults (teachers included) are never sure which form the teenager's actions will take. This situation has several consequences. One is that most teenagers adopt contradictory views. They reject and accept the adult world—at the same time. One psychologist has commented:[2]

> On the one hand, they see themselves as participants in the youth culture, and by virtue of that fact committed to nonadult values and distrust-ful of the adult world. On the other hand, most take for granted that they

---

[1] Albert Bandura, "The Stormy Decade: Fact or Fiction?" in *Contemporary Adolescence: Readings*, Hershel D. Thornburg, ed. (Belmont, California: Brooks/Cole, 1971), p. 194.

[2] John W. C. Johnstone and Larry Rosenburg, "Sociological Observations on Privileged Adolescents" in *Understanding Adolescence*, James F. Adams (Ed.) (Boston: Allyn and Bacon, 1968), p. 329.

will one day enter adulthood and see themselves as preparing themselves for it.

Most middle class high school students, in other words, are attached to a youth culture which rewards attributes such as athletic ability, personality and popularity with the opposite sex *and* at the same time holds high educational aspirations. Indeed, youth who are distressed when they receive mediocre or failing grades at school would at the same time rather be remembered for their popularity than their scholastic brilliance.

The tensions and uncertainties of the teenager's in-between status encourage reliance on peers, in some cases greater than their dependence on parents. The need for acceptance by one's peers is very strong during adolescence, and accounts for the fact that teenagers conform to fads in dress, grooming, and behavior, even when they don't particularly like or agree with these fads. Joining an exclusive club or gang is appealing because such groups afford a sense of security.

The importance of peer acceptance quite naturally causes tension between adolescents and adults. Sometimes parents feel helpless to exercise any guidance, especially when confronted with the declaration that "everybody does it." Teenagers generally do not even want to be singled out for praise, since this too is a form of separation from their peers. It partially explains why teenagers don't appreciate students who try too hard to win a teacher's approval.

Involved with the process of becoming an adult is the *development of a self-image*. By early adolescence the young person has become aware that he is an individual with his own personality. The ability to mentally stand off and ask, "Who am I?" develops during these years. And so does much sensitivity about appearance and capabilities, which in turn encourages tension.

> The teenager learns to develop defenses that the simplicity of his earlier life did not demand. He may show physical evidences of emotional turmoil —general restlessness, nail-biting, frequent minor physical complaints. There are usually emotional signs as well: daydreaming, withdrawal, excessive anxiety over mistakes, inability to concentrate, uncontrolled laughing or crying, sudden attachments to older people, extravagant expressions of emotion. Boys are likely to show off, brag, bully, violently resent authority, or become generally destructive.
>
> In his struggle with the often contradictory demands of his own inner urges and those of his environment, the individual may behave in ways that in a more stable period, would be considered neurotic.[3]

---

[3]Ruth Strang, "The Transition from Childhood to Adolescence," in *Understanding Adolescence*, James F. Adams (Ed.) (Boston: Allyn and Bacon, 1968), p. 31.

The adolescent is confronted with new social situations, especially as he learns to get along with members of the opposite sex. The *emergence of sexual desires and feelings* is another powerful and often bewildering force that occurs during adolescence.

Conditions Aggravating Adolescent Adjustment

Several conditions in contemporary American society make a smooth transition from childhood to adulthood more difficult. One is that adolescence in a highly developed society lasts far longer than it does in simpler societies. In New Guinea, for example, a ceremony is conducted at the advent of puberty. Before the ceremony the person is a child, and after it, he is suddenly and formally an adult. There is no in-between stage. Such a clear-cut definition is not possible in civilizations generally requiring a high level of education for widely different and complex jobs, ranging from replacing an automobile transmission to interpreting tax laws. Young persons who are physically grown must still live for years in a state of dependency on their parents and society. It isn't surprising that the situation sometimes rankles both adolescents and adults. The delayed assumption of responsibilities also postpones marriage for many years after the development of sexual powers, and this frustration intensifies the problem of adjustment.

Another aggravating factor in adolescent development is the pluralistic, confused roles of male and female in American society. For example, "a woman's place is in the home" was at one time, by consensus, an accurate description of a woman's role. Today this belief is more the exception than the rule. And no clear concept of a woman's role has replaced it. A young woman can choose from a wide variety of roles. In fact, the role and influence of the family has diminished in contemporary American society. Clearly defined social guides are also lacking in many other areas—sex, military service, drug use, religious belief and practice, economic well-being, and so on.

A third aggravating force is society's mixed concept of adolescents. Some adults perceive young people as primarily pleasure-seeking, while others think of them as violence-prone, in need of firm control and discipline. Some see the giggling, awkward, but good-hearted youngster depicted in the movies and on radio during the 1930s and 1940s. Still other adults, perhaps to compensate for their own aging in a culture that esteems physical beauty and youthful vigor, admire everything youthful and ascribe to adolescents the purest and wisest of insights, motives, and understanding, even of life's most complex problems. The fact that none of these stereotypes is true of more than a small minority of teenagers has not prevented people from holding such views. Unfortunately, expecting trouble from teenagers encourages a self-fulfilling prophecy. So pervasive is the expectation of trouble that one adolescent psychologist reports:[4]

> . . . I have often been struck by the fact that most parents, who are experiencing positive and rewarding relationships with their pre-adolescent children are, nevertheless, waiting apprehensively and bracing themselves for the stormy adolescent period. Such vigilance can very easily create a small turbulence at least. When the prophesied storm fails to materialize, many parents begin to entertain doubts about the normality of their youngster's social development.

Finally, the adolescent is affected by all the social and world problems that affect adults—unemployment, racial tension, international conflict, pollution of the environment, breakdown of respect for law and authority, and the changing mores relating to sex and marriage.

The Culturally Disadvantaged Adolescent

Research in the area of social and ethnic minorities becomes dated rapidly. What was true 30 years ago of children of East European immigrants is not very applicable to the black or Chicano students of today. The recent tendency of some persons to view almost everything in life from a racial standpoint presents the schools and society with problems of unprecedented complexity and seriousness. If he is to help the culturally disadvantaged student, the music teacher should be familiar with the most objective and rational scholarly works on how best to educate students who are not middle class and white.

Several points need to be kept in mind about culturally disadvantaged students. One: such a student is often not *just* from a lower socioeconomic group, *just* a member of an ethnic or racial minority, or *just* from a broken home. He often bears multiple disadvantages, two of the most common being poor health and a low level of aspiration. A black student from a broken home struggling to live on welfare in the inner-city of St. Louis is probably quite a different person from a black child whose father is living with the family and is regularly employed in a factory in Bloomington, Indiana. Often it is the combination of difficult circumstances that causes the student to fail in school or become a social problem.

Two: it is reassuring to realize that many culturally disadvantaged

---

[4] Albert Bandura, p. 196.

students eventually lead happy and productive lives. It is only a small percentage who commit serious crimes or who give up in their attempt to function within society.

Three: the disadvantaged teenager thinks more in terms of a person-to-person relationship with teachers, and less in terms of the total school and its curriculum. As Lindgren points out:[5]

> Throughout the studies comparing middle-class with lower-class school performance, the personal relationship between pupil and teacher has loomed large. The lower-class student . . . is less likely to react positively to ego rewards and more likely to respond to direct and immediate reinforcement. He will work hard for teachers who are supportive and who show their interest in him, but will become apathetic or even hostile in classes where teachers are cold, discipline-oriented, or interested solely in the cognitive aspects of learning.

Four: disadvantaged students come from all races and areas. Many such students are black, many are Indian, many are Spanish-American (Chicano), and many are white. As many disadvantaged people live in the rural areas as live in the cities. Many disadvantaged students reside in the southern states, but every region has such students.

Admittedly attempts to generalize about people are never true for all persons in a classification, as pointed out in Chapter 4, but valid generalizations contain enough fact to be helpful if not treated as stereotypes. Disadvantaged students often exhibit the following tendencies: they find it harder to adapt to the routine of school life (being on time, for example), find it more difficult to learn, are less able to handle abstractions, have a shorter attention span, are less verbally able, lack curiosity, have a limited range of experience, and tend to live for the moment with little thought for the future.[6] Some of these characteristics affect what the disadvantaged student will do in music. For example, these students are usually less likely to read music, to understand abstractions (impressionism, for example), and to persevere in learning the music for a program that is scheduled well in the future.

There are some advantages — and certainly some compensations — when teaching disadvantaged students. Because these students have fewer material comforts and enriching out-of-school activities, music usually means more to them. It is not just another nice activity that competes with ballet lessons and summer trips, as it is to some upper-middle class students. Furthermore, the "rags to riches" experience of many popular performers

---

[5]Henry Clay Lindgren, *Educational Psychology in the Classroom*, 3rd Ed. (New York: John Wiley & Sons, 1967), p. 559.

[6]Lindgren, p. 559. See also Robert F. Biehler, *Psychology Applied to Teaching* (Boston: Houghton Mifflin, 1971), Chapter 10.

provides motivation for many disadvantaged teenagers. And no music teacher should overlook the rich ethnic music background of many of these students. Although no music curriculum should be confined to a particular type of music, no music teacher should ignore (or disparage!) the richness that ethnic musics add to American culture.

The Teacher's Role in Adolescent Adjustment

Understanding the teenager's nature may not solve all the problems that arise, but if it makes a teacher more patient and sympathetic, that attitude in itself often leads to improved learning in the students. Understanding adolescent psychology can help focus attention on the real reasons for students' actions, not simply on the symptoms of their difficulties. For example, one high school faculty attempted to discourage student smoking through an educational campaign about its harmful effects. But like most teenage smokers, the students had begun smoking because they felt it marked the attainment of adulthood. They were unconcerned about health conditions 30 years in the future. The faculty might better have concentrated on the connection in the students' minds between smoking and being sophisticated.

Because adolescents do not feel secure about their status, they are extremely sensitive to condescension and patronizing attitudes. They want to be regarded as adults, even though they may at times slip back into childish behavior. They want (and need) teachers who are honest and straightforward with them, and who take time to consider students' ideas seriously. Adolescents want no favoritism, no tricks, and no evasiveness.

In addition to being understanding and fair, the teacher should be an adult. Sometimes it is tempting for him to be "one of the gang" in an effort to be liked by his students. Not only does this rob them of the leadership, guidance, and adult model they need; in the long run it doesn't work. If adolescents sometimes have trouble trusting adults in general, imagine how much less they can trust an adult who tries to act like a teenager.[7] The act is phony, and they know it. Adolescents realize, as the cartoon on page 133 illustrates, that they need to have parents and teachers—adults—as well as their own teenage friends.

The teacher should be a leader, not in the sense of being aloof and dictatorial, but rather with the ability to direct, persuade, and inspire. If the teacher drops his role and becomes just another member of the group, the students lose confidence in him. Research studies indicate that the con-

---

[7]It should be pointed out that to an adolescent, any teacher is by definition an adult, as are most people more than a few years older than he.

fidence students and workers have in their leaders affects their learning and productivity, as well as the morale of the group.[8]

The teacher should realize that he cannot, and should not, do everything in the way of music for his students. Because some degree of independence is important to adolescents for establishing their self-image as adults and competent persons, they need to have a type of popular music that is theirs, a type of music that they know more about than the music teacher does. To rob them of the satisfaction of knowing "This is ours" or "We did it ourselves" is to deny them something valuable.

Finally, strange as it may seem, adolescents need some order and routine in their lives. As Strang says:[9]

> It seems obvious that internal disorder can only be intensified by a disorganized family life, a lack of reasonable routine in school, or a cluttered physical environment. Organization of these external factors may help the confused child to organize his thoughts. In one school the basic treatment for emotionally disturbed children was to give them the experience of following a planned daily schedule.

If routine helps disturbed children, it can probably help the normal adolescent through the unstable times of his life.

Physical and Vocal Development

Particularly in the seventh and eighth grades, girls are often physically and mentally more mature than boys. This condition exists to some degree throughout high school, although boys tend to catch up by their early twenties. Individual variations are striking, especially in junior high school. Differences in height of a foot or more are not uncommon. Because growth can occur rapidly, especially in boys, there is a tendency toward physical awkwardness and a limited level of endurance.

Less well understood are the changes that occur in the voice. When the boy reaches puberty, the voice box enlarges to about twice its former size. Because the vocal cords double in length, the pitch of the voice drops about one octave. More boys experience voice change at 13 years of age than at any other, with a lesser but equal number changing at ages 12 and 14, and an even smaller number at 11 or 15.[10] In most cases, the voice change occurs at

---

[8]Lindgren, p. 155.

[9]Strang, p. 31.

[10]Glenn V. Ramsey, "The Sexual Development of Boys," *American Journal of Psychology,* LVI, No. 2 (1943), 217.

approximately the same time as other bodily maturation. With the change in the size of the vocal apparatus, the boy experiences difficulty in regaining muscular control over the voice. He is about as awkward vocally as he is in other physical movements. In a real sense he must learn to use his voice all over again. Because the changing voice is marked by instability and inconsistency, some boys for a period of a month or two can sing either a treble or bass part with equal ease. Teaching boys whose voices are changing is discussed in some detail in Chapter 14.

Girls' voices change also, but because there is no drastic change of pitch, there is no particular vocal problem. Most girls in early adolescence have voices which are light and fluty in quality, with limited volume. Maturation brings about the distinctive tonal characteristics that differentiate between alto and soprano. There is usually a widening of range also. The voices of both boys and girls deepen and become richer in quality with maturity.

Teenage Musical Development

It is easy for musicians who have had training at the collegiate level to overestimate the musical background of most teenage students. The disparity in background between teacher and pupil becomes more striking when one considers the musical history of a typical school music teacher. He had private instruction in voice or an instrument before entering high school; he continued private study and played or sang in several high school organizations; he was one of the 50 percent of high school seniors who went on to college. At this stage he was already marked as being above average musically. In college, music was his major field of study, and in addition, he may be working on a graduate degree. One would have to search among hundreds of people from the general population to find another with as much background in music.

Little wonder, then, that it is often hard for the music teacher and the student to understand each other. Granted, some students are exceptional, but the average student is musically so far behind his teacher that it is even difficult to communicate with him about music. He is likely to regard Broadway musical comedies as "classical" music, and he may think that Baroque refers to a salad dressing. When a trained musician sees an A sharp appearing on a piece of music in E major, something clicks within him that says this is an altered tone or a modulation. This same A sharp means very little to most adolescents. The teacher has developed a concept of tone quality for a good singing voice or a rich cello sound. But what about the teenager? Where has he had the chance to hear a good tone? on radio or television? from pop records? in the movies? How many good concerts does a high school student hear in a year? In small towns there are almost no performances except by local amateur organizations. In the cities, concerts are expensive and distances to the downtown area are great. Besides, children from the lower economic areas and minority groups sometimes feel out of place among the well-adorned patrons of many concert halls, and this further discourages their attending such programs. The teacher has had experiences with music that his students have not had. He may have played or sung under a fine director when the music thrilled him "to his toes." Can anyone describe this experience to a person who has never been exposed to anything like it?

A teacher must be careful about what he says when he tries to convey his feelings to the students.

> A fine, devoted choral director from a college was leading a massed high school choir at a festival. The music was a beautiful Bach chorale. Throughout the rehearsal in an effort to inspire the singers, he yelled directions such as, "Now you are on your knees pleading before God! Shake your hearts! Shake your hearts!"
>
> When the students returned to their schools the next day, they asked their own teachers, "Was that director a little 'off' in the head?"

It is easy for the trained musician to understand what the director meant by his exhortations. The students, however, simply did not have enough experience to understand.

Some music teachers talk about "covered tones" to their vocal students. This is fine *if* the covered tone has been demonstrated to them. Words such as "light," "intense," "intonation," and "sustain" also need careful demonstration, and the difference between tone quality and pitch has to be clarified. The teacher must be constantly aware of the lack of musical background in his students, so that he can present the material in an understanding and patient manner.

Motivation and Interest

There is little agreement among psychologists and educators about why and how a person is motivated. They state that:

(1) Students are naturally interested, and the teacher need only open the doors of learning so that interest may be satiated.

(2) Students are interested in something when it becomes involved with self.

(3) Students are interested in something which has a fascination for them.

(4) Interest is intrinsic (coming entirely from within the person) and is based on the student's prior experiences; therefore the teacher can do little to whet this interest.

(5) Interest is a state of tension in the student, which can be relieved by fulfilling some purpose.

(6) Interests are the result of basic biological needs that must be satisfied.

Clearly, more than basic physical needs motivate humans. In addition to physical requirements, there are basic psychological needs, of which *love* (sometimes termed *attention* by psychologists) is foremost. Numerous studies have shown the importance of love for infants, who require TLC (tender loving care) to thrive. Adolescents and adults also need a sense of belonging; they want to be a member of a group or family. Somewhat related to belonging is the need for *recognition* and *respect*. Another need is variously known as "self-development," "need for achievement," or "self-actualization." The individual wants to find life challenging, interesting, and worthwhile. This desire is closely related to the need for aesthetic experiences discussed in Chapter 3. When the mountain climber explained why he wanted to climb the Matterhorn by saying, "because it's there," he was giving evidence of this motivation. Another need is the feeling of *competence*, of being informed and capable. Many of these needs of course are interrelated and overlapping.

Three points are significant for the music teacher. One concerns the relationship between the intrinsic and extrinsic theories. It is clear that interest is not entirely extrinsic. If it were, then everyone would be interested in the same things. On the other hand, interest is not totally intrinsic. It has to come from somewhere; except for biological motivations, people are not born with interests. Clearly, a person's experiences are a prominent factor here. For the music teacher, then, the answer lies in a synthesis of the two positions. Extrinsic motivation, yes; but the teacher cannot expect lasting success merely by concocting a mechanical rabbit which the students by their natures will chase. Intrinsic motivation, yes; but the teacher must not assume the fatalistic attitude that he can do nothing to spark the students' interest.

The second significant fact is that adolescents' interests are not yet fully stabilized. To many adults, teenagers appear fickle and impulsive, and to an extent this is true. A boy or girl at 15 has not established permanent beliefs and interests. A student may like music under one set of circumstances, and heartily dislike it under another. There are a few students whose intrinsic interest in music is so great that it can scarcely be daunted no matter what the conditions may be, and there are others who will remain uninterested, regardless of favorable circumstances. But for the majority of students, interests are flexible enough to be influenced by the quality of teaching.

The third point is that people become interested in activities by which they can enhance the status of self. Interest is further stimulated when the self becomes identified with the group. Who has not observed the brother and sister who say nasty things to each other? Yet when an outsider makes a disparaging remark about either of them, almost miraculously they are united. What has happened is that an attack on one necessarily involved the ego of the other.

Techniques of Motivation

The best and most effective motivation occurs when the student senses that what he is learning will help him meet a personal goal. For example, because of the status and recognition it provides, boys will spend hours in strenuous physical drill to make the track or basketball team. A future doctor will study chemistry diligently because it is necessary for his professional preparation, which will eventually provide him with economic security, the satisfaction of helping people, and an impressive self-image.

The teacher's challenge is to associate music with the fulfillment of some need, without forfeiting the validity of the subject. The process can be depicted graphically: *Student* $\longrightarrow$ *Music* $\longrightarrow$ *Goal or need*. Making a subject seem vital to the fulfillment of a need is more easily advocated than accomplished. Many students have a short-range view of the future; they simply will not or cannot discipline themselves sufficiently to succeed at tasks that require careful planning and years of rigorous study. Others may be willing and able to work hard, but they can't see that studying a particular subject contributes to their goal.

The teacher cannot overcome these problems fully, but he can point out the benefits of the subject, and show how music meets relevant human needs.

Eileen Morgan, music teacher at Dalton Middle School, makes displays featuring prominent men and women who have an interest in music. She posted a picture of the President of the United States holding a violin that he played in his school days, and another of a well-known professional football player performing his own composition with a symphony orchestra. Eileen hopes the pictures contribute to the motivating ideas that "successful" people know music, and that music is for men as well as women.

In most music classes it seems that the easiest intrinsic motivation to cultivate is the students' need to feel competent or informed. The "You-don't-want-to-be-stupid" position (more subtly phrased, of course) works with most students. Gaining knowledge and understanding is an intrinsic need, more noticeable in some persons than in others, but normally present in people to some degree. To see this desire in operation one need only visit some of the national parks in the United States and observe people informing themselves about geysers, glaciers, and Indian ceremonial rites—subjects that have little relevance to their lives during the rest of the year.

Most of the methods a teacher can use to motivate pupils *directly* are extrinsic. Because of the very personal, individual nature of a person's intrinsic motivations, they cannot easily be structured by someone else.

> Bob Jenkins is shy and nonathletic. He finds in playing the drums a way to compensate for his lack of prowess in other areas of life. Even though he has only average ability, his drive to learn to play percussion well has propelled him through study and hard work to first division ratings in state festivals and to the position of drummer with the school stage band.

The teacher did not create Bob's motivation. The need for a compensating activity was already present in Bob; the drums happened to be the medium he selected. Perhaps Bob was guided in his choice by the teacher's counsel, but the need for a choice was pre-existent. Another young person might have selected something else—taking lessons to be a magician, or serving as set designer and prop man for the drama department. Sometimes compensatory activity takes the form of antisocial behavior.

Not all students can succeed at particular activity to the extent that they will achieve recognition or enhance their self-image. Most of us succeed at breathing and walking, but these achievements hardly mark us as exceptional persons. So the music teacher should not think that he has failed if some students turn to activities other than music to achieve self-fulfillment.

In discussing motivation in music, some distinction must be made between a performing organization such as a band, and a class such as music theory. A student in band develops a sense of belonging that the student in theory does not experience. A theory class does not present its efforts before the public, hence it is not evaluated as a group; the students succeed or fail on an individual basis. But an orchestra succeeds or fails primarily as a unified ensemble, with each person bearing responsibility for the group as well as for his own improvement. Both theory class and performing organization should derive their motivation from the attraction of music, and from the excitement and satisfaction of learning it.

The teacher of a musical organization can use several techniques to involve the students more fully in the welfare of the group, and provide additional nonmusical motivation.

(1) Give awards for service rendered. This recognizes the faithful, and lets the rest of the students know that good service is esteemed. There is

divided opinion about the use of awards. Some educators feel that the student should give a course his best efforts not because he will receive an award, but rather because the course seems worthwhile to him. Also, awards can lose effectiveness if they're distributed too freely and too often. Nevertheless, in our society public recognition is so much a part of life that the teacher may find awards advantageous. True, awards are a form of extrinsic motivation. If they are not overemphasized, they can be regarded not as a mere motivating device but as a means of recognizing those students who under any circumstances would do better-than-average work.

(2) Have a group uniform for use in public performances.

(3) Let the students invest in the group. This gives them some equity in the success of the organization. One choir has each new member buy a stole with the school letters embroidered on it. The stoles are worn with the robes for performances, and each year a service bar is added. The stoles give the choir a better appearance, and hence a morale boost. Members are encouraged to keep their stoles permanently after graduation. Most students in band and orchestra have purchased an instrument, so they already have a sizable investment in music.

(4) Invite the graduates of the group to come back and sit in on rehearsals when they can. One choir has a particular number that it performs at every spring concert. All the choir alumni in the audience are asked to come up on stage and sing with the group during that number.

(5) Make sure that names of all members are printed in the concert programs. Double-check to make certain that they are spelled correctly and that none has been omitted.

(6) Involve as many students as possible in the operation of the organization—set-up committee, uniform committee, library committee, student officers, and so on. What director would object to being relieved of some of the routine duties! Occasionally teachers complain that the students do not do a good enough job, and that a few students do not take any assignment seriously. In the first case it should be remembered that the students are younger and generally less capable than the teacher. They need much guidance and frequent supervision to see that they are doing their jobs properly. As for the students who cannot fulfill their obligations, it is wise to talk with them in private about the situation. If they are not interested, let them resign and have the group elect someone else to replace them.

(7) Help the students plan a "Parents' Night," when their parents come for an informal orientation to the organization. Hold a potluck supper, after which the group can perform some music. The numbers need not all be learned and ready for performance, since parents frequently enjoy seeing the stages of development through which the music is perfected. The group might even try sightreading a number. Then the students can explain about awards, committees, and other features of the organization.

(8) Make use of good group pictures. Besides being reproduced in the

school yearbook, they can be placed in the school and town newspapers and on posters advertising the performances.

(9) Make a recording of the group. Several record companies make a standard microgroove disc, complete with a printed label, from tapes supplied to them. If desired, the company can improve the sound of the finished product by adding reverberation, a technique used in most commercial popular recordings to add life to the sound. No company can make a good recording from a bad tape, so get the assistance of a professional recording engineer who has high-quality equipment. The finished records can be bought by the group members. More important then the keepsake value of the recording is the obvious incentive this gives the students to produce a high-quality performance.

Group Morale

An effective means of increasing interest and ego-involvement on the part of the members is to develop group spirit. Persons have made tremendous efforts and sacrifices for a group, team, or nation. Group consciousness is a major reason for the use of uniforms, flags, emblems, and organized cheers — all symbols of solidarity. In musical performance, *esprit de corps* has a decided effect on the actual musical results that are achieved, and the musical result, in turn, is a strong influence in building group feeling.

Morale, motivation, and group success are valuable in achieving good performing organizations in which a high level of learning takes place. Teenagers hunger for a favorable response from other young people, and few are unmoved by an appeal for group success. The teacher should realize that he is on firm ground psychologically when he says, "Look, no one wants to be a member of a group that's the laugh of the school. The way for you to succeed is to learn the music so that the audience will enjoy hearing it." The teacher should realize, too, that the vast majority of teenagers do not want the less motivated students to detract from the group's efforts. The teacher must protect the interests of the conscientious students.

Because "success" is crucial to the motivation and morale of teenagers, it is necessary for them to understand what constitutes "success." How they arrive at an evaluation of the group's work is a matter of first importance. Three opinions influence the students' evaluation of their performing ability. The first, though perhaps not the most important, is the opinion of the teacher revealed through his comments and reactions. The students are interested in specific comments; they want to know how well or how badly they did. For instance, "It was quite good (very good, rather good), but we still need to be more careful about our attacks and entrances."

Second, the students would not be human if they did not value the response of the audience and the audience's remarks to them after the program. Because of the importance of peer groups, the musicians are particularly sensitive to the audience's response at a school assembly. A wise teacher makes an effort to receive a positive opinion from this diverse group. The topic of presenting performances is covered in detail in Chapter 12.

In time, a third evaluation should become more important, and that is the members' own opinion. As the year progresses, the students should be given standards by which to judge their own work. This is an integral part of their education in music. They should learn to be alert for poor attacks, faulty intonation, and inappropriate tone quality. Developing critical listening is the key to mature evaluation.

Attitude of the Teacher

A significant factor in the morale of a performing group is the general spirit established in the rehearsal by the teacher. Because the subject of music is so closely intertwined with feeling, a music group requires a higher degree of pupil-teacher rapport than almost any other organization. The teacher cannot help being aware of the feelings of his students, and the students, in turn, are quick to assess a teacher's attitude and his mood. If he is unenthusiastic, so are they.

Students will not try to improve if they are criticized constantly. Everyone is sensitive to criticism, music teachers included. Therefore, the teacher should adopt an attitude of "honest optimism." He must honestly evaluate the playing or singing; no good is accomplished if he tells his group their work is fine when really it is not. Optimism is essential, too, because teenagers need encouragement, and the teacher must constantly set goals for the group. There is no need to become overwrought if one section can't master a particular point. They will get it in time, if the task is a reasonable one. Certainly they should not be punished over the passage: "Listen, we're going over this until you do it right!" It is infinitely better to be good-natured and say, "Go home, get a good night's sleep, and eat a good breakfast. Then, when you come to class tomorrow, it will seem easy!"

It is important to be diplomatic in criticizing student musicians. In fact it is a good idea to preface a criticism with a compliment: "Trombones, your tone was good right there at letter B, but the intonation was off. Check your pitch on that E natural; you were flat the last time you played it." The teacher should impress on the students that their music has good points, but it can be better still. He should encourage them to improve and yet not frustrate them with ideals that are beyond their reach.

Much of the classroom atmosphere depends on the teacher's attitude toward the students' mistakes. Most adolescents are not sure of themselves and are genuinely afraid of making an error. As a result, when they feel inadequate, they will fake their way along. The teacher must let them know that mistakes are common to every member of the human race, including the teacher. It is wise to encourage openness about errors. The teacher might say something like this: "Don't be ashamed of making a mistake; we're ashamed only of those we make over and over. If you're going to make a mistake, make it a *good* one; then we can correct it. Don't fake in rehearsal and save your error for the concert. It's too late to do anything about it then." Such a statement is psychologically and educationally sound, because it leads to the correction rather than the suppression of errors.

The effectiveness of the teacher's admonition here depends, of course, on the degree to which the students feel confident in his word. He must be able to look at the student who has made an error and say, in effect, "That's all right." The natural tendency is to be irritated and impatient. It is easy to forget that the football player who drops the touchdown pass in the end zone feels worse about his fumble than any of the spectators; the same is true in music. On the other hand, there are some instances in which a student makes the same mistake many times. If he is unwilling or unable to rectify his error, he needs private assistance. Studies by educational psychologists have compared the results of reward and punishment in effecting learning. Most of the experiments consisted of praising one group, reproving another, and ignoring a third group. The best results, which are statistically significant, were achieved by the praised group. The next best performances, though not statistically significant, were by the criticized group.[11] Not all students reacted in the same way to the treatment, however. The generally well-adjusted students responded best to praise; the overly conscientious students and the poorly adjusted student having strong need for approval produced more when criticized.

Good rapport between students and teacher is essential in the music class. It is achieved primarily through the attitude of the teacher. In neither of the illustrations that follow does the example represent a single act that won the students over forever. Rather the incidents were typical of the teacher's actions throughout the year.

At the conclusion of a general music class which had been excellent in every regard—learning had been going on, participation had been high, singing enthusiastic and of good quality—Ralph Johnson found that he had less than two minutes left; not enough time to start something new. It was nearly 12:30 and the students would leave directly for the cafeteria.

"Let's read the menu," he suggested. A boy was asked to go to the bulletin board which contained the week's menu, along with other school announcements. "Wait till I set the proper mood, Jeff," and he began to

---

[11]Lindgren, p. 220.

improvise on the piano the most pompous, booming fanfare he could muster. One would have thought the king was coming. Finally, the climactic, final chord. Jeff began to read, "Onion soup," then more thunderous piano music; "Wiener on a bun,"—more music—all to shrieks of glee from the class.

The class was attempting to play a tune on the melody bells, with eight class members each holding one pitch of the octave. At a point that required one student to play her note twice, Sharon Worthington said to the player, "Mary, hit the A twice."

"Oh, no," Mary said quietly, "it's the G that should be struck twice."

Mary was right; the teacher had inadvertently given the wrong note. "Oh dear!" she quipped, "First mistake I ever made in my life! Mary's right. Judy, it's your G that's struck twice."

In the first instance the teacher stopped taking himself so seriously, and sent the students from the room with a relaxed, positive feeling. In the second case, instead of becoming tense and embarrassed or making excuses, the teacher let the error pass for what it was: a simple mistake.

A touch of humor helps immensely to maintain a relaxed feeling in the rehearsal room. Good humor does not consist merely of telling jokes and engaging in humorous antics. It is an attitude of having fun while you work. Start at "letter G as in goulash" or "E as in eggroll." Humor can be worked into the directions given to the group. "Sopranos, you should hand the phrase over to the altos on a silver platter. But you know what you did last time? You tossed it to them on a garbage can lid."

Another factor in teacher attitude which influences rapport involves the cohesiveness between the teacher and students. Never should the teacher allow a "wall" to develop between the students and himself. There should be no teacher versus students; the teacher should not even think in terms of two separate interests. Rather, there should be a feeling of "we're doing this together." Inclusion, not separation, will achieve the best results. The students must be included in the plans, hopes, and the operation of the class.

A pleasant, optimistic outlook on the part of the teacher does not negate the need for firmness and consistency in dealing with young people. Consistency in this relationship gives the students a sense of security and confidence. If they never know what the teacher's reaction is going to be, they will never be quite sure how they should act.

Miss Martin was determined that there be no horse-play in chorus rehearsal. On Monday Jim Norton, a weak bass, was caught tossing a bit of paper at another bass. Miss Martin immediately asked him to leave the room. He was given five hours of sorting music.

On Wednesday Peter Ott, the only good tenor, was caught tossing a little piece of dried mud from off his shoe at another chorus member. Miss Martin just glowered at him and said, "Now look! Let's leave the horsing around to horses." Peter was given no penalties.

The attitude of the teacher is not the only factor that contributes to a pleasant atmosphere within the group. There should be a ban on destructive criticism by the students, especially in performing organizations. Some adolescents go through a stage of making smart and cutting remarks, even when they are totally uncalled for. Bad attitudes can easily "snowball" from a few people to many in a short time. Students who persist in talking negatively should be handled as behavior problems. On the other hand, the teacher should not be afraid of constructive suggestions from students. They should be invited to express their thoughts about class activities, as long as their comments are sincere and responsible. What should be avoided is the pointless, chronic complaining in which a few students like to indulge.

Finally, the teacher can now and then talk about good attitude. This does not mean long lectures or pep talks, but rather some occasional statements about the meaning of group endeavor. Say to the students, "You should be proud to be a member of the band. You don't have to go around the school beating on your chest and shouting 'I'm in the band!' But you should feel glad that you're in it, and when you know you're doing good work, don't be afraid to say so." It never hurts to tell the performers, "There are 65 people in band, right? So when you hear the applause at the end of a number, one sixty-fifth of that applause is for you. Enjoy it."

Securing Adequate Membership

A problem that concerns only elective performing organizations is recruiting and maintaining adequate membership. It is fine for a textbook to state that a 65 piece band should have 20 B flat clarinets and two bassoons, or that the choir should have a tenor section nearly the size of the soprano section. But this does not mean that the teacher on the first day of school will find the prescribed membership in band or choir. What can he do about incomplete membership?

The music teacher should be clear in his own mind, and make clear to the administration and other teachers, the reason for seeking students for music groups. It is *not* to build a little "empire" for himself. Rather it is to have a group of sufficient variety and size to provide a better musical experience. An orchestra without violas and string basses is just as incomplete as a football team without a guard and tackle. The presence of a tenor section in a mixed choral group significantly affects the kind of music that is sung and studied.

Recruiting Members

A singing group can be built much more quickly than an instrumental organization, which requires specialized instruction encompassing several years. The problems and their solutions, however, are basically the same for both vocal and instrumental organizations.

The most effective way to get new students to join is to have a successful organization. The clothing store that announced, "Our best advertisements are being worn" had the right idea. The activities and attitudes of present members are the best advertisement. A student who considers joining a music group is influenced in most instances by three things. First, he wants to know how the present membership feels about the group. If he hears grumbling, he isn't likely to join. Second, the student's own impression, gained from hearing the group perform, helps him determine how well he thinks he would like the activity. If the choir sings only sacred numbers, and he doesn't care for that type of music, he probably will not enroll, no matter how enthusiastic the members seem to be. Third, the impression the student gains about the teacher is important. Many high school students do not differentiate between liking music activity *per se* and liking the teacher. They gain their impression of a teacher from what they hear about him, and what they see of him in the halls and in assembly performances. So if the teacher walks around school with a long, glum face, students will assume that his classes are similarly dreary.

What can be done by a new teacher who starts the first week of school with only a small, incomplete enrollment of students who signed up the preceding spring? Here are some suggestions:

(1) Meet with the school principal or head counselor. Try to get his approval for schedule changes for students who might want to enroll in a music course.

(2) Obtain schedules of all students and list those who have time for an additional course. As much as the new teacher may wish to succeed, he must not proselyte from the classes of other teachers!

(3) Check the records to discover students who were members of music organizations in previous years but who are not now enrolled.

(4) See personally those students who are able to enroll. Be enthusiastic, but *don't plead*. Some students wait until they have a chance to "size up" the new teacher before committing themselves.

(5) Ask the present members for leads on likely prospects — students who have shown some inclination toward music.

(6) Solicit recruiting ideas from the members and use them on posters such as the one shown on page 147.

(7) In choral music, arrange a short, private audition for every new member. This allows you to assess the student's abilities, but it is also a chance to meet each student personally.

SO YOU SING LIKE A...

THAT'S OKAY
JOIN ANYWAY

EIGHTH GRADE CHORUS
(We'll teach you)

(8) Make the first rehearsal a successful and pleasant experience. Accomplish something the first day, even if it is only singing or playing some simple music, in unison if necessary. Save beginning-of-the-year routines for later (assigning music, robes or uniforms, and checking class lists). Be enthusiastic about the music organization! This is a prime requisite for a successful first rehearsal.

(9) Keep up the membership drive for no longer than five days. Then start to make the existing group into the best possible organization.

Some of the suggested steps may seem to encourage membership in the organization by any student regardless of his musical ability. Actually, few students who express an interest in joining a music group are innately incapable of profiting from the experience. Most of them need encouragement in undertaking music study because they have doubts about their ability.

Encouraging the Boys

So often music teachers, especially in vocal music, bemoan the lack of boys. "If I only had more boys," one choir director complained. "Right now I have only four, and one of them has an unchanged voice." In many schools there is a shortage of boys in the ranks of string players, and even in band. Getting boys into music, and keeping them there, is a special challenge. Generally, male teachers have an easier time involving boys in music. Yet there are many women who have successfully recruited whole boys' glee clubs, so the sex of the teacher is not the crux of the problem.

Sometimes boys feel that music is not quite manly. Fortunately this attitude has decreased considerably in the last 20 or 30 years, but its remnants still exist. Overcoming such an attitude is one important step in recruiting boys. The teacher can point out many well-known masculine musicians. There are fine men's choruses, outstanding bands in the military services which present excellent male vocalists, and the Metropolitan Opera Company which often features husky men as solo basses and tenors.

The idea that music and singing are not for boys is only part of their attitude problem. Many boys sincerely feel that they are unable to sing. This is probably a reaction to the change of voice and the accompanying uncertainty and frustration it causes. Boys must be given encouragement and understanding, and their singing should never be ridiculed. Specific advice on helping boys vocally is included in other chapters of this book.

In some schools boys have been attracted to singing by the appeal of a barbershop quartet. Barbershop singing is traditionally done by ear. Today, however, a sizable number of arrangements are available, which are best learned by having everyone sing the melody (always in the second tenor) in unison on a neutral syllable. The S.P.E.B.S.Q.S.A. (Society for the Preservation and Encouragement of Barber Shop Quartet Singing in America), Inc. offers aid in organizing and training such groups.[12]

For some reason, a group of boys who sing with a big, strong tone can capture an audience, even though they are singing a simple unison song with not much polish. The boys may be in a group of their own, or the male section of the chorus may sing alone. In either case, the group should appear before an audience at a reasonably early date, because a long wait before performing causes interest to wane. It is best to begin with simple music in

---

[12]S.P.E.B.S.Q.S.A., Inc. P. O. Box 575, Kenosha, Wisconsin 53141

unison or two parts. After a successful performance, everyone will be convinced that boys can and should sing. The more exacting work in parts should come after morale and interest have been established.

Both choral and instrumental music teachers usually welcome a member of the school's football or basketball team. The younger boys look up to athletes, whose entrance into the group seems to place the seal of approval on music—an approval that weighs heavily with the rest of the student body. The blessing of athletes in music can be a mixed one, however. These boys are putting their best time and effort into their sports activities, and music is definitely in second place. Then, they are the object of so much attention that some of them are a bit harder to handle. The teacher is glad when he gets boys from the school teams in music, but his success need not depend on them.

Care must be used in selecting music. Boys do not take readily to songs they feel are frilly and meaningless. By contrast, the boys in one high school choir became fond of the work "In Solemn Silence" by Ippolitov-Ivanov. It is a slow, chordal piece—a prayer to God that the horrible sufferings of war may pass. Though not the type of work one usually thinks that a high school student would like, it had a message they could comprehend, and they sang it with dignity and understanding.

Talk to boys in concrete terms. Instead of directing them to try "a more intimate style," tell them to sing the passage as they would a romantic popular ballad. Rather than saying, "Boys, that sounded just lovely!" shout out, "Hey men, that's the way to do it—with some polish!" When boys talk at the wrong time in class or misbehave in any way, there is no subtlety to it. It is right out where everyone can see it, so don't be subtle about reprimanding them. Instead of squeaking out, "Boys, you behave yourselves now," bark out in a firm voice, accompanied by a forcefully pointed finger (and a twinkle in the eye), "John Jones, cut it out!" Be honest, unafraid, make yourself understood, and you'll get along fine with the boys.

The adolescent years are a challenging time in anyone's life. The transition from childhood to adulthood in present-day American society is not easy. Fortunately, a music teacher can contribute significantly to the teenager's education and well-being. He needs to understand them and teach them in a way that builds on (*not* stops with) their needs and interests.

Questions

1. Should students who sing in church choirs or play in community orchestras receive consideration for this in their grades? Why, or why not?

2. Since teenagers are especially concerned with personal status, what might a music teacher do:

(a) to prevent a student's embarrassment during an audition for a choral group?

(b) to tell a student his tone is poor without hurting his feelings?

(c) to encourage the student who worries a great deal about making an obvious mistake during a public performance?

3. If you were the director mentioned on page 136, whose flowery language left the students wondering, what might you have said that would have made the same point more clearly?

4. What type of attitude does each of these statements indicate? How would each affect the teenage student?

(a) "What's the matter, Pete! Is your third finger frozen? Let's play E flat next time!"

(b) "Altos, that was nice, except for one thing—you didn't sing the dotted quarter followed by the eighth correctly."

(c) "Whew! I've heard better tones from a New Year's Eve noisemaker!"

(d) "Sherman, I know it's hard to play low on a brass instrument and play it soft and in rhythm at the same time. But that's what the music calls for. Would you do some careful, thoughtful practice at home on that place?"

(e) "This melody you turned in doesn't seem up to your usual standard, Clarissa. Did you really write this?"

5. Think of instances in which you have observed a music teacher develop good rapport with the students through something he did or said. What points did these instances have in common?

6. Why shouldn't a teacher plead with students to join a music organization?

7. Teenagers are sometimes impressed with a group if they feel that it is exclusive or difficult to get into. Should "snob" appeal be used to build up music organizations in the public school? Why, or why not?

8. What factors contribute to development of a "youth culture" and its music in the United States?

9. What are the general similarities and differences between culturally disadvantaged students and other students?

10. What is the proper relationship between teacher and students?

11. At what age do most boys' voices change? Do girls' voices change? If so, in what way?

12. What are the differences between intrinsic and extrinsic motivation? What are some techniques a teacher may use to motivate students in music?

8

Guiding Student Behavior

In some ways, a detailed discussion of student behavior focuses too much attention on an area that should be peripheral. However, peripheral or not, the subject is very much in the minds of most beginning teachers. Its seriousness is brought out in a study by Lawrence E. Vredevoe, who asked 3,000 prospective teachers, "What gives you the greatest concern or worry as you plan for your first teaching position?" Of these, 2,480 answered, "Discipline."[1]

The problem of discipline needs to be brought out into the open, therefore, and examined. Just as one learns first aid with the hope that he will not have to use it, a young teacher should be prepared to deal with students when their actions deviate from the accepted standard. By knowing how to handle such situations, the new teacher is more confident and better able to concentrate on the essential business of teaching the students some music.

True, a teacher can prevent some behavior problems by entering the classroom with a positive attitude. But he must be realistic about the total situation. Music lacks the concreteness of other academic subjects; students are less often told to read a certain chapter or write a term paper. An eighth-grader may be held back in school if he fails English, but not if he fails only music. These facts affect a teenager's thinking about how he behaves in music class. Furthermore, with students adjusting to all the changes that teenagers undergo, and with schools attempting to educate all the youth of the nation, it would indeed be amazing if student behavior were flawless.

Necessary Precautions

Five precautions should be kept in mind while reading about guiding the behavior of teenagers in music. First, no discussion can cover every situation that might arise. There are so many different ways in which a

---

[1] Henry Clay Lindgren, *Educational Psychology in the Classroom*, 3rd Ed. (New York: John Wiley & Sons, 1967), pp. 370–1.

human being can act, and as many different circumstances in which each act can occur. John talked in class when he shouldn't have. How much did he talk? What did he say? How did he say it? How much did it disturb the rest of the group? Was this the first or the fiftieth time John has talked in class? When did the talking occur—when the teacher was explaining something? when the group was changing from one activity to another? when a record was being played? What type of home background does John have? Is someone else involved with John in this incident? If so, to what extent? Do other students in the group talk when they shouldn't? What has been done about them?

As if the students do not provide enough variables, the teacher brings his share to the situation. For a minor misbehavior, two teachers might call out "John!" with vastly different effects, depending on the personality and prior actions of each teacher. It is a matter not only of *what* is said and done, but also of *how* it is said and done. Sometimes a student teacher is surprised to find that an action, successful for the model teacher, produces the opposite results when applied by the student teacher with the same pupils as before. What happened? The situation is no longer the same, the personality of the teacher is different, and the experience of the students with that teacher is different. The best that any book can offer the reader is some insight into the most common problems, their significance, and how they might be handled.

As a second precaution, the teacher must not fall back on rules and books as the one means of dealing with classroom misbehavior, while ignoring the development of good, positive teaching. Good teaching is essential, and no teacher should become so preoccupied with worries and fears about student behavior that he neglects for one moment the positive side of his job. In fact, good teaching is the best way to prevent student misbehavior because it draws the students' attention to the benefits of learning and thus discourages them from engaging in divergent activities.

Third, the teacher's effectiveness in personal relations also bears directly on his effectiveness in guiding classroom deportment. All that was said in the preceding chapter about the proper relationship between teacher and students applies here. Lindgren says about teacher-student relationships:[2]

> The beginning teacher wants specific suggestions—techniques, if you like—that will enable him to handle such problems. It is difficult for him to grasp the point that discipline is partly a point of view, partly a feeling of self-confidence, partly a kind of relationship between the teacher and his class, but mostly a feeling that the class develops about its own behavior. These are the kinds of concepts that defy verbal description. They are the approaches teachers must learn through actual experience.

[2]Lindgren, p. 371.

As a fourth precaution, no recommendations should ever be considered as ironclad rules. The suggestions here are based on much experience in teaching music to teenagers, but the recommendations can certainly be altered when circumstances warrant it.

Fifth, the suggestions in this chapter are designed to apply to what might loosely be called the "average student." Dealing with the incorrigible, the psychotic, or the alienated sociopath is a job for specially trained persons working in specially designed schools and programs. Teaching such students is beyond the scope of this book. This is not to slough off those seriously disturbed young people and the teachers who work with them. It is to say that dealing with severe problem behavior constructively requires education beyond what is usually required for certification in music. Furthermore, the results of teaching problem youth under experimental conditions can seldom be applied to more "average" situations, or even be transferred from one atypical situation to another.

Although the teenager can be a joy to work with, teenage groups may not be a pleasure to instruct before some attention is given to the delicate task of developing a good relationship between students and teacher. The plural form *students* is used advisedly here. Teachers have long known what the den mother of a Cub Scout troup found out: "Individually those boys are so nice, but when they're together . . ." Most teachers have little trouble handling a private lesson or an ensemble class. It is when the numbers become larger that unexpected things sometimes begin to happen.

Although maintaining order is by no means a teacher's most important duty, *a music teacher must be able to guide students.* This is as much a part of his job as teaching the quality of the melody in a sea chanty. The better a manager he is, the less he will have to concern himself with discipline.

Teacher Discipline or Student Self-Discipline?

If a class of 50 students felt like it, they could get out of their seats, dash out the door, and run down the hall waving their arms and yelling. No teacher would have sufficient physical strength to stop them. Of course, it doesn't happen. Why? Because the vast majority of the students realize that the action would not be in their best interests. Eventually there would be penalties, true, but more important, the students see the sense of what they are doing in class and the lack of reason for running out of the room screaming. In short, they themselves exercise some self-discipline, the ideal form of classroom control. The teacher's objective should be to encourage development of that self-discipline. It is necessary if learning is to take place, because no teacher can control all the actions of all his students.

Self-discipline is encouraged when the student is motivated by the classwork—when the course meets a specific need or interest. Discipline is involved not only with the act of teaching but with the students' responses to the teaching.

To promote the ideal of self-discipline, it is a practical fact that teacher-imposed guidelines are also needed. Even adults, who should be capable of self-discipline, need police to enforce traffic regulations, because grown people driving automobiles do not always exercise self-restraint. No teacher should feel bashful about enforcing compliance with reasonable regulations, especially considering that all sorts of students with all sorts of problems are in schools (discussed in Chapter 7). Adolescents want to know what the rules are. They want the security of knowing what they can and cannot do, even though they may still try to get away with doing the forbidden. Lindgren states the matter in this way:

> One of the perplexing characteristics of children . . . is their need, on the one hand, to have someone set limits for their behavior and, on the other, to test or challenge the very limits that have been set. We often find ourselves drawn into a kind of trap because of these ambiguous and often contradictory motives. Some adults, when confronted by complaints of children that limitations on their behavior are too severe, react by doing away with all or most limits. Thereupon they are appalled when children respond to greater freedom by actually worsening their behavior and blaming the adult in charge for what has gone wrong. On the other hand, adults who attempt to deal with this ambiguous situation by being severe, restrictive, and punitive cannot understand why children are so apathetic and why the behavior of some children actually becomes worse.
>
> Such experiences show that the behavior of children cannot be handled on an "all-or-none" basis. The effective teacher is one who can allow children freedom to develop naturally and spontaneously, but who can also set limits to their behavior at appropriate times. The better the morale of the group and the better the learning situation, the less need there should be to invoke limits.
>
> The problem of the teacher with respect to discipline may be seen in terms of a problem in leadership, to which some of the findings psychologists have made in this field may be applied. One approach to the study of leadership identifies two dimensions: *initiation of structure* and *consideration*. Leadership activities concerned with the initiation of structure include direction, control, punishing, setting limits, rewarding, manipulating, organizing, scheduling, maintaining standards, and the like. Consideration includes such behavior as extending sympathy and understanding, compromising, helping, inviting and using suggestions of group members, and being supportive.[3]

---

[3]Lindgren, p. 352. Reprinted by permission.

Guiding Students Democratically

The words "democratic" and "autocratic," when used to describe teaching, are prejudged by many people because of misconceptions about what the words mean in the schoolroom. Often one gets the impression that teachers are either autocrats or believers in freedom, when in fact most teachers are between these two poles — fortunately. True, some teachers who profess to be democratic operate autocratically, while others who talk like Prussians are really rather democratic. Being human, teachers are not always consistent. On some occasions and on some questions they will be more demanding than on others.

Both positions have merit. Autocratic teaching is not automatically bad; there is a place for what might be called "teacher maintained control." Experimental evidence indicates that democratic methods are superior. But in most of these studies (which were not conducted with music classes) the autocratic teachers were inflexible and lacked compassion for the students, while the democratic teachers were flexible and warm — a correlation of method and teacher personality which is not always present.[4] Because music classes often engage in group activity in which all participants act simultaneously, democratic practices are limited. Group activities require good leadership to be successful, and music is such a complex group activity that leadership is not easily or successfully delegated to the students. With or without democracy in the classroom, the music teacher will still have to be the leader. The performing music organization especially is basically a leader centered activity, and this cannot be changed, no matter how much one might wish to promote democracy in the school. What might be called "benevolent" autocratic procedures have a necessary place in music teaching. For example, the students cannot stop and decide every time what part of the music should be practiced again. Usually they are not musically competent enough to do this, and such a procedure is too time-consuming.

Yet democratic practices should play a significant part in the music class. The overall objectives of the school demand no less. Besides, democratic practices can be used to increase the musical benefits. Students take more interest in an activity when they have had a hand in its operation than they do when they are simply led around, no matter how kindly, like a flock of sheep.

The answer to the autocratic–democratic dilemma in teaching is to incorporate as much democracy as possible into the classroom without sacrificing learning. The classroom should not be a field of battle in which the students and teacher struggle for control. It is a place for learning, a place in

[4]Lee J. Cronbach, *Educational Psychology* (New York: Harcourt, Brace & World, 1954), pp. 451–52.

THE PROBLEM

The kids in your class are disrespectful and unmanageable . . .

THE WRONG APPROACH

All right . . . I've got all day, and all night! Either the person who threw that eraser admits it, or this entire class will sit here till Midnight, if necessary! I've had it with you kids!

You don't study! Most of you are going to flunk anyway! And none of you have an appreciation for the marvelous opportunity that's being given you here to prepare for later life! You're a bunch of lazy slobs and I'm fed up with the whole darn lot of you!

THE MAD APPROACH

One . . . one of you just hit me on the head with . . . an eraser!!

Please don't be short with me! I know my faults—that I'm not qualified to teach this course, and my methods are old-fashioned! Help me to find myself! Just tell me what you want to study! Teach me how to teach you!

I need this job! I've got a wife and kids! So please don't express your contempt for me by throwing erasers! The Principal might see it and fire me! Tell me what to do! You're the students Naturally, you know best!

Somewhere between the "wrong" and the "Mad" approach there must be a "right" approach.

which both "sides" can "win" by fulfilling their roles in the educational endeavor.

Characteristics of Democratic Practices

Democratic education should not be considered a political system. Grambs and Iverson state:

> After all, the classroom is not at all the area of politics where citizens of equal voting stature discuss, debate, and then cast a ballot. The teacher has knowledge, the teacher is an adult, the teacher is vested by law with authority, and the teacher is surrounded in part with the aura of the parent. These "authorities" of the teacher, both open and hidden, make an important difference. The students had no say in choosing Mr. Griffin as their teacher. Neither of course did Mr. Griffin choose belligerent Tim Atkins or arrogant Jane Boothe for his class. Reluctant subjects and arbitrary leadership do not, in our usual sense of the word, make for a very democratic situation.[5]

Democratic education, then, is a social system that is concerned with human relationships, and not just with the act of voting. Good teaching in music depends on discovering the proper balance of group centered and leader centered techniques.

There are four characteristics of democratic practice applicable to the music class. The first characteristic, and the basis for the other three, is the acknowledgment of *the dignity and worth of the individual.* This tenet of democracy indicates for the classroom that the opinions and interests of both students and teacher must be respected. It hardly need be said that the teacher should be sincere in setting up circumstances that give the students a feeling of being important and valued. Such situations should not be arranged merely to achieve ends desired by the teacher.

As a part of its interest in individual worth, this nation has protected the right of an individual to worship as he pleases. Because of the sensitive nature of religious freedom, care must be taken in the presentation of vocal music with a religious text. Some students object to singing songs with certain religious words. Sincere objections to such music should not be treated as evidence of misbehavior. If there seems to be a religious problem in a particular school, the teacher should talk with the superintendent or principal to find out what policy exists regarding religious music. If the school maintains no specific position the teacher can quietly discuss the

---

[5]Jean D. Grambs and William J. Iverson, *Modern Methods in Secondary Education* (New York: William Sloane Associates, 1952), p. 58. Reprinted by permission.

matter with the student officers of the group. Generally the student can simply refrain from participation, with the assurance that this will in no way affect his grade. He should inform the teacher *before* class starts, just as he would report laryngitis or other physical incapacities. Notes from home should not be requested; this demand serves only to spotlight a situation that can inflame emotions. The less religious differences are emphasized, the better it is for everyone.

Some confusion regarding the place of religion in the public schools has resulted from the Supreme Court rulings of the 1960s. The Court did not ban religion from the schools. On the contrary, it specifically encouraged the *study* of religions. Declared unconstitutional were religious *practices* in the schools—prayers prescribed by school governing agencies, worship services, and the like. The issue can be resolved quite simply by answering the key question: Is the activity being presented for religious or educational reasons? The former are unconstitutional; the latter are encouraged.[6] Therefore, the teacher should choose a song for its musical value, not for its religious message. This distinction should be explained to the students. The music teacher should not discard a good song because of religious objections by a minority, any more than a school cafeteria should be required to serve *only* a certain food on a certain day because of the religious beliefs of some students. If possible a cafeteria director should offer a choice, but he should not require the majority to eat a certain food because of the demands of the minority. For the sake of religious broadmindedness and good music education, the music teacher should select a variety of good music from different denominations and faiths.

Freedom Within Rules

This is a second democratic condition. Initially it is the teacher who sets up rules for the class. To expect the students to enter an unfamiliar organization and establish their own rules is unrealistic. It is expecting something of the students which they cannot reasonably produce without prior experience and an understanding of the unique nature of a music performing organization.

Remembering that he must work within the overall student behavior policies of the school, the teacher should select the precise points at which guidelines are required. For instance, should the student raise his hand and be recognized by the teacher before speaking? Why? It is wise to discuss each suggestion briefly. Thus the attention of offenders can be called to the rules on which they themselves reached consensus as a class.

---

[6] For a thorough and practical discussion of these decisions see: *Religion in the Public Schools* (Washington, D.C.: American Association of School Administrators, 1964).

The degree of student sophistication largely determines how much stress to place on regulations. Younger, less advanced students may need the security of concrete behavior guidelines. However, to an intelligent group of juniors and seniors, such techniques as passing out copies of the rules appear degrading. The more mature and capable class usually exercises greater self-discipline and has less need for specific regulations. The teacher must use discretion in these matters. Rules must never become ends in themselves.

Suggested Points of Regulation

There are areas in which policies have to be made by every music teacher. Here are some suggestions that may serve as an initial guide.

Talking.   It is difficult for anyone to sit for a whole hour without talking to someone. A teacher can check himself on this point sometime when he is a member of a group instead of a leader. So it seems unreasonable to expect absolute silence from teenagers. They should understand, however, that there is a time for talking and a time for silence. Talking might be permitted for about a minute between changes of music, before class starts, and any time that the teacher is not before the class. *Uncontrolled talking should be prohibited at other times.* Action is necessary early in the school year before bad habits are established.

The two times that will cause the most trouble are when the teacher is working with one section and leaves the others sitting unoccupied, and when he stops the group to make a comment on the music. *He should not give directions to the class if some students are talking.* The persons who miss the directions will make the same errors again, and the directions will have to be repeated especially for them. If this happens often, the class becomes a boring waste of time. In a large group, each student must raise his hand and be recognized by the teacher before he speaks. Unless a group is quite small and composed of the better students in the school, this procedure is necessary to preserve order.

Just as there is an obligation on the part of the students not to talk out of turn, the teacher is obligated not to demand group silence so that he can make irrelevant statements. If students talk habitually while he is speaking, it would be a good idea for him to assess the significance of what he is saying.

Inability to Participate.   In vocal music classes students are sometimes present but unable to sing because of colds or laryngitis. The instrumental teacher must deal with broken or forgotten instruments, cut lips, and sprained fingers. These situations should be handled in basically the same way. The student should report his affliction to the teacher *before* class begins. Then he should sit in his regular place and follow the class activity, learning as much as possible.

Some students who cannot participate ask permission to do homework during class. If doing homework under such circumstances is allowed, it is sometimes surprising how many students develop throat troubles or broken instruments on days in which there are important examinations in other subjects!

Attendance.   Many schools have a detention hall or eighth hour to handle excessive tardinesses and unexcused absences. When a schoolwide setup exists, there is little that the music teacher need do about this matter. If there is no such program, then the teacher must establish his own policies concerning attendance.

If a teacher demands that his students be punctual, then he himself must not be lax about starting class on time. This is necessary not only for the sake of consistency, but also for good teaching. Much time can be wasted in getting classes under way. A teacher who is slow about starting class gives the impression of lacking interest.

Music teachers, who for the most part have been taught throughout their lives a sense of obligation and responsibility, are sometimes shocked to discover that one or two students have failed to appear at a performance of the organization. This action cannot be allowed to pass without penalty. It mocks the efforts of the rest of the students who did show up; it makes a sham of granting credit and it demonstrates a complete lack of regard for what the group is trying to do. The seriousness of the matter should be emphasized *before* the program, so that errant students will have had adequate warning.

Occasionally a new teacher encounters students who are contrary and stubborn. Reasonable requests for out-of-school meetings and other extra efforts are greeted with groans and muttering. Why? A few students, feeling loyalty to the former teacher, may resent the new teacher. Perhaps they are just being adolescent and trying to show their independence from authority. They may want to draw attention to themselves. Such actions are usually of little consequence, and it is best for the teacher to ignore them. Rather than retorting, "Now listen, you *will* do it!" and putting the students in the position of losing face if they back down, it is wiser to pass over the remark and go on, assuming that the students will follow the request in time. In most cases they will. If a student actually does not follow the directions, penalties should be imposed.

Other Facets of Behavior.   Gum-chewing and music do not go together. Students should be asked to dispose of their gum before class begins. Until the students take responsibility for doing this themselves, some teachers appoint one student as "chief gum-collector" to pass around the waste-basket.

Members of performing groups must maintain good posture. It increases alertness and improves behavior. Sloppy posture usually indicates inatten-tiveness. A sloucher can be reminded that he is beginning to look like a question mark or a pretzel. A good-natured remark usually succeeds in bringing about improved posture. In choral organizations, slouching can be corrected temporarily by having the class stand. Even in instrumental groups, sections can get on their feet occasionally when they play.

The students should put notebooks and purses on the floor underneath their chairs. This will keep them from fooling around with pencils, mirrors, pictures, and other items.

Minor behavior problems are sometimes encouraged unwittingly by a teacher whose attention is focused more on his music than on the class. If he continually hovers over the score, it is likely that some students will lag in participation — they may even engage in activities quite unrelated to music. If looking at the music is such a temptation, it should be closed.

The teacher should work with at least one eye on the students. Not only must he know the subject sufficiently to teach it to someone else, but he must also be able to put this subject matter into second place, and focus his major attention on the students' response to what is being taught.

Areas of Choice

A third characteristic of democratic education is providing for significant areas of choice by the students. There are several ways in which students can be given choices in music. Two have already been mentioned: considering policies and handling routine jobs. A third area for significant choice lies in the selection of music. Students cannot be expected to select the major share of the music they will study, but they can choose several numbers that interest them.

A fourth area for choice by the students will be mentioned in some detail in Chapter 17 in connection with staging music for concerts.

Development of Responsibility

A fourth outcome of democratic education is the development of re-sponsibility in the students. The educational process must gradually prepare the student to direct himself, and give him practice in doing so. The student must be made aware of his responsibility for his own behavior. Some students have the notion that it is the teacher's job to make them behave. The other aspect of training in self-direction is to give the student responsibility for the successful operation of the group.

In most cases of misbehavior, the student who is guilty knows it. So the problem for him is seldom one of not knowing how to act, but rather one of acting as he knows he should.

> Ray Johnson found that this reminder was effective with his students: "Look, you're big boys and girls now. You know the rules that we all worked out together for conduct in band. So do what you know is right. If you act like adults, you'll be treated as adults, and everything will be just fine. When you act like children, everyone, including me, will treat you as children. It's up to you. Now let's get to work on this music."

The appeal is essentially a good one because it puts the responsibility on each student. Teenagers want to be free from adult authority, so they need to be given a chance to take care of themselves.

Managing Rule Violators

Sometimes teachers wonder: "How strictly should I enforce the rules? After all, the students are human beings. How can I find out when to clamp down and when to relax control?" This question is difficult to answer. Because feeling and attitude affect music learning, student reaction cannot be ignored. The teacher must learn to sense when he is approaching the middle ground between too much and too little control. The midpoint is not something that he finds and then rigidly maintains every day and in every situation; no two situations are quite the same.

There is a practical answer to the amount of attention given to rules and behavior. When concern with behavior even approaches the amount of concern for the learning of music, then behavior is being overemphasized. The point of education is not to attain proper classroom manners. These are only means to an end. The results obtained in the classroom are most revealing in assessing the proper amount of control. If student conduct is interfering with learning, then stricter behavior controls are called for. The difficult thing for the teacher to decide is whether the lack of learning is due to class deportment or something else, such as ineffective teaching methods. Equally difficult to determine is whether the class is approximating its potential for learning. Sometimes the class' accomplishment is acceptable, but because of classroom behavior problems the educational results are less impressive than they could be.

The teacher should be alert to whether the misbehavior is serious or just "pulling the teacher's leg." Usually it is the latter. It's hard to put into words how one can tell, but with a little experience one can sense a certain look in the eyes and lack of conviction in the voice of a student when he is just trying to get away with something, often for no other reason than to add a little zest to a humdrum school day.

To think in terms of penalty rather than of punishment is psychologically more healthful for both student and teacher. The word "punish" connotes the infliction of pain, whereas "penalty" implies a loss due to nonfulfillment of a stipulation, without the involvement of personal feelings. The case against punishment *per se* is well-established. Although punishment or threat of it may appear to work, in the long run it does not obtain genuine compliance in the teenage student.

Many a young teacher is afraid that if he reprimands a student, he will be disliked by the class, even though the student concerned is obviously wrong. This fear is unjustified. If the rules are democratically formed, the action of the group will support the teacher in maintaining order. The majority of the class wants the violators dealt with because they feel that if they behave themselves, so should everyone else.

Objective Attitude of the Teacher

There are several ways in which a teacher can handle the students' conduct more smoothly and effectively. The first involves his attitude toward dealing with rule violators. No matter how disgusted, disappointed, or exasperated he may become, he must not lose his temper. He should be adult enough to avoid the trap of acting childish. A teacher admits defeat when he allows a student to make him angry. Firm, clear, reasonable, and unemotional directives achieve control without harmful aftereffects. More important, anger denotes the teacher's personal involvement. By remaining uninvolved personally and emotionally the teacher will be better able to deal with the students. Noninvolvement is a cardinal rule in handling student misbehavior.

It is difficult for a new teacher to realize that misbehavior by students is seldom directed at him personally. When confronted with their acts, the students sometimes say, "But we didn't mean anything against you." And what they say is true. Students will vent all types of repressions at school. The "smart" talk by the adolescent boy in school may well be his releasing resentment of an overly strict home. A student's behavior in class may have little relation to what has happened in that particular class, and this is one reason why even a good teacher must expect some behavior disturbances.

The teacher has to make a distinction between disliking the student personally and disliking the things he does. The student must realize, if at all possible, that the teacher makes this distinction.

> Jim Baker found it necessary to penalize his principal second violin for persistently talking out of turn in rehearsal. "Look, Bill," Mr. Baker said, "personally I like you and you're a good fiddler. But in orchestra there are rules about talking and we all agreed on them. You seem to have trouble following them. I don't like this, and neither does the rest of the orchestra. Not only aren't you learning anything, but you're keeping the others from learning. So I think you'd better put in an hour after school. There are some bowings to mark in the violin parts. Why, I'd have to penalize my own mother if she talked as much as you do."

This reprimand is a good one for several reasons. First, it is direct and easily understood. Second, it separates Bill as a person from his actions; and it is the actions that need changing. Third, it tells Bill why his behavior is unacceptable. Fourth, it derives its authority from "we" or "the group," and not from the teacher's personal demands. Fifth, the talk ends on a note of humor, letting the students know that the teacher has not involved himself personally in the matter.

Specific Teacher Actions

There are a few suggestions that may help maintain order. For example, a wise teacher is careful about the seating placement of talkative students. When possible, combinations of good friends should be separated. In mixed choral groups, for goodness' sake (literally) have the boys sit in the front rows. It may be musically fine to have the lower part soaring out from the back of the group. But before this can occur, the boys have to sing their part well, and before that is possible, it is necessary for them to have training, which requires that they behave themselves and learn something. In performing groups the seating should be arranged with aisles between the chairs so that the teacher can walk among the musicians to observe their work more carefully. This discourages small offenses and encourages better rapport between teacher and students.

In handling behavior, *the teacher should mean what he says and follow it up!* If he cannot or does not intend to follow up what he says, he shouldn't say it. Students are quick, very quick to discover idle threats. They will sometimes "test" a teacher to see if he really means what he says. This test has to be met, or the teacher is in for a miserable time. He must mean what he says from the beginning of the year on. It is too late to wait until things have gone badly for several weeks or months.

The chorus students at Farnsworth High School soon discovered that Miss Painter's threats didn't mean a thing. When they came into class, they stood around the room in small groups, talking and laughing. Some students sat down in the wrong seats. Finally, after shouting and pleading, Miss Painter got the chorus seated. She then started to talk about the day's work.

Some members of the chorus began to converse with one another, and Miss Painter barked out, "If you people don't stop talking, I'm going to assign extra homework!" The talking stopped for a few moments, then started again. Miss Painter raised her voice so that she could be heard above the sound of shuffling feet and conversation. Finally, after more admonitions to be quiet, the chorus started singing, almost ten minutes after the hour began.

A few students had not bothered to pick up their folders, and Miss Painter noticed that they were just singing along without music. The song stopped. "Where's your folder?" she asked Joe Hinman. "Guess I left it in my locker," Joe replied lazily. "Listen, you people who forgot your folders," she said, "tomorrow I'm going to check each one personally for his folder. If you don't have a folder, I'm lowering your grade." The students weren't worried. Miss Painter had made the same threat before, but had always forgotten to carry it out.

Students have an uncanny way of knowing when a teacher is confident in what he is doing, and they are especially discerning when he is hesitant. He must make sure that the rules have been clearly established, that the class understands them, and that students are dealt with in some manner when they violate the rules.

It is often wise not to make an issue of a small offense. Everyone makes small infractions of rules on occasion. When a motorist is caught over-parking his time on the meter, he gets a ticket. He is wrong and he knows it, but he doesn't want to be treated like a criminal. Students feel the same way about their small offenses.

When a student misbehaves, what should a teacher say and do? This depends largely on the seriousness and frequency of the misbehavior. There are many ways to pass out mild reprimands for rule infractions, however. The following illustration shows how one case *might* be handled.

Helen Oliver was telling the Girls' Glee Club about the procedures they would follow at the concert for getting on and off the stage. Judy turned and whispered to her neighbor. Miss Oliver stopped talking for a moment, looked at Judy and said in a firm voice, "Judy." She waited a moment more for her to stop whispering. Judy stopped, and Miss Oliver went back to explaining the stage procedures for the concert.

Most small violations can be handled in a similar manner. With less sensitive students it is necessary to be quite blunt, but most teenagers will respond to a short reminder.

What does a teacher do if a student continues to talk even after a reminder? This probably will not happen, but it can. Here is how it might be handled.

> Glen Winter was working with the tenor section. One of the basses turned around in his seat and started to talk and laugh with one of his friends. Mr. Winter said, "Jack, sometimes I think you should've joined a speaking chorus instead of a singing one."
>
> Before Mr. Winter could finish working with the tenors, Jack resumed his talking and laughing. Mr. Winter then said in a firm voice, "Jack, you were just told to stop the chatter. Now do it!" Mr. Winter kept looking at him until Jack turned around and gave him his full attention.

What would happen if Jack still persisted in violating the rules? Mr. Winter would have no choice but to deal with him outside the class situation. The methods for doing this will be discussed shortly.

Another type of situation involves no particular individual but rather a sizable segment of the entire group.

> To Sandra Babcock, it seemed as if the whole general music class was talking and not yet ready to work. She held up her hand and said in a clear voice, "A moment of silence, please." She waited about 15 seconds for the group to quiet down, meanwhile catching the eyes of several students and looking directly at them. After a few seconds of silence she said, "Ah, what a wonderful sound — silence." Then she immediately started to work on the day's activities.

How much better this solution is than standing in front of the group and shouting for attention, making everyone tense and irritable. For the technique to be effective, the teacher must wait for real silence, and by his manner he must insist on it. His duty is to keep a cool head, get the attention of the students, and give firm, clear requests. He should put the group to work as soon as possible and make his own remarks pertinent to teaching the class.

Handling Persistent Rule Violators

If a student persists in violating standards of conduct in spite of good, positive teaching and the employment of reminders and mild reprimands in the classroom situation, he should be dealt with outside class. According to educational psychologists, a friendly private conference is the most effective means of dealing with students. It does not bring any additional class attention to the troublemaker, and attention in some form is frequently what he is seeking. Furthermore, it avoids embarrassing him before his peers.

Students who reach this degree of rule violation are motivated by psychological needs and forces that they themselves may not understand. The private conference is informational because the teacher tries to determine the cause for the misbehavior, and correctional because he can work with the student to remedy the situation. If possible, the teacher should get information about the student from the guidance personnel of the school before the conference.

As for the conference itself, there are several points to remember when talking with a student under such circumstances:

(1) Be friendly, honest, and unhurried. Remember to differentiate between disapproval of the student personally and disapproval of what he does. Sarcasm, ridicule, and anger are as ineffective when used in private as they are in a group situation. Allow enough time for a thorough and easy-going discussion.

(2) Approach the student positively. Something like this is effective: "Look, John. You could be a lot of help to the chorus. We need tenors, and especially tenors who can carry their part well. You could be a big plus sign in chorus, if you wanted to be. Why don't you spend your energy building up the group, instead of tearing it down?" This type of approach is much better than the negative admonitions, "Don't do this. Don't do that."

(3) Give the student a chance to talk. This helps to convince him that he is being treated fairly. Learn more about him. Ask him whether there is anything that can be done to help him behave better in the future. He may ask to change his seat, and this may solve the problem.

A student will often attempt to talk his way out of a difficult situation. His statements usually fall back on predictable arguments. Some of these defenses are examined briefly here to see how a teacher might handle them, again remembering that the best reply would necessarily depend on the total situation. The first argument is basically, "Why are you picking on me?" The student usually knows full well that he is not being singled out unfairly, but he feels in need of some defense to save face.

Mike's plea was, "Why are you picking on me?" Miss Hartman replied, "Believe me, I don't have time to pick on you or anyone else. The only reason I single out one individual is that he's doing something he shouldn't; and that's why I'm talking to you."

A variation of this student defense reaction is one that goes, "Every time there's trouble in my section, you look at me." This argument is, of course, limited to students who have been dealt with on previous occasions.

> Fred Travis tried such a defense with Mr. Collins, who answered, "Well, you've caused a disturbance so often in the past that there is a temptation for me to look first in your direction. But it doesn't matter where I look first; the only people I single out are the ones who are actually causing trouble."

If the student chooses one type of defense more than any other, it is probably this: "George was doing it too, I wasn't the only one."

> When Fred used this excuse, Mr. Collins replied, "I'm just like a referee in a game. When I see an infraction of the rules, I blow the whistle and hand out a penalty. I saw you this time, so you're being penalized. If George causes trouble, he'll be penalized too."

The statement of the persistent, petty rule violator goes essentially, "All I did was write a note, and I got in trouble."

> When Susan explained to Miss Arnold, "I just asked Judy a question," Miss Arnold answered, "If you had a question about the music, why didn't you raise your hand and ask me? It's my job to answer questions about the music. If your question was *not* about the music, then you should have waited until after class to ask Judy."
> On another occasion, Susan explained, "All I did was laugh at something Donna said." Miss Arnold answered, "What you haven't thought of, Susan, are all the many other times you've disturbed the class and prevented the others from learning. Remember there was once a straw that broke the camel's back. Well, this incident today is like a straw. So you're being penalized for many small offenses, including today's."

The teacher must not plead with the student to behave. Pleading makes the position of the teacher seem weak, almost desperate. Besides, it seldom improves the student's behavior in the future.

Handling Serious Infractions

If private conferences with the student do not work, then definite penalties are necessary. A word of caution is in order here: a teacher may be tempted, at the first sign of trouble, to simply lower the student's grade, or send him to the principal's office or the study hall. But such actions are generally negative. Granted they may be necessary in some cases, but they can be justified only after the teacher has taken the time and trouble to work with the student privately. Probably there should be at least one talk with the student before resorting to negative measures.

It is best to work with the principal or head counselor on serious behavior problems. A pupil who is causing the music teacher some headaches is probably causing trouble for other teachers as well. The principal wants to know about such a student so that an organized program of correction can be effected. He can study the total situation and make recommendations. He may wish to talk to the parents, or he may have the teachers act together to bring about some changed behavior in the student. Whenever possible, the principal should be informed ahead of time if a teacher suspects that he is going to have a serious problem with a student.

Minor behavior problems should not be sent to the principal or head counselor. Principals do not like being thought of as school disciplinarians. They want each teacher to take care of his own problems as much as possible, because they realize that eventually the teacher is the only one who can maintain order in his own room. No one else can do it for him. The school administration, of course, will help with serious and unusual problems.

Besides working with the school principal, the teacher can try several other courses of action. Precisely what is done depends on each situation. For instance, keeping a student after school or giving him an assignment to do is usually successful only with less mature students.

(1) The student can be assigned time to put in after school. This time should be spent constructively doing such things as sorting music or undertaking special assignments. Using this type of corrective measure is limited because it is often the teacher, not the student, who is penalized by staying later. If the school operates an after-school detention room, the teacher is not inconvenienced by requiring a student to stay after hours.

(2) The misbehavior of the student can be reflected in the grade he receives. Usually the persistent violator cares little about grades, so this is of limited value.

(3) The student can be removed from the group for a period of time, and required to sit in the office or study hall. There is one disadvantage to this approach: when a student is absent from class, he is obviously not learning, and the teacher will have to help him catch up.

Permanent Removal from Class

When should a student be removed permanently from class because of poor behavior? Briefly stated, he should be removed whenever the positive benefits to him as an individual are outweighed by his negative influence on the group. Any sincere teacher thinks long and hard before removing a student from class. Many times the student who gets into repeated and serious trouble also has an unfortunate home background. Most teachers feel a special obligation to help such a student overcome his environment. A sympathetic teacher will tolerate misbehavior from a disadvantaged child that he probably would not accept from other children. On the other hand, he has a clear obligation to the majority of the students who do conduct themselves properly. He owes his cooperative students the best music education he can give. So comes the hard decision: the chronic troublemakers cannot be allowed to remain. Removal from class then is entirely justifiable.

A new teacher will sometimes be given this advice by an experienced colleague: "Kick out a few people the first week or so, and you won't have any more trouble." There may be some truth to this advice, but like an iceberg, only a portion of the matter is visible. To begin with, the teacher is doing more than removing troublesome students; he is defining his beliefs about the purpose of education. Second, the new teacher must have an understanding with the school administration before such action is undertaken. If classroom behavior was bad during the previous year, drastic steps may be necessary to achieve order. But such steps should be taken only with the administration's knowledge and support. Third, a teacher must be able to present good reasons for removing a student, and it is hard to build a case in only a week, especially when the teacher is new. Fourth, a new teacher is often mistaken about who the real troublemakers are. At the beginning of the year, both teacher and students need time to adjust to the new situation. An overzealous teacher can ruin a music group in the first two weeks by wielding the ax too hastily and indiscriminately.

Although the extremely serious school disruptions—threats of physical violence, knife pullings, fights—are rare in music classes, a word should be said about them. Under no circumstances should a teacher attempt to wrestle a weapon from a student or hold two combatants apart. Besides inviting injury, physical intervention complicates the determination later of what really happened. Instead, send a fleet-footed, responsible student for the principal, male physical education teacher, or school security officer if the school has one. Do not panic outwardly or lose self-control. Meanwhile, in the most determined, forceful tone of voice possible, tell the student or students to stop fighting or put down the weapon. Surprisingly, this will sometimes work. But in any case, unless the teacher issues a clear directive, during a later investigation it may not be possible to establish the point that the teacher did all that was reasonably possible to maintain control. Again, such violent behavior problems are rare, but for a number of reasons they have been increasing in the last decade. A little forethought helps in handling a potentially dangerous situation that might arise.

Effective teaching should of course be the focus of the teacher's efforts.

Then if a student gets out of line, the teacher can show firmly but pleasantly that he is concerned for the student's improved behavior, and his educational well-being. As the teacher demonstrates consistency and reasonableness in handling these problems, the students will gain increasing confidence in his judgment, and the specter of discipline will gradually disappear.

Questions

1. Why does the matter of classroom management become more important as the size of the class increases? In what way do the techniques for managing a group of 80 vary from those used in teaching a group of five students?

2. Should a student with an unfortunate home background be expected to adhere to the rules just as much as a student from a good home? Why, or why not? If equal adherence is desirable, how might the music teacher make allowances for such a student, while still retaining the integrity of the class?

3. In providing students with significant choices in music, which of these matters are more properly left to the teacher and which can involve a large amount of student participation?

(a) The selection of one of two serious numbers to be performed at a program.

(b) The decision of whether or not the band needs to rehearse again a certain section of an overture.

(c) The selection of the type of stole that will be bought to go with the choir robes.

(d) The decision of whether or not a piece from the Renaissance period shall be studied in the course.

(e) The determination of the order in which the music will be performed in the spring concert.

4. What should the teacher do to manage each of these incidents?

(a) Bob, a sophomore, is somewhat of a "show-off." A student running errands for the principal's office enters the room with a note for the teacher. Bob shouts to the girl bringing the note, "Marge! Baby!"

(b) Linda is a quiet freshman in the clarinet section. As the teacher is explaining a point, he notices Linda talking quietly to her neighbor.

(c) Howard has caused trouble in the eighth grade general music class. Feeling that he is seeking attention, the teacher assigns him a report to make to the class, with the hope that this will provide him with attention and the class with useful information. While giving the report, Howard talks and talks, uses the occasion to be a "clown," and is clearly not interested in giving a useful report.

(d) The seventh grade general music class is attempting to adapt an autoharp accompaniment to a song. Herbie is usually reasonably well-behaved. But as he holds the instrument waiting to play the chords the class decides on, he can't resist strumming lightly on it.

(e) The ninth grade girls' glee club is practicing its music for a performance at the annual Mothers' Tea. As the teacher walks by frivolous, talkative Diane, he notices that she is looking at a movie magazine behind her folder.

(f) A nearby store is featuring inexpensive plastic water pistols this week. Nearly every boy entering Mrs. Hixson's seventh grade general music class has a loaded water pistol in his pocket as he enters the room.

5. Why is a private conference the best way to deal with a student whose behavior has become a problem?

Suggested Readings

Biehler, Robert F., *Psychology Applied to Teaching.* Boston: Houghton Mifflin, 1971. Ch. 15.

Jessup, Michael H., and Margaret A. Kiley, *Discipline: Positive Attitudes for Learning.* Englewood Cliffs, New Jersey: Prentice-Hall, 1971.

Larson, Knute G., and Melvin R. Karpas, *Effective School Discipline.* Englewood Cliffs, New Jersey: Prentice-Hall, 1963.

Lindgren, Henry Clay, *Educational Psychology in the Classroom,* 3rd Ed. New York: John Wiley & Sons, 1967.

Section Five

How: The Methods of Teaching Music

How to teach music is the final topic considered in this book, not because it is the least important, but rather because it is the largest and most varied. Chapter 9 begins the section with a discussion of basic guidelines for teaching music. Many of the specific actions the teacher should take in teaching can be developed from the fundamental generalizations presented in that chapter. For example, students will remember more if the teacher reviews near the conclusion of the class the material presented earlier in the class period. Although one could make up a number of rules (for example, "Review all factual lessons within one half hour of presentation"), if the teacher understands the principles of how the human mind retains information, he can apply this information to teaching a wide variety of topics in many different situations. A general understanding is more adaptable and is therefore more useful than a specific fact. Besides, one usually remembers basic ideas better than isolated specifics—another fundamental principle about the retention of information.

Chapter 10 deals specifically with the junior high/middle school general music class. Here, as in much of the content of the remaining chapters, the suggestions presented are based on the principles discussed in Chapter 9. This chapter also presents outlines for 19 units of study for these classes.

Chapter 11 covers the rehearsal and teaching of performing groups. Because the same basic information is valid for both choral and instrumental groups, the two types of musical organizations are considered together, with a few exceptions.

Chapter 12 covers teaching musicianship and interpretation in musical performance; Chapter 13 treats intonation. In these chapters too, choral and instrumental music are discussed together.

Chapter 14 is devoted to teaching singing, including the important topic of voice change in boys. Chapter 15 is the instrumental counterpart of Chapter 14 and includes basic playing techniques of families of instruments.

In 1963, when the first edition of this book was written, some reviewers of the manuscript suggested deleting the chapter on theory and music appreciation. "It's a pipe dream," they said. "Almost no schools teach such courses." Before the 1960s ended, the most frequently received suggestion was that the chapter be expanded—

such has been the increase of interest in this area of music education. Chapter 16 not only covers teaching theory and music appreciation, but discusses the humanities/fine arts courses as well.

Because public performances are an integral part of secondary school music, an entire chapter, Chapter 17, is devoted to the topic.

9

Guidelines for Teaching Music

Below is a true-false quiz containing some "common sense" beliefs about learning music. It can be an interesting springboard to a comparison between what everyone "knows" about teaching and what research into the learning process reveals. The answers to the questions will be disclosed at various points in the chapter. Prior to reading the chapter, you may wish to try your luck at the quiz.

T F 1. The most effective way to correct the performance of a particular rhythmic figure is for the teacher to tell the students how to do it.

T F 2. It's a good idea to have a choral group sing back and forth many times between the notes of different intervals, such as the augmented fourth, so that they can sing each interval correctly when it's encountered in actual music.

T F 3. Repeating a point many times is a good way to make sure the students remember it.

T F 4. Thinking, especially in solving difficult mental problems, is a skill that is developed through practice in much the same way that physical exercise builds muscles.

T F 5. General ideas are usually remembered better than particular facts.

T F 6. If a performing group can't get a passage right, the students should go over it again and again until they can do it correctly.

T F 7. In learning new music, a performing group should first get the notes right, then work on interpretation.

T F 8. There is one best way to teach a new number to a band or choral group, and the prospective teacher should learn and use that method.

T F 9. Because people remember so little of what they learn in school, teachers should concentrate on seeing that the students enjoy music, whether learning occurs or not.

T F 10. Students will learn better if they understand the reason for what they are doing.

T F   11. If you want to learn to play a Mozart sonata, you will get better results if you practice it for two hours on each of the last two days before your lesson than if you work on it for 30 minutes a day for the six days preceding your lesson.

Although there is a little truth in each of the eleven statements, nine of them are false. Which ones are correct and which are incorrect is not the point at this moment. The point is that each answer calls for an assumption about how music is learned best. Just as he reveals his beliefs about the purposes of school music through his actions (see Chapter 3), a teacher makes decisions based on his fundamental beliefs about learning, whether he realizes it or not. These basic principles have a strong bearing on what happens in the music class, and therefore should be clearly understood.

Two precautions should be mentioned about employing the guidelines suggested in this chapter. One: None is absolute; none should be allowed to work to the detriment of other principles. Reason and discretion are necessary in their application. Two: Most principles do not apply to all types of learning. Mastering the skills required to perform a piece of music, and gaining an understanding of how the sounds of a piece are organized, involve different learning principles.

Learning is a many-sided word. It can refer to kinesthetic or muscular-physical skill, as when a violinist learns to shift from first to third position. Learning also refers to memorization of facts: the students may learn that A above middle C vibrates 440 times each second, or that Mozart was a composer of the Classical period. Learning may mean problem-solving. For example, a student may have studied some Impressionistic music and its phrasing. When presented with a Debussy work that is unknown to him, he is able to phrase it properly because he has learned how to perform such music. Finally, a person has learned a piece of music when he can listen to it with understanding or play it and convey its aesthetic meaning.

And so the idea that there is only one right way to teach music is incorrect. The answer to question 8 is "false." The appropriate method depends on the situation, the students, and what the teacher wants the group to learn.

Suitability of Goals

Closely related to the "to whom" aspect of the teaching mixture mentioned in Chapter 1 is the teacher's reasonableness in his expectations of what a class can learn. Because this guideline applies to all learning, it is presented first in this chapter. *The teacher must view realistically the variables affecting the level at which a class operates.* Stravinsky's *Rite of Spring* is a monument of modern music, but it is not suitable for performance by a junior high school orchestra. No choral teacher should expect a group of 13-year-olds to sound like a choir of college voice majors, nor should he anticipate that an unselected glee club meeting twice a week will achieve the standard set by a highly select choir that practices daily. Significant variables, which apply to both the performance and the study of music, are:

(1) The age of the students. This is especially important in choral music.
(2) The degree of selectivity of the members.
(3) The amount of class time available.
(4) The previous musical experience of the students.

The formula for having one of the best bands or choirs in the state is a simple one: mature students + a high degree of student selection + sufficient time + good previous training + a competent teacher = a top group. Of course there is a correlation among these factors. Notable schools have good teachers because able people naturally gravitate toward prestigious teaching situations, and their skilled teaching in turn makes the program even stronger.

Sometimes the statement is made that all students are pretty much alike everywhere, so the differences in performance quality are due to the teacher's ability; that is, the performance is only a reflection of the teacher. Such a sentiment is wanting in logic. Can anyone say that a band from a small school with limited financial resources and frequent changes of teachers reflects poorer teaching than a group from a large school with good resources and a long tradition of instrumental music?

Young teachers sometimes despair because, try as they may, they cannot reach the standards attained in the best schools of the state—schools whose groups are heard at professional meetings and workshops. Prospective teachers should realize that the vast majority of groups across the nation are not highly selected and experienced. One hears about the few high-quality performing groups simply because they are exceptional, not because they are typical.

Acknowledging the existence of less-than-ideal situations does not mean that a teacher should be content with sloppy performances or casual scholarship among his students. The plea is for realism and progress toward better performances and intellectual understanding. Striving for unrealistic standards in music makes no more sense than accomplishing a seven-foot high jump (close to the world's record) as a requirement for passing a physical education course. Neither does a one-foot high jump requirement make much sense, because it represents virtually no accomplishment. Suitable expectations are an important condition in educating students.

Cognitive Learning

Because not all learning is of the same type, some guidelines apply more to one kind of learning than another. For the sake of clarity, the discussion will be divided into the three broad categories mentioned in Chapter 6: the cognitive domain (facts and ideas), the psychomotor domain (skills), and the affective domain (attitudes).

"Learn by Doing"

In the 1930s and 1940s this phrase, derived from the eminent philosopher-educator John Dewey, was the motto of what was then called "progressive education." There is much truth in these words, although they need some qualification. As the seventeenth-century essayist John Locke wrote:

> Let us then suppose the mind to be, as we say, white paper, void of all characters, without any ideas; how comes it to be so furnished? . . . To this I answer, in one word, from experience. . . . I find I am absolutely dependent upon experience for the ideas I can have and the manner in which I can have them.[1]

People learn about the beat in music by feeling it, not by memorizing a definition of the beat. Activities such as tapping feet and clapping hands clarify the experience of the beat. Even with relatively complex ideas — romanticism, for example — one must see (experience) romantic characteristics in paintings and read (experience) romantic pieces of literature to acquire a concept of romanticism. Therefore, the answer to question 1 about teaching a rhythmic figure is "false." Talking about rhythm is not an effective way to teach it.

Two qualifications are necessary to validate the "Learn by doing" directive. One: The experience must be the right kind, because a person can easily do the wrong thing — hold an instrument incorrectly, for instance. Two: Not all learning experiences are equally instructive. Some require a large expenditure of time and effort for a small educational return. What is needed (and was probably assumed by Dewey when he wrote the phrase) is to do significant things correctly, and not just to do tasks for the sake of activity. The guideline for teaching is that *learning should be based on carefully structured experiences.*

---

[1] J. E. Russell, *The Philosophy of Locke,* extracts from *The Essay Concerning Human Understanding* (New York: Holt, Rinehart and Winston, 1891), p. 35.

Valid Musical Experiences

Certainly each activity in a music class should be as musical as possible. The hour long solfège drill mentioned in the first chapter is one example of how music classes can be unmusical. Such instruction reminds one of the old joke about the doctor who said, "The operation was a success, but the patient died."

There are several ways in which musical qualities can be lost or ignored. Some teachers are satisfied with the students' performance when the notes are learned. But music is more than producing the sounds called for by the notation. Even though learning the notes in many cases represents no small accomplishment, the teacher should not stop there. Phrasing, nuances, and expression are necessary to make it music, and not merely a mechanical exercise in making sound. The answer to question 2 is "false." Extensive isolation of intervals is neither musically valid nor educationally successful.

Sometimes students rehearse a work so much that they perform it mechanically. To maintain the quality of freshness in a piece of music, work on it should be distributed evenly throughout the weeks prior to the performance. Ideally, rehearsal on a piece should be so regulated that it reaches its acme of development at the time of performance. This peak occurs at the point that represents the greatest amount of technical perfection coupled with a feeling of musical spontaneity. When groups go "dead" in a program, it is often because they reached their peak of interest too far ahead of the performance.

If an organization is performing ten numbers, it is clear that all ten cannot be brought to their height of technical accuracy and freshness simultaneously. What can be done? A piece that is nearly ready for performance weeks ahead of the program will have to be placed in a musical "deep freeze"; it should be withdrawn from regular practice for a few days. Curiously, this seasoning often improves the performance of the work. A few days before the performance, the number can be rehearsed again and given the final polishing touches.

Sometimes it is necessary to set aside portions of a piece temporarily. Some melodies are easily learned, and it is easy to tire of them. This can result in a peculiar situation, especially in vocal music. The students love to sing certain melodies, but the more they sing them, the worse the music sounds! The number of repetitions of these passages has to be carefully rationed. It may be necessary to avoid the easier sections of a work in class, and expend effort only on the more difficult passages.

To demonstrate how several numbers might be spaced over a period of time, let's assume that a group has eight weeks in which to prepare a program of eight works. In this plan all the music is assumed to be of equal difficulty, a most unlikely possibility.

First week — Introduce and learn most of pieces 1, 2, and 3.

Second week — Introduce piece 4 and learn most of it. Continue work on pieces 1, 2, and 3.

Third week — Introduce piece 5 and learn most of it. Finish work on pieces 1 and 2, and save them for review.

Fourth week — Introduce piece 6 and learn most of it. Continue work on pieces 4 and 5. Save and only review pieces 1, 2, and 3.

Fifth week — Introduce piece 7 and learn most of it. Continue work on pieces 5 and 6. Save and only review pieces 1, 2, 3, and 4.

Sixth week — Introduce piece 8 and learn most of it. Continue work on pieces 6 and 7. Save and only review pieces 1, 2, 3, 4, and 5.

Seventh week — Continue work on pieces 7 and 8. Begin polishing pieces 1 and 2. Occasional review of pieces 3, 4, 5, and 6.

Eighth week — Polish all eight pieces. Dress rehearsal and performance.

In addition, the teacher should pace the students psychologically to help preserve freshness and interest in the music. No teacher should try to maintain the same psychological intensity in all rehearsals. The students will have a vastly different attitude toward a class early in September than toward the dress rehearsal for the Christmas concert.

Aural Experience

Music is an aural art. To be valid, *learning in music should involve listening in some form* — critiquing a performance of a passage, hearing the timbre of a voice or instrument, or listening to a rhythmic or tonal pattern.

The need for aural experience is especially significant in learning to read music. It is a necessary antecedent to visual experience. This view, expounded by Pestalozzi in 1801,[2] is summed up today in the expression "Ear it before you eye it." The order is important here. Teaching musical comprehension by proceeding from printed symbols to aural experience is successful only when adequate listening has preceded the reading.

The manner in which a child learns language is similar to the way he learns, or should learn, music. By the time a child enters first grade, he already has an understanding vocabulary of about 24,000 words and three or four years' practice in speaking the language before he first sees the printed symbols that represent what he has been saying.[3] These facts about language

---

[2] *Grove's Dictionary of Music and Musicians, American Supplement* (Rev. Ed.) (New York: The Macmillan Co., 1947), p. 333.

[3] Ruth G. Strickland, *The Language Arts in the Elementary School*, 2nd Ed. (Boston: D. C. Heath and Co., 1957), p. 230.

development, along with research by Penfield,[4] have brought about some new approaches to language instruction in the schools. Today many language specialists introduce foreign languages to elementary school children by working mainly on an aural-speech basis, and only after two or more years have passed is the child shown the printed page.

Involvement

In 1964 two researchers reported a study in which fifth graders were taught Spanish. One group of classes used teaching machines, a second group a programed textbook, and a third group was given traditional classroom instruction. The teaching machines were early models, and broke down frequently. The more highly trained teachers put aside the machines and instructed the students in other ways. The teachers with less training told the students to fix the machines as best they could and to continue. In some classes as much as one-fourth of the time was spent repairing machines. Which group of students learned the most Spanish—those with the more capable teachers who were clever enough to move to other modes of instruction, or those with less able teachers who said in effect, "Fix it yourself and learn what you can"? Surprisingly, higher achievement was shown by the students who were told to fix the machines, a fact true at every IQ level.[5]

In another study, students were given two sets of arithmetic problems. On the first set the students were provided with principles that helped them solve the problems. On the second set of problems the student had to derive the principles themselves. A week later they were tested on solving the two types of problems. The results: Students did better on the problems for which they had to derive the principles than they did on the problems for which they had been given the principles.[6]

What do the results of these and similar studies indicate? They show that what we do for ourselves seems more important to us; we learn it better, and are more likely to remember it. What we get "free" just doesn't mean as much. For this reason, students should be encouraged to *put a reasonable degree of thought and effort into the learning activity.* The principle of involvement has long been known to observant teachers, and has in recent years received renewed attention under the heading "discovery method," also called inaccurately the "Socratic method." One of the reasons for the success

---

[4]Wilder Penfield and Tamar Roberts, *Speech and Brain-Mechanisms* (Princeton, N.J.: Princeton University Press, 1959).

[5]Henry Clay Lindgren, *Educational Psychology in the Classroom*, 3rd Ed. (New York: John Wiley & Sons, 1967), p. 388.

[6]Lindgren, p. 271.

of programed learning is the fact that it requires frequent responses from the student.

The principle of involvement, like the other guidelines mentioned in this chapter, is not absolute and overriding. It must be used with judgment. Discovery has a limited scope; there is simply not time enough in anyone's life to discover everything for himself. Some things must be accepted and remembered. Otherwise progress is impossible, because with no sharing of prior experience, each generation must cover the same ground as its predecessor.

Of course, not all involvement need be discovery, although this is one of its more prominent forms. Other types of involvement include the responding called for in programed learning, preparing reports and compositions, and joint decision-making between teacher and students. To a degree, involvement includes singing along in the soprano section or playing second trombone. Participation is better than passivity. But there should be more to school music than merely training students to produce the sounds represented by symbols on a page of music and to follow the conductor's directions. The student makes no judgments, nor does he feel he has a voice in deciding what the group does. Granted, the students should not have ultimate responsibility for deciding on the tempo of a work or determining whether the altos are singing too loudly. But merely allowing students to make sounds does not always mean that they feel involved.

Understanding the Purpose

No one likes to work on a project without some idea of what is being accomplished and why. *The purpose of what is taught should be made clear to the students.* It isn't enough for the teacher to say, in effect, "Trust me." If the beginning violinist is expected to maintain a straight left wrist, he should be shown that this helps him finger notes on the G string well, and makes it easier for him to shift to higher positions. If the director asks the choir to sing a piece of music over again, the singers should be told why.

The teacher of general music classes faces the same demand. The class may have a project of filling 12 water glasses, one for each semitone. The teacher sees the usefulness of this as an illustration of pitch, tuning, and all that goes with it. But do the students? When the group tries to "tune up" a chord they are singing, the teacher should point out the connection between the activities: "Remember the water glasses we tuned yesterday? What happened when we got to a point where we needed just a little more water or a little less? We had to listen and work very carefully, didn't we? Listen to your singing in the same careful way you did then." Unless the students know the purpose of what they are asked to learn, they will not learn it as well nor remember it as long. The answer to question 10 is "true."

Technical drill must be as functional as possible. Exercises extracted from a piece of music being studied are more successful because the students can see how the exercise applies to what they are doing. Playing the G sharp minor arpeggio when they have never seen it in the music they're performing is neither stimulating nor useful for most students.

Multisensory Approach

Some years ago examiners in the Belgian Department of Instruction noticed that students from a certain small rural school were consistently scoring unusually high on the national examinations in mathematics. It was evident that the teacher at that school had a superior method of teaching mathematics to children. Thus the Cuisenaire rods were discovered. The rods are actually small sticks. Each of the ten sizes comes in a different color, and they are proportioned so that ten of the "one" rods equal one "ten" rod in length, two of the "two" rods equal one "four" rod, and so on. If properly taught, six-year-old children using the rods can work problems that were once thought possible only for much older students.

Why are the Cuisenaire rods so successful? One reason is that the youngsters can see and feel $2 + 2 = 4$; no longer are the numbers abstractions, manipulated without any real comprehension. The rods provide a concrete "doing" experience, as recommended in the first learning guideline presented in this chapter. In addition, seeing *and* feeling provide a stronger impression than either experience alone. Another principle of learning, then, is that *the more ways in which something is experienced, the more likely it is to be understood and remembered.*

One application of this guideline can be seen in the prevalence of visual aids such as films, film strips, and overhead projectors. The teacher can help the students associate sound with musical notation through the use of books, chalk and flannel boards, and similar equipment. As the guideline suggests, seeing an opera is better than merely hearing the music. And a sense of musical style can be more easily achieved by hanging appropriate paintings when a class is studying the Baroque or Romantic era so that the students *see* the style as well as *hear* it.

Conceptual Learning

Why are concepts educationally important, in addition to their value as mental tools? They are valuable for two reasons: One: Concepts—generalizations, principles, and ideas—can be applied to more than one situation. Two: Concepts and general understandings are far more likely to be remembered. The answer to question 5 at the beginning of this chapter is "true." In fact, experiments indicate that the ability to interpret and apply basic ideas does not diminish after the course is over—a permanence that is not characteristic of factual learning.[7] Because concepts are retained, in addition to some specific information, the answer to question 9 is "false." *The music teacher should work for the development of general understandings on the part of the students,* rather than the memorization of a great amount of detailed information.

A teacher doesn't impart concepts directly. They result from generalizations the student makes, not from something the teacher does for him. The teacher can arrange a presentation so that the student is more likely to make significant generalizations, but unfortunately there is no way to guarantee that such understandings will develop.

Some teachers and curriculum planners have developed impressive plans around concepts. For example, one unit or lesson is spent on beat, another on meter, another on syncopation, and so on through to polyrhythms and irregular meters. The progression of topics reminds one of a string of box cars in a train, one car for each subconcept of rhythm, melody, and the like. While such a progression of topics seems logical, it is not psychologically or musically valid. People do not learn concepts as they might memorize a list of rules or definitions. To arrive at a concept requires many different experiences with the same idea. Music is neither conceived nor heard in isolated fragments; all musical concepts are interrelated.

An increased understanding of concepts is marked by clarity of verbal expression, precision and accuracy in use of terminology, and the ability to see appropriate relationships with other concepts. For example, a six-year-old may think of an orchestra as a large number of people playing instruments. By the age of 12 he may understand that an orchestra plays only certain works written for it and that one should listen carefully to its music. By the end of a high school music appreciation course he may understand the instrumentation of the orchestra, be able to name specific works, recognize the various forms of symphonic music, and appreciate the aesthetic and social role of the orchestra in the life of the community.

Concepts are not learned once and for all. Each learning experience enables the student to form a more precise concept. Any concept, no matter how sophisticated, is always in the process of formation.

Whole and Part Learning

Establishing concepts is closely related to whether people learn by wholes or by parts. Forty years ago psychologists were disagreeing strongly on this

---

[7]Ralph W. Tyler, "Permanence of Learning," *Journal of Higher Education,* 4:203–204, 1933.

issue. One group, represented by the Gestalt school, maintained that it is only the whole or the total configuration that has meaning; therefore, a teacher should work to give the student insight into whole sections or ideas. The other, equally esteemed group, called "stimulus-response" psychologists, stressed the learning of parts as components of the whole; accordingly, the teacher should present a learning task in segments. There were several reasons for the differing viewpoints: too much theory and not enough practical research, dissimilar testing situations, and differences of opinion about what the term "learning" means. Today most psychologists realize that each position has merit, and that learning involves both approaches. Bits of information are examined, but at the same time mental processes fit the item into a meaningful pattern. Even a small child tries to make sense out of what he encounters. The persistent question "why?" directed to his elders is proof of this fact.

The music teacher should "work both sides of the street" on the question of whole and part learning. If a song is being learned, he helps the students understand its text and its general mood. At the same time, he may stop to correct a missed final consonant or an out-of-tune C sharp. The Gestaltists are right in maintaining that the whole is greater than the sum of its parts, because each part receives extra meaning by virtue of belonging to something larger. But the opposing stimulus-response oriented psychologists are also right in insisting that without valid portions—correct notes and rhythm in the case of music—there is no accurate whole to comprehend. Generally, the answer to question 7 is "false." The right notes (parts) and the proper interpretation (whole) are learned almost simultaneously. Certainly there should be no lengthy separation between them.

Memory

The retention of what has been learned is a requisite of education. Sometimes the necessity of remembering is downgraded by saying that all students do is "regurgitate facts." But without memory, we would live only on a level of instinct and impulse. The real issue should not be the merits of remembering, but rather the value of what the student is taught and asked to remember. This is, of course, a curricular question, dealing directly with content and method.

There are ways in which remembering can be encouraged. One way is to present the material in its best light, so that its interest and usefulness are apparent. People on a sinking ship will remember much better a set of instructions about how to find their lifeboat than will jovial passengers just sailing out of the harbor. While the teacher can scarcely make what he teaches seem to be of life-saving importance, he can help the students see where it fits into the subject in particular and life in general. When students understand the purpose of the material to be learned — a guideline mentioned earlier in this chapter — they will remember better.

Although examinations are often condemned, learning material for a test does aid in remembering.[8] A test provides the students with an immediate reason for learning. The criticism directed at "learning to pass a test" would be better aimed at *what* the students are tested on, rather than at the practice of giving examinations.

The teacher can also urge the students to concentrate on the "big ideas" of the material, not on isolated, detailed information. Again, broad conceptual ideas are remembered best. A few years after having taken a course in chemistry, for example, most people will remember generally what the atomic theory is, but will have forgotten the atomic weight of iron.

The quality of remembering is affected by the quality of the original learning. Often what is forgotten was never thoroughly learned in the first place. This fact does *not* justify going over the same material repeatedly, but it does suggest the need for adequate clarity and comprehension when something is first taught.

Remembering is aided by the impact with which something is learned. This is one reason for using films and other visual aids in teaching. The more vivid an experience, the better it will be remembered. For example, placing key words in a lesson on the chalkboard does make a difference. One general music teacher played a fanfare from a recording and then announced in stentorian tones, "Today we will study *syncopation.*" If he does not overuse this device, it will grab the attention of the class and contribute to remembering.

Memory is aided when the student recognizes a pattern. Research studies indicate that nonsense material is much less likely to be retained. A series of numbers such as 1 11 12 5 14 2 8 7 is more difficult to learn and remember than a series such as 1 5 2 6 3 7 4 8. In the latter case the learner discerns a pattern in the sequence. This fact is closely related to the formation of concepts, but operates at a less comprehensive level.

Finally, remembering is aided by frequent review. Most of what is forgotten is forgotten soon after it is learned, usually within one hour. Ebbinghaus conducted the classic studies of memory.[9] The general curve of forgetting has been confirmed by other psychologists, including Luh, whose name appears in Figure 4.[10] In practical terms, the forgetting curve indicates that the students will retain more if there is review at the conclusion of the class, in the next meeting of the class, and every so often after that.

---

[8] George J. Mouly, *Psychology for Effective Teaching,* 2nd Ed. (New York: Holt, Rinehart and Winston, 1968), p. 371.

[9] Hermann Ebbinghaus, *Memory,* trans. H. A. Ruger and C. E. Bussenius (New York: Teachers College, Columbia University, 1913), pp. 68–75. First published in German in 1885.

[10] C. W. Luh, "The Conditions of Retention," *Psychological Monographs,* XXXIII, Whole No. 142 (1922).

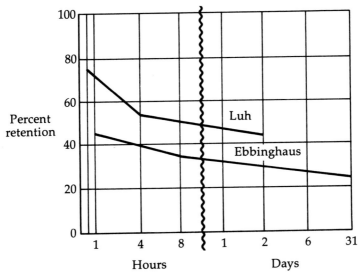

Figure 4   Ebbinghaus curve of forgetting

The forgetting curve does *not* say that we forget 60 percent of anything we learn. It's not that simple! Remembering depends on what is taught, how it is taught, the interests and abilities of the students, and much more. So question 9 is "false." Not only are concepts retained, but with good teaching methods many details and specific skills can likewise be remembered and carried over into adult life.

Transfer

Transfer occurs when something learned in one area is applied to another area. For example, some teachers believe that learning mathematics will enable a student to understand rhythmic notation—a belief that is largely untrue. For literally thousands of years educators had faith that much of what they did would automatically transfer to other areas: geometry was a builder of logical thinking, and Greek and Latin developed one's ability to use the English language. In the twentieth century these beliefs have been tested experimentally, and the results have been disappointing in their support of transfer. Latin helps a little in improving English, but not nearly as much as studying English itself. Students who learn the logic of geometry seem to reason no more logically in other areas than students who do not take geometry.[11]

---

[11]Lindgren, pp. 232–235. See also Mouly, pp. 374–379.

The misplaced faith in transfer stemmed from a basic misconception about how the human mind works. Since the mind is not a muscle, exercises do not build up certain mental faculties that can be applied to any mental task. By contrast, the muscles of the arm can be strengthened through exercise, and the increased strength can be used for lifting, holding, or hugging almost anything. The brain can work mathematical problems day after day, but improvement will only be shown in the ability to work mathematical problems. No general, overall improvement in thinking ability will occur. So the answer to question 4 is definitely "false."

What does this fact indicate about transfer? First, it means that there is no such thing as *automatic* transfer. Second, transfer depends on the degree of relationship between two areas, and the extent to which instruction is designed to achieve maximum transfer. Studying the development of notation will not improve the students' understanding of Brahms' music, but studying Liszt's techniques of theme transformation will transfer because Brahms uses theme transformation extensively. *The greater the similarity, overlap, or number of common elements between two topics, the greater the possibility of transfer.*

The teacher can teach for greater transfer. If the students play a particular rhythmic figure by rote, they may not do much better on the figure when it is encountered in another work. On the other hand, if the teacher shows them how to recognize aurally and visually the relationships among the note values in the figure, the teaching has a greater chance of being applied to other situations. If the basic 2:1 rhythmic structure is understood intellectually and musically, it can be transferred to a variety of meters and rhythmic figures. The same is true of concepts as diverse as "accompaniment" and "impressionism."

The teacher should jog the students to think about other applications of what they are learning. One way to do this is by questioning. "How does the articulation in this piece compare with the articulation in the piece we just finished rehearsing?" "What kind of cadence occurs just before the tempo changes?" Another way to increase transfer is to teach topics in a more unified way. There are classes for the academic study of music and there are performing organizations, and seldom do the twain meet. Too often students do not apply their knowledge of theory or literature to their performance of music, and in academic classes there is little music making. Such situations do not encourage transfer.

Psychomotor Learning

Skills do involve the intellect, but the emphasis in the psychomotor domain is on mastering a task in which a physical skill is central—playing a passage from an overture, sight-reading, aurally recognizing a particular triad. Because rather different processes are involved, some different guidelines are necessary in psychomotor learning.

Distributed Effort

Educational psychologists have found that *it is far more efficient to learn a skill in numerous short sessions than it is to learn the same thing in a few long sessions.* Some psychologists refer to this as "distributed effort," others as "distributed practice" or "spaced practice." In an experiment by Lyon,[12] the subjects learned stanzas of poetry. When two stanzas were learned in one sitting, it required .38 of a minute per stanza. However, when 100 stanzas were learned in one session, it took 3.85 minutes per stanza, *ten times as long* for each stanza! The significant figure here is the amount of time required *per unit* or *line* being learned. Many other experiments, ranging from juggling to addition, have reached the same conclusion.[13] Thus it is many times more efficient to practice an instrument for one hour each day of the week than it is to practice seven hours in one day. More learning takes place in the first ten minutes of practice than takes place in the next ten, and with each additional amount of study there is a corresponding reduction in the amount learned. The answer to question 11 is "false."

There are other reasons for encouraging distributed effort in teaching. One: Fatigue and boredom set in during long practice, and the desire to improve is diminished. Two: Mistakes are more likely to be repeated in a long session, thereby becoming fixed in the response pattern. Three: Forgetting is a learning experience since it shows what elements have been inadequately learned. If there are additional practice sessions, these weaknesses can be overcome. Four: A person tends to resist immediate repetition of an act, and this resistance continues as the repetition continues. Five: Incorrect acts are forgotten more quickly than correct ones, and spaced practice allows incorrect responses to be dropped.[14]

The music teacher must realize that it is better to leave something unfinished, and come back to it another day, than it is to overwork on it. The principle of many learning periods precludes negative threats such as, "We're going to stay on this until it's right." On the other hand, distributed effort must not serve as a means of escape from hard work. Persistence is still vital to good teaching. But persistence should not be confused with dull repetitiousness. The answer to questions 3 and 6 is "false."

---

[12] D. O. Lyon, "The Relation of Length of Material to Time Taken for Learning and the Optimum Distribution of Time," *Journal of Educational Psychology*, V (1914), 85–91.

[13] See H. B. Reed, "Distributed Practice in Addition," *Journal of Educational Psychology*, XXVI (1935), 695–700. See also C. G. Knapp and W. R. Dixon, "Learning to Juggle: I. A Study to Determine the Effect of Two Different Distributions of Practice on Learning Efficiency," *Research Quarterly*, XXI (1950), 331–36.

[14] Lee J. Cronbach, *Educational Psychology* (New York: Harcourt, Brace & World, 1954), p. 368.

The maximum amount of time that should be spent on any one activity varies with the amount of concentration required, the age of the students, and their interest in the activity. Students can work for about ten to twenty minutes on a piece of music or on a musical topic in the general music class. In a drill activity, which may require more concentration, the time should be shorter.

Distributed effort does necessitate frequent changes from one piece of music to another, or from one activity to another. Far from being a drawback, however, such changes are desirable in the education of a musician. Musicians need to be adaptable, able to adjust quickly from one piece of music to another. When a group performs, it will have little time to recast its mood for each musical work.

Singleness of Concentration

A person can concentrate on only one point at a time. When concentrating, he lets the remainder of his activities continue without conscious thought. The necessity for singleness of attention raises problems of priority when one considers all that is involved in making music. Tone, words, notes, and style are all present together, yet an individual can think about only one aspect at a time. The answer lies in emphasizing different phases of the music at different times and in forming good habits quickly, so they can become automatic responses as soon as possible.

Singleness of concentration has significance for the music teacher in determining how rapidly the students can progress. The well-trained musician is tempted to cover ground too quickly.

> A supervisor from a large city was discussing the abilities of persons who were teaching voice classes in the various schools. "You know," he said, "year after year the best singers in our all-city recital are from Lincoln High School. And the surprising thing is that George Nelson has a voice like an old crow; he's the worst singer of all the vocal music teachers in the school system. But he sticks to the fundamentals of singing so well that his students get a solid vocal foundation. The teachers who are better singers, it seems, can't resist hurrying on to the 'fine points,' and their students just don't have that wonderful foundation that George's students have."

Probably George Nelson was well aware that certain things were lacking in the students' singing. He apparently realized, however, that teenagers cannot jump in a year or two from musical immaturity to a high degree of musical development, any more than a boy can grow into manhood in a year or two. He achieved results by concentrating on the most important things first, and leaving the "fine points" until the students were ready for them. He knew the students were learning, so he was not impatient with them for falling short of a professional performance level.

Developing good habits in making music is much like learning to drive a car. When a person first begins to drive he must consciously think of each step: turn the ignition key, release the brake, set the transmission, step on the accelerator, turn the steering wheel. But eventually these actions become automatic; he can simultaneously drive and carry on a conversation.

Although the degree is exaggerated for illustration, young violinists are occasionally instructed something like this:

> "Hold the violin under your chin so that it points halfway between straight front and straight to the side. Keep your left elbow well under the violin and your left wrist straight; hold the neck of the instrument between the thumb and the index finger, like this; turn the left hand so that the little finger is nearest you.
>
> "Now, the bow is held in the right hand with the thumb curved a bit so it touches the angle between the stick and the frog; lean your hand inward so the stick crosses under the index finger at the middle joint; the little finger regulates the balance and is curved so only the tip touches the top of the stick. The wrist is flexible but not flabby; the muscles of the bow arm are relaxed, just tense enough to move the bow properly. Now, the bow is drawn at a 90 degree angle to the strings. Don't let the angle change as you approach the tip. Remember you *draw* the bow gently across the string— don't scrape or bounce it."

Then pointing to the music, the teacher says:

> "The note on the second space of the treble staff is A."

If the student hasn't given up by now, the teacher may go on:

> "There are four beats in a measure. You know what beats are, don't you? Each note of this kind, with no stem and not filled in, gets four beats. Now we can figure out all the other note values mathematically."

At least one good thing can be said about this example of teaching, which can only bewilder most students: it is thorough.

Levels of Technical Requirements

Few in number are secondary school music groups that can perform a work correctly the first time it is presented to them. Usually the students must simply learn to execute the music. To help them do this, the teacher needs to have in mind a hierarchy of difficulty for the tasks he is asking the students to master. In choral music, for example, he should be aware that each of these group efforts is increasingly difficult:

> one part with piano doubling
> one part with the complete piano accompaniment
> one part unaccompanied
>> (The order of the last two depends on the nature of the accompaniment in the particular piece.)
> two parts with piano doubling each
> two parts with piano doubling one or the other
> two parts with the complete piano accompaniment
>> (Again the order will depend on the piece.)
> two parts unaccompanied
> three or more parts in the same order of increasing difficulty

If the teacher finds that the class can sing easily at one level of difficulty, he might skip over some of the intervening levels. If the group cannot do one step properly, say sing in four parts, then the teacher should back up and attempt something easier, such as two or three parts, or he can work with the one part that is causing the problem. The same general procedure also applies to teaching instrumental music.

The teacher need not always have a class work at the same level of musical advancement. New learnings require that the student be challenged, and old learnings need to be reinforced by thoroughly reviewing material that may seem easy now.

Affective Learning

Chapter 6 pointed out that *attitudes are learned indirectly,* as a by-product of instruction. Beliefs and feelings cannot be forced on people; at least in a democratic society they should not be so promoted. Attitudes are shaped by many factors, including the teacher's personality and the attitude of the peer group. There is a human tendency, especially present in teenagers, to "follow the pack," to adopt the beliefs of the immediate social group.[15] Attitudes differ in their susceptibility to change. Superficial feelings are easily altered, but deeply held beliefs are remarkably durable.

Attitudes are very much involved with a person's ego. The school's chess champion is certain to like the game better than the student who al-

---

[15] Howard Gibbs Inglefield, "The Relationship of Selected Personality Variables to Conformity Behavior Reflected in the Musical Preferences of Adolescents when Exposed to Peer Group Leader Influences," unpublished doctoral dissertation, Ohio State University, 1968, pp. 175–176.

most never wins a match. His attitude toward the game is colored by his attitude toward his performance. In the same way, a person's self-image in a music course influences what he learns. People tend to fulfill their self-made prophecies. The person who has decided he has no talent for music will probably not learn much music, and the reverse is true for the student who considers himself talented. The self-image about musical talent is probably formed in the early years of elementary school, so the general music teacher in seventh grade will in some cases need to break down old feelings of inadequacy, as well as work toward positive attitudes. If it should happen in American society that the image of an educated, mature adult includes music understanding and competence (as has happened in some societies, both past and present), then it will be easier to establish positive attitudes toward the subject.

There appears to be a moderate positive correlation between valid information and a favorable attitude. This positive relationship is not surprising. As he gains information, a person can see more sense in the subject, he has a greater feeling of competence, and he has an investment of time and effort in the subject. The word "valid" is included to describe the appropriate type of learning, because sometimes what was taught in no meaningful way increases a student's competence. Spelling the G sharp melodic minor scale doesn't help teenagers to appreciate Bartók's music, for example.

Attitudes cannot be separated from the other principles presented in this chapter. A student's feelings influence what he learns, and vice versa.

Applying the Principles

Before an Air Force plane takes off, the crew goes through a checking procedure in which gauges are read and equipment is tested. The analogy between flying an airplane and teaching music is not a perfect one, but there are similarities. Prior to teaching, the music teacher should "check out" the guidelines presented in this chapter.

Will the lesson be of reasonable difficulty for the students?

Will the students experience music, or just hear explanations about it?

Will the aesthetic qualities of the music be brought out?

Will the students be involved in the learning activity? Will they have an adequate aural foundation for what they will be asked to learn?

Will they understand the reason for what they are studying?

Will the teaching techniques involve several senses and different methods of presentation?

Will the students gain general understandings in addition to useful facts?

Will the student gain some comprehension of the whole musical work?

Will the material be presented in a way that encourages remembering and transfer to other musical situations?

If the learning involves acquiring skills, will the effort be distributed over a span of time? Will the students' attention be focused on one point at a time? Will differing levels of technical demands be accounted for?

Will the learning be presented attractively, to encourage positive attitudes toward music?

Will there be a balance among the principles?

The principles of good teaching are valuable not only for preparing teaching plans, but also for diagnosing why a class did not learn a point very well. Just doing more of the same routine does not mean improvement. Adding hamburger to hamburger will not produce steak, no matter how much you add; the result is only more hamburger. Often the content or method must be changed, not just repeated. Finally, the principles presented in this chapter are not a set of rules for teaching music that one should memorize word by word. Rather, they are guides for teaching music effectively.

Questions

1. Which guideline or guidelines does each of these examples probably violate?

(a) The students in Pat Schilling's general music classes spend much time filling in workbooks on musical notation — items such as the number of beats a dotted-half note gets in 3/4 meter.

(b) Jack Garcia rehearses the orchestra for an entire period on the introduction to an overture.

(c) Jimmy Johnson has just been told all of this by his clarinet teacher: to watch his embouchure, especially the lower lip; not to lift his fingers so far off the keys; to make sure he taps his foot *evenly*; to play all the first-line E flats with the third finger of the left hand, except where impossible; to be sure to tongue with the tip of the tongue on the tip of the reed.

(d) The band finishes playing a march with a decisive chord. "Well," says the director, "let's run through it again." He has the band start again.

(e) Kevin McClean has just taken his first teaching position as band director in Milton. Before leaving for a summer camp job, he orders some music for the band he will meet for the first time in the fall. As he glances through a stack of music, he notices the march "Fairest of the Fair" by Sousa. "Hey," he thinks to himself, "I'll get that. We played it in the band at State U., and I really liked it."

(f) Alice Merkle has her choir work on vowels for five minutes at the beginning of each period. On Monday she works on *ay*, Tuesday *ah*, Wednesday *ee*, Thursday *oh*, and Friday *oo*.

(g) Charles Newcomb was anxious for the chorus to win a high rating at the festival. He picked the three pieces that the group would sing and worked on them intensively through January and February up to the festival in March. Now, during its performance, the chorus is flatting and lacking vitality in its expression.

(h) In order to improve the sightreading ability of the girls' glee club Mary Jane Snyder has the girls practice interval reading. She puts two intervals on the board daily, and then has the girls sing back and forth between the two pitches of each interval.

(i) David Barrow's junior high flutists are encountering difficulty getting into the upper octave when playing B flat, B natural, and C. "Come on! Come on! Try a little harder," he says in a nice tone of voice.

(j) Carol Springer has this routine for each new piece her singers attempt: (1) Sing the rhythm of notes on the tonic note until done correctly. (2) Sing through each part until the proper notes are learned. (3) Sing through with the parts together. (4) Put in the expression.

(k) Ted Albert is a thorough instrumental music teacher. For each important program his band presents, he totals up the number of measures in the works to be played. Then he divides that number by the number of class meetings before the program. Each class session covers the exact number of measures to be learned.

2. What characterizes valid musical experiences? Give examples of valid and invalid learnings in music classes.

3. Describe how concepts are learned.

4. Name six ways in which a teacher can increase the chances that the students will remember what they have learned.

5. What is transfer in learning? How can it be aided?

6. Why is a student's self-image of his abilities in music so important in determining what he learns in music classes?

Projects

1. Select one work each for band, orchestra, and choir. Study the work and then decide how you would introduce it to the students so that they can grasp the idea of the whole piece.

2. Observe the same type of class or organization (high school band, junior high girls' glee club) in three different schools. Evaluate each class in terms of (1) age, (2) selectivity of students, (3) time available for instruction, and (4) students' previous musical experience.

3. Select a concept related to music. Indicate the depth of a student's first understanding of that concept, his understanding during a middle stage of development, and then at a nearly complete level of comprehension.

Suggested Readings

Basic Concepts in Music Education, 57th Yearbook, Part I, National Society for the Study of Education. Chicago: University of Chicago Press, 1958. Chapters 6 and 7.

Biehler, Robert F., *Psychology Applied to Teaching.* Boston: Houghton Mifflin, 1971. Chapters 5–8.

Bloom, Benjamin S., *Taxonomy of Educational Objectives Handbook I: Cognitive Domain.* New York: David McKay Company, 1956. See also *Handbook II: Affective Domain,* 1964.

Gordon, Edwin, *The Psychology of Music Teaching.* Englewood Cliffs, New Jersey: Prentice-Hall, 1971.

Leonhard, Charles, and Robert W. House, *Foundations and Principles of Music Education,* 2nd Ed. New York: McGraw-Hill, 1972.

Lindgren, Henry Clay, *Educational Psychology in the Classroom,* 3rd Ed. New York: John Wiley & Sons, 1967.

McDonald, Frederick J., *Educational Psychology,* 2nd Ed. Belmont, California: Wadsworth Publishing Company, 1965.

Mursell, James L., *Music Education: Principles and Programs.* Morristown, New Jersey: Silver Burdett Company, 1956. Chapter 3.

The General Music Class

Steve Kowal's father has changed jobs four times in the last two years. Each time the Kowals move, Steve changes schools. The new principal has just now given him a schedule, and as he answers the phone he says, "All eighth-graders take general music every other day. I think it works best in your schedule second hour."

"General music . . ." Steve's mind runs back over the other general music classes he's had. "I'll never forget old Miss Farot at Middleville," he thinks. "She was nice; a lot like my grandmother. But I sure did get tired of filling out those workbook sheets for her. Don't care if I ever figure out another time signature or harmonic minor scale. Hope we don't do that here; I'd have to learn it all over again because I don't remember that stuff any more. Now at Edgerton, there was a class! That variety show we did for the PTA open house sure was fun. We thought up all our own jokes too. Of course, those songs got kind of boring after a couple of weeks. Mr. McIntosh in Ohio Heights must have been born in a library. If the piece was real old, he thought it was great. Some of the songs were awful—singing cuckoo and all that stuff. That trumpet piece by Purcell and some of the other pieces weren't bad, though. Wonder what general music will be like here?"

A good question, Steve! Educators have been trying for years to agree on what type of school should exist for students between the ages of 10 and 15. There isn't even agreement on the name of the school. Seventh-graders, for example, are included in any one of several organizational plans: "elementary" schools containing grades 1–8, "secondary" schools containing grades 7–12, "junior high" schools containing grades 7 and 8 or 7–9, and "middle" schools containing grades 5–8 or 6–8.

What Is General Music?

Music educators have also shown little consistency in naming and teaching the music course taught to almost all students of this age. The term "general music" is widely applied to the junior high/middle school nonperformance course consisting of varied musical experiences and learnings, and is so defined in this book. There are a few "general music" courses taught at the high school level, however, and the term is also applied by some music educators to the elementary school basal music curriculum.

Some teachers conceive of the general music class as a feeder program for high school organizations. Others see it as a recreational period, and still others consider it an extension of elementary school music. Many teachers have not given general music classes as much attention as they have their bands, orchestras, and choirs, so in some schools the course has fallen into second-class status. Since the 1960s, however, some music educators have recognized the importance of general music.

The organizational pattern of the school affects what is done in the general music class. Some of these classes meet daily throughout the year or for a portion of the year, some meet twice a week, and others only once. Some schools require the course for one, two, or three years, while others don't require it at all. Occasionally the classes are composed entirely of either girls or boys, a plan that has much merit because it makes it easier to meet the special musical needs and interests of each sex. Some schools group students homogeneously according to academic ability, and this grouping carries over into music. Sometimes students who take instrumental music are included, but oftentimes not. As if these are not enough variables, the elementary music program of a district largely determines the musical development of the students and influences their ability to do well in general music class; so variations in the elementary schools help to explain differences in musical development at the junior high level.

These many variables mean that there can be no single "right" content and method for all general music classes. There is a difference between a heterogeneous seventh grade class meeting twice a week, and an eighth grade elective, composed mainly of girls of advanced ability, meeting daily. What is good for one is not necessarily good for the other.

As in the total music program, the first purpose of the class is to teach music. But what is special about general music? One outstanding feature is the child/adult status of the students involved. All that was said in Chapter 7 about new patterns of social behavior, varied physical development, the lack of ability to express themselves, the easily triggered emotions—all these become very real in the junior high or middle school. A second feature is the fact that for students whose only music experience has been under the direction of an elementary classroom teacher, the general music class is their first experience under the tutelage of a music specialist. Third, in many instances the class is compulsory and heterogeneous. Students of every type are there, whether they like it or not. The teacher must take into account the goal (teaching music), the conditions of the class (age of students, departmentalized organization, compulsory enrollment, homogeneous or heterogeneous grouping), and then teach the subject so that it can be successfully assimilated by the students. It is not an easy assignment, but it is vital in music education.

Goals of General Music

General music classes operate under the same overall objectives as the rest of the music program. They should provide aesthetic experiences and varied opportunities for increased appreciation of music. There should be no double standard implying that general music is less important than a performing class in meeting these goals. The general music class, however, has one objective that is especially significant. Many general music students are taking their last formal instruction in music, unfortunately. In the future the majority of them will be involved with music only as interested consumers. These students need instruction in music analogous to the instruction a musician would value if he took golf lessons or an evening class in making pottery. He needs a rudimentary competence to get around the golf course in a reasonable number of strokes or make a decent looking vase. These students need a basic understanding of the music to enable them to appreciate the work and skill of others.

Because the general music class should be a microcosm of the world of music, the three broad areas of music should be included: (1) performance— singing and playing instruments; (2) analysis—listening, demonstrating knowledge, and understanding; and (3) composition and improvisation— writing and creating music. Playing instruments or composing in general music class does not mean playing violin concertos or composing cantatas, of course. But valid musical learning can take place when basic activities are pursued in an intellectually honest way, no matter how rudimentary the level of instruction. An instructor working with the novice golfer or pottery maker teaches essentially the same things that he teaches an advanced student, but the beginning instruction is less refined and less detailed.

Performing music is an appropriate part of the general music class not only because it aids learning and maintains class interest, but also because adults are often involved in singing or playing simple instruments after completing high school. Opportunities for participation range from the casual (playing guitar and singing for one's own enjoyment) to more structured situations (church choirs and amateur theatrical productions).

Listening is the most prevalent musical activity in adult life. Millions of dollars are spent each year on sound reproducing systems, concert and opera tickets, and constructing magnificent art centers such as the Kennedy Center in Washington, D.C. But do people know what to listen for in the music that strikes their eardrums? They should at least start to develop this skill in general music class.

Why should a future real estate salesman or truck driver try his hand at composing or improvising music? Not to challenge Mozart or Louis Armstrong, certainly, but to encourage himself to think musically, to consider how one sound is combined with another, and to make musical judgments. Besides, it's an excellent teaching device. A student beomes more interested when *his* song is played for the class. Creating music is psychologically valuable because it is something he has done himself, not something that has been done for him—a situation that helps establish him as a unique individual.

The 1965 publication *Music in General Education* summarizes the objectives of general music instruction.[1] Notice that the ten objectives refer to the three basic musical activities—performing, analyzing, and creating—and to the three general types of learning—knowledge, skills, and attitudes. By the time he finishes high school a broadly educated person should have the following competencies in music:

Skills

I. He will have skill in listening to music.

The generally educated person listens with a purpose. He recognizes the broad melodic and rhythmic contours of musical compositions. He is familiar with the sounds of the instruments of the orchestra and the types of human voices. He can hear and identify more than one melody at a time. He can recognize patterns of melody and rhythm when repeated in identical or in altered form. He can concentrate on sounds and the relationships between sounds.

II. He will be able to sing.

The generally educated person is articulate. He uses his voice confidently in speech and song. He sings in a way that is satisfying to himself. He can carry a part in group singing. His singing is expressive.

III. He will be able to express himself on a musical instrument.

A generally educated person is curious. He is interested in how instrumental music is produced and willing to try his hand at making music, if only at an elementary level with a percussion instrument, a recorder, or a "social-type" instrument. He experiments with providing accompaniments for singing and rhythmic activities. He is familiar with the piano keyboard.

IV. He will be able to interpret musical notation.

The generally educated person is literate. He understands arithmetical and musical symbols. He is able to respond to the musical notation of unison and simple part songs. He can follow the scores of instrumental compositions.

---

[1] Edited by Karl D. Ernst and Charles L. Gary (Washington, D.C.: Music Educators National Conference, 1965), pp. 4–8.

Understandings

V. He will understand the importance of design in music.

The generally educated person understands the structure of the various disciplines. He knows the component parts of music and the interrelationships that exist between melody, rhythm, harmony, and form. He is able to recognize design elements aurally, and he uses musical notation to confirm and reinforce this recognition. He realizes that the active listener can, in a sense, share in the composer's act of creation. By understanding how music communicates he has come to gain insight into what it communicates.

VI. He will relate music to man's historical development.

The generally educated person has historical perspective. He recognizes that music has long been an important part of man's life. He understands that its development in Western civilization is one of the unique elements of his own heritage. He is familiar with the major historical periods in that development and the styles of music which they produced. He has acquaintance with some of the musical masterpieces of the past and with the men who composed them. He relates this knowledge to his understanding of man's social and political development.

VII. He will understand the relationships existing between music and other areas of human endeavor.

The generally educated person integrates his knowledge. He has been helped to see that the arts have in common such concepts as design resulting from repetition and variation. Sociology and politics are recognized as pertinent to the development of art as well as to economics. He understands how literature and music enhance one another and together illuminate history. The mathematical and physical aspects of music are known to him through aural experiences as well as through intellectual inquiry.

VIII. He will understand the place of music in contemporary society.

The generally educated person is aware of his environment. He understands the function of music in the life of his community and he accepts some responsibility for exercising his critical judgment to improve the quality of music heard in church and on radio and television. He is aware of the position of the musician in today's social structure and understands the opportunities open to him to engage in musical endeavor both as a vocation and as an avocation.

Attitudes

IX. He will value music as a means of self-expression.

A generally educated person has developed outlets for his emotions. He recognizes music not only as a source of satisfaction because of its filling his desire for beauty, but also because of the unique way in which it expresses man's feelings. If he is not prepared to gain release by actually performing music, he has learned to experience this vicariously. He looks to music as a source of renewal of mind and body, as an evidence of beneficence in his life. He recognizes the importance of performers and composers and is grateful for the pleasure and inspiration which they give him.

X. He will desire to continue his musical experiences.

The generally educated person continues to grow. He seeks additional experiences in areas in which he has found satisfaction. He looks for community musical activities in which he can participate. He attends concerts and listens to music on radio, television, and recordings. He keeps informed concerning happenings in the world of music by reading newspapers and magazines.

XI. He will discriminate with respect to music.

The generally educated person has good taste. He has learned to make sensitive choices based on musical knowledge and skill in listening. He evaluates performances and exercises mature judgments in this area. He is not naive about the functional use of music for commercial purposes, nor to the commercial pressures which will be exerted to obtain what money he can spend for music.

The General Music Teacher

There is no area of music teaching to which the idea of the "complete" music teacher, as presented in Chapter 2, is more applicable than the general music class. The course demands ability, knowledge, and resourcefulness. Especially important is the rapport that the teacher must establish with the class. Unless this is present, the most perfectly planned lesson is relatively worthless. The teacher must understand and accept what one successful general music teacher calls, partly in jest and partly with respect, "the junior high mind." Teaching general music to adolescents is as much a matter of feeling and attitude and understanding as it is of knowledge and intellect.

The characteristics that work best for the teacher are enthusiasm and a sense of fairness. The problem for the successful teacher at this level often is not how to evoke enthusiasm from the students, but how to keep it within bounds. The response of early adolescents to good teaching is probably more fervent than at any other level. And the converse is true: at no level will the response to poor teaching be more vexing. It should also be added that at no level is the response likely to be more unpredictable.

General music teaching requires considerable knowledge of the subject matter. Suppose the teacher is preparing a unit on the music of the three major religious faiths in the United States—Judaism, Catholicism, and

Protestantism. Are there hymns with different words but essentially the same melody found in all three faiths? In two? What source books are available to help answer such a question? In Palestrina's day, it was common practice to assign boys to the treble parts; when and where was this custom changed? Are there choirs that still use boys for the highest parts? The *Shema* in Judaism and the *Credo* in Catholicism are each a basic statement of faith. Why are the two settings so different? These questions have barely scratched the surface of the topic. And the teacher had better be prepared for such questions. The 13-year-old boy with big, clumsy feet and the 12-year-old girl who giggles at everything can at times ask the most probing, serious, and difficult questions!

The teacher must be inventive and willing to try new things. This requires effort and a certain spirit of adventure. There are real rewards for the imaginative teacher. He will find new zest in his work, to say nothing of the feeling of pride when an idea works out well. Suppose he wants the students to understand the significance of the half steps between 3–4 and 7–8 in the major scale. How can this be done so that the students *hear* the tonal relationships and remember them? Suppose the teacher wants to present operatic music so that it draws a favorable reaction. The class is made up of students who are well-versed in the latest hit tunes, but are openly skeptical about opera. How can he circumvent the obstacle of attitude without standing before the class and saying, in effect, "This is good music. Now sit still and listen to it"? Suppose he wants the students to see a certain music program on television. How can he motivate them to watch without coming right out and requiring that they do so? How can the program be followed up in a meaningful way? Multiply these questions many times and you have some idea of the need for inventiveness on the part of the general music teacher.

A comprehensive discussion of the general music teacher should mention the importance of skill at the piano. While the teacher does not need to be a virtuoso at the keyboard, he must play accompaniments easily and well.

Characteristics of Successful Teaching

Successful general music teaching is marked by seven conditions, all pertaining to the age of the students and the nature of the course.

Concreteness

Young teenagers need instruction that is simple, unvarnished, and direct. They react best to the straightforward approach that was discussed in some detail in Chapter 8. Students at this age are often literal in their interpretation of learned material. In one school a fine musician presented to his class a song called "Nymphs and Shepherds." The response of the class was disappointing, but to an experienced teacher it would have been predictable. Teenagers know there's no such thing as a nymph, they have never seen a shepherd, and they haven't the slightest intention of dancing and singing on the lea. To them, the whole idea is silly. They are too old to accept without question whatever the teacher gives them, and they are not yet old enough to look beyond the literal aspects of the work and enjoy the beauty and charm of the music. They are no longer naïve, but neither have they a mature perspective.

The correlation of learnings must be direct and concrete. A study of neumes, the *Bay Psalm Book*, or the harmonic form of the minor scale is worthy, to be sure. But a class of 13-year-olds will not grasp the significance of any of it unless it is carefully related to what they know and can use. Copland's *Lincoln Portrait* is a work about a real person. Some of its music is derived from music sung and played by Americans of the mid-nineteenth century. It has power and a definite mood, plus the concreteness of narrated words. This is a work that seventh grade students can understand and appreciate.

There are several practical ways to make the learnings more concrete. One is the "Song Bag" described by Andrews and Leeder:

> A "Song Bag" is made by covering a cardboard form with burlap, bound at the neck with brightly colored twine, and labeled "Song Bag." The class then discusses the project and its objective, which is to place the name of each song, printed on a cardboard note (which may be half, whole or otherwise) on the song bag when the song is sung acceptably by the class. In this way the cumulative repertoire of the class becomes visible. The next step is to decide just how the class will interpret "sung acceptably." The class may set up certain standards, such as these:
>
> (1) The song must be sung correctly, and with good tone quality.
> (2) Everyone in the class must join in singing the song.
> (3) One verse should be sung from memory.
> (4) The song should be sung in the right mood, according to the composer's markings and the spirit of the words and music.
>
> These requirements or standards may vary according to the class that is setting them up. The teacher participates in the discussion which may be led by him or by the class chairman.
>
> Once the standards are agreed upon and accepted by the entire class, a committee is elected to judge when the song is ready to go "into the bag." This committee is changed frequently, so that all members of the class will have a chance to serve on it. When the class indicates its singing is ready to be judged, the committee listens to the singing of the song and renders a

verdict, giving reasons why it does or does not believe the song is "sung acceptably."[2]

The significant feature of this procedure is not so much the concreteness of the song bag itself (the use of which is perhaps best confined to seventh grade), but the concreteness of the specific standards by which the students can judge their singing.

Another practical step is a music notebook or log. A notebook is kept by each student as an account of what the class has done — the songs sung, the records heard, the facts learned. The student is encouraged to supplement the notebook with pictures and articles from newspapers and magazines, reports on reading or records listened to outside the class period, a list of questions that come to mind as something is studied. Periodically the teacher calls for the notebooks and looks them over, possibly using them in determining a grade. The notebook idea does have one drawback. Verbally able students can handle such a project easily, but the student who is weak in communication skills finds music another course in which success depends on reading and writing. The teacher must stress to the class that the notebook represents a personal view of events in music class and indicates the degree of the student's interest in music activities, but that it cannot say much about the depth of the student's understanding or the permanence of his learning.

"Satisfaction Fast"

Early adolescents are normally impatient; they lose interest in an activity that does not lead to satisfactory progress within a reasonable time. Accordingly, Irvin Cooper's suggestions for finding the cambiata voice (see Chapter 14) allow for no delay or dawdling. In less than 15 minutes, the major undertaking of checking voices is finished. An experienced music teacher knows the importance of working quickly.

A second reason to strive for "satisfaction fast" is the limited time.[3] In most schools the class does not meet daily. It is hard for students to leave an interesting point on Wednesday and take it up again on Monday. Much of the impact of Wednesday's lesson will have dissipated in the intervening days. For this reason, every class period should be planned to give the students some sense of accomplishment, a feeling of "We can do that" or "We know what that means and how it relates to us."

---

[2]Frances M. Andrews and Joseph A. Leeder, *Guiding Junior High School Pupils in Music Experiences* (Englewood Cliffs, N.J.: Prentice-Hall, 1953), p. 72. Reprinted by permission.

[3]The author is indebted to Mary E. English for the phrase "satisfaction fast." Professor English and Allen L. Richardson are the authors of *Living with Music* (New York: M. Witmark & Sons, 1956).

In practical terms this limits the complexity of class activities. In one class period, the students might learn to sing a song with a descant, but they would have to leave unfinished a work in four parts. It is better to listen to the third movement of Tchaikovsky's *Symphony No. 4*, which takes about five minutes, than it is to take the arm off the record in the middle of the 20 minute first movement and say, "We'll hear the rest of it on Monday."

The teacher must be amenable to the use of shortcuts. Rather than teaching the tonic and dominant chords in the common keys, naming the notes in each chord, describing the tonal relationship between them, and explaining how to derive the proper chord from the symbols I and V⁷ or F and C⁷, the teacher can say, "Here's the autoharp. When we sing 'The Cowboy's Lament,' John, play the F chord when I hold up one finger. Play it once on each heavy beat. When I hold up five fingers, push the C⁷ button, one chord to the measure. Just follow my directions."

Shortcuts, which get quick results without understanding, may raise the question "When do the youngsters finally learn what they're doing?" There are several ways to bring about understanding after the act. The teacher might ask, "How far is it from F to C? . . . All right, suppose we wanted to start singing with the G chord instead of F. What chord would we substitute for the C chord?" Or the teacher might say, "Donna, tonight I'll let you take the autoharp home. Sing 'Down in the Valley' starting with a G chord. Don't look at any music. Just experiment with the chords until your ear tells you they sound right with the melody. Then write the names of the chords, one for each heavy beat you hear. When you come to class Thursday, we'll compare what you found with what the book tells us, and we'll see if the ears of the class agree with yours."

Another approach might be to say, "Class, when Greg presses the F button, he's playing more than the note F. Susie, go to the piano and experiment, playing tones other than F until you find those that match what the autoharp is sounding. The class can be the judge of whether or not a note fits properly."

For songs with simple harmonies, vocal chording is a good activity, especially if there are a few changed voices in the class. The teacher can write

the I, IV, V, I chords with symbols and names on the board. The structuring of the chords will vary depending on the division of voices in the class. The class can sing them on a neutral syllable. Then they can sing the appropriate chord as the teacher calls it out by name or number while he plays the melody on the piano. Better yet, the teacher can hold up the right number of fingers for the chord number, so that there is no extraneous sound intruding upon the music. He can try various inversions, having the class decide which they prefer. Finally the class can divide, with one section singing the melody while the other sings the chords.

There are many more techniques to instill in the students a feeling for harmony and an understanding of it. But the underlying procedure and timing of the instruction are the important considerations. In the class that used the autoharp, the students were given "satisfaction fast" in a musical experience — they sang a song with an attractive accompaniment. *Then* they proceeded to find out why certain chords made the music sound better.

There is a limit to how thoroughly a general music class needs to understand the tonic-dominant relationship and the intricacies of harmony. At some time in their schooling the students should be led to comprehend this, but not in a heterogeneous class of young teenagers that meets on alternate days. Further understanding must await a theory class or at least an advanced class more homogeneous in its study.

Relate to Students

Relating the subject to the students is crucial at the junior high/middle school level. Sometimes teenagers feel that much of what they do in music class is not immediate or vital. Often the material seems distant in both time and geography. A song about flowers or a girl in Italy may be pretty, but it strikes adolescents as insignificant. That Bach inverts the theme and that Bartók uses scordatura tuning for the violin does not seem vital to most young people.

One way to relate general music more closely to the students is for the class to keep up on current musical events. Some teachers assign each student one week during which he is responsible for reporting music news to the class, or preparing a bulletin board or large wall calendar. If students keep a music notebook, one section of it can be reserved for current items. In covering the current scene, the class reporter should mention more than local concerts or musical events at the White House. Motion pictures, and radio and television programs that have good music should also be mentioned, as should announcements, articles, and commentaries about music in newspapers and magazines. One class followed the writings of the music critic in a large metropolitan newspaper, found them written in a language difficult to understand, and wrote a letter to the critic asking her why such big words were necessary. Not only did the critic send the class a thoughtful and sensitive reply, she published the students' letter and her reply in the paper. Alive and relating to the students? Very much so!

The need to relate also affects the selection of music and activities. Gian-Carlo Menotti has written operas that have wide appeal as well as musical value. *The Telephone* is short and clever, while *Amahl and the Night Visitors* is longer and essentially serious. *The Telephone* involves the plight of a young man who is desperately trying to propose marriage to a giddy girl gossiping on the phone, laughing (usually as she sings), and inquiring about the well-being of her friend's pussy cat. This kind of story does not set a 12-year-old boy's heart to pounding with excitement. Amahl, on the other hand, is a crippled boy of about 12. He's quite human, telling tall tales and even thinking considerately of his mother on occasion. With which opera do the students identify themselves? *Amahl.*

Not everything the class studies or sings must have a 12-year-old boy or girl as protagonist. But to the extent possible in a group situation, the learning should start "where the student is"—to cite one of the oldest saws in education—and move on from there. Not all relevance comes from obvious external relationships, however. The removal of ignorance is valuable in itself for most students (see Chapter 7). Learning, then, is motivated when the students realize they are gaining something they didn't have before, whether the new understanding is about African music, the boy's changing voice, or the characteristics of Baroque music.

Another practical way to relate students and music is to set up a "Student Talent Day." At the sixth and seventh grade levels quite a few students are still studying piano privately, and others may be in band or orchestra. Students who have studied guitar or accordion, or have simply taught themselves to play the harmonica or ukulele, should also be included in the activity. The purpose of the student performance is to demonstrate that music can be made in many ways. Simple efforts as well as more advanced performances can be enjoyable and worth hearing.

If the use of popular music is justifiable in the schools—and it is, to an extent—it's in the general music class. Because popular songs are familiar to students, they can be a good springboard for studying other music. Many aspects of popular music—ostinato, syncopation, chord progressions, and so on—are found in art music as well. Including some currently popular tunes also contributes to the rapport between students and teacher. Class members are pleased that their teacher doesn't "look down his nose" at such music, and they are relieved that he is not hopelessly out of contact with what's happening in the world. But popular music alone *cannot* make up for inadequate teaching, hold the interest of a class week after week, or provide adequate coverage of the vast world of music. Furthermore, the teacher should not assume that the popular music he knows and likes is the popular music his young teenage students prefer. There's a big difference in the musical tastes of a 23-year-old college graduate with a degree in music and a typical 13-year-old.

Involvement

An excellent way to stimulate involvement in general music classes is through techniques such as games and challenges that capture the students' interest. The "Spelling Bee" is as old as American education (probably older), but it is a simple technique that motivates many a youngster to learn to spell and makes the class more interesting. The music teacher can ask the students names of notes, musical symbols, themes, or songs, sending those who answer incorrectly to the end of the line. Or he can propose a game of "Stump the Class," in which he plays portions of musical works, types of scales or chords, or compositional techniques such as augmentation to see if anyone in the class can recognize what he has played. A student can keep score. A contest between teacher and class, or between the boys and the girls, seldom fails to spark attention.

Students feel involved when their opinion is requested. They can be invited to determine when the second part of a round should enter, to create the second half of a phrase, to decide which chord should be played at a certain point in the music, to decide which instrument should accompany a song, to write new words to a known melody, to make a rudimentary analysis of what is heard or seen in the music, or to decide where a particular chord belongs on a consonance–dissonance "thermometer" that has an octave and an "elbow chord" as its two extremes. Another device to encourage student judgments is the "Song Bag" described earlier in this chapter.

Building on Student Maturity

As Chapter 7 pointed out, teenagers want to be adult; they feel that they have left childhood behind. The teacher should recognize this desire and predicate his planning on it. The type of music he chooses, and even its appearance, should differ somewhat from that used in the elementary school. More than one general music class has wanted to sing from individual octavo music rather than books, because it felt that basal series books are for children! The interests of junior high/middle school students begin to broaden, and at times their perception can be surprisingly profound. The choice of music should reflect this. Gone from their repertoire, unfortunately, are many of the fine songs from elementary school days. They are not gone forever, though, for as the students become more secure in their adult image, they will again enjoy the music they learned earlier.

The teacher can use the adolescents' desire for maturity to attain other desirable objectives. At this age, teenagers often dislike and reject what they do not know or that which differs from their expectations. The teacher can say to the class, "One of the things that distinguishes an adult from a child is his attitude toward people and ideas that are unfamiliar. Call it 'fairness' or 'tolerance,' but a person who is growing up always gives a fair chance to that which he doesn't know. Now, this Spanish folk song may strike you as being pretty strange. It's free in its use of rhythm. It sounds sort of made up on the spot—and it is. But different as it may seem, see if you can find three things about it that you like—three reasons why the song makes good sense musically." Students at this age are capable of viewing the world with tolerance, of understanding those people who believe and act differently, of respecting music and customs of other nations. Several of the units suggested later in this chapter will build on the developing maturation of the students.

Emphasize Musical Qualities

If the essence of music is lost, the music class will be hollow and meaningless. This can happen when the instruction becomes "literary" or "academic" in the least desirable sense of these words. A student may learn that Mussorgsky was born in 1839, that he held a clerical position with the government, and that he was one of "the Russian Five," yet never comprehend his music. A student may be able to figure out meter and key signatures, call out note names correctly, write scales, and still be musically ignorant. Such knowledge is fine *if* the students have grasped the musical idea first. Steve's teacher at Middleville, Miss Farot, failed when she sought to make facts synonymous with music.

A second way in which music can be lost is by making the class period solely a recreation time. Steve's class at Edgerton came dangerously close to doing this when it devoted its efforts to a variety show. No one is against enjoying music, but the indispensable combination is fun *and* learning. A good teacher can have both in his class. There is a place for the lighthearted song and the relaxing diversion, but then the students should move on to other things. General music classes exist to teach music.

Account for Variety

Variations are present to some degree in every class at every age level, but in general music, the variety that is the spice of life nearly overpowers the recipe. Attempting to take care of these variations is no small undertaking. Essentially, it is best done by avoiding concentration on any one phase of class endeavor. A variety of activities is required. The principle is similar to the theory behind multi-packages of cereal; among the assortment at least one will be liked. The boy who is self-conscious about his singing can succeed by giving a report on sound reproduction systems. The academically slow student who has trouble understanding the factual material may possess a pleasant singing voice, and in this way find some satisfaction in the class. As a bonus, the assortment of activities guarantees that the class will be stimulating for the teacher as well as the students.

Activities and Materials

While hard and fast formulas should be avoided, the teacher should usually plan for two or three different activities in each class period. Most sessions should include singing. Further work can revolve around listening, studying about music, playing instruments, or developing creative projects.

Singing in General Music Classes

Singing in a choral organization and singing in a general music class have different purposes and should be approached differently. Singing in general music class is less concerned with technique because the music is simpler and perfection is unnecessary. Singing gives the students a personal experience with the music, develops their most important means of making music, and contributes insight into a particular work.

How is singing best taught in the general music class? First, the teacher must select songs carefully for range, number of parts, text, musical quality, application to other class activities, and variety. Then he must make himself familiar with the music—accompaniment as well as voice lines—and think through several possible ways to teach the song.

There are three possible approaches. One is to have the class hear the song without seeing the notation. This rote method is especially good if the song has a mood that the class should grasp. The second is to let the students hear the song as they follow the music in their books. This procedure is the one most frequently used and contains elements of both rote and reading. When a song is presented to the class by either of the above methods, the teacher may sing it or play a recording of it. The teacher's singing is preferable, however, because a live presentation seems more immediate. If the teacher is a skillful pianist, he can play the accompaniment while he sings the new song, but the piano should never *substitute* for the voice, since the piano's fading tones do not present a good model of singing style. A third method of presentation asks the students to attempt reading through the song at sight. This method should be employed occasionally because it develops skill in reading music. Whichever method is used to introduce the song, the teacher should be certain the students know which part they are to sing and that they have clearly in mind the initial pitch. The teacher may

The Minstrel Boy

Irish Folk Song
Arranged by Darrell Peter
Words by Thomas Moore

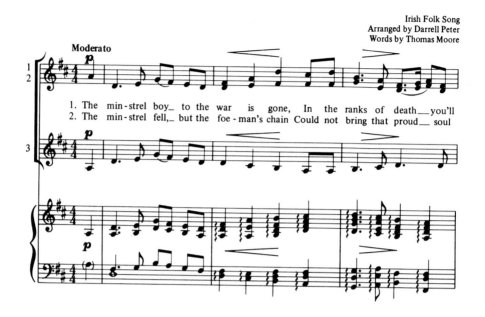

1. The min-strel boy_ to the war is gone, In the ranks of death__you'll
2. The min-strel fell,_ but the foe-man's chain Could not bring that proud__ soul

find____ him; His fa-ther's sword_ he has gird-ed on And his
un - der; The harp he loved_ ne'er_ spoke a-gain, For he

indicate with a nod of his head or by pointing his finger when the voice parts should enter.

The teacher should draw attention next to the song's musical content. The song "The Minstrel Boy" (pp. 214–215) will serve as an illustration. The teacher can ask general questions first. "What's the mood—happy? sad? powerful?" If the students are experienced in sightreading, they can sing the melody at this point. In most cases, however, they should hear the song through and sing it themselves. The teacher can then point out features of the melody and ask questions. "Notice that the notes for the words 'the war is gone' in the first line outline a major triad. Which lines are repeated? Are they repeated exactly? What dynamic changes occur in the first and second lines? All right, let's hear you make a difference. It's a crescendo; then get softer again."

At this point the teacher must decide what the class should do next with the song. Wrong notes may be the main flaw, or the students may indicate a lack of concept of the mood of the song by singing mechanically or in a style inappropriate to the music. Perhaps the dotted rhythm is sung carelessly, or the class doesn't know what to do about the pick-up note 'A' before "Land of Song!" in the first verse. Maybe the students are taking breaths at the wrong places, or failing to notice dynamic markings. The class should work on trouble spots, then sing the entire song again.

Depending on how quickly and how well the class has learned the song thus far, the teacher must decide whether to go on or set it aside for the day. In any case, further study should ensure that the music remains technically correct and properly expressive. The class might be divided in half, with each side singing for the other and offering suggestions for improvement. A stanza may be read aloud and its mood, important words, and its melody discussed. The teacher can ask, "What about the accompaniment? Why are some of the chords rolled out in this song? Here's a hint—what instrument does the text focus on?"

So far the students have sung only the melody of the song. As in other music of this type, the melody is the essential vehicle for artistic expression, so the students should explore it completely before learning the harmony parts. Most general music classes are able to sing simple part songs, so teaching the three parts in this number presents no serious problem. If the class is composed largely of soprano voices, as it sometimes is in seventh grade, all students should learn the lower parts as well as the melody. This stimulates interest and encourages flexibility in adapting to another part. The class can be divided arbitrarily, each section singing its part alone and then with the others. Later the parts may be reassigned if the range of the music permits.

For boys with changed voices, it may be necessary to choose songs having a bass clef part. But when treble clef music is of sufficiently good quality, it would be regrettable to withhold it from the class simply because there is an imbalance in voice distribution. These boys can sing one of the parts an octave lower, or a simple part can be worked out for them by the teacher.

When the song is sung well, the teacher may want to add other elements to enrich it. In "The Minstrel Boy" the military mood can be supplemented by a simple drum part in the *a* lines of the form. Other techniques include

clapping, tapping feet, or other bodily movement, chants, rhythm or orchestral instruments, and dramatizations. The textbooks themselves often suggest good possibilities. Generally, songs that contain a picturesque text ("The Caravan") or definite rhythmic patterns ("Ezekiel Saw de Wheel") are most suitable for additional musical elements. With other songs, the addition of clapping or rhythm instruments would be an artistic travesty ("Let Us Break Bread Together on Our Knees"). If piano accompaniment is used, a student can profitably be assigned to learn the part and play it. The accompaniment should not be continually present, however, because it tends to cover up errors in singing.

Listening in General Music Classes

Procedures for developing listening skill are basically the same for a general music class and for other situations. But a few suggestions may be helpful for this type of class.

(1) The students should always listen for something. They must know the reason for paying attention to what they hear. Never, never should they be told, "Just sit and listen." In the "Song Bag" activity, their purpose in listening is to determine if their performance of the song meets the predetermined criteria. In other situations the purpose of listening is to discover how a theme is developed, or to identify a rhythmic pattern or a specific instrument.

(2) Whenever possible, the class should be actively involved while listening. The students can keep track of the number of times a theme or subject occurs, they can tap beats and rhythmic figures, follow a chart or simple score, or sing along with a theme. Appropriate activity seems to focus mental attention.

(3) The students should learn to analyze what they hear. Commensurate with their level of musical sophistication, they should be able to answer the

questions: "What did the composer do and how did he do it?" This suggestion does *not* mean that seventh-graders should make the detailed analyses expected of college music majors. It means being able to tell if a theme is developed or varied, if an introduction is slow and soft, if a melody is song-like, or if the music works up to a mighty climax of sound. A student is on the right path when he says, "Well, the music started with a burst of sound, with lots of fast notes in the higher instruments, mainly the violins, I guess. Then this was followed by a smooth, slow, song-like melody that wasn't high or low. It was an oboe or some instrument like that. I think the composer wanted a lot of contrast. He sort of grabs your attention by writing a fast-loud part followed by soft, song-like music."

(4) Listening sessions should seldom exceed 15 minutes (including discussion) on any one work, or 30 minutes in any one class. Early adolescents generally have a low threshold of boredom. Besides, they need activities other than listening. Since the 15-minute limit does eliminate the lengthy first movements of some Romantic symphonies and concertos, either the movements can be heard in installments, or shorter works in the same style can be substituted. The latter solution is usually the better of the two options.

Chapter 16 discusses listening more fully and offers many suggestions that can be applied to teaching listening in the general music class.

Creating in General Music Class

As mentioned earlier in this chapter, individual creative efforts are one of the three main outcomes of music education. How can they be achieved? By setting up a structured situation in which the student is allowed as much freedom of choice as he can profitably handle. Whether the activity is improvising or composing, he is *not* told: "Create some music." A person is not taught swimming by being tossed into the water and told, "Swim." In music, the student should be given some suggestions: He can be provided with rhythmic values for notes of his own choosing, he can select rhythms for given pitches, or still more simply he can be asked only to choose among several measures, phrases, or taped excerpts composed by the teacher. He may be asked to select one element of a melody and vary it with each appearance, while retaining the same pitches, timbres, or whatever he chooses to keep constant.

Although such structuring may seem excessive, it is worth remembering that very little music is composed or improvised "out of thin air." Bach, Beethoven, Brahms, Bartók, and most other composers worked with existing styles, which they modified only slightly, if at all. When improvising —whether it be Indian music or American jazz—the performer usually works within understood "rules of the game." To give a 13-year-old a definite structure within which to create a composition is certainly not demeaning. Instead it suggests what actually happens in composing music.

Unless a student possesses a high degree of skill on an instrument, he should confine his improvisation to a simple medium such as the autoharp, bells, or one finger piano playing. The improvisor's attention should be on the musical effect he's creating, not on the technical skill of putting his musical ideas into sound. He should be asked to improvise first on something he knows, because success is more likely while tinkering with a familiar melody. He gains confidence through manipulating small ideas. In time, he can and will become more inventive.

Craft Projects

Many teachers of general music have guided a class through such activities as making puppets, cigar box ukuleles, miniature stage sets, shepherd's pipes, and soap carvings of instruments. These projects provide variety and concreteness. However, making puppets and carving soap are not musical activities, and such projects take about twice as much time as the teacher expects. Time is so limited, especially when classes do not meet daily, that using music time for crafts work cannot be justified. For teachers who want to "keep the kids busy," a crafts project seems heaven-sent, but the concern should be for the teenagers' musical education. If a crafts project can be undertaken jointly by the music and art or practical arts departments, so that the time need not be taken from music class, then the project may be beneficial. Also, crafts work can be done on an individual basis outside of class. A musically less gifted student can contribute to the class and feel a sense of accomplishment through manual endeavor.

Audiovisual Aids

The teacher of general music has many occasions to use films, filmstrips, flat pictures, tape recorders, record playing equipment, and other audiovisual aids. The nature of the course decrees that the students should explore every avenue of musical experience to uncover its infinite variety and scope. Such a comprehensive goal requires the use of varied tools.

Audiovisual materials cannot in and of themselves teach a class, but when properly used they can bring about increased learning. Several studies, one involving seventh grade music, indicate that a presentation by sound motion picture is between 18 and 34 percent more effective than traditional methods of teaching.[4]

---

[4]Walter A. Wittich and Charles F. Schuller, *Audio-Visual Materials* (Rev. Ed.) (New York: Harper & Brothers, 1957), p. 392.

Films and recordings must be of high quality. A generation ago students accepted almost anything because there was novelty involved, but today teenagers are accustomed to color television, dazzling motion pictures on wide screens, and stereo recordings played through equipment of the finest quality. No teacher can hope to win over a class by playing a scratchy record on an inferior record player. When films are shown, the room should be darkened enough to get the utmost contrast from the picture. Every film or filmstrip should be previewed before being shown to a class, to ensure its appropriateness and quality.

Finally, never should the teacher say, "Class, today let's watch a film." The students must know what to look for, and the teacher must know what he wants the class to get from the film. Some teachers overprepare a class, spending an entire period on specific build-up for a 20 minute film. To some degree the film must speak for itself, otherwise why show it at all?

Bulletin boards and wall displays help inform the class about current affairs in music and add concreteness to many of the learnings. The material should be displayed attractively, with a message or title that is unmistakably clear. It's wise for the teacher to keep a permanent file of good pictures suitable for mounting and display. Material can be purchased or collected from magazines and newspapers. Many music manufacturing firms put out attractive and educational wall charts, which are worth ordering. The bulletin board can provide a record of class activities by showing charts of individual voice ranges, a list of the current song repertoire, and drawings or written reports by students. Because the message of most bulletin board displays is quickly grasped, the teacher and the class may decide to alter or replace the display about once a week. Preparing bulletin boards is an excellent way to involve students in the operation of the class, so their help should be invited.

Books and Equipment

Both teacher and students benefit by more than one set of books. Some contain more factual material, others more music. In either case, an increased amount of resource material means more flexibility in choosing songs and planning units of study. Fortunately, in a departmentalized arrangement in which the classes come to a music room, the number of books that need to be purchased is equal to the number of students in the largest class, so the purchase of supplementary books is not a prohibitive expenditure.

The teacher should see that the records played in class are available to students through a school or city library. It is not uncommon for a student to become sufficiently interested in a work heard in class to want to hear it again at home. The recordings manufactured for use with each book series are often exceptionally well done, and should be purchased by the school.

The following equipment should be available for teaching general music classes:

A good piano that is kept in tune
A tape recorder of good quality with a good microphone
A good record player
Recordings
An autoharp
Enough ukuleles or guitars for half the class
Simple rhythm instruments such as claves, large and small drum, maracas, tambourines, castanets, triangle
Xylophone, glockenspiel, or Resonator Bells
Motion picture projector, slide projector, screen
Room darkening shades
Bulletin board
Plastic or cardboard simulations of piano keyboard

The Unit Plan — Why?

Traditional planning for general music classes has been based on units, each involving songs, recordings, and other class activities centered on a unifying theme, such as "Songs of the South" or "The Sight and Sound of Music." The unit idea adapts well to a course that tends to be more extensive than intensive in its approach to the subject, because units allow for variety while retaining a thread of unity. It is not the only means of organizing lessons in the general music class, but it is particularly well suited to the demands of the situation.

The unit plan can be overdone. Conceivably, an entire year could be spent on the music of Russia, with all theoretical learnings, songs, recordings, and class activities revolving around that single theme. Instead of aiding learning, such an excess would be an intolerable bore.

A unit will have little value if it is essentially nonmusical. One could be developed around Shakespeare in music: Berlioz' *Romeo and Juliet* could be compared with Tchaikovsky's, and with *West Side Story; The Taming of the Shrew* could be compared with *Kiss Me, Kate*; the various songs alluded to in Shakespeare's plays, or derived from them, could be studied, and so on. The trouble is that the unit starts with Shakespeare and then examines music associated with his plays. Shakespeare is first, music is second. The difference is subtle, but nevertheless crucial to the teaching of music. Music may be brought in incidentally in social science when the class studies coal miners or rivers, and this is fine. But in a music course rivers and coal miners are relevant only as they increase the students' understanding of music.

Because class situations vary greatly, and each unit has its own particular requirements, it is impossible to provide a model plan that is applicable to all units. Basically, the unit should focus on some phase of music, integrating as much as possible singing, listening, creating, discussing, and reading. It is neither possible nor desirable for every unit to encompass the variety of activities that should be found in each class period. Some topics suggest singing, while others invite more discussion and study. The teacher should not strain to achieve integration where it does not logically exist. If a prospective unit does not in itself suggest appropriate songs, then the class can work on songs that are not directly related to the unit, and neither the unit nor the singing will be of any less value for it. When possible, films, books, displays, field trips, and appearances by outside authorities should be integrated into the unit of study—not forcibly, but as a logical extension of a particular learning experience.

The following 19 units represent types of learning that are appropriate for general music classes. These suggestions, along with moderate singing activity, probably provide more than enough material to occupy a class meeting every other day for one year. The units are presented in a simple, three part format. "Value" states why the unit is particularly appropriate for the general music class. The second part, "General Procedure," suggests ways to present the unit. The suggestions are general since the wide differences among classes make detailed outlines impractical. Each teacher must work out the details to fit his teaching situation and the resources he has available. The third part, "Possible Extension," lists topics that might be studied as a result of the work on the unit. Some of the ideas in this section could be used in place of the unit. The titles can be made more personal or eye-catching for the students if the teacher so desires. The units are presented in random order. There is some overlapping among units, but this is not altogether bad, since the learnings can reinforce one another.

"The Nature of Sound"

Value.   Correlates well with science courses and has special appeal for students who have an interest in things scientific. Helps in understanding pitch, volume, and other musical factors.

General Procedure.   Play a recording or tape containing experiments with sound, or possibly some electronic music. When the curiosity of the class is aroused, describe and demonstrate how sound starts, how it travels, how the ear and brain function in perceiving sound, and how pitch and amplitude are determined. For demonstrations, prepare a trough holding marbles and manipulate it to show the chain reaction from one molecule to another. Suspend balls of cork close together on strings to illustrate the same reaction. On a string instrument, pluck or bow one of the larger strings to show the blur of vibration, and let the students feel the vibration by touching their fingertips lightly on the back of the instrument. Discuss the difference between sound and noise.

Possible Extension.   Learn about recording and sound systems. Many students have fine record-playing equipment at home, so this topic is useful and appealing. Make tape recordings of various sounds, and explore some of the types of electronic music. Experiment with tuning and pitch: take eight to twelve glasses or pharmaceutical bottles of varying size, and fill each with water until the desired pitch is reached. A further extension of this activity is a "jug and bottle band," for which music has been published.[5]

"What's Rock?" (Nashville, Motown, etc.)

Value.   Encourages students to think about and listen to music analytically. Makes comparisons with other musical types and styles. Is also a good unit for arousing the attention of the class.

General Procedure.   Ask the class to select one rock or some other currently popular tune. Select another work—Louis Armstrong, Josquin Des Prés, Debussy, country–western, Spanish–American—as a basis for comparison with the piece the students select. Listen for two minutes to each work and make a comparison on only one aspect of the music—melody, harmony, instrumentation, vocal timbre, tempo, text, phrase length, and so on. Resolve any differences of opinion about the musical factors by replaying portions of the two works. Move on to another aspect of the music. Occasionally change to other numbers so that unit does not become tedious. Have the class make a wall chart of the musical factors in the style they selected.

Possible Extension.   Prepare sheets outlining the musical factors of pieces selected by the students. For example, four measures of a rock drum-

---

[5] Adam P. Lesinsky, *Fife, Jug and Bottle Band*, 2 vols. (Rockville Centre, N.Y.: Belwin, Inc.), Book I, 1952; Book II, 1956.

mer's pattern may be illustrated, or a typical chord progression written out. Find examples in art music of the musical factors of the rock tune. Make a second wall chart listing these works according to the musical factors. Listen to portions of the paired works. Students in the class who play electric guitar or other popular instruments can briefly demonstrate them to the class. Discuss with the class the business aspects of the popular music field, especially the promotion of songs.

"Music in Religion"

Value.   Relates to an area of adolescent interest—spiritual and religious ideas. Impresses students with the importance of music in all religions, and encourages tolerance toward people of all faiths. Opens to the students a vast store of the world's great music.

General Procedure.   Present musical high points of Protestant worship service, Catholic mass, and Judaic service. Show how the text affects the type of music used. Sing and hear recordings of Protestant hymns, chorales, or anthems; chants from the Catholic mass and chant-like melodies in modern notation; and musical portions of the Judaic service. Examine songs that have a background in more than one faith: "O Come, O Come, Emmanuel," or "God of Abraham" (Yigdal).

Possible Extension.   Listen to instrumental works such as Respighi's *Concerto Gregoriano* for violin, Mendelssohn's *Reformation Symphony,* or Bruch's "Kol Nidrei."

"Man Expresses His Feelings through Music"

Value.   Makes the students conscious of the universal nature of music and impresses on them the oneness of humanity in its need for expressing feelings.

General Procedure.   From differing cultures and countries, select several folk songs that have essentially the same aesthetic feeling and thought in the text. Many textual themes are possible: human suffering ("Go Down Moses," "The Peddler," "The Pratties They Grow Small"), or an ability to laugh at imperfect conditions of livelihood ("The Little Old Sod Shanty," "Eating Goober Peas"), or men at work ("Drill, Ye Tarriers, Drill," "The Ox-Driving Song," "Song of the Volga Boatman"). If the class consists only of girls, make a collection of lullabies from around the world. Become familiar with as much literature as possible, using folk song collections and other sources to supplement the regular series material published for junior high school students. Listen to recordings of good folk songs. On a world map pinpoint the locations from which the songs have come.

Possible Extension.   Study a folk opera such as Weill's *Down in the Valley*. Listen to orchestral works that utilize folk music as thematic material (d'Indy's *Symphony on a French Mountain Air*, Op. 25; Tchaikovsky's *Symphony No. 4*, fourth movement; Dvořák's *Slavonic Dances*).

"Jazz"

Value.   Acquaints the students with a significant area of American music and presents an opportunity for creative activity.

General Procedure.   Have the students listen to a selection and then help them analyze what they heard—instruments, tempo, form, rhythmic features, vocal style, and so on. Explain that most jazz is improvised, that it is a "players' art" instead of a "composers' art." Teach the class to tap or clap prominent syncopated figures by rote; then direct them to listen again and count the number of times the figure is heard. Demonstrate the blues scale on the piano by playing a major chord in the left hand, and the lowered third, fifth, or seventh in the right hand. Two students can come to the piano, one to play a major chord in bass clef range and the other to figure out and play a lowered note in treble clef range.

Encourage improvisation by providing the student with a simple chord progression such as I-IV⁷-I-V⁷-I. Then with the voice or a simple instrument, he can work through these four steps: (1) Play or sing a chord outline, one note to the beat for two measures (C E G C/C G E C), several times to get the pitches of the chord solidly in mind. (2) Maintain a steady beat, but make one or two small changes in the rhythmic pattern, or in the order in which the notes are performed. (3) Vary the rhythm and melody more extensively. (4) Gradually add a few nonchord tones. The students' efforts at improvisation can then be performed for the class, with a recorder background or an accompaniment on piano or autoharp. Urge the students to keep their early improvisation efforts *simple*. As Gabriel Fauré is reported to have said to a composition student, "Don't try to be a genius in every measure."

Possible Extension.   Explore the further techniques and terminology of jazz: riffs, breaks, tone colors, mutes on brasses.[6] Study the "relatives" of jazz — dixieland, boogie-woogie, swing or big band sound, bop, progressive, free form. Present concert works that incorporate jazz characteristics: Copland's *Music for the Theatre,* Debussy's "Golliwog's Cakewalk" and "Minstrels," Lukas Foss' *Concerto for Improvising Solo Instruments and Orchestra,* Milhaud's *Création du monde,* Stravinsky's "Ebony" Concerto, *L'Histoire du soldat, Ragtime for Eleven Instruments,* and Gershwin's works.

"Styles in Music and the Fine Arts"

Value.   Explores music of high quality and develops an awareness of style in music. Increases appreciation of the interrelation of culture and music.

General Procedure.   Play two contrasting recordings such as "Bydlo" (Peasant Cart) from Mussorgsky's *Pictures at an Exhibition,* and Boccherini's famous "Minuet." Ask, "What kind of people are represented by this piece? Are they people who rush through revolving doors? Are they calm, simple? How do they think and feel?"

Investigate many types of music in addition to the usual Baroque and Classical works. Try Civil War songs, original American compositions for band, and music of one time period from a single country. When pointing out similarities or contrasts between pieces, stay within the same medium when possible — orchestra, piano, chorus. At this age students find it hard to hear the similarity of style between a piano piece and a choral work by the same composer.

---

[6] As part of this instruction the teacher may wish to use one of the several records on jazz produced by songbook publishing companies, or play Leonard Bernstein's recording "What Is Jazz?" (Columbia Records).

Possible Extension.   Present not only the music of a certain place and time, but also a sampling of the art, architecture, dress, and culture of a period. Prepare bulletin boards and other displays to give the students information quickly without making demands on class time. Look for films that are appropriate in content and difficulty.

"Singing and Your Voice"

Value.   Leads to a better understanding of the processes involved in correct voice production and explains the change in boys' voices. Some presentation of voice change is essential at this age.

General Procedure.   Through drawings, pictures, and films (*Your Voice* is an excellent film for this[7]), show the physical processes involved in singing and speaking. Pay special attention to the change in boys' voices, answering such questions as when it will happen, how fast, and what happens to the vocal cords. Explain how this will affect the choice of music sung. Have the students experiment with the physical setup recommended for correct singing: feel the abdominal wall move out during inhalation and in during exhalation; sing a high pitch and then a low pitch with the hand lightly on the larynx, noting the change in vibration and position. Check the singing range of each individual.

Possible Extension.   Let each student make a range chart and keep it in his notebook, or post the class results on a wall chart. Keep the chart up to date throughout the year. Play recordings that represent the various voice timbres and classifications. Then quiz the students on their ability to identify the easily recognized voice types.

"The Virtuoso and His Music"

Value.   Expands the students' interest and knowledge of music. Presents music with "showy" qualities, which young people at this age find attractive.

---

[7]Encyclopaedia Britannica Films, 11 minutes.

General Procedure.   Put the word "virtuoso" on the board and explore its meaning with the class. Mention the names of Liszt and Paganini, the great virtuosos on their instruments. Listen to a representative composition of each, giving special attention to the virtuoso techniques employed. Discuss the word "virtuoso" again, this time enlarging its meaning to include its use as an adjective to describe a certain quality in music. Listen to a movement of a virtuoso concerto, noticing especially the features that distinguish the cadenza.

Possible Extension.   Present the concerto grosso and notice how it differs from the solo concerto. Play a movement of Vivaldi's *The Four Seasons* to illustrate the combination of both. Listen to the virtuoso pieces associated with bands in the early part of this century—Herbert Clark, Arthur Pryor, and others. Invite an outstanding instrumentalist to visit and demonstrate the techniques possible on his instrument.

"Rhythm in Music"

Value.   Explores rhythm, one of the most basic and appealing aspects of music.

General Procedure.   Group rhythms into loose classifications according to their complexity and similarity. Point out the simple, strong beats that underline the rhythm in marches and popular songs; the syncopation of most types of Latin American music; the triple pattern of the waltz and minuet. Have the class clap and tap out patterns and beats, and write them on the board. Clarify the difference between the rhythmic pattern and the beat. Let each student take a simple melody, perhaps "Frère Jacques" or "Twinkle, Twinkle, Little Star," and rewrite it with several different rhythmic patterns.

Possible Extension.   Study the more intellectual, complex rhythms as found in Tchaikovsky's *Symphony No. 4*, first movement, and twentieth-century pieces with irregular measures and polyrhythms. Try Copland's *El Salón México* to demonstrate twentieth-century rhythms.

"Some Uses of Music"

Value.   Leads to an understanding of the various roles of music in contemporary society.

General Procedure.   Ask the students to think of situations in which music contributes to a nonmusical goal—creating a pleasant atmosphere in supermarkets and air terminals, relaxing people at social occasions such as dances and campfires, setting a mood of devotion in religious worship, increasing the dramatic impact of motion pictures, and so on. Ask them to analyze examples of such music, perhaps at home. For example: Is the music complete in itself? (This is generally not true of television or film scores.) How long is the piece? Does it have enough quality that you would want to listen to it apart from its nonmusical setting? Are the musical ideas developed or varied in some manner?

Discuss how people use music—somewhat as they use clothes and grooming (or lack of it)—to identify themselves as members of a group or to associate themselves with certain beliefs and attitudes. For example, music of the main-line Protestant denominations differs from that of the more fundamentalist churches; a 50-year-old has different tastes in popular music from a 15-year-old; blacks sometimes favor music that is not well-known or liked by middle class whites, and so on. Different musical preferences are fine, as long as they do not encourage separatism and animosity among races, age groups, or religious faiths.

Possible Extension.   Relate this discussion to the units on "Music in Religion" and "Man Expresses His Feelings through Music," because much folk and religious music serves a functional role. Study the field of music therapy, in which music is used to treat mental disorders. The techniques of coupling film and music can be studied,[8] and some students may wish to fit music to a few minutes of silent film.

"Music Reading"

Value.   May comprise virtually the first organized presentation of music reading the students have ever received, if the elementary program

---

[8]Aaron Copland's *What to Listen for in Music,* 2nd Ed. (New York: McGraw-Hill, 1957) contains an interesting discussion of the subject.

was weak on such training. In other cases will provide review of skill previously learned.

General Procedure.   Move the teaching along quickly and limit the amount of time given to explanations of fundamentals. A student at this age level who requires extended explanation lacks either interest or ability, and should not be allowed to slow the pace of the entire class. Handle fundamentals in a concise and interesting fashion, as suggested by this phrase used by English and Richardson: "Let's get our signals straight."[9] Limit teaching efforts to these three areas: note names, time values, and common signs found in music.

Let the students clap easy rhythmic figures at sight. Make a game of it by dividing the class into two teams and giving each person a slip of paper with a simple rhythm printed on it. Each player taps his rhythm for someone on the other team, who must either describe the note values he hears or write them on the board.

Choose simple music for sight singing, usually in unison. Stress the importance of keeping one's place in the music and of not giving up as long as the music is continuing.

Possible Extension.   Try *Two Part Reading Fun* and *Three Part Reading Fun* by Carl Vandre.[10] Make brief use of flash cards containing a measure of melody or rhythm. Have the students experiment at the piano keyboard, learning to play simple melodies and chords from notation. Let the class silently follow a score (without a vocal text) as the music is played. Emphasize the need for keeping track of the beats in each measure. To find out how closely individuals are following, stop the music and see who can point to the exact spot in the score.

"So You Want to Conduct!"

Value.   Contributes to an understanding of beat and rhythm, and leads to insight into how musical groups play or sing together. Provides a degree of physical activity that is well received at this age level.

---

[9]English and Richardson, Vol. I, p. 4.

[10]Carl Vandre, *Sight Reading Fun* and four similar books (New York: Mills Music Co.).

General Procedure.   Start with the two beat pattern. Draw it simply on the board, and have the students practice conducting the pattern while you

conduct with your back to them, looking over your shoulder occasionally. When the pattern is done properly, have the class sing through a song in the proper meter with no anacrusis, conducting as they sing. "Joy to the World" can be used for 2/4. Proceed in the same manner to the three beat, and then to the four beat patterns, writing them in this way:

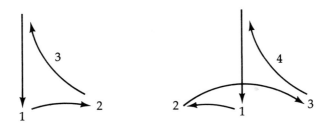

In subsequent class sessions try "America" for 3/4 and "Alouette" or "All Through the Night" for 4/4. Next teach the procedure for conducting an anacrusis, at which time almost all common songs can be added to the conducting repertoire. Let the students take turns conducting the class as it sings. Instruct the class to follow the conductor even when he is wrong.

Possible Extension.   Teach the conducting of a hold and a cutoff, and proceed to the use of the left hand. Encourage the students to maintain the conducting pattern in the right hand while at the same time indicating dynamic level and other points with the left. It is possible to conduct to records, but this technique is of limited value in teaching conducting.

"Instruments of the Orchestra"

Value.   Increases the students' appreciation of instrumental music. Value of the unit may be limited if the students have covered the material in elementary school.

General Procedure.   Obtain some of the excellent teaching aids that are available—filmstrips accompanied by recordings; good pictures and wall charts in color and black and white; and recordings of individual instruments, to say nothing of works of music such as Britten's *A Young Person's Guide to the Orchestra* (available also in motion picture form as *Instruments of the Orchestra*[11]), and the ever-popular *Peter and the Wolf* by Prokofiev. If there are instrumentalists in the class, have them demonstrate their instruments, or invite outside students to give brief demonstrations. The students who demonstrate should be competent players but need not be virtuosos, since class interest will be high anyway. Divide the presentation into families of instruments to help the class recognize instruments by sight and, more important, by sound. Make a special effort to show instruments such as bassoon and oboe, which are not so well-known.

Possible Extension.   Study the orchestra as a complete entity, its seating arrangement, instrumentation, and the conductor's score. Listen to a more advanced work featuring sections of instruments, such as Bartók's *Concerto for Orchestra*, or a record such as Howard Hanson's discussion of the orchestration of *Merry Mount*.[12] Compare the range and timbre of particular instruments with classifications of human singing voices, or study the use of instruments to represent characters in programmatic music. Study the instrumentation of bands, and of groups that perform popular music.

*"Contemporary Concert
Artists, Conductors, and Composers"*

Value.   Brings life and currency to the art of music, and introduces contemporary works.

---

[11] Black and white, 20 minutes, British Information Service.
[12] "The Composer and His Orchestra," Mercury 50175.

General Procedure.   Select about 20 of the most outstanding names among present-day concert artists, being careful to choose equally from the ranks of pianists, singers, instrumentalists, conductors, and composers. Present each briefly, his accomplishments and his background, making sure that the artists come across as human beings, not supermen. Show the class a picture of each musician, and give an occasional "flashcard" test on recognizing the pictures. Since spelling some of the names may be difficult, it's wise to allow the use of phonetic spellings, so that emphasis will not be diverted from music to spelling.

Possible Extension.   Relate contemporary musicians to current musical events, giving special attention to well-known musicians when they appear in the local area. Make an inventory of the recordings owned by the families of class members to determine the number that were recorded by the contemporary musicians studied in class.

"Simple Instruments"

Value.   Teaches the fundamentals of harmony and provides experience in music making. Increases interest in recreational music, which is a worthy outcome of such classes. Provides an opportunity to improvise.

General Procedure.   Teach one simple instrument until the class has gained enough mastery to play it with little help. A logical first choice is the autoharp, because it is easy to play, and publishers of general music materials often include markings for autoharp accompaniments. The ukulele has been used successfully in some schools. It is more difficult than the autoharp, but it is an inexpensive recreational instrument that enjoys periodic revivals of public interest. The guitar is in much favor currently and is the instrument most likely to be owned privately. Each of these three harmony instruments is appropriate in the general music class, and each can be mastered in a group situation. Remember that the main function of these instruments is to accompany songs.

Possible Extension.   Teach the class a few recreational songs that can be accompanied by the instruments taught in class. Try improvisation. In

Living with Music, simple parts are written for string bass, drums, piano, and other instruments.[13] The "other instruments" part uses a technique (called "vocalstration" in the book) which is common to the jazz musician: instrumentalists in the class are asked to create their own part using only the notes of a certain chord in one measure, another chord in the next measure, and so on, until a line based on the fundamental harmonies of the piece has been written. The new lines are then played with the original melody as an accompaniment or countermelody.

"The Music of England"
(Russia, Spain, Latin America, etc.)

Value.   Allows for comprehensive study of one culture.

General Procedure.   If England is the country chosen, have the class sing several English folk songs such as "Turtle Dove" and "Early One Morning," and some of the hymns of the Anglican Church such as "For All the Saints" *(Sine Nomine).* Choose several works that represent various periods of history—compositions by Purcell, Elgar, Vaughan Williams, and Britten. Compare the works of Vaughan Williams; some are arrangements of folk music, while others are more complex and dissonant. Share with the class the Britten opera *The Little Sweep.* It is about an 11- or 12-year-old boy and includes a song for the audience to sing. Purcell's *Trumpet Voluntary in D* is especially appealing to a general music class, as is Elgar's *Enigma Variations.*

Possible Extension.   Learn about Handel and the *Messiah,* the organ at Westminster Abbey, the tradition of boy choirs, the music for the coronation of the King or Queen, English folk songs that have become American folk songs, English sea chanteys, musical settings of great English poems, plus the music of several other fine composers not mentioned in this outline.

"Musical Comedy and Opera"

Value.   Builds on the teenagers' interest in current musical comedies and dramatic shows. Expands the students' comprehension and acceptance

---

[13]English and Richardson, Vol. I, pp. 21, 66; Vol. II, p. 17.

of dramatic vocal forms by proceeding from the known to the unknown. Aids teacher-pupil rapport.

Selection of Music.   Much of the success of the unit depends on the works selected for study. Avoid works that to a 12-year-old appear pompous and long-winded, overly romantic, or odd and silly without being funny. Plots dealing with illicit love or romance on too mature a level are inappropriate. At best, the matter of love leaves a red-blooded 12-year-old boy "cold," but idealized romance, as found in the poems *Evangeline* and *The Courtship of Miles Standish,* is quite appealing to girls. Of the standard operas a few are usable: possibly *Cosi Fan Tutte* and *The Marriage of Figaro* by Mozart, short operas such as *Gianni Schicchi* by Puccini, and perhaps one act from a few others. Explore the works of Britten, Menotti, and others which are more "down-to-earth" and hence more meaningful to students at this age. Gilbert and Sullivan produced many fine operettas, but much of the subtle English humor and satire is lost on young Americans unless it is carefully explained. Contemporary American musical comedies usually find quick favor.

General Procedure.   Start with a musical comedy, giving the general idea of the plot and pointing out the function of the overture, the relationship between orchestra and singers, and the variety in the songs. To present opera most effectively to the class, invite fine soloists to come and sing excerpts from the opera. The impact of live performance does much to win favor for operatic music. If the opera is very long, choose one scene for concentrated attention, and merely tell the class about the plot involved in other scenes. Do not emphasize the interest that the plot alone creates, because on the basis of dramatic action, musical presentations come off a poor second to novels, motion pictures, and television plays. Rather, focus attention on the relationship between the drama and music. In *Amahl and the Night Visitors,* the roles of two distinguished kings are written for deep voices. Why? How is the music affected when Amahl's mother slowly creeps toward the gold that she wishes to take for her son? Why does the oboe theme appear at both the beginning and end of the opera? Why was an oboe selected to play this melody?

Possible Extension.   Take the class to see a live performance of an opera, or if this is not feasible, obtain one of the several films on opera. Study in advance an opera that will be shown on television in the course of the year. Prepare a bulletin board display on operas and opera singers, or on current musical comedies, and compare these forms with the oratorio.

"Songs and Dances from around the World"

Value.   Builds on the students' feeling for rhythm, and expands their knowledge of the music of foreign countries. Adds variety to the class through experimentation with simple folk dance steps.

General Procedure.   Group together those dances, preferably from different countries, that have similar steps, tempo, and style. This makes it easier for the students to learn and remember each dance, and it impresses them with the similarities among all peoples. Choose dances that call for a singing accompaniment, so that singing is involved in the unit. Point out that many folk dances are performed to music sung by the people participating in or watching the dance. Do not limit the class to the more usual type of dance and music. Instead, include music of African tribal dances and American Indian dances.

Many young teenagers do not respond well to dancing in a classroom. They feel self-conscious and become uncooperative or boisterous. Sometimes simple square dances are effective, though. Generally, students appreciate competent dancing by someone else. The physical education teacher may provide assistance in locating and rehearsing dancers.

Possible Extension.   Study ballet music and ballet sections of musical comedy.

"Music as a Vocation or Avocation"

Value.   Gives the students a comprehensive idea of the vocational and avocational possibilities in music. Helps them understand why music is offered in the school.

General Procedure.   Present the various careers in music with descriptions of training, working conditions, and opportunities. Include the following types of music occupation: music education (public school, college, private studio), professional performer (concert artist, symphony musician, dance band musician), music therapist, music merchant, church musician. Several publications, such as *A Career in Music Education,* and *Careers in Music,*[14] describe the different areas of specialization. As part of the discussion on music education, ask the students to think through what they feel to be the purpose of the present class and of school music courses in general. Let them discuss curriculum content from the standpoint of need. They will undoubtedly agree that the three R's are necessary, but the need for music and the arts may not be as evident to them.

Mention the possibilities for participation by interested amateurs. Stress performing organizations such as church and community choral groups, as well as community orchestras, especially if there is a local one. The students should know that one out of every six Americans between the ages of five and 75 plays an instrument regularly, and that there are choirs in nearly every church.[15] Intelligent listening to music is an avocational activity that should not be overlooked. Americans spend more money on quality music than on spectator sports.[16] Acquaint the class with newspapers, magazines, and books that review recordings and concerts, as well as reference books such as Percy Scholes' *The Listener's Guide to Music,*[17] that are written for the nonprofessional.

Individual Lesson Planning

Planning for a class in general music is similar to planning for a performing group. The preparation should take into account the three main parts of the "teaching formula" presented in this book: What?, How?, With What Results? The question "Why?" does not need to be rethought for every class, although it does affect the teacher's selection of what he will teach. Differences in approaching the two types of classes arise because the role of performance varies in each, and there is more diversity of activity in a general music course. The nature of on-the-spot decision making in each situation, therefore, requires a different orientation.

One technique that is especially helpful in a plan for general music is the preparation of "cues." These are reminders or questions for the teacher, briefly indicating how something will be taught or what question should be asked to bring out a point. Not everything the teacher plans to say can or

---

[14]Music Educators National Conference, Washington, D.C., 1965, 1970.

[15]"Report on Amateur Music, 1971" (Chicago: American Music Conference, 1971), p. 6.

[16]M. B. Schnapper (Ed.), *The Facts of American Life* (Washington, D.C.: Public Affairs Press, 1960), p. 270.

[17]Percy Scholes, *The Listener's Guide to Music: With a Concert-Goer's Glossary* (10th Ed.) (Oxford: Oxford University Press, 1961).

should be cued in, of course. The cues are merely to indicate blocks of activity.

Many prospective teachers find it difficult to allocate time in planning a lesson. Although one's ability to do this improves with experience, no one ever becomes 100 percent accurate at it. Some reasonably accurate estimates can be made, however. The teacher knows the length of songs or recorded examples. Also, he can place limits on the amount of time he wants to spend discussing a point. The same is true of learning a song. Time estimates should be made for the simple reason that without them the teacher may run short of enough to do in the class or omit some important things that he planned. Of the two time errors, the latter is far less serious, because omitted portions can be included in the next class.

Following is a plan for one class period of seventh grade general music. A unit has been selected that does not logically include a film, field trip, or any other single time-consuming activity. Songs are selected on the assumption that some of the boys in the class are singing in bass clef range. The class numbers about 30 students of average ability and interest. For clarity, the plan has been written in more detail than is normally necessary in a teacher's plan book. Most teachers develop their own unique abbreviations and one-word reminders.

Lesson Plan for General Music

Write "virtuoso" on board. (3 minutes)
—What does it mean?
Piano virtuoso—Liszt
Have students think of word to describe the following music as they listen.

Listen to *La Campanella.* (5 minutes)

—Is the piece sad? serious? wild? happy? breathtaking? (6 minutes)
—What kind of man was Liszt? thoughtful? shy? a show-off?
—Piece is *La Campanella,* "The Bell"
—What kind of piece best depicts a bell?
Have students decide how the music differs from other music they know, while they listen a second time.

Play last minute or two of piece again. (4 minutes)
—What did you decide? How is this music different?
—Is it meant to be played by a talented amateur?
—Does it require you to think in order to understand it?
—What about this piece could be called "virtuoso"?

Tell class the next instrument they will hear is a violin.
Play half of Lalo's *Symphonie Espagnole,* fifth movement. (4 minutes)
—Is this for a virtuoso? Why?

Teach new song "Whoopee Ti-Yi-Yo," *Exploring Music*, Book 7, p. 132. (10 minutes)
—Is song for a virtuoso?
—Is it serious? simple? Does it tell a story?
Remind about good singing technique.
Try for *appropriate expression;* observe dynamic markings.

Review "Oh, Won't You Sit Down?" *Making Music Your Own*, Book 7, p. 140. (5 minutes)
Work on second part especially.
—What is the effect of F natural in 2nd part in chorus?

Have class listen to the phrase.
—What are the words about?
—How important are they to the music?

Sing "Pretty Saro," *Making Music Your Own*, Book 7, p. 147. (3 minutes)
Hear Julie, Wendy, and Sue on the autoharp part they thought they could play.

If time is left, sing "Hey, Ho! Nobody Home," *Making Music Your Own*, Book 7, p. 182.

According to the plan, neither the unit on the virtuoso nor the singing of "Whoopee Ti-Yi-Yo" will be finished during the period. "Oh, Won't You Sit Down?" may be, if the class does it properly. "Pretty Saro" is a song the students know, and three interested class members wish to add another line to it. The "if time is left" category allows for adjusting the timing of the class activities. Naturally the plan may be altered in other ways if the situation warrants. Like all plans it outlines a workable direction for the class and ensures more thoroughness than is likely to occur through haphazard, random teaching efforts.

Projects

1. Share with other class members some of your experiences as a student in junior high school general music class. Describe the organization of the class, the type of activity carried on, and the strong and weak points of the course.

2. Examine the following books published for use in seventh grade general music classes:

> *Making Music Your Own* (Morristown, N.J.: Silver Burdett Company, 1968)

Exploring Music (New York: Holt, Rinehart and Winston, 1971)

Discovering Music Together (Chicago: Follett Publishing Company, 1970)

Growing with Music (Englewood Cliffs, N.J.: Prentice-Hall, 1966)

This Is Music (Boston: Allyn and Bacon, 1964)

3. Plan in detail a unit of your own choosing. If songs are included in the unit, indicate a source for each, listing the book title and page number. Identify precisely any films or filmstrips that might be used, and collect several pictures that are suitable for display. Describe any field trip or other activities that will be involved.

4. Using the unit developed for question 3, make a lesson plan for a single 45-minute period. Estimate the amount of time consumed by the various activities.

5. The unit "Rhythm in Music," suggested on page 228, contained general procedures for its presentation. Select specific songs, dances, and recordings that you would use in teaching the unit (a minimum of six to eight pieces). Include in your plan any clapping or similar rhythmic activities that would be helpful.

6. Decide on two compositions or sections of compositions by each of the following modern composers; choose music that is characteristic of the composer's style and suitable for use in a general music class: Bela Bartók, Igor Stravinsky, Aaron Copland, Dmitri Shostakovich, Paul Hindemith, Samuel Barber.

7. Examine these three portions of operas and evaluate them for their suitability for a junior high school general music class:

Richard Wagner—*Tristan und Isolde*, Act II

Giacomo Puccini—*La Bohème*, Act II

C. W. von Gluck—*Orfeo ed Euridice*, Act III, Scene 2

8. Study *The Old Maid and the Thief* by Gian-Carlo Menotti. Plan how you would prepare a class for hearing this work, what learnings should precede its presentation, how much the class will hear in one period, and what you will say to the class about it.

9. Study the list of objectives presented in *Music in General Education* (pages 202–204). Think of one or two ways in which a music teacher can help the students achieve each of the eleven goals.

10. Select two currently popular songs that you think would be especially appropriate for use in a general music class. Give reasons for your selection.

11. Think of two games or challenges to encourage the students to listen to the exposition of a fugue. Think of two such techniques for encouraging the students to read musical notation.

12. Write a simple bass clef part to "The Minstrel Boy" (pages 214–215).

Suggested Readings

Andrews, Frances M., and Joseph A. Leeder, *Guiding Junior High School Pupils in Music Experiences*. Englewood Cliffs, New Jersey: Prentice-Hall, 1953, Chapters 3, 4, 6, and 9.

Andrews, Frances M., *General Music Classes in the Junior High School*. Englewood Cliffs, New Jersey: Prentice-Hall, 1971.

Cooper, Irwin, and Karl O. Kuersteiner, *Teaching Junior High School Music* (2nd Ed.). Boston: Allyn and Bacon, 1970.

Glenn, Neal E., William B. McBride, and George H. Wilson, *Secondary School Music: Philosophy, Theory, and Practice*. Englewood Cliffs, New Jersey: Prentice-Hall, 1970, Chapter 5.

Hughes, William O., *Planning for Junior High School General Music*. Belmont, California: Wadsworth Publishing Company, 1967.

Monsour, Sally, and Margaret Perry, *A Junior High School Music Handbook* (2nd Ed.). Englewood Cliffs, New Jersey: Prentice-Hall, 1970.

Reimer, Bennett, "Development and Trial in a Junior-Senior High School of a Two-Year Curriculum in General Music" (U.S. Office of Education H-116), 1967.

Singleton, Ira C., and Simon V. Anderson, *Music in Secondary Schools* (2nd Ed.). Boston: Allyn and Bacon, 1969, Chapters 3 and 4.

Sur, William R., and Charles F. Schuller, *Music Education for Teen-Agers* (2nd Ed.). New York: Harper & Row, 1966.

11
Teaching Music in the Rehearsal

It is a bright, warm day in early September. Joe Fontana, just graduated from college, steps before his band. Before the students is a piece of music, which he promptly undertakes to have them play. Cacophony results! His high school students can't read through the music as the groups back at college always did. A feeling on the order of panic strikes him. What should he do now? What precisely can he do to teach this or any other piece of music?

To begin with, there may be precise answers, but there can be no perfect answer. There are too many variables involved—the musical development of the students, the particular piece of music, the personalities of the teacher and students. Nevertheless, it is helpful to see how a problem can be handled under one set of conditions.

Planning

As for Joe Fontana's state of panic, it need not have happened. He should have planned for such an eventuality. Beginning teachers sometimes have mistaken impressions about planning. In their collegiate musical organizations and in their observation of master teachers, there is seldom visible evidence of a lesson plan or other specific preparation. To all appearances the director improvises, relying on his good musicianship and quick wits. In a few cases this is true. Usually, however, much thought has gone into planning what appears to be made up on the spot, even though the preparation may not be written down in a formal lesson plan. The fact that the college or professional director may have rehearsed a work many times during his career is one reason why he is well prepared on a number.

Planning can start as soon as the teacher decides what he wants to accomplish in his teaching. He should start with a general, long-range idea of what he hopes to accomplish during the year: the music to be played or sung, the programs to be performed, the skills to be developed, and the theoretical and historical knowledge to be integrated into the year's work. Then he is ready to plan what he will do in the particular class period.

No single teaching outline is suitable for all class meetings. The method and content will vary according to previous learnings, the closeness of a performance, and the type of music being studied. Many teachers begin the period with a combination warm-up and technique developing routine. This portion of the class must be varied from day to day and must be relevant to the other activities in the course. In singing, for example, attention can be centered on producing the sound correctly or singing in tune. In instrumental music, playing techniques can be stressed, or a scale or exercise can be played to practice correct fingering or bowing. This type of work should be brief—not longer than five or seven minutes. To close a class, the students can review something they do well, or put together something on which they have been working. The idea is not to leave the group hanging in the middle of a specific learning task when the period ends. Between the opening and closing of the class, the group can begin studying new music, review familiar works, perfect its current repertoire, and learn aspects of theory and literature relevant to the music being rehearsed.

To prepare for a particular class, the teacher must decide which pieces will be studied, which places in the music should receive special attention, and what learnings should be achieved. In addition, he needs to study the score and parts to music he does not know well. The teacher studies the music in advance to learn it and decide on the proper interpretation ahead of the students. Also, the study should anticipate spots that are likely to be difficult for the group. When the students reach a troublesome passage, he must be quick to come up with the alternate fingering for G on the trumpet, a bowing technique that will help the strings coordinate the bow with the left hand, and a suggestion for getting the woodwinds to play a particular rhythmic figure correctly. *No teacher should be caught unprepared for problems in the music; he must have plans for overcoming them.*

Need the plans be written down? For the beginning teacher, yes. After a year of experience, his own good judgment can guide him in this. A lesson plan should include a statement of the long-range goals and how the particular classwork fits into those goals. More important, it should include suggestions for warm-up, a list of the music to be worked on, reminders of the points to be covered in each piece, and an estimate of how much time will be required to accomplish the planned learning.

Meanwhile, back at the school, Joe Fontana is wondering what to do about his first class. If the students' folders contain less difficult pieces, he should try a simpler number, one so easy that it is certain to be performed with some degree of success. This will salvage some order from a potentially chaotic situation.

But teaching is not merely leading a group through music simple enough to be performed at sight. For the next meeting of the class, Joe Fontana must be prepared to teach, in the fullest sense of the word. Let's see how the process should be undertaken.

Understanding the Work as a Whole

As soon as he presents a piece of music, the teacher begins the interplay of whole and part learning. The first step in the study of a new work is some activity to give the students the sense of the whole work.

Several procedures are available for this. The number may be read through at sight, especially if it is quite easy, even though it is a far from perfect rendition. To emphasize the mood in vocal music, the number can be sung the first time on a bright or dark vowel sound, whichever is appropriate. The text of the music may be read aloud in unison with expression, or the accompanist may play the voice parts while the students follow the music. A representative section can be played or sung to give the students a clear and immediate idea of how the piece sounds. A recording of the work can be played. In contrapuntal music, the teacher can take a thematic phrase and have each part perform it as it comes along. The theme can be learned first, the countermelody second, and the free material left until later. If the melody does not appear until a third of the music has passed, the first reading can start with the melody section. If the emphasis is to be rhythmic, the words or rhythms may be chanted or played in unison. In some cases, a technical or rhythmic problem may be studied just prior to learning the new piece. To give the students a better idea of the music, they can be told something about the history or the style of the work.

Whatever the procedure, it should move quickly. The students want to sing or play; they do not want to be told about problems that *might* arise. Sometimes teachers spend as long as 20 minutes preparing to sight-read a number, an amount of time that is entirely too long.

Instrumental Music Teaching

The logical groupings of instrumental parts vary with each piece of music, and from place to place in the music. For example, the traditional march of the Sousa period has about five groupings. The excerpt from "Semper Fidelis" contains these groupings in a repeated section: a melody—mainly cornets and trumpets; a bass line; a decorative part in the piccolos and clarinets; a harmony part for horns, trombones, and baritones; and a percussion part (seldom indicated in condensed scores). To teach this section of the music, the following steps are recommended:

(1) Start with the melody, since it carries the main burden of the musical idea. Briefly help the players find the correct notes, rhythms, and expression. Before leaving them to work with another grouping, make sure the essential musical idea has not been lost while working out the technical problems.

(2) Work with the bass instruments. In this case, considering the ability of most high school players of the tuba and the difficulty of this portion of the music, it might be wise to suggest that the bass instruments practice the part individually outside of class. Better yet, say, "I'll work with you on this again during study period or during sectional practice tomorrow." In any event, avoid holding a·bass sectional during full band practice. As soon as they can play the part reasonably well, combine it at once with the melody.

(3) Listen to the high woodwind part. Rhythmic precision is important here. When sufficient clarity is evident, combine it with the other two parts.

(4) Work with the horns and low clarinets. This simple part should require little assistance.

(5) Help the percussion as much as necessary, recognizing the need to fit their part into the ensemble.

(6) Have the entire band play the section, with special attention to style and balance.

To assist or help means to do whatever is necessary to get the music performed correctly. In the melody parts, it may call for making sure that the students play the line in bugling fashion with the first and third valves for all notes. It may mean achieving rhythmic accuracy by holding the dotted-half note over into the first eighth of the next measure. It may involve singing to the players the style in which the notes should be tongued. It may require checking the players' fingerings on the high woodwind line to see that they use the easiest and best sounding combination on their particular instrument. And so it goes through each line—counting rhythms, demonstrating style, checking fingerings, adjusting dynamics, bringing out accented notes, and pointing out other parts to listen for—until everyone's playing fits into the mosaic of sound that is music.

The teacher must exercise good judgment in how much attention to devote to the various sections. For example, if a harmony part has many afterbeats, it is fruitless to spend much time on the part alone because it makes sense only in conjunction with the other parts. Discretion is needed in the amount of time given a part and the degree of perfection expected in the first few practices. A teacher might spend 50 minutes with the cornets and might even come close to getting their playing just right. But what about the rest of the band during this time? Their interest has not been stimulated, nor is it likely that their musical insights have been deepened. Besides, if each section receives such attention, the cornets will probably have fallen from perfection when the teacher gets back to them a few days later. The

Semper Fidelis

teacher should content himself with correcting as many errors as possible in about three or four playings by a section. Further improvement should be left until another day.

Choral Music Teaching

The choral teacher follows an approach similar to that of the instrumental teacher. After giving the singers a sense of the whole work, he may let them sing the entire number together, if this was not done initially. He must make a judgment at this point, based on how well the students succeed in their attempt at singing the music. It may be that the tenors and basses need only sing their parts again with the accompaniment. Perhaps the altos need to sing their part while the other lines are hummed. More often than not, each part needs some specific help. The procedures suggested here are on the "bedrock" order; that is, they assume that the singers need a maximum amount of assistance. The amount of help called for will vary from one day to the next, from one piece of music to the next, and from one passage to another within the piece.

The usual method for helping singers is the unimaginative procedure called "pounding parts." The author dislikes the term, but mentions it here because it is in such common usage. "Pounding" implies an unmusical activity, and suggests that music must be abandoned to learn music — something of a contradiction. Sectional work is necessary, of course, but it can be done musically.

The teacher can do much to retain musical quality by working in musically logical segments, and by pointing out and performing the similar phrases of music that appear throughout a piece. Students are often surprised and pleased to realize that by learning one phrase they have mastered others that are nearly identical. Above all, *interpretation and notes should be learned together.* Sometimes inexperienced teachers think that they will first teach the notes, and then the interpretation. But this idea does not work in actual practice, nor is it consistent with the principles of music teaching. After several sessions on a piece, the interpretation has largely jelled, and changes come only with difficulty after that. Unlike well-trained musicians, adolescents seldom see any difference between learning the notes and learning the style in which the notes should be performed. With teenagers, first impressions are lasting ones.

When the musical substance of the work has been established, the choral teacher should follow these steps:

(1) Select a phrase of two, four, or possibly eight measures. If the music is a typical homophonic SATB[1] work with the melody in the soprano, have

the accompanist play the bass line. (A male teacher may want to sing it.) Then have the basses sing their part back in full voice. Ask the tenors, altos, and sopranos to sight sing the bass part *softly* with the basses. Singing along with other parts strengthens the students' ability to read music in both clefs and contributes to their understanding of the music and its harmony. Naturally, the girls will sing the bass parts an octave higher than written. Repeat this unison singing a time or two more if necessary. Then have the section sing the passage alone, unaccompanied by the piano or other singers. Another way to check the section is to select one or two individuals at random to sing the phrase. At this point, whatever is not learned adequately will have to be left until the next class.

(2) The tenor part should be covered in much the same manner. The girls can sing the tenor line with the boys. When the tenors have learned their own part, direct them to sing it with the bass part, while the accompanist plays the two lines on the piano and the girls drop out. The use of accompaniment depends largely on the difficulty of the vocal line. Piano support can be omitted entirely, or the written piano accompaniment can be used, or the accompanist may play all four voice parts.

(3) Repeat this procedure for the altos. The sopranos may join in softly on the alto line. Girls are usually better sight readers than boys, so one singing of the phrase may be enough. The altos, tenors, and basses should then combine their respective parts to sing the phrase.

(4) The soprano part is approached last because it is frequently the simplest and most easily learned. The entire group then performs the phrase.

In this procedure, a phrase of music is built up layer by layer, with everyone singing during most of the process. There are several reasons for rehearsing the bass and tenor parts first in a mixed group. (With glee clubs, the lowest part should also be learned first.) Inexperienced basses and tenors find it tempting to sing the melody an octave lower, rather than to put forth the effort to learn a separate harmony part. This is especially true if the boys know the melody before they learn the bass or tenor. Because the bass part is sometimes the most difficult, the boys need the practice of singing in several combinations. Boys at this age are usually less competent musically and vocally than girls and thus need more attention. Also, more girls than boys audition and enroll in choral music, so in a select group the girls have probably been screened more carefully.

Some teachers prefer to have the other parts remain silent while one

---

[1]A mixed chorus consisting of sopranos, altos, tenors, and basses sing music arranged for SATB, the acronym made up of the first letter of each part. A similar scheme is carried out for girls' glee clubs which sing SA or SSA music, the two S's standing for first and second soprano. Music written for boys' glee clubs is arranged in two parts for tenor and bass (TB); in three parts for tenor, baritone, and bass (TBB); or in four parts for first tenor, second tenor, baritone, and bass (TTBB).

section is receiving special attention. They object to asking the girls to sing along on the boys' parts for two reasons: a few of the notes are out of range, and singing four different lines by the sopranos may confuse them. Some of the notes may be out of range for some of the singers, but as a practical matter a few notes in the soprano part are usually out of range for some of the sopranos, and the same is true of every section. As for confusion, it is likely to result only if the practice is continued after the initial work on a piece.

The basic teaching steps are the same whether or not the girls sing with the basses and tenors. Although having the higher parts sing with the lower parts is not essential, it does keep singers from sitting around with nothing to do. Because singers do not have the concrete experience of fingering an instrument, telling them to follow their part silently is not as successful as it is with instrumentalists.

In the early stages of the learning process, humming a part while another section sings is not recommended because it may contribute to learning wrong notes and careless vocal habits.

Further Rehearsal Techniques

It is often more efficient and effective to communicate with the students *while* the music is being performed. A good teacher is one who foresees a point on which a quick reminder will save a minute of class time. Noticing the pattern in the trombone part, the instrumental teacher can call out to

the trombones, "Sixth position on F" just before the figure is played. It is not necessary to stop the band and say, "Trombones, in the third measure after letter C, play the F in the alternate sixth position." Not only is time lost stopping the group, giving instructions, and starting again, but the musical flow is impeded. The successful music teacher calls out "Smooth, smooth" at the approach of a legato passage. When the students are slow to cut off a tone before a rest, he snaps out a sharp, distinct, "Off!" just at the beginning of the rest. He may wish to hold his hands still during the rest to indicate stopping of the sound. The verbal command thus serves the additional purpose of calling attention to his conducting. Commentary from the teacher is a vivid, live way to present the live art of music. Its only limitation occurs when the music is too loud for the teacher to be heard. The technique should not replace decisive conducting, nor should it continue into the time of performance.

Indicating Musical Entrances

A problem that causes grief among inexperienced teachers is how to indicate attacks and entrances. Inexperienced students are seldom able to watch conducting motions and follow their music at the same time. In fact, some of them can scarcely keep from getting lost even when their entire attention is on the music. So in the initial stages of learning a work, some way must be found to supplement the conducting motions. The teacher can mark time by clapping his hands or tapping on a hard surface. Or he can provide verbal commands. After the starting place has been indicated, and in vocal music the opening pitches given either by voice or piano, the teacher says *in the tempo of the music,* "Ready, go," or "Ready, begin." After the first few times, verbal commands should be dropped completely so that the students do not become dependent on them.

In choral music it is sometimes necessary for the teacher to sing with a section the first time or two. It may be especially useful for a man to sing with the boys, because they sometimes lack the confidence and zeal to get started on the right note at the right time. A teacher may occasionally have the unsettling experience of giving a start, and having no one come in. He should check to make sure the students understand what he wants, and try again. When students do not come in on an entrance, it is usually due to inattentiveness, lack of understanding, or lack of confidence, rather than to contrariness on their part.

Isolating Trouble Spots

One of the keys to more efficient and effective music teaching is the teacher's ability to determine the exact point on which the students are having trouble. Sometimes one note in a phrase is the cause for incorrect performance. It is not necessary, or even wise, to practice all the notes in a phrase again and again just to get a certain note right. For example, the basses in the chorus are learning this phrase from the "Hallelujah Chorus" from Handel's *Messiah.*

And He shall reign for ev - er and ev - er

The basses may falter on the F sharp, B, and D, missing the B and losing their accuracy. It is useless to sing the entire phrase over and over, mistakes and all. The pianist should play the three tones while the basses sing the pattern.

When they do it correctly, they should go over the three notes about three times. Between each repetition the teacher need only say "A-gain" or "Once more" in the tempo of the piece. The whole process would be: SHALL REIGN FOR—once more—SHALL REIGN FOR—sing the whole phrase—AND HE SHALL REIGN FOREVER AND EVER. Sometimes it helps to tape-record the correct piano or teacher version, and then the incorrect version so that the students can hear their mistakes more clearly.

Some teachers make a list of such trouble spots and use them for "spot practice" in the class. This provides a quick review of the troublesome passage without performing the entire work, thus speeding the learning process and making it more thorough and accurate. To keep the group alert and to check the learning of a passage, the teacher can say suddenly, "We're having trouble with the F sharp, B, and D above the words 'shall reign for.' Perry, let's hear you sing the passage," and have Perry sing it. Then, "Stan, let's hear you sing it," followed by one or two others.

Prior to working on a trouble spot in the music, the students should be acquainted with the entire phrase or piece so that they understand as fully as possible its rhythmic, harmonic, and melodic factors. In short, they should have a concept of the whole.

Students should be encouraged to inform the teacher of passages that they find difficult to perform correctly. They know, better than any listener, which passages make them feel insecure. This technique is more useful for advanced groups, since they don't need to go over music so often to learn it, and they have a better sense of their capabilities.

Keeping All Students Occupied with Learning

A rehearsal of a professional group is marked by long waits for some players, but in the schools a music class should be a learning situation for all students. They must be involved in the classwork as much as possible during the entire time. Long waits encourage discipline problems and boredom and waste time for most of the class. What's more, long waits are usually unnecessary.

The problem can be alleviated by efficient teaching techniques. When an instrumental group is in the early stages of work on a piece, the students can be told to finger silently through their parts as another section rehearses. (Silent fingering is a good practice pedagogically.) The teacher does not ask students to do this on a piece that they have been playing for some time. By then, the work with single sections should be mostly over.

Many a baritone player is not interested in listening to the clarinet part, even though the second and third clarinets may be playing the same musical line that appears in his part. The same is true of singers in choral groups.

Student musicians seldom realize that there is much they can learn by following what goes on in class, even though it may appear not to pertain to them. The teacher should not hesitate to ask questions of unoccupied students. "Altos, at what place are the tenors missing the rhythm?" "Mary, why should the second and third trumpets play the accompaniment figure staccato?" Drawing attention to other sections is especially important in instrumental music because each player sees only his own part.

There are striking differences among the members of most high school music groups. On the one hand is the gifted musician with years of private instruction and summer music camp experience, who can sightread just about everything the group performs. At the other extreme is the below-average student with little musical background. Able students can be excused from some rehearsals to (1) practice individually, (2) participate in a small ensemble, (3) study aspects of music such as those suggested in *Performing Music with Understanding*, and (4) coach the less able or younger students. Many a teenager has been motivated toward a career in music education through serving as a student conductor, section leader, coach, or cadet teacher of younger students. Such experiences are beneficial to everyone involved. The less able students who remain with the teacher in rehearsal also benefit, because the teacher has more time to help them.

Reviewing Learned Music

After the students have grasped the basic style of a piece and are able to execute the correct pitches and rhythms, they should review the work to retain what they have learned. The amount of forgetting that is characteristic of the mind, as pointed out in Chapter 9, means that review is certainly a part of every teacher's job. Not only will some of the learning be forgotten by the next time the class meets, but a few students may be absent and miss the initial presentation entirely. The teacher need not go back to the very first step of the learning process. Instead, he might have a small group or section perform its part alone. In choral music, for example, the piano can play the accompaniment with the singers. If the result is satisfactory, then two sections can perform their parts together. The parts can be hummed while the section in need of help sings the words. Essentially, what the vocal or instrumental teacher does is move *quickly* through some of the teaching procedures.

Another helpful device in reviewing music is to have a section stand while performing its part (cellos excepted). This provides a change of position and allows the standing students to be heard more easily. It also strengthens the confidence and independence of a section and encourages alertness and better posture.

Critical Listening by Students

To allow for critical listening, the teacher can set up "teams" consisting of four to eight students. They should be drawn from a cross section of instruments or voice parts to avoid depleting an entire section. They can be called on quickly to hear the rest of the class perform, or possibly to perform themselves. The team listening should be invited to stand near the teacher to hear better.

After listening to the class perform, the team members can offer comments. Sometimes the listeners will accuse the group of making some error that it did not make, or they will fail to notice a glaring mistake, especially when first given the chance to listen. The teacher should not be discouraged when this happens. As long as the students are learning what to listen for in music, and are improving in sensitivity and in the accuracy of their evaluations, the procedure is achieving its goal. The teacher must guide the students in this evaluative listening process. Here is an example of what might take place after a team has just listened to the rest of the choir.

MISS GORDON: Now, what was the biggest error in the singing?

PETER: The alto part was too weak, I think.

MISS GORDON: Well, that's partly true. But that isn't what I was thinking about.

DIANNE: Well, the tenors let their tone sag as they went for the high note.

MISS GORDON: Yes, a little, but still not what I was thinking of. What was the main fault in the singing?

BILL: They didn't put the "d" on the word "heard."

MISS GORDON: Yes, we're still missing a lot of final "d's." But what I heard was the harsh tone quality. It's entirely out of place in this piece. (*To the singers*) Listen, let's sing at letter E exactly as you did it the last time.

Group sings phrase.

MISS GORDON: (*To the singers*) Now let's do the same thing again; only this time, sing it very gently and warmly. Imagine you're saying goodnight to your boyfriend or girl friend.

Group sings phrase.

MISS GORDON: (*To the team listening*) Now, can't you hear the difference? The first version sounded very much like our school fight song, while the second had a tender, serious sound—just what this piece needs.

Admittedly, this process is more time-consuming than telling the group what to do. But the educational values make it well worthwhile. A student whose opinion is considered is less likely to feel lost in the large group, and he will pay more attention to details if he knows he must understand them to form an evaluation. This type of listening adds interest and variety to the class. In fact, students are sometimes so eager to listen that the teacher will find it necessary to keep a record of the number of times each team is asked to evaluate the group.

Another benefit of this technique is the clarification it gives the words of the teacher. Such problems as balance among sections, precision, phrasing, accents, tone quality, and intonation become more understandable to the student after he has heard them in live performance. Serving on listening teams gives students additional aural experience, which is basic to music learning.

Because a teenager's musical development should include proper listening habits concerning his own performance, he should develop a sense of when he has an important part in the music and when he hasn't. On a level commensurate with his maturity and musical development, a high school musician should be aware of what is happening in the music from the standpoint of both aesthetic understanding and effective performance. The teacher should stop the group and ask, "Who has the melody here?" "What's happening in the music at this point?"

Sensitive judgment is also required for accompaniment—the performance of a subordinate part within a musical arrangement. Just as it is essential to recognize the main ideas of a piece and know who executes them, it is also necessary to allow those ideas to be heard. If a person on a subordinate part cannot hear the melody, it is likely that either he or the other members of his section are too loud. When the students have learned to execute the accompanying part softly enough, the next step is to vary its dynamics, phrasing, and tone quality to correspond to the melodic line.

In contrapuntal music the awareness of thematic material can be developed by bringing out the subject or main theme strongly while the contrasting lines are performed softly. In a choral group, subordinate lines can be hummed. Sometimes the seating can be arranged according to the order in which the sections perform the thematic material. Or the sections can be turned toward each other in a circular arrangement to enable the performers to hear one another better. When their positions are changed, the students may have trouble at first. The piece will sound different to them, and they may feel uncertain.

Objective Listening by the Teacher

Teachers need to listen objectively to their own classes. In one large high school the teachers periodically trade groups. While one director rehearses the students, the regular teacher sits in the back of the room and listens much more objectively than is possible when he himself is on the podium. In a smaller school the choral teacher might exchange classes with the instrumental teacher, or student conductors can be trained. If these procedures are not feasible, the teacher can start the group on a familiar number and back away from the group as far as possible. Holds, rubato passages, and the like can be conducted with oversized motions from the place where he is standing.

The objective quality in listening needs to be emphasized. After the arduous labor required to prepare a performing organization, objectivity does not come easily, but it is necessary if the teacher is to evaluate his group accurately. He might on occasion imagine that he is an adjudicator at a festival. What criticisms would he make? What suggestions would he offer?

As an aid to objective listening, good recordings of the organization are useful for several reasons. They give everyone a chance to listen. The teacher can take them home for study and listen to a passage as often as he needs to. They can be saved as a record of progress throughout the year, and from one year to the next. One recording can be compared with another so that the students can be instructed by hearing changes in their performance. Furthermore, a local radio station may be interested in broadcasting the recording, if the performance and fidelity are satisfactory.

A word of caution: making tape recordings correctly is time-consuming. More than one teacher has suddenly realized on Friday that a whole week has been spent preparing a few tapes. The first tape will probably require more time than succeeding attempts. Additional time must be allowed for listening to playbacks, because students seem to have an irrepressible desire to hear everything that they have recorded. To conserve time, one or two of the recorded pieces can be played back in class, and the entire tape can be heard at noon hour or after school.

Even if the teacher can objectively hear what his group is singing or playing, he faces a second question: How good should the execution of the music be? Should the teacher adhere to the standards of a professional group, or should he accept almost anything short of cacophony? A school group should *execute the notes and rhythms of the music with a pleasing tone quality and with the essential musical expression of the piece.* If the students cannot perform the music to this extent, it should not be performed for the public, regardless of the age of the students or amount of musical progress they have made. No teacher should be lulled into thinking, "Well, they're just kids," and accept sloppy, unmusical performing. Failure to meet this standard indicates the work is too difficult, or requires additional rehearsal, or both. The words "with essential musical expression" are crucial. Debussy should not sound like Sousa; a Palestrina motet should not be sung with the same expressive qualities as a Poulenc choral work.

Individual Attention

Since performing groups are usually larger than other classes, there is a tendency for the student to feel as unimportant as a little stick in a large woodpile. And the teacher often tends to think in group terms. When he says, "You did that well," the "you" is usually plural. As a result, a student may not feel sufficiently responsible for his own work. One way to overcome the problem is to offer short individual assistance sessions.

Bill is an average student and an average clarinet player. Just as the band period ends, John Stafford asks him to remain in his seat for a moment. Bill isn't upset, because Mr. Stafford usually has someone stay after class.

"Okay, Bill," he says, "let's hear the third clarinet part at letter C in the *Water Music*." Bill plays in a satisfactory manner.

"That's fine, Bill! You know some of the clarinets were having trouble with that place, and I wanted to make sure that you could play it. You'd better get to your next class now. Keep up the good work."

This technique is excellent for keeping the students alert, because they realize that anyone can be called at any time. In addition, it lets them know that the teacher is observing their progress and is interested in each person.

Another way to hear students individually is to have them go to another room and tape-record a specified portion of the music, a procedure suggested in Chapter 6 for grading purposes. In this instance, the students would receive only comments, not grades.

Work Outside of Rehearsal

There are several ways to arrange for additional practice. In one school, the sections of the band have a rotating schedule that allows for a sectional practice weekly outside of the regular period. In another school, the junior high vocal teacher is able to attend two practices of the high school chorus each week. Boys and girls are divided and one group moves to another room so that both can rehearse simultaneously. In another school the teacher has the chorus meet three days a week, with another day set aside for work with the boys and another for work with the girls. Some teachers have students practice in a supervised fashion during a free period. The attempt to find a way to work with small portions of an entire group is a matter on which the music teacher will need to advise the administration. It can significantly affect what the teacher is able to accomplish.

The teacher should not overlook the benefits of homework for students in performing classes. Besides practicing parts at home, they can keep a music notebook that includes information on the music studied, facts about composers' musical style, technical problems encountered, and other material. The Teacher's Editions of *Performing Music with Understanding* contain many suggestions for individual work and study.

Time-Savers

Class time in performing organizations can be saved if the teacher will take these easy, practical actions.

(1) Write the titles of the music in order on the chalkboard so that the students can locate it in their folders and put it in order before class begins.

(2) Ask the librarians to service the folders by passing out or collecting music during study period or after school, rather than during class time.

(3) Appoint student assistants to take attendance. One person can be responsible for checking each section in a choral group or large family in instrumental groups. Pupil absences should be indicated on a card for each student or on some kind of class roll, not in the teacher's gradebook.

(4) Provide an electronic tuning device or several tuning bars so that instrumentalists may tune themselves before class.

Rehearsal Procedures

In a rehearsal, where time is at a premium, a director must be both efficient and pleasant. The following example of how *not* to operate a class will indicate some errors a teacher should try to avoid.

Choir is stopped by Mr. King.

MR. KING: Well . . . (*pause*) . . . Why don't we start at letter A and sing it over again . . . (*pause*) . . . Ah . . .

Piano, give us the notes after letter A.

ACCOMPANIST: Do you want to start with the pickup?

MR. KING: Yes, I guess so . . . (*pause*) . . . Anyway, give us the notes.

Three things wrong here:
(1) Director should know what he is going to say before he stops the group; there should be no delay.
(2) There should be a reason given for going over the music again.
(3) Exact starting place was not made clear.

Notes are played. Choir starts singing, but is soon stopped by Mr. King.

MR. KING: I think you should put a crescendo on the words "o'er all the earth," so that "earth" is louder than the three words preceding it . . . Uh . . . I guess we'll start at letter A again.

Good suggestion.

More delay. The students can't help wondering if the man knows what he wants.

Choir sings phrase exactly as before with no crescendo; sings to end of piece.

MR. KING: (*pause; stands looking down at the music*) . . . That was a pretty good job, I guess . . .

What about the crescendo? He guesses it was good. Doesn't he know? Still is working much too slowly.

Well, let's get out "The Heavens Declare the Glory of God"—the Beethoven.

Good number; the students like it.

You know, I ordered this music from Smith's Music House, and they sent me the music all right, but it was in a book with about ten other pieces. So I sent it back to them and told them about the mistake they had made in sending me the right music but in the wrong book, you know. Well, you know what they did? They sent me the right music after a couple weeks of delay, but they billed me for the postage *both ways* on the books *they* had sent me by mistake. Was I ever disgusted! So when I sent the money to them for this music, I didn't send the money for postage, and told them why. They sent me a letter apologizing for their error. Guess you have to be firm sometimes.

Be sure the story will be interesting to the group before you tell it. This one might be—it depends.

Just like the time I got a parking ticket because the parking meter was broken. (*Mr. King goes on in detail about how he refused to pay the fine, and was finally vindicated.*)

What, another? When does the group get to sing? What happened to Beethoven?

Oh yes, we were going to sing "The Heavens Declare." (*He smiles at students . . . pause*) . . .

At last!

Oh, oh, another delay. He'll be lucky if he doesn't have some behavior problems before the period is over.

Now, at the beginning you should sing with a full, round sound. Basses, do the best you can on that low note. The music is in unison so you shouldn't have any trouble with that part . . . Ah . . . Now along about the middle we have a modulation. Does anyone know what a modulation is? John?

How helpful to the students are these comments?

A question — good.

JOHN: It's when the music goes into a different key.

MR. KING: Right! You'll have a good chance to hear this modulation because the piano plays it for several counts before you come in . . . (*pause*) . . . When you have the same note repeated, remember to make a crescendo up to the eighth chord. That word "heavens" should go HEAvens . . . Ah . . . Also you . . . Ah . . . um . . . notice that the first melody comes back here near the end.

Delay again.

Hesitating manner and further delays.

Any questions? . . . (*pause*) . . . Gary?

GARY: Here (*points to the music*) the basses have some little notes written in above the larger notes. What do we do about them?

Good for Gary! Mr. King should have mentioned this.

(*Mr. King walks over and looks at Gary's music.*)

MR. KING: Oh yes! I nearly forgot. Well . . . ah . . . let's just omit them. I think that those notes are there in case you can't get the low ones. You won't have any trouble with those low ones, will you?

He did forget. His lack of preparation on this music is showing.

Any   other   questions? . . . (*pause*)

This technique of openly inviting questions is all right once in a while, but it can turn into a great time-waster if used often.

O.K. Let's get going!

Choir begins singing.

Finally! How many minutes have been lost?

This little drama represents only a few minutes out of a single class. Mr. King's slow pace, personal revelations, indefiniteness, and piling up of suggestions could be tolerated for a little while. But just imagine what it would be like to sit through this sort of thing one hour a day, five days a week for an entire semester or school year! It would take an extremely patient person, or one who simply hardened himself to be impervious to conditions around him, just to stand it, least of all to be interested and educated by the experience.

Mr. King had no discipline problems, even though this type of teaching is an ideal propagator of misbehavior. Neither did he say things that were obviously foolish or contrary to good musicianship. He appears to be a sincere and devoted teacher with an adequate musical background. He did, however, make errors in handling the rehearsal.

One was his slow pace. To the students, music is only as alive as the teacher makes it. If the learning experience does not move, the students either become mentally numb, or attempt to create excitement themselves. *A quick-moving class is a must.*

Another foible of Mr. King's was his indecisive manner. A lack of self-confidence is shown by tone of voice, lack of eye contact, and general attitude of the individual.

A third error was that Mr. King talked too much. This is not to say that a teacher must never talk about personal matters in front of the group. But a beginning teacher should generally avoid this habit until he has had enough experience to sense the type of anecdotes that interest students. Conversational ramblings should be indulged in sparingly, if ever, because they seldom contribute to learning.

There are two ways for a teacher to check himself on overtalkativeness. He can make an audio or video tape recording of an entire class period, and then play it back at a later time. Or he can place a reliable student in the back of the room with paper, pencil, and a watch with a second hand. The student then lists every activity and the amount of time it consumes. For example, a portion of the sheet might look like this:

	Min.	Sec.
Band played first phrase		8
Teacher talked		10
Played first phrase		8
Teacher talked		12
Played to end of piece	3	57
Changed to "Noël Français"	1	2
Teacher talked		48

The amount of time spent in the various activities can then be totaled. The resulting figures are often a revelation to a teacher with a penchant for talking.

Closely related to the problem of overtalking is that of making explanations and directions clear. Mr. King had trouble with this. Directions must be complete and exact; if the group starts at a letter where there is a pickup, they must be told whether the pickup should be included. The instructions should be kept brief, however, in line with the slogan "Don't write; wire."

Developing Music Reading

So far little has been said about music reading. In fact, the steps outlined for choral teaching are basically rote procedures, in which the students hear their part performed and then repeat it. This type of learning is slow, and because it involves small segments of music, it is difficult to keep musical. The best solution is to teach the students to comprehend more fully the symbols seen on the page.

Teach music reading? Isn't that the job of the elementary music teacher? Some students can and do sight-read well, but most teenagers *cannot* read correctly at sight the music put before them. There are several causes for this situation, most of which are not relevant to the main purpose of this book. One fact is pertinent, however: many elementary school children are taught to read music—*music of a difficulty appropriate to the elementary school*. Since the music studied in the secondary schools is more advanced, the reading ability of the students will have to be furthered if they are to perform it at sight. Furthermore, human beings lose a skill that they do not use regularly. No one should be surprised when a student, who has not been in a music class for two years or more, walks into an audition for the glee club and is unable to sight-read some simple music put before him. Certainly no music teacher, who can tell the difference when he fails to practice for two or three days, should expect teenagers with moderate ability and interest to retain for years a complex skill such as music reading.

The ability to read music is a continuum, not a "can or cannot" proposition. Very few people (even trained music teachers!) can individually and unaided sight-read perfectly every piece of music. On the other hand, most persons can ascertain something about the music from looking at it. The elementary schools may be doing their best, but at the secondary level more skill is needed because the group is divided into a greater number of parts, there are changed voices, the works of music are longer, and the technical demands of the music are greater.

Fortunately, the reading ability of a group is always better than the individual abilities of its members. If one person misses a note, his neighbor can often supply it. In addition, students are more confident and have less fear of mistakes when doing something as a group.

Although reading procedures are nearly identical for vocal and instrumental music, a few differences should be mentioned. The main reading problem in vocal music is to maintain pitch. Once a singer loses the proper pitch, he must depend on experience and ability to find it again. Not so with instrumental music. On a clarinet, if a certain arrangement of holes and keys is covered, the player can be sure that he is playing a certain pitch. If he misses a note, he usually can find the next one. The singers can be told, "When the notes go up, move the voice up; when they go down, move the voice down; and when they remain the same, do not change." The teacher can then explain that the staff is a graph of musical pitch. Even this simple and limited approach can produce marked improvement in the singers' ability to comprehend the printed page.

Another reading problem in vocal music is the presence of two lines for each part; one of music and one of words. Not only do the eyes of the singer move from left to right; they must also move up and down to take in the words. To complicate matters, the position of the words below the notes, used throughout elementary school, is now reversed for the boys whenever the tenor and bass parts share a single staff below the body of text. Because of the more complex eye movements required, the students should sing most pieces through the first time on a neutral syllable such as "loo" or "lah."

The reading problem in instrumental music arises from the greater number of parts (in some cases there is only one player on a part) and the need for keeping in mind key signature and correct fingerings. The reading ability of the instrumentalist is determined largely by the speed and accuracy of his reaction to the visual stimuli of notation. A particular F is fingered a certain way, and the wind or brass player reacts to the symbol with a certain combination of fingers and feeling in the lips and mouth.

The way to learn how to read music is to read music. There are no secret systems, tricks, or easy formulas. The author has observed teachers successfully employing a number of different systems for teaching reading. One way to teach interval recognition is to associate each interval with a known song: the perfect fourth is associated with Wagner's "Wedding March," for example, or "I've Been Working on the Railroad." Another reading method is the fixed *do* or solfège, complete with extensive use of chromatic syllables. Another is the movable *do* system used in Hungary and America. Other systems stress tonal patterns. Some teachers ask the students to read letter names or numbers. The fact that such different approaches have been made to work indicates that success lies not in a particular method but rather in persistent practice at reading. Notes and rhythmic patterns must be experienced so often that they can be recalled quickly and easily. Reading can hardly be said to occur when a student requires one minute of time to figure out a rhythmic figure. He is reading only when he recognizes the pattern and executes it almost instantaneously.

To give students experience in reading, the teacher should have them read a piece of music at most of the class meetings. The music should be simpler than the numbers normally performed. When students try to sight-read material that is too difficult for them, they become frustrated because they leave the piece without performing it satisfactorily. Some states, such as New York, have music graded by difficulty for use at festivals. If a group is performing grade V music, then its sight-reading training pieces should be grade III or IV, with an occasional V. As the group progresses, more difficult music can be tried. In every sight-reading effort, the performers should keep going unless there is complete chaos. It's hard for a conscientious teacher with sensitive students to keep going when the music doesn't sound good. The temptation is to stop and give some help to make things sound better. The teacher can call out rehearsal or page numbers, letters, or other assistance, but the music must be kept moving, if at all possible.

Functional Music Reading

Sight-reading technique can be developed on an informal or functional basis. Various patterns in the music can be pointed out, so that the students gain a concept that is transferable from one piece to another. When the problems are derived from actual music, the training seems logical and necessary to the students. This is certainly preferable to formal schemes which in effect say "You learn this because you might need it some day."

Informal coverage will encompass almost all the reading problems found in the school music repertoire. The more complex patterns will have to be taught by rote. They are few in number, however, and do not appear to be a serious drawback. Even with a background of training in a formal scheme, in which the student has covered all the possible combinations of notes and rhythms, he almost always seems to have forgotten the exceptional patterns when he finally encounters them in the music, and the teacher has to revert to rote methods for a moment.

The functional approach has another feature to its credit: it allows for retention of the whole-part principle. Students should learn to read rhythm and pitch together, because that's the way music is. A teacher may temporarily isolate a rhythmic problem so that it can be studied. But the occasions during which rhythm and pitch are separated must be short. These elements have to be quickly associated again with the music.

Even the functional, informal approach requires teaching such basic music knowledge as common note and rest values, meter signatures, accidentals, interpretive signs, and note names. This much knowledge is necessary so that the students will have a basis for their concepts. Although much of this information has been learned in elementary school, review is often necessary.

As for the teaching of rhythm, it is important to stress the 2:1 ratio, which is the basis of rhythmic notation, and to clarify the role of the beat in determining the duration of notes. In this way, a student is not so disturbed when, after being told that a quarter note lasts for one beat, he encounters music in 3/2 meter. Dotted notes can be explained as an addition to the note. Actually, some students just have to learn that a dotted-half note usually receives three beats and a dotted quarter one and a half beats.

Counting Systems

To help the students read rhythm, the teacher should teach them a system for counting it. Several methods of counting rhythm are available. The beats are almost universally counted off "one," "two," "three," and so on. Eighth notes in duple time are usually counted by adding "an" or "and." Sixteenth notes are easily counted by "one-ee-an-da," or "one-a-an-da," and triplets by "one-tee-toe," or "trip-o-let" or "one-la-lee." Unless one syllable such as "ta" is used for every note, the counting system should avoid using the same word symbol for different rhythmic figures:

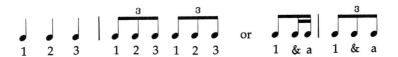

A trained musician can count these patterns correctly, but a beginning student is more confused than helped by them.

Occasionally words can be associated with rhythmic figures, such as

Am - ster - dam.

The following rhythmic pattern is seen often:

It can be remembered as the "here-comes-the-bride" phrase because of its prominence in Wagner's well-known "Wedding March" from *Lohengrin*.

It is important in teaching rhythmic understanding to separate the beat from the execution of a rhythmic pattern. Many students are not clear on this point. They are inclined to think that music with a pounding, obvious beat has lots of "rhythm." To keep the distinction as clear as possible, the teacher can have the students tap the beat with one foot and confine the execution of the notes to either the mouth or the hands. Inexperienced students find it difficult to produce even a rudimentary rhythmic pattern while simultaneously maintaining a steady beat.

A concept of rhythm can be promoted through warm-up routines without notation. The teacher calls out the type of note just before the beginning of a measure.

Singers can also perform with neutral syllables if desired: "may," "me," "mo," and so on. Instrumentalists play the note values as written.

The exercise offers practice in counting and thinking ahead, both of which are necessary for accurate reading of rhythm. It can be varied by moving the pitch up a semitone on each measure and then returning by half steps to the original pitch. Triplets may be added later.

The best method for presenting 6/8 or compound meter has long been debated by music educators. What is sometimes forgotten is that since they first learned "Pop Goes the Weasel," students have been singing and hearing music in compound meter. So they know about it through experience, even if they don't recognize it in notation. The most practical approach to 6/8 meter is to consider it as six beats in a measure, with a strong emphasis on "1" and "4," sometimes stressed by tapping the foot. In this way, counting 6/8 meter remains the same whether the tempo is slow or fast. The 2:1 ratio is maintained when this is done:

With a little practice the students can read 6/8 or 9/8 as easily as any other meter.

Reading Patterns

Psychologists have discovered that when a person reads, his eyes do not move letter by letter or word by word, but rather by groups of words.[2] The better the reader, the larger the groups of words he encompasses in a single eye movement. The same principle applies to music reading. A musician is taught at first to react to each note, but eventually he learns to group notes together and perform them as a single entity by drawing on his previous experience with music. Thus, when a competent flutist sees:

he can grasp the eight notes at once and react with the proper kinesthetic movements in the fingers and embouchure.

The perception of interval patterns is especially valuable to the vocal student, because he does not read by a set reaction of fingers but rather by a sense of relative pitch, which utilizes his mental imagery of the tone and his memory of the physical sensation involved in singing it. The pitch B just

---

[2]The first experimental evidence was provided by William A. Schmidt, *An Experimental Study in the Psychology of Reading* (Chicago: University of Chicago Press, 1917). See also William S. Gray, *The Teaching of Reading and Writing: An International Survey,* Monographs on Fundamental Education, X (UNESCO, 1956), Chapter III.

above the bass clef feels one way for the male singer, and B on the second line feels another. Through experience in associating notes and their sounds, the singer develops a sense of pattern that helps him read. Although successful reading does not usually consist of an "interval-plus-interval-plus-interval" approach, common intervals and patterns should be pointed out by the teacher as they occur in pieces of music. For instance, when the basses begin to see and hear the similarity between

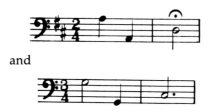

and

they are learning to read music. The same is true for reading rhythmic patterns. The more the students see a particular pattern in different settings, the more quickly they can understand and read it.

A vocal teacher can offer some direct reading practice by writing a major scale on the chalkboard in C, or any key that is comfortable to sing. Under the notes he writes solfège syllables or the numbers 1 2 3 4 5 6 7 1̄. (A dash above or below a number indicates a pitch in an upper or lower octave.) Solfège syllables are satisfactory if the students are familiar with them, otherwise they should be avoided, since the students feel that they are too mature to spend the time that is required to make the syllables meaningful. They are more suitable vocally because their pure vowels are without diphthongs, and there are no two syllable words such as "seven." On the other hand, numbers are in the same language in which the students sing most of their music, and a number series by its nature implies a relationship between the numbers. When used to define the distances between scale steps, a number system clarifies the concept of intervals.

The teacher can start by asking the singers to sing a major scale with the numbers. This establishes a feeling of key center. Once the tonic feeling is established, the students will have some basis for relating intervals to one another. By pointing to notes on the board, the teacher can direct the class to sing simple three- or four-note groups which begin and end on the tonic: 1 3 1, 1 3 5 1, 1 2 3 1, 1 2 3 4 5 1. Later, longer and more difficult patterns can be sung at sight—1 2 4 5 7̲ 1, 1 3 5 6 1.

After some practice with a scale written on the board, simple tonal patterns in various keys can replace the scale. These patterns should not be haphazard groups of notes, but short combinations similar to those found in the music the group is singing. When the patterns are sung in unison, the bass clef may be used occasionally in place of the treble clef, because it will do no harm to have the girls become familiar with the bass clef, too.

Because of transposition and greater clef differences, the instrumental teacher finds it harder to use the chalkboard for simple reading work. Fortunately, many supplementary books have been published in recent years. Some of these stress technique, while others emphasize rhythm, style, scales, or chords. The materials are written at varying levels of difficulty.

Sight-reading practice should not become separated from the main thrust of the classroom effort — fostering skills and understanding. Exercises in reading are valuable only to the extent that they teach something better than it can be taught through reading actual music. Good sight-reading is only a tool, a means to learn music. Reading will help the student reach that goal, but it will not replace it.

Teaching Musical Understandings

This chapter has discussed techniques for teaching students to perform music. Performing, however, is not all there is to music, and it should not be the only aspect of the subject that is taught in secondary school performing groups. Just as one should eat more than one type of food, students should be given more than one aspect of music. The plea here is not to do away with performing music, or to be satisfied with carelessness and minimal skills. Rather the hope is for some enrichment of what has been the traditional musical experience of students in a band, orchestra, or choral group.

Most college music majors — after years of experience in performing organizations — have some notion of how to rehearse a group. Not so with the idea of bringing additional musical learning into a rehearsal situation. Because only a few directors have made an organized effort to include basic musical information in the rehearsal, both prospective and experienced teachers have had little chance to observe and evaluate how such information is taught.

Here are some guidelines for teaching more than performance skills.

(1) As much as reasonably possible, integrate understandings about music theory and literature with the pieces of music being rehearsed. One director, who believes that his band members should know the fundamentals of notation, sets aside two rehearsal periods following each big concert. The students are told to leave their instruments in their lockers on those days, which are spent learning to write scales and figure out meter signatures. Although he should be commended for realizing that his students need to do more than play their instruments, his method leaves something to be desired. First of all, the students are tacitly led to believe that theory consists only of scales and meter signatures. A more basic flaw, however, is that looking at a suspension or a rondo *apart from works of music* is not very successful with most teenagers. A trained musician finds segments meaningful

because he can relate them to music he knows. But most secondary school students can't do this because they don't have enough background in music.

(2) Organize active learning. The director mentioned above was content with a passive study of theory, which does little to interest the average student. If the learning revolves around the music being rehearsed, the material comes alive through playing or singing. One of the advantages of a performing group is its potential to perform *and* study a piece of music. The sum of the two aspects of music is educationally greater than either activity alone, and students do learn more in this way. Sometimes it is impossible for a group to perform a particular work. Perhaps it's too difficult, or written for another medium. In such cases, a recording should be played.

(3) Plan the content for such learning according to a definite scope and sequence. Tossing out tidbits of information won't "add up" for most students because, again, they don't have the background to assimilate bits and pieces. Also, the "tidbit approach" often results in gaps and repetition in coverage. Long-range planning is necessary.

(4) Provide in-rehearsal follow-up. A textbook such as *Performing Music with Understanding* is helpful for presenting information, but the importance of personal contact in reviewing the material can hardly be overestimated. No book can do the job by itself. Thirty or 45 minutes each week spent demonstrating and discussing what has been learned can make a significant difference in the students' understanding and retention.

(5) Include both the student's performing skill and his nonperformance knowledge in determining his grade. This makes clear the importance of such understandings as the difference between polyphony and homophony, the tertian pattern of chords, and the characteristics of a concerto grosso or cantata.

Thomas Morley's late Renaissance madrigal "April Is in My Mistress' Face" (pages 271–273) can illustrate how basic learnings will be related to performance. The exact information that the students learn along with and by means of this piece of music will vary according to what they have learned previously and will learn in the future, and the results are further affected by all the other variables cited in this book. In addition to performance skills, some of the learnings that can be derived from this madrigal are:

(1) Notation, including key signatures.

(2) Polyphonic style, especially the imitative entrances that are clearly present in measures 23–35.

(3) Intervals and minor chords. Especially noticeable are the intervals prevalent in counterpoint (measures 1–2, for example). The students can learn to identify basic intervals such as thirds and fourths without specifying whether they are major, minor, perfect, and so on.

(4) The madrigal as a type of music literature: its text, the number of singers originally involved, the typical performance setting, a few composers, and similar information.

(5) Characteristics of Renaissance music and other fine arts. In Morley's

madrigal students can see the partially systemic harmony, the lack of a stable tonality (measures 9–11), a restrained style, and suspensions (measures 29 and 37). The characteristics of the Renaissance period can be presented, and the rehearsal room given some interest by hanging a few Renaissance prints on the walls.

(6) Aesthetic aspects of the music: the effect of the falling lines in measure 21, the overlapping entrances in measures 23–24, the suspensions, the missing third in some chords, the ascending bass line in measure 11,

April Is in My Mistress' Face

Thomas Morley (1557–1603)

and the change to major on the final chord. In the case of aesthetic qualities it isn't so much knowing so that one can answer questions about them, but rather noticing and being aurally sensitive to these qualities in the music.

Instrumental teachers may wonder how studying a madrigal applies to them. First of all, "April Is in My Mistress' Face" has been transcribed for band (*Two Madrigals* arranged by McLin, published by Pro Art). Transcriptions of Renaissance music for band or orchestra are rare, which is unfortunate. Although transcriptions are not as appropriate as original music for a particular medium, it is better to use transcriptions than to neglect an area of music entirely. If the instrumental teacher chooses not to perform a madrigal transcription, at least once in two years the students should hear a madrigal from a recording, so that they learn a little about this type of music. For study purposes an instrumental teacher can show the choral version on an overhead projector, or make copies, or borrow from the school choral library. The student instrumentalists should figure out which part of the choral version they are playing, and then look over the text carefully for clues to the appropriate style. In fact, it's a good idea for band and orchestra members to sing through the madrigal. They will be better musicians for doing so.

Flexibility and imagination are necessary in deciding when to include nonperformance learnings. Many teachers find that devoting half a period twice a week is most successful. Others prefer to spend five or ten minutes during each rehearsal period. Directors find that even a few minutes of such study can add welcome variety to rehearsals. During the week or so prior to an important program, the study of theory and literature may not be undertaken at all, but during other weeks the teacher may give it substantial attention. Sometimes the students become so interested in what is being discussed that it's difficult to stop after a short time. When this happens, a good portion of the class period can profitably be spent on the material.

For "April Is in My Mistress' Face," two short sessions of about ten minutes each might be spent helping the students hear and understand its polyphony. Other sessions can be devoted to (1) recognizing that the most frequent intervals are thirds and sixths, (2) determining the pattern of the minor triad, and (3) learning about Morley and the Elizabethan madrigal. Of course this list can be expanded or contracted according to the director's wishes.

It's a simple proposition, but one that sometimes gets lost in the rush to get ready for the next concert—a school performing organization exists for educational purposes. More important than high ratings at a state contest or hearty applause from an audience is the learning that takes place in the students' day-to-day encounter with music. Because most performers seldom take other music classes during the years they are in these groups, their education should include broad and basic information about music. Acquiring technical skills—fingering dexterity, pure vowel production, and brisk détaché bowing—is not enough for a good education in music.

Selecting Music for a Particular Group

A music teacher should select music for its usefulness in furthering the music education of the students. Two requirements must be met for a piece of music to contribute to the students' musical education: the music must be high quality (a topic discussed in Chapter 4), and the music must be suitable to the musical understanding and technical ability of the group. No music teacher should choose a number that sounds best with 100 musicians and attempt to perform it with 30. Neither should he pick music that is far beyond the ability of the student musicians. Some of the points a teacher must consider apply to selecting both vocal and instrumental music. They are as follows:

Repetition.   If sections of a work are repeated, this clearly will cut down on the amount of time required to learn the music. If a rhythmic or melodic pattern is repeated often in the piece, this also reduces the amount of music to learn. Repetition is especially helpful if the music is to be memorized, as is often the case in choral music. One of the annoying problems in memorization occurs when the melody returns with different harmony parts; it is easy for the students to become confused.

Length.   All other things being equal, the longer the work, the longer it will take to learn it. In addition, there exists a certain amount of fatigue and loss of interest in learning music that requires a lot of time and effort. Teenagers, especially in junior high, are not noted for their ability to stick to one activity for a long time.

Rhythm.   Adolescents are attracted to music that has rhythmic interest. They are able to perform difficult patterns, if these occur in almost all parts simultaneously, and if they contain much repetition. Rhythmic problems begin to appear when greater independence is required of the performer.

Meter.   Meters that are less familiar to the students require more learning effort. Students find the music somewhat more difficult when the meter or the tempo require that the beat note be an eighth, half, or dotted note. A few choral works are written with no meter sign, and this sometimes bothers inexperienced musicians.

Musicianship of Students.   There is an essential quality in music that is more than pitches and their durations. The piece "How Lovely Is Thy Dwelling Place" from Brahms' *Requiem* requires a concept of tone color and, more than that, maturity of feeling. The notes of this work can be sung by a good high school choir, but the proper expression is not easily attained. If such a number is undertaken, it will need to be worked on intermittently over a period of time, so that the music has time to "settle" in the students.

A work that is soft, slow, sustained, and subtle demands much musicianship and control. Debussy and Palestrina were great composers, but much of their music requires subtle interpretation, slow tempos, and sustained phrases. This is not to say that teenagers should not perform anything that is too mature for them, but there is a limit to which adolescents can be pushed in subtleties, symbolism, or profound emotion. The teacher wants to broaden horizons for the classes, but he does not want to lose the students in the process.

Quality of Music.   There are some works of music that are so logically written, and so clear in their musical intent, that many of the technical barriers are overcome. This explains why some high school choral groups can sing choruses from Handel's *Messiah* and why some bands can play difficult contemporary compositions. The phenomenon may be due in part to the added zest of working on such music. Because most school groups must expend quite a bit of effort before a piece of music is ready for performances, the music itself should have lasting quality. Much entertaining music that has only a glittering surface cannot maintain its original appeal.

Vocal Considerations

Text.   It is necessary to determine the purpose of the work, then to evaluate it. Here are two texts comparable in purpose, but hardly similar in quality.

How Do I Love Thee?

How do I love thee? Let me count the ways.
I love thee to the depth and breadth and height
My soul can reach, when feeling out of sight
For the ends of Being and Ideal Grace.
I love thee to the level of every day's
Most quiet need, by sun and candlelight.
I love thee freely, as men strive for Right;

I love thee purely, as they turn from Praise.
I love thee with the passion put to use
In my old griefs, and with my childhood's faith,
I love thee with a love I seemed to lose
With my lost saints. I love thee with the breath,
Smiles, tears, of all my life! and, if God choose,
I shall but love thee better after death.
                    —Elizabeth Barrett Browning

When Roses Bloom

When roses are in bloom, my love, I think again of you,
And hear the lark that once did sing of love so pure and true.
'Twas in a garden far away beside a trellised wall
Where first we pledged eternally our hearts, our lives, our all.

And now the spring is here again; my heart should be in bloom,
But deep within my soul there is no rose amid the gloom,
Nor is there any lark to sing, since we did drift apart.
How silent now the garden spot that dwells within my heart!

The difference between the two examples is clear. The first is profound and imaginative, while the other is trite. Teenagers are more discerning about good and bad poetry than adults sometimes realize. They may not be able to say why one poem is better than another, but they sense the difference.

Teenagers, especially boys, are often critical of the words to which music is set. Unfortunately, students tend to be critical of any text which is abstract or symbolic. "Lo, How a Rose E'er Blooming" is a fine text, but its symbolism must be carefully explained to the singers to avoid a lackadaisical effort on the song. In schools with little choral music tradition, it is wise to select good music with concrete texts, ones that the students can comprehend easily. A distinction should be made between texts that are abstract and those that are serious. Teenagers usually will undertake willingly a serious text that they can understand.

Some works of music have texts written in dialect. Too often these attempts at writing in the vernacular are grossly inaccurate, because most dialects contain tonal characteristics that are impossible to indicate fully on the printed page. Furthermore, adolescents can seldom phonate them accurately, even though they may spend some time in practicing the strange pronunciations. The teacher should seriously consider whether the use of dialect in a particular number will produce the intended feeling of realism or unintentionally convey an impression of comedy and ridicule.

Range.   The ranges of the various adolescent voices will be discussed in Chapter 14. Generally, the problem is not so much with those few notes that lie at the extremes of the range, but rather with a tessitura that is consistently too high or too low. Singers may be able to hit a few high notes, but they cannot sing many of them in succession without distorting their tone or singing with bad intonation. So in rating music for its difficulty, the tessitura of the parts must be carefully checked, especially when changing voices are involved.

Tenor Part.   The tenor part is very important in SATB music, but few teenage boys have the experience and vocal development to sing it well. Tenor sections in school choral groups vary in their strengths and weaknesses, so each teacher has to know his tenor section. If the section is made up largely of boys whose voices are still changing, then high notes may present no problem. In other tenor sections, high notes are out of the question. One of the problems is that composers and arrangers have never quite agreed on what a tenor voice is. Some tenor music demands a light quality, and some a dark, dramatic quality; some parts go to a sixth above middle C, others go to an octave below middle C. Adolescent tenors usually sing best about B flat or A below middle C, and they cannot be relied on for much volume.

Accompaniment.   Choral groups that are not musically advanced will usually sound better in a work that is accompanied. The piano gives them a feeling of confidence and supports their sometimes shaky pitch. There are two conditions under which an accompaniment might hinder rather than help a choral group. One is when the accompaniment is quite different from the singers' parts. In some modern works the rhythm is not the same, and the singers have to sing intervals such as E natural against an E flat in the accompaniment. The other occurs when the piano part is too difficult for the accompanist to play well, a not uncommon condition.

Chromaticism and Modulations.   Teenage singers can usually handle a small amount of chromatic movement and modulation to closely related keys. They find it more difficult, however, to sing accurately a piece containing many chromatics, frequent modulations, or modulations to remotely related keys. This is especially true if the work is sung *a cappella*.

Intervals.   Singing augmented seconds and fourths and unusual leaps in a melodic line presents obvious difficulties. A less conspicuous problem is created when certain intervals are sounded harmonically. The trouble lies not so much in the actual intervals themselves, but in the way they are approached. The minor second in the following example can usually be sung with accuracy:

But when the approach differs, the same harmonic interval may become extremely difficult to perform well.

The character of the lines also affects the difficulty of the interval. For instance, if the singers are divided into two groups, and one group sings "Three Blind Mice" in G while the other sings "America" in F, they could probably sing the dissonances without too much difficulty. However, if the same dissonances occur between two lines that are unfamiliar or have little melodic character, the students find them almost impossible to sing accurately.

Unfortunately, the interval problem makes it difficult for secondary school groups to sing some fine works of the twentieth century. This does not mean that all difficult intervals should or can be avoided. On the contrary, every group should sing some modern works each year. They may be difficult, but they are worth the effort if the teacher plans properly for them.

Arrangement by Voice Classification.   Octavo music is classified by and arranged for different types of choral groups. In general, the more voice parts a piece contains, the more difficult it will prove to be. A TTBB work for boys' glee club is decidedly more difficult than a TB work. This is true for several reasons. The number of singers on each part is cut in half, requiring more independence from each singer. The length of time required to learn the notes may be much longer because there are twice as many parts. Also, the highest and lowest parts are likely to be harder since the notes must necessarily be closer to the extremes of the voice range, and with each additional part there is a greater chance of error in notes or pitch. For inexperienced glee clubs, then, two part music is much more suitable. The change from SA to SSA or from TB to TBB can be made without extensive reorganization of the group. In the girls glee club some sopranos and altos will be able to sing second soprano on three part numbers. The same is true of the boys in changing from TB to TBB music.

In boys' voices the tenor voice is usually the slowest to develop. Some mixed choruses, especially in the smaller schools, have a hard time finding enough tenors to make up a section. Arrangers have attempted to overcome this problem by providing SAB arrangements, in which boys with changed voices take the baritone part and boys with unchanged voices take the alto or sometimes the soprano. Although these arrangements are not completely satisfactory in harmonic structure, they do provide acceptable music for such groups.

The change from SAB to SATB is not made as easily as the change of voice groupings within a boys' or a girls' glee club. There is usually a greater difference between SATB tenor parts and SAB baritone parts than there is between the first and second tenor parts in glee club music. The change can be facilitated if the teacher emphasizes to the prospective tenors that the "B" in SAB stands for baritone and not bass. However, it is no easy matter to create a tenor section out of a group of boys who are used to singing baritone. For this reason, SAB arrangements should not be used to the exclusion of all SATB arrangements, unless the prospects for a tenor section are nil.

Occasionally arrangements for one voice grouping may be used successfully for another grouping. For example, an SATB arrangement can sometimes be used by a boys' glee club that contains unchanged, changing, and changed voices. The music may have to be transposed, depending on the demands of the soprano and bass parts. The unchanged boys' voices can sing the soprano line, the changing voices sing the alto line, and the changed voices the tenor and bass parts.

If the first tenors in the boys' glee club are weak, the most suitable arrangements are those that place the melody in the baritone or second tenor part.

Musical Arrangement.   Arrangements that teenagers sing best are solid, "clean," and uncluttered with close harmony or excess parts. Members of school choral groups are not always talented, well-trained singers, so the

Prairie Home

presence of complicated effects and extra parts can make the music sound worse, not better. There is nothing wrong with some of these arrangements, except that they are not suitable for most secondary school groups.

"Prairie Home" (p. 281) is essentially a simple American folk song that has been subjected to a grandiose treatment. This song is effective as a solo with a simple accompaniment played on the guitar. The choral arrangement would sound better if it had emulated the solo version of the song. The melody here is almost lost in the complex fabric of parts. The parts are not merely doublings in different sections or at the octave, as they often are in eight part music, but rather they present as many as six distinct lines. The first and second soprano parts represent the type of passage that must be sung well, or it will sound terrible. Effects such as this do not usually enhance the music, and a few of them go a long way with most listeners. Then there is always the question: Is the effect achieved worth the time and effort required to learn it properly? In many cases the answer is "no."

Too many teachers and arrangers have forgotten the beauty of hearing the simple done tastefully. A well-sung unison is thrilling and beautiful.

The plea here is not to do away with eight part music; there are some fine works that must be sung in eight parts. Rather the plea is for clean, simple arrangements, and the elimination of musical bric-a-brac. There is no virtue in singing a work in eight parts when four parts will do just as well. Collegiate and professional choral groups can easily sing the more complex arrangements, but not most secondary school glee clubs and choirs.

Instrumental Considerations

Key.   The easiest key for a band is B flat, while G and D are easiest for strings. The next easiest keys move toward more flats for the band and more sharps for the strings. In both cases the construction of the instruments and the traditional keys used for instruction encourage this difference.

Scalewise Runs.   Sometimes the assumption is made that if the page looks rather black (that is, if it contains many sixteenth notes), it is automatically difficult. Although this is sometimes true, it makes a difference whether the notes jump around without much pattern or move scalewise. Almost all students have at least minimal experience in playing scales, so they know scales better than any other musical pattern. If the passage is in an easy range and key, the demand for alacrity in playing does not present too serious a problem.

Range.   On woodwinds and strings, range affects the timbre and quality of intonation, and involves certain technical problems of fingering. On brasses, however, range is of first importance. Tones that are too high for the brass player may be missed entirely or played with strain and poor intonation. A high tessitura in a brass part is exhausting for the less mature player.

Amount of Technique.   The length of difficult passages must be considered. For example, the clarinets might rather easily play

but have trouble playing sixteenths of similar difficulty if they appear on four or eight consecutive beats. The longer runs require just that much more skill and training.

Musical Arrangement.   As with choral music, the easier, and often the better, arrangements for teenage instrumentalists contain clear, basic outlines without needless decoration. There is, of course, considerable variation between music that is suitable for players with only a year or two of experience, and music that is possible for select players at the high school level. The simpler music requires fewer different parts and less independence of each part. The reduced number of independent parts may not be readily apparent in the score; even though the same number of instruments may be mentioned, many of the parts are doubled. With less experienced players, doubling is desirable because of the additional support it provides. But when the players are more advanced, it steals color and interest from the group's performance. An overuse of doubling tends to make the group sound the same no matter what it is playing.

Another difficulty in judging an instrumental arrangement is the disparity in the number of instruments on a part and in their amount of tone. On the score, the first trumpet, oboe, and flute each occupy a line and appear to be equals. The flute, however, is not as strong as the oboe, which in turn is not nearly as strong as the trumpet. Neither can the E flat alto clarinet play a concert B flat below middle C as fully as can the six third clarinets. The teacher must understand instruments well enough to evaluate an arrangement for its potential to permit the important parts to be heard. He is advised to be on the lookout for bassoon solos that are accompanied by the brasses!

The band has suffered throughout its existence from an unstable instrumentation. The fluegel horn, saxhorn, valve trombone (often written in treble clef), C melody saxophone, E flat alto (peck) horn, B flat soprano saxophone, E flat soprano clarinet, E flat cornet, bass saxophone, all have come and gone. But the significant change has not been in the instruments that have undergone trial in the organization; the orchestra has tried out a few instruments itself, such as the tenor saxophone, cornet, and euphonium. The important change has been in the concept of what the band is, which in turn has greatly affected the nature of musical arrangements for bands.

For many years the band was thought of in "town band" terms; that is, a small but noisy group that existed primarily to give concerts on hot summer nights in the town park. It played a repertoire consisting of novelties, light overtures, marches, and an occasional dazzling solo. Nobody took it very seriously.

Following World War I and on into the 1940s, the band took on a new dimension. However, it could not shake some of its old habits, one being that it must produce a big enough sound to be heard well outdoors. Because good original compositions for band were rare, the repertoire became heavy with transcriptions—"Elsa's Procession to the Cathedral" from Wagner's *Lohengrin*, and many more. This style of band, which is probably still the dominant one in secondary schools, calls for many players, sometimes nearly 100. When the band is good, the effect is that of a mighty organ. Because of its strong and sensuous tone, it is at its best with transcriptions of nineteenth-century masterpieces and Bach organ music.

Since World War II another concept has appeared in bands and band music. It strongly favors original compositions, which of course are largely by contemporary composers. Since these composers live in the twentieth century, they do not write for the romantic sound of yesteryear. Their music calls for fewer players and a less lavish use of instruments. This concept of a band sometimes prefers to call itself a wind ensemble. No longer is it interested in the lush, rolling effects of the generation before; rather, it is more intellectual and detached in its approach.

The instrumental music teacher, especially at the high school level, will find music that fits both concepts of band. What he chooses will depend on his own taste, and the size and ability of his group. Unlike the orchestra director, who can look at the first violin part and know that the composer intended it for 14 or so players, the band director has to consider the music and its style and arrangement in order to determine what the intention of the music is. "Elsa's Procession to the Cathedral" is intended for a big band, and is not as effective when done with 45 players. And the reverse is true: Persichetti's *Divertimento for Band* is not as effective when played by 100 players. It is not a question of which style is "right," because both have musical value when properly used, but rather getting the right music with the right concept.

The orchestra teacher's most serious problem is having too few strings to balance the wind and percussion, which are usually at full strength. Therefore, when looking over music, the teacher should check to see that the strings are given a chance to be heard. Some of the earlier arrangements for school orchestras seemed most concerned with keeping the music sounding, no matter how many strings might be lacking. The result was a "band with strings" effect that did not do justice to the orchestra. One collection written some years ago had violins on the melody part, and no viola part, yet the music could be played by a band using the wind parts of the set, and thereby do without strings entirely.[3]

A final word on orchestra arrangements. The piano appears infrequently in the symphony orchestra, and should be just as scarce in the school orchestra, except for groups that have studied only a year or two. The arrangement should be complete without the piano. The only justification for using a piano in a school orchestra, beyond those valid for the professional orchestra, is for limited assistance to the strings in learning the music, and for strengthening a particular part that lacks adequate instrumentation.

Program Requirements

Sometimes there is a mistaken idea that certain music needs to be selected to fill a void in a concert, or to round out the program. Much of the problem is solved automatically if the teacher chooses music of different types from different historical periods. Also, each year he can vary his program format. One year the choral groups might do a cantata, another year a program of folk music and dancing. The instrumental groups might present a concerto program featuring three or four outstanding students, and another year the more usual program of concert music.

The teacher should try to determine the musical development of the community. He should maintain the ideal of presenting the best music without losing his students and audience. There should be a little give and take between the teacher with his musical standards, and the students and the community with their lack of experience in music. It is a rare community that appreciates an all-serious program. On the other hand, there is no community in which some serious works cannot be presented.

It is difficult for listeners to sit through an entire concert of unfamiliar music. At Christmas time they want the program to include "The First Noel" or "Silent Night." A good arrangement of "The Battle Hymn of the Republic" is a stirring experience to them because they know the song. The average

---

[3]Cited in Charles B. Righter, *Success in Teaching School Orchestras and Bands* (Minneapolis: Schmitt, Hall & McCreary, 1945), p. 69.

adult listener would much rather hear the familiar, established songs than current popular tunes.

Some teachers attempt to entertain their audiences by performing complex arrangements of "Polly Wolly Doodle" and similar music. They achieve their goal of pleasing the audience, but at what a price! There is nothing wrong with doing "Polly Wolly Doodle," but why a tricky, big arrangement that demands many hours of valuable class time? In choosing the few songs that are chiefly for audience appeal, whether folk or popular, the teacher should select the easiest, best sounding arrangement he can find, and save the hours of rehearsal time for music that is worthy of meticulous care and attention.

Finding Appropriate Music

Where does a teacher find music for his performing groups? First, many pieces of music are presented in methods classes. The college student can start immediately to build up a music list or professional library of numbers that appear to be good and within the capabilities of the teenage student.

Second, there are several graded listings of music appropriate for school groups — lists such as those included in state festival guides. Other suggestions are contained in the following publications:

Choral Music

Charles G. Burnsworth, *Choral Music for Women's Voices: An Annotated Bibliography of Recommended Works.* Metuchen, New Jersey: Scarecrow Press, 1968.

Robert L. Garretson, *Conducting Choral Music,* Second edition. Boston: Allyn and Bacon, 1965.

Arthur Ware Locke, and Charles K. Fassett, compilers, *Selected List of Choruses for Women's Voices.* Northampton, Mass.: Smith College, 1964.

National Education Association, *The CMP Library,* Vol. 3. Washington, D.C., 1970.

Selective Music Lists. Washington, D.C.: Music Educators National Conference — American Choral Directors Association, 1968.

Instrumental Music

Kenneth Berger (editor), *Band Music Guide.* Evanston, Illinois: *The Instrumentalist,* 1964. Addendum published in 1968.

Margaret K. Farish (editor), *String Music in Print.* New York: R. R. Bowker, 1965.

George N. Heller, *Ensemble Music for Wind and Percussion Instruments.* Washington, D.C.: Music Educators National Conference, 1970.

National Education Association, *The CMP Library*, Vols. 1 and 2. Wash., D.C., 1970.

Orchestra Music Guide. Evanston, Illinois: *The Instrumentalist*, 1966.

Mary Helen Rasmussen, and David Mattran, *A Teacher's Guide to the Literature of Woodwind Instruments*. Durham, New Hampshire: *Brass and Woodwind Quarterly*, 1966.

Mary Helen Rasmussen, *A Teacher's Guide to the Literature of Brass Instruments*. Durham, New Hampshire: *Brass and Woodwind Quarterly*, 1964.

Albert W. Wassel, and Charles H. Wertman, *Bibliography for String Teachers*. Washington, D.C.: Music Educators National Conference, 1964.

A third practical step is the "program exchange" idea. Some teachers have standing agreements to exchange printed concert programs. A few music houses and instrument manufacturers publish programs that are submitted to them. Some professional organizations, the National School Orchestra Association among them, make an attempt to circulate programs among the membership.

Fourth, music can be ordered on approval from music stores and publishers. If a teacher does not know what pieces to ask for, the lists of music printed by various publishers can be examined and works by recognized composers selected from them. These numbers should be surveyed leisurely at the piano, then the pieces that seem musically inferior or unsuitable for teenage groups can be returned. Choral teachers can keep those works that have good possibilities, and begin to build a personal library of single copies of choral music. This is somewhat expensive at first, but within a few years a valuable reference file will develop. This file can be catalogued by voice arrangement and difficulty, and comments can be written in the margins. The instrumental teacher can keep a written record on each piece, and maintain a file of free sample scores.

Copyright Law

Before discussing the ways in which music may be changed to better fit the requirements of a group, it is necessary to examine what can and cannot properly be done under the copyright law as it now exists. The law states that copyrighted music cannot be copied. It does not matter whether the music is to be used at a performance for profit or in a classroom, and it makes no difference whether it is mimeographed or copied by hand on manuscript paper or on the chalkboard. It is even illegal to copy the words on a slide and project it, or to print the text of an anthem in the church bulletin on Sunday morning. This is the letter of the law. Fortunately, laws are carried out by human beings and the spirit of the law as presently administered is more flexible.

Music publishing houses do not prosecute school teachers and church choral directors for *slight* infractions of the letter of the law. They are human, and do not want to be Shylocks about the copyright. Nor do they want unpleasant publicity. What the publishers are concerned about are the obvious violations of the law—the teacher who saves some of his budget money by making photocopies, ditto, or mimeograph copies of the music.

If it is absolutely necessary for a teacher to make written changes in the music, he must write the publishers requesting permission. *If* the music is not published in the form in which he needs it, and *if* he has purchased several copies of an existing arrangement, the publisher will almost always give permission. This means that a teacher can, for example, arrange SATB material for SAB, if he has purchased copies of the SATB music, and if no SAB version is available. If an SAB version is available, he should buy the necessary copies or do without.

Music publishers want children to have music. But they do not want them to have it if it means robbing the composer or arranger of the income to which his ability properly entitles him, or depriving the publisher of his return on the investment in each piece.

The copyright law protects a piece of music for a period of 28 years. This period can be, and usually is, extended for another 28 years. After the 56 years have passed, that work or arrangement becomes public domain, and such material can be copied and reproduced at will. As one can surmise, all music copyrighted before 1917 is not now covered by copyrights, and this includes a vast field of fine music. A distinction should be made between music that is copyrighted, and an arrangement that is copyrighted. The original versions of such songs as "Home on the Range" are not copyrighted, but published arrangements of them are. A person can make his own arrangement of such pieces from the original but he cannot copy someone else's arrangement that is covered by the copyright law. The year in which the copyright was issued must be printed on the music, along with the symbol ©.

Adapting Music

There are several ways in which the teacher can simplify the music without infringing by rewriting it. Since the range of the voices in vocal music is frequently a problem, it is sometimes helpful for the accompanist to transpose the entire work. Intonation can frequently be improved by moving the key up or down a half step.

A second way to simplify and often to improve a work is to cut the number of parts or reduce the number of performers in one section of the music. In both instrumental and vocal music the amount of doubling can be reduced. In choral music the singers can be told to sing other parts, while in instrumental music the player will have to rest unless a new part is written out for him.

Two other simplifications are possible in choral music. If a group is not very advanced, a section of a song can be sung in unison by one part or by a combination of parts. The amount of time required to learn the full arrangement may not be justifiable in terms of its worth.

In some numbers the harmony parts are changed when the melody is repeated. The music can be simplified by merely instructing the singers to repeat the harmony parts as they were first learned — sometimes with different words. A good example of this is the Christmas carol "The Twelve Days of Christmas." The song can be complicated or quite easy, depending on the presence of repeated harmony parts.

The music teacher should not be hesitant about trying changes in the music. Perhaps a soloist can perform one portion, or the teacher can compose a descant, a countermelody, or simple harmony parts. The need for teacher-arranged music is greatest at the junior high school level. The changing voices with their range limitations and the unique nature of each group make it desirable for the teacher to try his hand at occasional arranging. The instrumental teacher may also find it advantageous to do some arranging, especially if the group is of unusual size and instrumentation.

Questions

1. In the early stages of work on a piece, why is it suggested that a particular section be worked over only a limited number of times? What principles of music teaching are pertinent to this practice?

2. How would you explain to an uninterested student why it is important for him to follow what is going on when you work with another section?

3. What principles of music teaching are involved when trouble spots are isolated?

4. When practicing music reading by pointing to a scale on the chalkboard, why is the major scale suggested for the initial work? Shouldn't students learn both major and minor? Is a teaching principle involved here?

5. In teaching parts to an instrumental group it is suggested that the melody be rehearsed first, while a choral group should learn the lowest part first. What are the differences between vocal and instrumental music that would account for this inconsistency of approach?

6. In concluding work with one section, it is suggested that the part be played or sung with other parts previously learned. Why?

7. In teaching students to play or sing subordinate parts, should these parts be studied by themselves or in conjunction with the melody? Why?

Projects

1. Select a choral or instrumental work. Decide what information you can teach the students with that particular piece of music.

2. Study the score to a march and a choral number, marking out the melody and other parts as though you were going to teach it for performance. Also mark those spots at which the students may encounter problems of rhythm, pitch, and so on.

3. Select three easy pieces (one each for band, orchestra, and chorus) which would be appropriate for a first meeting of the group.

4. Using the same three numbers, decide how you might present the music so that the students gain a concept of the whole piece.

5. Using the scale-interval technique suggested on page 268, direct the class through some simple melodic figures. Use both clefs.

6. Practice starting your college class on a song with verbal commands and without conducting.

7. Observe a teacher rehearsing a school performing group. Note his effective and efficient actions, and those that are not so. Note the amount of time lost between changes of music and in unnecessary talking by the teacher.

8. Visit two secondary school choral teachers and two instrumental teachers. Find out from them

(a) what arrangements are made for sectional rehearsals,

(b) what homework is expected of the class,

(c) what steps they take to enable themselves to hear their own group as objectively as possible.

9. Find out how compound meters are taught to children in the elementary schools. Attempt to determine whether a consistent approach is used, and how much experience pupils have with compound meters. Recall how you were taught to read such meters, and judge the effectiveness of that method.

Suggested Readings

Andrews, Frances M., and Joseph A. Leeder, *Guiding Junior High School Pupils in Music Experiences.* Englewood Cliffs, New Jersey: Prentice-Hall, 1953, pp. 149–59.

Boyd, Jack, *Rehearsal Guide for the Choral Director.* West Nyack, New York: Parker Publishing Co., 1970, Chapters 6, 9, and 10.

Colwell, Richard J., *The Teaching of Instrumental Music*. New York: Appleton-Century-Crofts, 1969, Chapter 6.

Kuhn, Wolfgang E., *Instrumental Music: Principles and Methods of Instruction* (2nd Ed.). Boston: Allyn and Bacon, 1970.

Roe, Paul F., *Choral Music Education*. Englewood Cliffs, New Jersey: Prentice-Hall, 1970, Chapters 6 and 9.

Singleton, Ira, and Simon V. Anderson, *Music in Secondary Schools* (2nd Ed.). Boston: Allyn and Bacon, 1969, Chapter 6.

Sur, William R., and Charles F. Schuller, *Music Education for Teen-Agers* (2nd Ed.). New York: Harper & Row, 1966, Chapter 12.

12

Teaching Musical Style and Interpretation

Interpretation is the lifeblood of music. Without it, music is like a corpse — a form lacking vitality. Music, dance, and drama depend on someone's ability to re-create them, to bring them to life. The exclusively visual arts need no mediator between the creator and the observer. But in music (except for tape-recorded works), the performer is the intermediary between the composer's directions and what the listener hears. The performer's interpretive skill — his treatment of the music's expressive qualities — can make the difference between a rewarding aesthetic experience and a monotonous waste of time.

Although music has a notational system, it is inadequate. It indicates pitch level and duration rather accurately, but directions about dynamic level and style are broad and subject to personal judgment. Music notation is like the script of a drama. The words are there on the page, along with a few general directions about stage action and the way in which a line should be delivered, but the actor is responsible for bringing the words to life. In the same way, the performer's interpretation is a necessary aspect of music.

What does this mean for the school music teacher? First, it means that as the musical leader of a group he must make the interpretive decisions, just as a professional conductor or solo performer must. Second, he must teach his students to perform the music with correct interpretation and to make valid judgments on their own. The two tasks — deciding on the interpretation and then teaching it — are related, of course. Let's begin by examining the decision making process.

Deciding on Interpretation

Where does a school music director get his ideas about how a piece of music should be interpreted? From the existing body of information about how the work is performed and from his own musical ideas and judgments.

Of the two sources, the former is more reliable. It's a fact: the school music director rarely has as much training and experience in interpreting orchestral music as the conductor of the Boston Symphony, in interpreting band music as the band director at Indiana University, or in performing Chopin's music as the scholar who has studied the interpretation of Chopin's piano works. Therefore, it behooves the school music director to consider seriously how persons in recognized positions of musical leadership have treated a work.

Performance Practices

The largest source for interpretive ideas is recordings. There are regular commercial releases on familiar labels, and "service" recordings provided by publishers.

A second source is the written body of knowledge about performance practices. Conductors of major professional ensembles who make commercial recordings are well aware of the writings and traditions about performance styles in music, so what is heard on the recording is partially a manifestation of that knowledge. In the case of a teacher, interpretive skill is like a return on an investment—it is a practical benefit gained from the hours spent in courses in music history, literature, and theory. Books such as Donald Grout's *A History of Western Music* (New York: W. W. Norton & Company, 1961) and the musical styles series published by W. W. Norton, Prentice-Hall, and others provide information about performance practice. In addition, there are specialized and authoritative books on particular styles or types of music. Some of them are:

General

Richard L. Crocker, *A History of Music Style*. New York: McGraw-Hill Book Company, 1966.

Robert Donington, *The Interpretation of Early Music*. London: Faber & Faber, Ltd., 1963.

Frederick Dorian, *The History of Music in Performance*. New York: W. W. Norton & Company, 1942.

Early and Renaissance

Thurston Dart, *The Interpretation of Music*. New York: Harper Colophon Books, 1954.

Joseph Kerman, *The Elizabethan Madrigal*. New York: Galaxy Music Corporation, 1962.

Gustave Reese, *Music in the Middle Ages*. New York: W. W. Norton & Company, 1940.

———, *Music in the Renaissance* (Rev. Ed.). New York: W. W. Norton & Company, 1959.

Baroque

Manfred Bukofzer, *Music in the Baroque Era*. New York: W. W. Norton & Company, 1947.

Claude V. Palisca, *Baroque Music*. Englewood Cliffs, New Jersey: Prentice-Hall, 1968.

W. Gilles Whittacker, *The Cantatas of Johann Sebastian Bach*. London: Oxford University Press, 1959.

Classical

Reinhard Pauly, *Music in the Classic Period*. Englewood Cliffs, New Jersey: Prentice-Hall, 1965.

Romantic

Alfred Einstein, *Music in the Romantic Era*. New York: W. W. Norton & Company, 1947.

Ray M. Longyear, *Nineteenth-Century Romanticism in Music*. Englewood Cliffs, New Jersey: Prentice-Hall, 1969.

Twentieth Century

Erhard Karkoschka, *Das Schriftbild Der Neuen Musik* (in German). Celle: Hermann Moeck Verlag, 1966.

Frank Pooler, and Brent Pierce, *New Choral Notation*. New York: Walton Music Corporation, 1971.

Instrumental

Richard Franko Goldman, *The Wind Band: Its Literature and Technique*. Boston: Allyn and Bacon, 1961.

Choral

George Howerton, *Technique and Style in Choral Singing*. New York: Carl Fischer, 1957.

Authenticity

How carefully can or should a performer adhere to the sound the composer had in mind? There are strong arguments for authenticity. A Baroque concerto grosso played in a passionate romantic style is hardly genuine. It's like illuminating a great Rembrandt painting with blinking colored neon lights. And it does seem that the judgments of the composer or ethnic group should be honored. After all, they created the music in the first place, and if it is worth performing, it should be done competently and honestly. A black spiritual should not be sung like an English folksong, and a Bach organ fugue transcribed for band should not be souped up with snare drum and cymbal.

There are some counterarguments, however. Maybe Bach would have written for snare drum and cymbal had he been able to work them in. Such a question can never be answered, of course. But more important is the fact that fully authentic performances of early works can never be achieved. In some cases, modern instruments such as clarinets and trumpets are clearly superior to original models and are different both acoustically and technically. Furthermore, it is impossible to know exactly how music was performed 200 years ago. Musicologists can make only educated guesses about the presence and style of vibrato, the execution of certain rhythmic figures and embellishments, and tempos.

Practically speaking, about all that the school director can do is be as authentic as he reasonably can be. He certainly should avoid gross errors in interpretation and style, but he must accept the fact that his teenage voices cannot render authentically all types of music from Irish folksongs to early Renaissance Masses. Similar limitations exist for the instrumental teacher.

Even though there are limitations on the degree of authenticity a student group can attain, the young people should at least know what type of sounds they are trying to achieve, even if they can't execute them perfectly.

Personal Judgment

The director should neither overinterpret nor underinterpret the music. Both extremes are equally undesirable. The director who abuses his license adds many "personal touches" to the music: extreme tempos, additional sforzandos, sustained *m*'s, *n*'s, and *ing*'s in choral music, excessive rubato, exaggerated dynamic changes, and so on. The opposite type of director seems to think that as long as he fulfills "the letter of the law"—gets all the notes sounded in tune and on time—he has done his job. His conducting beat is the same size and style whether the music is loud or soft, staccato or legato, fast or slow. He never talks about the implications of the text. He has a mechanical view of music.

Both of these poles in interpreting music indicate a lack of understanding about music. The director should use, not abuse, his license to interpret. Knowing accepted interpretations of the style in general and the work in particular, he exercises discretion, judgment, and good taste. *Some* latitude is available in tempo, dynamics, articulation, and the like, but radical departures from the norm merely detract from the music.

Techniques of Teaching Interpretation

When the teacher has decided on the proper interpretation, the more difficult task of teaching it begins. Most teachers face several problems at this point. One is the mistaken belief that interpretation is something to be reserved primarily for advanced students. This notion is based on the assumption that skills must be perfected *before* musical expression is considered. An extreme example of technique before interpretation appears in the case of a principal player in a major symphony, a graduate of a fine European conservatory, who assigns his private students only scales and exercises for at least the first two years; no piece of music is studied during that time. Some teachers speak of first giving their students the necessary "equipment" to perform musically. Such thinking is probably better suited to setting up a factory or buying a baseball team bats and balls. It doesn't apply very well to human beings; people learn playing techniques and interpretation at about the same time. If learning style and expression lags behind technical skill, it should be only a brief lag, certainly not two years!

Technical skill and musical expression complement each other, because each provides a sense of purpose for studying the other. Clearly, no teacher should ask a student to do something he is unable to do; a youngster cannot play something in a lyrical style if he can't play the notes. But as much as possible, the teacher should teach a sense of phrasing, style, and expression. Even the simple songs in beginning instrument method books can be played musically instead of the "duh, duh, duh, duh, duh" so often heard.

A second problem is the teenager's apparent lack of interest in subtlety. There are several probable causes. Adolescent behavior is characterized by enthusiasm, impatience, and straightforwardness. And many young people have such a limited musical background that they simply don't know there are different styles in performing music. Furthermore, conditions in a student's environment sometimes encourage him not to notice subtleties. The youngster who lives in a home with a blaring television set or record player and people yelling at each other soon learns not to listen.

A third problem in getting teenagers to interpret music is that they are taught one aspect of expression here and another there, with no attempt to pull together the total effect. They may practice making crescendos and decrescendos in warm-up, but when they turn to a piece of music they are rehearsing, nothing more is said about dynamic changes. The students should be aware of the overall effect of a musical work, so that they can see beyond isolated particulars.

The adjudication forms created by the National Interscholastic Music Activities Commission (NIMAC) of the MENC, three of which are reproduced in Appendix E, categorize the total performance of a group into various elements, so that the adjudicator can discuss them properly. However, at the top of the sheet the adjudicator gives the group one final rating, which represents a summation of all the factors considered. The music teacher must treat the area of interpretation in the same manner by considering the parts that go into it, but then making sure that the whole does become greater than the sum of its parts.

Integrating particular aspects of interpretation into the total musical expression can be aided by the right kind of work on interpretive elements. For example, a choral director may devise some experiences in which the attention of his girls' glee club is devoted almost entirely to dynamics. They gain further understanding of the concept of dynamics, experience the actions necessary to sing softly and loudly, and become more sensitive and proficient in their responses to dynamic markings. If he relates the study of dynamics to the music the group is singing, the members will realize more fully how the dynamic contrasts affect the qualities of the music.

Sensitivity to interpretive concepts can be fostered by focusing attention on them as the music is being learned, and by providing structured experiences that make the students aware of each element. Both techniques are necessary for successful teaching to take place. The major effort of this chapter is to present specific, structured experiences for making students more sensitive to music.

Rhythm

Rhythm is essentially a physical phenomenon, not an intellectual one. Physical experience must accompany or precede learning the symbols that indicate it. Groups that are not musically advanced need many physical experiences with rhythm—tapping feet, chanting words, counting patterns. The rhythmic reading methods suggested on page 265 involve this type of response. There is a need to feel the rhythm, and especially the sensation of the beat, which the musician should maintain inwardly at all times.

When problems are encountered in performing a rhythmic figure, the pattern should be isolated temporarily, and then returned to its proper musical context as soon as possible. The concentrated attention need not be extensive. Here are two examples of this, the first one from Wagner's *Die Meistersinger von Nürnberg* and the second from "Mary Had a Baby."[1]

Count with syllables, then play:

Then practice with the tie:

Count with syllables,
then sing on "tah":

[1]SSA, arr. Theron W. Kirk (Westbury, L. I., New York: Pro Art Publications, Inc., 1959). Used by permission.

Specific rhythmic problems can be approached through rote procedures, in which the teacher demonstrates the proper execution of the figure and the students imitate him. In this way the students get a feeling for style and accentuation at the same time. Most rhythmic teaching should be done in a singsong voice. Suppose that a group of singers is experiencing trouble with the following phrase:

Go down   to   Mex - i - co

The teacher can start by asking the singers to repeat exactly what he says, regardless of rhythm or words. Many times when he works out a rhythmic error he has to break down the wrong pattern before he can establish the correct one. So it is best to start with a simple rhythm entirely different from the problem phrase, in order to break away from the incorrect pattern. A quarter note phrase is simple and enables the students to imitate the teacher and feel the beat (see page 301).

The procedure illustrated should be lengthened or shortened according to the needs of the group and the difficulty of the music. The instrumental teacher can use the same technique. The students say the syllable "ta," then play a unison tone, and then proceed to the particular phrase of music.

Some teachers, rather than have the students singsong the words or repeat a neutral syllable, have them clap out rhythms. This is a good technique, but clapping is not as fast or precise as the articulating action of the tongue.

A rhythmically dynamic work should occasionally be rehearsed without stops so that the surging momentum of the rhythm is not impeded. Small errors on such occasions should wait for correction until the piece is done. Rhythm in such a work should be alive, exciting, and pulsating. A teacher must not lose those qualities by allowing his teaching to become academic and banal.

Blend

Although "balance" and "blend" are used interchangeably by some music teachers, the two words do not mean exactly the same thing. *Blend* refers to the homogeneity of sound, usually within a section, although the term can apply to the uniformity of timbre between sections. *Balance* refers to the distribution of volume and emphasis among the various sections.

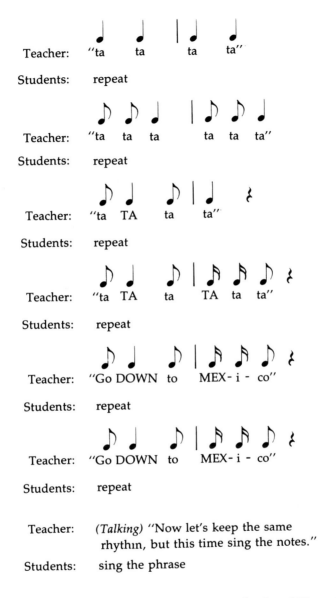

Teacher:	"ta ta ta ta"
Students:	repeat
Teacher:	"ta ta ta ta ta ta"
Students:	repeat
Teacher:	"ta TA ta ta"
Students:	repeat
Teacher:	"ta TA ta TA ta ta"
Students:	repeat
Teacher:	"Go DOWN to MEX- i - co"
Students:	repeat
Teacher:	"Go DOWN to MEX- i - co"
Students:	repeat
Teacher:	(*Talking*) "Now let's keep the same rhythm, but this time sing the notes."
Students:	sing the phrase

Thus Ronald's voice may not blend with Allan's (if it is a different quality), or the cornets may overbalance (be too loud for) the clarinets.

A teacher should not assume that a blending of tone quality is always desirable or necessary. In choral music, some teachers make such a fetish of blend that they drain all the color and character from the voices of the singers. Some instrumental teachers work on blend by striving at all times for a homogeneous tone, even though the instruments are basically different and have highly individualistic tonal qualities. In some cases the desired tonal effects are lost in achieving uniformity.

The most suitable degree of blend is determined largely by the type of music being performed. A reverent, chordal piece requires far better blending of sound than does an exciting, barbaric selection. In the latter work a teacher should not expect or even want a perfect blending. How much more effective it is to let the individual color, emotion, and vitality break through the barrier of blend! Again, good musical judgment must be the guide.

If it is determined that more blend should be achieved, the first step is to make the students conscious of what it is. The teacher should remind them persistently that it is not necessarily the best musician who performs loudest and has the most "piercing" quality. The comparison with a speaker (the best speaker is not always the one who talks loudest) can be made to advantage here. The importance of unity must be emphasized again and again. Each section should sound like one performer, and not like 15 or 20 soloists crowding into the same part. The idea of each performer fitting his sound into the whole group must be carefully nurtured.

In many respects, the secondary school choral teacher does not find the problem of blend as serious as does the collegiate director (or the church choir director!). The lack of mature voices may hinder the school teacher in many respects, but blend is one area in which an immature voice has an advantage. Few teenage singers have an inordinate amount of vibrato or highly individualistic voices.

Chapter 14 presents some basic singing techniques for choral groups. A good technique encourages uniformity of tone production, and this in turn contributes much to the blending of voices, as does a uniform vowel sound. With advanced groups, the teacher may instruct the singers to form a somewhat rounded *oh* position of the lips on vowels such as *ee* and *ih*.

The proper method of tone production improves the blend in instrumental music, too. Unusual embouchures with pinched lips and squeezed tones do not contribute to uniformity. With strings, a healthy tone and a consistently produced vibrato improve blend. Instruments and mouthpieces should be as similar as possible. A brass player with a shallow-cup mouthpiece will not normally blend with a player who has a deep-cup mouthpiece. Nor will trumpets blend well with cornets, or a wide-bore trombone with a narrow-bore instrument.

Several specific techniques will increase the students' consciousness of blend.

(1) Choose two singers with the same range, or two players on the same instrument, who do *not* blend with one another. Have them play or sing a phrase together. Then select another performer who blends well with one of the original two, and have the new duo perform together. In this way, the students can hear blend, or the lack of it, for themselves. One variation of this procedure is for the teacher to sing or play with a student. The teacher can at first use a timbre that does not blend, and then one that does blend with the student.

(2) Start with one voice or instrument and then add another. When the two sounds are blending perfectly, add a third, and so on. This technique is generally more successful with college students than with secondary school students, perhaps because it is time-consuming, and to younger musicians it seems rather far removed from the actual performance of music.

(3) Organize student listening groups, as was suggested in Chapter 11.

(4) Make tape recordings of the rehearsal. When students hear music played back with individual sounds popping out all over, they are more likely to appreciate the problem. Be sure that the recordings are representative of the sound of the group. It would be unfair to leave a microphone so close to one individual that his sound would stand out unduly on the recording.

(5) Work on good unison singing or playing. Outlining triads is excellent for developing accuracy in pitch and blend; singers may try various vowel sounds in so doing. Unison songs are good for choral groups because the same words will be sung by all voices at the same time, and this frequently does not occur in part music. During unison playing or singing, the students can strive for a more homogeneous tone. In band the cornets can be told to sound more like the French horns, and vice versa; in chorus, the tenors can work toward a quality that blends better with the basses.

(6) Develop the group's ability to play or sing softly.

(7) Remind individual students whose tone stands out in a section. If handled with delicacy, students do not mind being asked to hold back, especially if a compliment can be paid them for their above average work.

(8) Encourage the more timid students to sing or play with more assurance.

(9) Work with individual problems in extra, private sessions. In singing, unusual quality can be caused by tension in the throat or overarching of the tongue. An instrumentalist may possess a freak embouchure or an improper sense of tone production. No amount of classwork on blend is likely to remedy these problems. Individual instruction is the most direct and successful solution.

(10) Perform at moderate dynamic levels. Loud playing or singing encourages individual voices or instruments to stand out.

Finally, poor blend is sometimes a symptom of more basic problems, such as poor intonation, bad ensemble, or faulty tone production. In such cases, the teacher must work on the cause and not the symptom.

Balance

The school music teacher faces a problem which the professional conductor is spared: unbalanced sections. Except for select school groups, the teacher must work out the best balance among the singers or players he has available.

Achieving correct balance is largely the job of the teacher, because he is the only one who can listen to the entire ensemble, and it is his aesthetic judgment that will determine what the correct balance should be. Good music education requires that the students learn what balance is, and that they understand why one part should be stressed at a particular moment in a piece of music. But they can't tell if what they are emphasizing in their performance is being emphasized in what the listener hears. Only the teacher can determine this.

The director generally controls balance by indicating either verbally or through conducting gestures that one part should be louder and another softer. There are several ways to fortify a part that needs emphasis. The instrumental teacher can rewrite parts into a better range, or assign two players to a solo passage, or ask an instrument to play a cued-in part. A choral teacher can assign a few students to be "travelers." These singers sit near the boundaries of sections and move from tenor to bass, or from a first to a second part, as necessary. Such changes may slightly alter the timbre of the line. This may or may not be acceptable, depending on the particular passage in the music.

Good balance does not necessarily mean equality of parts. In almost all works, there is an interplay between parts, as one section is more prominent and then recedes to allow another section to bring out its more important line. This interplay exists even in homophonic music when all parts are marked at the same dynamic level. A particular chord member can be more important, as in the case of a Tierce de Picardie or major triad at the conclusion of a work in a minor key.

Balance is often better achieved by reducing the volume of the less important lines, rather than by encouraging the performers of the more important lines to come out more loudly.

Dynamics

Good control of dynamics depends on two things: a consciousness of dynamics on the part of the students, and facility in making dynamic changes. It may be desirable to offer specific training in performing at six dynamic levels (*pp, p, mp, mf, f, ff*) and in making crescendos and decrescendos, accents, and *sforzandos*. Many students are hazy about such matters when they first enroll in music. The choral teacher can make up any combination of dynamic markings to serve as exercises, and write them on the board or call them out verbally. An especially good exercise combines arpeggios with crescendos and decrescendos:

There are several other routines that stress dynamics. One is to hold a long tone or chord for 20 slow counts. The dynamic markings can also be reversed in this exercise. In either case, the training develops the ability to spread out a crescendo or decrescendo and to sustain long tones.

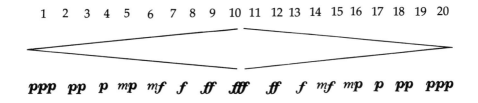

Another exercise is to take a technically simple figure and have the students perform it in whatever manner the teacher indicates by his conducting. This makes the students conscious of both dynamic level and conducting motions.

Fine as such exercises are, they are not part of a musical context. A group may master an exercise designed to gain dynamic control, and yet not play or sing expressively when performing a work of music. The principles of meaningful teaching demand that work on various elements of music be made functional by centering on the context of the music being studied.

In the initial stages of learning a number it is usually necessary to exaggerate the dynamic levels. The students need to realize that there is a big "fall-off" between what the performer thinks he is doing and what the listener actually hears. What seems to the performer to be a noticeable crescendo may seem to be almost no crescendo at all to the listener. The students need to be prodded into exaggerating dynamic levels by such statements as "Make twice as much crescendo as you think you should." A tape recording may be valuable here. Tape recorders often do not produce the changes of dynamics that are actually present in the performance. As a result, the dynamic levels must be exaggerated to have any effect on the recording, and an exaggerated performance is good training for the students.

Probably the most important factor in achieving variation in dynamic level is the use of proper methods of tone production. Although it may seem illogical, a good tone is more easily produced on winds or in singing at *forte* than at *piano*. As described in Chapter 14, when singing with a full tone, the chest seems to stay up more easily, the throat is relaxed, and the tone seems to roll out. In soft singing, the chest wants to cave in, the throat muscles become tight and lack responsiveness, and the tone is squeezed out. The result is a flatting of the pitch and tight little tones that do not project. The singers should be reminded repeatedly that in singing softly *nothing changes except the amount of air that is released*. The rib cage remains expanded, the lungs are filled with air, and the throat remains at ease. What happens? The muscles of the abdominal wall hold the air back, the mouth is open, and the throat muscles are relaxed. Enough breath escapes to support a very soft tone. It is tiring to maintain an expanded rib cage and open throat without the aid of a full stream of air flowing by. For this reason, time and conditioning are required for good *pianissimo* singing.

To help the students sing softly and yet maintain intensity in the tone quality (some teachers call this "spinning" the tone), have the group sing a chord or a tone *ff*. Then repeat the chord *pp*, but maintain the identical body feeling, except for the holding back of air, that accompanied the singing of the *ff* chord. Another way to maintain intensity in singing *pp* is to start by humming the passage. Then sing it, keeping as much of the humming style as possible — a somewhat closed mouth, minimum jaw movement, and a continuous feeling of hum and resonance.

With wind instruments the technique for soft playing is almost identical to that required for soft singing. The correct method of tone production demands adequate breath support and attention to the basic steps outlined in Chapter 15. The throat is not pinched, squeezing the air out and distorting the tone. As in singing, the air is held back by the muscles of the abdomen and the diaphragm.

On string instruments there are three variables: the pressure of the bow on the strings, which is regulated by the forefinger of the right hand, the speed with which the bow is drawn across the string, and the position of the bow in relation to the bridge and fingerboard. String instruments are designed to produce their biggest tone with the bow drawn quite near the bridge. The farther the bow is from the bridge, the softer the tone becomes.

Unless the adolescent possesses above average voice development and/or tone production technique, his dynamic range is narrow. Junior high school singers especially cannot produce volume. There is only so much *forte*. Any attempt with singers or instrumentalists to go beyond their ability results in a frenzied, distorted tone. An effective *pianissimo* can be achieved by reducing the number of performers on a part, a technique not unknown to professional music organizations.

It is important to remember that dynamics are relative. Driving 100 miles per hour may seem fast in an automobile, but for a jet plane this speed is slow. Similarly, a *forte* in the music does not mean the same thing to all composers or in all periods. The basic element in dynamics is the principle of contrast. If a performer wants climactic passages in the music, he must save some volume for them. The accented note is a good example of this. If all the notes in this measure are performed *ff*, it will be impossible to make much of an accent on the notes so indicated. However, if the unaccented

notes are executed *piano*, the accented notes will be more prominent. A good way to practice music that contains many accents is to go through it performing only the accented notes. The rest of the notes are heard in the "mind's ear" of the students. Most of the effort should be directed toward keeping the unaccented notes soft, while the accented notes are allowed to spring out in full volume. The action is that of letting the accented note escape, rather than "punching" or "kicking" it.

Sustained Tones

At times it is more difficult to interpret long, sustained tones in the melodic line than short ones, perhaps because the greater movement of short tones hides a lack of expression by the performer. Sustained tones must somehow convey a feeling of progress. Something must always be happening within a sustained tone, because good music is always evolving.

Two types of sustained tones should be cited here. One is the final chord of a piece, and the other the long tone that leads toward some climactic point. The latter is well illustrated by a vocal work, Handel's "Thanks Be to Thee":

The long A progresses toward the apex of the phrase on the word "be." It is logical that the tone should increase in volume and intensity as it is held. A feeling of "holding back" at the beginning of such crescendos, and a faster rate of increasing loudness at the end, will make sustained tones more effective.

A final chord can increase or decrease in volume and intensity, depending on the character of the piece. If the work ends in a triumphant manner, the last tone, if it is long, will probably sound better with a slight crescendo. For some reason, a tone that is held at one dynamic level always seems to decrease slightly in volume, so a slight crescendo gives the impression of a steady dynamic level. On the other hand, if the composition ends in a subdued and pensive vein, the last tone can appropriately diminish in volume. A director can achieve a dramatic effect by slowly letting the closing tone fade into silence. Even after no more sound is audible, he and the group remain motionless for several seconds. This brief silence allows the effect of the music to become thoroughly absorbed by the listener.

Staccato

One of the more difficult elements of interpretation is to execute separate, detached notes. Staccato style is not as easily perceived by students as legato. The song style, which is basic to music and is the type of sound youngsters first learn, is flowing, not abrupt. Staccato is a more advanced and intellectual phenomenon. In addition, it is hard for teenagers to grasp the idea that there is more than one style of detached notes. The length of note, the separation between notes, and the crispness of attack vary with each musical work, and often within the piece itself. Composers and arrangers have not always been consistent in their use of staccato markings. Sometimes students are told, "Staccato means to cut the value of the note in half, so that the latter half of its value is silence." While the statement is true of some phrases, it is not true of others, and it can do harm if it discourages consideration of the musical intent of a particular phrase.

To teach the proper degree and style of detachment, teachers must rely largely on demonstration. The proper rendition may be played or sung by the teacher or by an advanced student who has prepared the passage. Verbal directions help to some extent. But "short" does not mean the same thing to everyone. The phrase "play it shorter than you did last time" is a little more precise, but it still may not convey the idea of the style adequately.

On string instruments, short notes are regulated by the style of bowing — staccato, spiccato, ricochet, détaché, martelé. Teachers who want to help their string players with various styles of bowing should examine one of the books on the subject.

Achieving staccato style and properly detached notes on wind instruments is discussed in detail in Chapter 15. Along with intellectual understanding, wind instrument players need good tonguing, proper breath support, and coordination between breath, tongue, and fingers. With them, the act of tonguing is more than an interpretive device; it is a necessity for good playing.

Staccato singing is difficult, and should not be attempted until a group has mastered the proper method of tone production. The difficulty seems to be that singers want to pronounce the words as slowly as they do in legato singing. The vowels must be executed very rapidly in staccato. Some distortion may result when certain vowels and diphthongs are sung short, but because of their brief duration this is not serious.

In contrast to wind instrument tonguing, singing requires a short pushing action of the diaphragm to produce the abrupt start that is necessary for each staccato note. This diaphragmatic action is similar to that required for the accent and *sforzando*. The latter require a greater push of the diaphragm, and a heavier initial sound.

Tones ending in consonants (except *m*, *n*, and *ng*), are concluded automatically by the formation of the consonant. If the final syllable ends in a vowel, the student is likely to stop the tone by closing his mouth, or by tensing his throat muscles as they clamp down to shut off the flow of air. A more effective way, however, is to keep an open, relaxed throat and to stop the flow of air by a holding-back action of the diaphragm. This method is more consistent with proper tone production.

Adolescent singers are prone to go flat on short notes. This can be caused by the practice of "scooping" tones, by failing to make the notes lean toward the logical culmination of the phrase, or by allowing the throat setup to collapse to some degree when starting and stopping the tones. Another cause for inaccurate pitch in singing short notes is the inability to think the correct pitch in the "mind's ear." Many young singers find the proper pitch only by "tuning up" the note as they sing it. If the notes are short, there is no time in which to do this, and the result in extreme cases sounds more like talking than singing. Experience with correct tone production methods is the best remedy for pitch problems in staccato singing. It is helpful from the standpoint of intonation to sing a staccato passage occasionally in legato style.

Legato

Music teachers spend a lot of time teaching the *beginnings* of notes. The system of counting beats decrees precisely where a note starts, and students learn to understand and abide by the system. The conclusions of notes are another matter. Many students think that a note that is three counts long stops on the third beat. At best they are hazy on this point. Therefore, both vocal and instrumental teachers have to counteract the students' tendency to rob some of the value from the ends of notes. Gaps caused by incomplete durations, of course, diminish the legato effect. Notes must be held for their full value, and students need to know exactly when a note should end.

Instrumentalists, with the exception of trombonists, do not have any particular difficulty in slurring and thus achieving a good legato. For an experienced singer, however, it's harder to master a good legato style. Much vocal control is needed to sing with an endless flow of tone that seems to permeate through each word and between words.

The best way to teach legato to the teenager is to stress again the idea of continuity of tone. Such expressions as, "Sing through the words," "Keep pulling the tone," and "Don't drop your words" will help establish the concept. The singer can imagine that the notes are glued together, their flow interrupted slightly only at phrase endings. Also, the singer might imagine that in his mouth is a ball of string, the end of which is continually being pulled out as he sings. Legato tone is like the string—an endless, constant stream of sound.

The concept of "pulling the tone" can be taught by singing the phrase on a neutral syllable, then adding the words while maintaining the same smoothness of sound. Another technique may be used occasionally during practice. The teacher may insert holds at different places in the music, particularly on the last note of the piece, to impress on the singers the idea of sustained sound.

Phrasing

It is rare indeed to find a phrase of music in which all notes receive exactly the same emphasis. A machine makes identical sounds, but human beings seldom do, in speaking or in music. Human beings put sounds together into phrases so that they have meaning and logic. Phrasing is the process of dividing the music into logical units, and then relating the notes within the units according to their importance and purpose. Phrasing is not merely a question of where to breathe or when to change bows.

A discussion of phrasing is limitless, because in music there are infinite numbers of phrases, each requiring a different treatment according to its unique construction. Proper phrasing is dependent on the musical judgment and sensibility of the music teacher. The most effective way to begin teaching correct phrasing is by rote. Words are inadequate for describing how to execute a phrase, how to make an appropriate tenuto, and how to integrate a decrescendo into the musical line. As in teaching staccato style, the teacher should sing the phrase first. An instrumental teacher may prefer to demonstrate on his horn or clarinet. Initially, the student must be told, "This is how it should be done." After a while, when he has absorbed many phrases, he can begin to figure out phrasing for himself. It is a rare secondary school student who by his own efforts phrases well, especially the more complex music of Debussy or Bach's unaccompanied sonatas. Both the running commentary suggested in Chapter 11 and good musical conducting will help establish good phrasing. But the essence of the instruction must be the teacher's demonstration.

There is another technique to make students more conscious of phrasing and interpretation. After they have gained an idea of how a phrase should sound, they can be asked to sing or play it with the dynamics and style markings reversed. The deliberately wrong rendition draws attention to the interpretation of the passage. A variation of the procedure is to offer two or three different ways of interpreting the same phrase. For example, the teacher might put the following examples on the board and invite the class to perform both. Then he can ask which is more suitable in the particular piece

of music.

By penciling a circle around a phrase unit, the students can indicate the notes that are combined into meaningful phrases. For instance, a figure may be written:

but it is musically thought out in this way:

A series of repeated notes can sound monotonous unless handled in a musical manner. The students may circle

to remind themselves about the tendency of the three notes to "lean" or be pulled toward the half. String instrument bowings, which are very much involved with phrasing, should definitely be marked in the music, as should breath marks in wind music.

In melodies containing short note values, the longer notes, *up to one beat in length,* frequently receive greater emphasis and volume. For example, in a syncopated figure such as

the eighth notes are generally only half as heavy as the quarter. In most cases a slight separation between the first two notes will improve the musical effect:

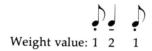

Weight value: 1   2   1

The same general idea applies to many other rhythmic figures, such as

and the combinations of

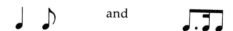

in 6/8 meter. To convey the idea of volume or weight, the teacher might refer to weight values as pounds—one pound for a quarter note, a half pound for an eighth note, or some such allocation. Middle school students may find it helpful to write weight values in pencil on several pieces of music, so that they understand the idea thoroughly.

The beat on which the note occurs likewise affects the amount of stress it receives. Usually the first beat of a measure receives the most emphasis, and the last beat, the least.

Interpreting Vocal Music

Unlike instrumentalists, singers pronounce words as they sing, and use their voices to create certain musical effects such as humming. These actions require special consideration.

Phrasing in Relation to Text and Rhythm

There is no fixed relationship between the relative importance of the text as compared to the music. The proper balance can range all the way from Gregorian chant in which the text entirely dominates the melodic line, to a work such as Randall Thompson's "Alleluia" in which the one word "Alleluia" is the text and the music is the essence of the work. The teacher must judge the proper relationship between the two when deciding on the interpretation.

In speaking, certain words are stressed more than others. The same is true of syllables within a word. The vocal teacher should read through the text of a particular work, judging which words are more important, and trying to make himself sensitive to the sounds, colors, and poetry of the words.

Sometimes the phrasing of text and music do not jibe. If no compromise can be worked out, the logic of the musical phrase should take precedence.

Tone Color

Because the tone color or timbre of the human voice shows a person's feelings so readily, and because a song is a musical setting of specific feelings, the tone quality of a choral group is important in interpretation. Different emotions projected in a song call for different timbres. It comes as a surprise to some students that there is no single, best singing tone.

When a teacher begins to stress to his students that different songs require different tone qualities, it is wise to work on the two poles of tone color: the light and the dark. When the tonal extremities are mastered, other timbres can be approached in relation to them.

Change in timbre is brought about partially by specific physical action. The dark tone color is nearer the basic tone quality, which will be described in Chapter 14. Adolescents usually find this dark quality more difficult to produce, since their voices tend to be light. The physical setup for the dark tone is a wide-open, relaxed throat, with the tongue relaxed and low. The position of the mouth and lips is similar to the one used for producing the sound *oh*. In fact, the *oh* vowel should be used to practice a dark tone quality.

The light, bright tone quality is produced by raising the jaw slightly from the *oh* position and narrowing the opening of the mouth, as for the vowel *ee*, by bringing the tongue up somewhat. Sometimes the simplest way for the teenager to think of the difference between the dark and light timbres is to think of the dark as being vertical and full, and the bright as being horizontal and flat-surfaced. The bright tone should not be squeezed out so that it sounds pinched and strained, however. In such a case the result would not be a bright tone, but merely a poor tone quality.

To achieve a change of timbre, students need not only a knowledge of physical procedures, but also a feeling for the music. The teacher or a good student may demonstrate or play a recording of the tone wanted, and in effect say to the singers, "This is the tone color we want. Go ahead and get it." This technique resembles an imitative rote procedure, but it encourages the students to base their responses on feeling for the music, rather than on conscious physical actions. When a person's voice is filled with anger, grief, or other emotion, he is not aware that he is tightening a certain muscle, closing or opening the back of the throat, tensing or relaxing the tongue. It all happens as the result of a certain feeling. Therefore, the efforts of the teacher to promote an understanding of the piece — its text, historical setting, and musical qualities — are helpful in getting the right tone quality. A song should be felt as it is being sung, and this feeling will affect the timbre of the voice.

Humming

Many teachers question the value of humming for choral groups. Like several other musical effects that have been mentioned, it should be used sparingly and with discretion.

Students should be taught how to hum properly. Too often the hum is produced by squeezing the throat muscles. The result is a sound that does not project. To produce a resonant hum, students should sing the basic *ah* vowel, and then close their lips. They must not close their teeth! The *ah* vowel can be varied at times with other vowel positions to give the humming tone a slightly different color.

Accurate pitch is hard to achieve when teenagers hum. Basically the problem is one of attitude. The singers seem to think that sloppy pitch won't be noticed during humming. In a musically less developed group, it is hard enough to make the singers aware of pitch when they sing, so the task is even harder when they hum.

Runs

Whenever more than one note is sung for a syllable of a word, there exists a situation that encourages sloppiness in singing. One way to achieve accuracy in such passages is to have the singers place a small "bump" or "pulse" at the beginning of each note, much as they were encouraged to do in staccato singing, except in this case to a lesser degree. The phrase

A - men

would then be considered as

A(a) (a) (a)men

with the *u* over the notes indicating the little diaphragmatic bump at the beginning of each note. Some teachers tell their singers to put a small *h* in front of each note. This technique is all right as long as it is made clear to the singers that they should not stop or break the air stream before each note. The bump or the slight *h* sound will eliminate the siren effect that singers sometimes get on such passages. If the technique is exaggerated, it can ruin the sound when only one person is singing. But when used with moderation by an entire group, it helps make the pitches clearer. Two more elements are needed to make a run sound clean: accurate pitch and accurate rhythm.

Pronunciation of Foreign Languages

When songs are sung in languages other than English, the words should be pronounced as correctly as possible. The most authoritative book on the pronunciation of ecclesiastical Latin is *The Correct Pronunciation of Latin According to Roman Usage.*[2] This book is especially useful in giving the correct pronunciation to such mispronounced words as *excelsis, coeli* and *nostrae.*

For modern languages such as French, Italian, Spanish, and German, several textbooks and dictionaries are available. Many schools own sets of language records or tapes that can be studied. In addition, the language teacher will probably be glad to assist if he can. If no teacher in the schools is competent in the particular language being sung, the music teacher might be able to find someone in the community who knows that language well. Accurate pronunciation helps to produce the correct timbre and unique tonal characteristics that add to the effectiveness of a work in a foreign language.

[2]Published by St. Gregory Guild, 1705 Rittenhouse Square, Philadelphia, Pennsylvania 19103.

Musical Feeling and Technique

In his eagerness for a good performance, the teacher should never become so preoccupied with such technical considerations as blend, balance, and rhythm that he loses the spirit of the music. It is better to let some technical aspect go unperfected than to destroy the heart of the work.

Both technique and musical feeling are necessary, and this fact presents a problem to which there is no easy solution. Constant and unhurried effort is required to bring each of the two elements into proper perspective. First, technical work should be integrated as much as possible with the pieces of music currently being studied. Functional learning, not isolated drill, is most effective.

Second, the teacher should help the students recognize the relationship between technique and musical feeling. A musician has much in common with the actor in this respect. Until the end of the nineteenth century, acting consisted of artificial, pompous, formal motions. Techniques were the basis of acting. Then Constantine Stanislavsky, in his books and in the Moscow Art Theatre, began a revolution toward a combination of feeling and natural technique. According to Stanislavsky, the actor must project himself as deeply as possible into the character he is to portray, but at the same time he must never lose sight of the fact that he is acting and that a certain amount of objective technique is necessary to project the part successfully.

When a group sings "By the rivers of Babylon, there we sat down, yea, we wept, when we remembered Zion," they must feel the anxiety and privation of the captive Israelites. But more than that they must know the technique required to project the correct feeling through the music to an audience. The students should know in exact, objective terms how to achieve a warm tone or a decrescendo, and at the same time they should understand and feel what the music is trying to convey. When objective technique and subjective feeling are united, a vehicle of artistic expression has been created.

Questions

1. Instead of chanting neutral syllables, is the use of words

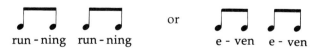

justifiable educationally in the junior or senior high school? Why, or why not? Is tapping the foot while playing or singing a good practice for the secondary school student?

2. Does achieving good blend mean losing individual quality for the performer in a group? Is this a good educational practice?

3. What can a choral teacher do to achieve good balance if he has 40 girls and 20 boys in the group? What can a band teacher do to balance eight clarinets against nine trumpets? What can the orchestra director do to balance a complete wind section with eleven violins, two violas, two cellos, and three string basses?

4. Is it desirable to have each performer learn an exact degree of loudness for each of the six dynamic levels (*pp, p, mp, mf, f, ff*)?

5. Suppose that the group you are conducting shows no flexibility and does not follow the tempo changes as you conduct them. What teaching device might you use to get them to be more responsive to tempo change?

6. Why is it important for students to learn the terms "blend," "phrasing," "tone quality" when they can perform rather well without knowing these words?

7. Examine the adjudication forms in Appendix E. Do these forms give proper emphasis to pertinent musical factors? Are they too much centered on the technical phases of music, and too little concerned with the overall effect? Why, or why not? What suggestions, if any, could you make to improve the forms?

8. Page 300 contained the example of a teacher using rote methods to teach his singers the syncopated phrase "Go down to Mexico." Would it have been better to make the students use a system of counting and figure it out for themselves? Which method, rote or reading, is more effective musically in this instance? Which will the students remember longer? Which is more efficient in its use of class time?

Projects

1. There are several recordings available of

(a) "Hallelujah Chorus" from the *Messiah* by Handel

(b) *1st Rhapsodie Roumaine* by Georges Enesco

(c) *Firebird Suite* by Igor Stravinsky

Listen to two recordings of each work. Compare and contrast the tempo, dynamic levels, tone color, style or articulation, and other interpretive factors at selected places in each work. Decide which is preferable and be able to state why.

2. Listen again to the opening section of Enesco's *Rhapsodie*, the section that features the clarinet. Decide how you would teach a teenage clarinetist

in your orchestra to play the solos with the necessary musicality and flexibility.

3. Listen again to the middle of the "Hallelujah Chorus." Note the smooth quality of the words "The kingdom of this world," as contrasted with the more martial quality of "and He shall reign forever and ever." Plan how you would work with a teenage choral group to achieve this difference in the style of singing.

4. Devise some simple unison exercises to be sung or played to give teenage students a clearer idea of the exact ending of dotted-quarter notes, half notes, dotted-half notes, whole notes. Decide upon the verbal explanation that should accompany the presentation of the exercises to the group.

5. Look through copies of choral and instrumental music for works, such as Handel's "Thanks Be to Thee," which are especially suitable for developing an awareness of dynamics and a technique for producing the proper dynamics.

6. Listen to commercial recordings of recognized choral groups singing

(a) a cowboy folk song

(b) a chorus from an oratorio

(c) an old English folk song

(d) Stravinsky's *Symphony of Psalms*

(e) Brahms' *Ein Deutches Requiem*

Note the different choral tone used for each work. Decide how you would work with a high school choral group to achieve the proper timbre for each type of music.

7. Select a phrase of choral music requiring some flexibility and imagination in phrasing. Take it to your class and insist that they phrase it in the way you suggest.

13

Achieving Correct Intonation

"Tune it up, altos!" the director admonishes a section of his choir. A good direction, no doubt about it. A trained musician knows what the conductor means. He responds by careful listening and the slight adjustment of fingers or voice necessary to "tune it up." But what about the 13-year-old violist now in his third year of study, all of it in group situations? What about the flighty freshman girl in the glee club? To her, "tune it up" may mean to sing in a more lively manner. What about the junior bass who is back in choral music for the first time since seventh grade? For that matter, what about the first baritone horn, a senior with eight years of instrumental music experience? How much does he know about intonation? The school music teacher faces a real challenge. Not only does he encounter the usual vicissitudes of intonation — acoustical problems of instruments, difficult places in the music, and fluctuations due to heat and cold — he also faces the job of teaching students what it is to be in tune, and what they must do to achieve proper intonation.

A few music teachers seem to accept poor intonation as a fact of school music life. Perhaps they assume that teenagers can't perform in tune, or maybe they don't know how to teach the rudiments of good intonation. Possibly they just don't listen carefully themselves. In any case, it is a mistake to regard poor intonation as inevitable. Skill and persistence are required to keep a group in tune. Although a teacher has not necessarily failed if his group sounds a few notes out of tune, he does bear a large share of the responsibility for achieving good intonation.

The problem for the school music teacher is not primarily to understand the physical properties of sound, but to understand why students are not in tune. Many of the causes are interrelated; that is, an instance of poor intonation seldom has only a single cause.

Intonation Illusions

There are many reasons, some musical and some physical, for poor intonation. In addition, however, there are two factors that give the *illusion* of faulty intonation. One is simply the presence of wrong notes. As an experienced band director once observed, "You know, when everyone's playing the right notes, it's remarkable how much better the intonation is."

A second illusion regarding intonation involves the relationship between timbre and pitch. Two tones may be sounding at the same pitch level but seem to be out of tune because of their differing qualities. This is one reason for urging work on uniform vowels in a choral group. Oddly, a poorer, less distinguished tone quality can more easily conceal its pitch. A fine, alive tone with a solid "center" cannot do this. The phenomenon is best illustrated by a good trombone player. If he blows a firm, well-rounded tone, any movement of the slide is noticeable to the ear. But if he blows a sickly sound, he can move the slide an inch or more without seeming to affect the pitch level. This should not be construed as an argument for poor tone quality, however. It merely means that the teacher must be able to distinguish between pitch and timbre, so that he can trace the problem to its real source.

Good intonation is another illusion that should be mentioned. Because of the effort involved in getting students to perform in tune, a teacher sometimes loses his objectivity in judging pitch as the days go by. Mentally he begins to correct out-of-tune notes, or to let them pass because they're an improvement over earlier efforts. Although a music teacher should think positively, he should not be satisfied with minimal progress.

Musical Inexperience

The musical inexperience of many teenagers, a basic cause of poor intonation, makes itself evident in three ways: poor listening habits, lack of control, and little concept of pitch.

Poor Listening Habits

People are constantly bombarded with sound in supermarkets, restaurants, and stores; their ears are assaulted by sounds ranging from jukeboxes to traffic noise. It is almost impossible to find refuge from this barrage. Even the silent prayer period in many churches is accompanied by organ music. The result is that a person psychologically "tunes out" much of what he hears, and no longer notices the clock ticking, the refrigerator turning on and off, or the noise of cars going by on the street outside. Unfortunately, he develops the habit of not listening. Such a habit makes it more difficult to teach students to listen carefully so that they can perform in tune.

To compound the problem of aural inattention, most teenagers have had even less experience in careful listening to parts or themes, or to accuracy of pitch. Their predicament can be appreciated by many a music major who discovered this fact for himself when he first started taking dictation in college theory class. If a musical novice is merely admonished to "correct the bad intonation," he is placed in an awkward situation. He is like a man who is sent to the scene of a crime to seek clues, but is given no idea of the nature of the crime.

Some music teachers think that only a few gifted individuals have the innate ability to discriminate between minute differences in pitch. But Carl Seashore (see Chapter 5) produced evidence to the contrary. His research indicates that the average individual can hear the difference between three double vibrations per second, or about .05 part of a tone at A440.[1] This amount of aural acuity he considers sufficient to make music activity worthwhile.[2] A student's ability to distinguish fine gradations of pitch may be hidden, but it is seldom lacking. The teacher must find ways to draw out this innate capacity for pitch discernment.

Lack of Control and Coordination

The second manifestation of inexperience is inability to coordinate the directions of the mind and ear with the voice and fingers. The adolescent violinist may falter when shifting to a new position not because he can't hear it and doesn't know better, but because his muscle movement is too inconsistent to enable him to find the same place twice. The same is true of the adolescent singer, especially the teenage boy. The teacher must remember that the first efforts in any endeavor are often ineffectual. Control in musical response will come with practice.

Lack of a Concept of Pitch

The lack of a concept of intonation is also evidence of musical inexperience. It's not enough to tell the student that intonation is "the quality of in-tuneness" or that being in tune is "the accurate reproduction of pitch." These are mere words, and no one can learn about intonation by definitions alone. Words can help formulate an idea, but they can't furnish a complete concept.

---

[1] Carl E. Seashore, *The Psychology of Musical Talent* (Morristown, N.J.: Silver Burdett Company, 1919), p. 45.

[2] Seashore, pp. 66–67.

Several analogies are useful in establishing the idea of accurate intonation. One analogy is that of a marksman with his rifle. The marksman aims to hit the center of the target—the bull's-eye. A musician also aims at a target with each note he performs, but the target in this case exists in sound, with the center determined by physical laws of sound. When the student hits the bull's-eye with his tone, his intonation will be good and the sound will have a "trueness" about it. When he starts hitting around the edges of the target, the pitch will be off and the intonation poor. If he just plain misses the target, then he produces a wrong note. In some ways wrong notes are not as hard to correct as faulty intonation, because they are so obviously wrong.

The teacher may also suggest the analogy of tuning in a television set. The selector may be on the right channel, but there is a fine-tuning knob to make the picture sharp and clear. Again, achieving good intonation is something like focusing a camera so that the picture is not blurred or fuzzy.

To provide a more concrete experience with pitch, the science teacher might be invited to give the class a short, simple demonstration of the physical properties of sound. Few students fail to be fascinated by a well-planned demonstration of acoustics. It is especially valuable for them to hear the simultaneous sounding of tuning forks that are two or three double vibrations apart. The "beats" created by this phenomenon are a revelation to the students.

Poor Methods of Tone Production

Poor methods of producing the sound have a detrimental effect on a group's ability to perform with accurate pitch. On wind instruments it is more a matter of consistency than of general pitch level, which is regulated by the tuning. There are few things as frustrating for a teacher as the presence of a brass player with a "mobile" embouchure. Each time he plays a tone with a different lip formation he produces a slightly different pitch. It is impossible to tune such a player. Some reed players tend to bite down on the reed when under tension, and a sharpness in pitch is the result. Some brass players when tense press the mouthpiece back hard against the lips, and this causes pinching and sharping, plus other complications.

Correction involves working not on intonation directly, because in this case it is a symptom, but rather on the fundamentals of playing the instrument. The cure for this type of intonation problem requires attention to points inadequately covered in the students' early instruction.

In singing, pitch is likewise affected when the sounds are strained or inconsistently produced. If the proper singing routine has not been established, the pitch of a tone is subject to every psychological and physiological vagary.

The practice of "scooping" or "shoveling" is harmful to accurate pitch. Although some popular solo singers use the device almost constantly, teenage students should be told of the damage this inflicts on a group. Frequently the cause of scooped notes is a lack of mental and physical preparation on the part of the singer.

Vowels that are not uniform are detrimental to intonation. This is primarily due to the different timbres present when the vowels are not produced in a similar manner by all the singers. Uniform vowel production is more easily achieved when the singers retain an open throat position and confine the changes for different sounds to the front of the mouth and lips.

Psychological Factors

Because music is so involved with emotion and feeling, it is not surprising that pitch is affected by psychological factors. As already mentioned, the best corrective for faulty intonation is alertness and understanding on the part of the students. Anything that dulls their acuity will impair intonation. One teacher has been known to spend an entire class period on a single piece of music. Any teacher, vocal or instrumental, who does this should expect alertness to wane.

Singing is especially susceptible to the psychological condition of the singers. They can become tired of singing in a particular key. Choral groups do perceive a tonal difference when a piece is transposed a half step up or down. Some songs are rarely sung in tune when performed in the original key. An example of this is the familiar "Silent Night," which is usually sung with better intonation when transposed up a half step from the original key of C major. Attention should be given to the range when transposing keys. If the top tones become too high, then perhaps transposing down is more practical. However, the basses must not be asked to sing so low that they either rumble or stop singing.

Sometimes students sing the wrong pitch because they are inattentive or indifferent. One individual picks up the pitch from his neighbor, who in turn may be doing the same thing from someone else. If many singers do this, the right pitch can become pretty well lost.

Singers are often affected emotionally and mentally by changes in the dynamic level of the music, and their reactions, in turn, affect the pitch level. This sometimes occurs after they have sung continuously at a *forte* dynamic level. When they attempt to sing a soft section, they will frequently go flat. Their attention decreases and psychological relaxation sets in, resulting in a feeble, unsupported tone. The singers should be made aware of these tendencies to relax or to overexert themselves as they vary the dynamic level. To overcome such reactions in his singers, the teacher can provide simple scale or chord exercises, with slow changes in dynamics, followed by rapid changes of *forte* to *piano* and back to *forte.*

The solution to psychologically caused intonation problems in both vocal and instrumental groups is to reexamine the fundamentals of music teaching discussed in Chapter 9. Especially significant is pacing the work on a piece of music, and distributing the effort. Some psychological causes, such as nervousness in public appearances, are overcome only through experience.

Closely related to a person's alertness is his physical condition on a particular day. Colds sometimes affect the ability to hear, and cause general sluggishness. The voice is especially susceptible to the physical condition of the body. Sometimes it is said of a person, "His voice sounds tired," and it is true. When the energies of many students in a group are consumed in an event such as a basketball tournament or a school play, this is apparent in the tired sound and the increased amount of out-of-tuneness. If students leave home at 5 A.M. and ride a bumpy school bus a hundred or more miles to perform in a contest or festival, intonation problems are almost inevitable because of sheer fatigue.

Environmental Factors

Atmospheric conditions can play havoc with intonation. Not only does hot, humid weather deplete the musicians, causing singers to flat; it affects the quality of tone from reeds. They sound soggy, flat, and listless. Other instruments are affected as well. The strings tend to lower in pitch, and the brasses and winds tend to rise. Probably the most critical problem exists at the outdoor concert on a cool night. The end of the horn nearest the player's mouth is kept warm with breath, while the far end is cool. Each time the player rests for a few moments, the instrument cools and becomes flatter.

Sometimes faulty intonation can be traced to environmental factors in the classroom. Chairs of the wrong type are a hindrance to proper posture. Poor ventilation and overcrowding have an adverse effect on the physical well-being of the students, so one of them can be appointed to be responsible for raising and lowering windows. Overcrowding has an adverse effect on the group. If string players are so confined that they have hardly enough room for a full bow stroke, their physical discomfort will be readily apparent in the sound. Such a situation can only encourage intonation problems.

Acoustical conditions vary from room to room. If the students are accustomed to rehearsing in a "live" room, and are confronted with an auditorium that is acoustically dead, they will tend to overextend in their effort to combat these altered conditions, or they will become frightened and emit only tight little sounds of uncertain pitch.

Characteristics of Instruments

The instrumental music teacher has an additional responsibility. He must cope with mechanical frailties and strive to overcome them, as well as develop a sense of proper pitch within his students.

Wind Instruments

Errors of pitch are inherent in all wind instruments. The first step is to convince wind instrument players that they do indeed have to be concerned with intonation. It is obvious to string players and singers that they make their own pitches, but the same responsibility is not as apparent to the student who gets a note by pushing valves or keys. As one student told his teacher, "But I know my clarinet is in tune. The man at the store who sold it to my dad said so." The techniques suggested on page 328 will help to drive home the need for attention to intonation. The teacher can say, "When you push down the right fingers, you're only in the neighborhood of the note, not exactly on it. Getting exactly on pitch is your job."

The student should be shown what tones are chronically out of tune on his instrument. Some of these are predictable, such as the 1-2-3 valve combination on brasses and the throat-tone B flat on clarinets, but others depend on the unique qualities of the student's instrument and his manner of playing it. These troublesome pitches become evident through the efforts of the group to achieve good intonation. It is the successful teacher who says to his first flutist, "Barbara, you know that D flat is sharp on your instrument, so humor it down as much as you can."

The teacher's directive to "humor" the pitch down raises the simple question: how? There are both technical and psychological approaches to doing this. Woodwind fingerings can be varied to change the pitch slightly. On the clarinet, covering the holes with the second and third fingers of the left hand when playing throat-tone B flat and using the little finger of the right hand on the E flat key on certain high notes are examples of this. Alternative fingerings are available on brasses, especially on the French horn, which can also vary pitch by the degree to which the tone is stopped by the right hand in the bell. Flutes may tip just a bit to alter the angle between the blowhole and the lips, tipping away to sharpen and turning in to flatten. When a flutist does this, he should think of moving his head slightly, and not the flute. The tension or "squeeze" of the lips and jaw on the reed affects the pitch of other instruments. An advanced player is very precise in manipulating this technique, and a secondary school player can master it if he has a well-established embouchure. Brass players also make slight adjustments by regulating the amount of tension in the lips.

Although it is hard for instrumentalists to realize, just thinking about sounding a pitch sharper or flatter will cause some changes of throat and tongue tension, intensity of the air stream, openness of the throat, and adjustment of embouchure that will effect a pitch change. So when the first flutist Barbara is told to lower her D flat, she is conscious of making certain responses to accomplish this, and she can also "think" of playing the pitch flatter.

Woodwind instruments with chronic intonation problems can sometimes be improved by a knowledgeable and skillful repairman. There is hardly a professional clarinetist or bassoonist who has not had pads raised or lowered, or a hole made smaller to flatten it or larger to sharpen it.

Sometimes instruments can be adjusted at points other than the usual tuning place. For example, if a clarinet is sharp on its usual tuning note of C, but in tune on throat tones, it can be "pulled" somewhat at the center joint. On brasses, the entire relationship between fingered notes is altered when the main tuning slide is changed very much. The procedure for getting the individual valve slides in tune is as follows:

(1) Play the second open tone (G on trumpet, F on bass clef baritone, etc.).

(2) Play the same tone with the first and third valves. Frequently this tone is sharp to the open tone.

(3) Pull out the first valve tuning slide slightly and the third valve slide twice as much.

(4) Experiment until the pitches of the fingered and open note match exactly.

(5) Play one whole step higher (A on trumpet, etc.) with first and second valves.

(6) Compare it with same note played with third valve only. If the first and second valve pitch is higher than the third valve pitch, the third valve slide has been pulled too far and the first valve slide has not been pulled far enough.

(7) Experiment until the pitch of the two fingerings is exactly the same.

(8) Check open tone G against the first and third valve G.

(9) If this is not in tune, repeat the procedure until the fullest possible pitch agreement has been attained.

The second valve is so short that its adjustment has little effect. It can be checked on the trumpet by comparing B played with the second valve against B played with the first and third valves.

The quality of a student's instrument has much to do with the quality of its intonation. Possibly the most noticeable difference between an economical and a quality instrument is in their tuning properties. The teacher should try to convince parents that a quality instrument, not necessarily a luxury instrument, is well worth the additional cost because of the satisfaction the student can get from it, to say nothing of the additional resale value.

A special problem with wind instruments is the influence of dynamic level on pitch. Clarinets tend to lower in pitch as they get louder, brasses tend to sharpen. Players must be taught to compensate for this, to avoid pitch discrepancy at the extremes of dynamic range. It should be added that the stiffer the reed on a reed instrument, the less the pitch is affected by dynamic level.

String Intonation

When instruction is first offered on strings, only students with a good sense of pitch should be allowed to start. A string student who cannot hear pitch accurately only frustrates himself and his teacher. To check pitch sense, the teacher may administer the Seashore or Gordon tests. Oddly, a lack of ability to sing in tune does not always indicate a poor sense of pitch.

The string teacher should stress slow and careful work. A primary cause of bad pitch on strings lies in asking the students to play something too difficult for them, something for which they have not yet developed adequate neuromuscular control. When string players are pushed into higher positions before they are ready, intonation will undoubtedly suffer. Sometimes it improves when the teacher has the group play the music at half speed. This gives the players additional time to think, move fingers, and listen, and the result is better pitch.

Faulty intonation on strings is often caused by a poor left hand position. On violin and viola, young players sometimes display three habits that result in a lack of consistency in the placement of the fingers on the strings. One: the player allows his wrist to bend or become unstable. Two: he turns his hand so that he sees the palm rather than the lateral edge. This places his fingers far from the strings and causes him to be less efficient in finding the proper pitch at the proper moment. Three: he allows the neck of the instrument to rest on the joint connecting the index finger and palm. This causes tension and cramping in the hand, and reduces the accuracy and facility of the fingers, particularly on the highest string. This habit can be observed best by viewing the player from the scroll end of the instrument.

Inaccurate pitch also results when the string player does not think of the pitch he is trying to get. He must hear the pitch in his mind and associate it with the kinesthetic feel of the correctly placed hand and finger. Slow and careful practice helps to establish this association.

The effect of vibrato on string intonation is an interesting topic, but it has little practical application for the school music teacher. Vibrato greatly improves the tone of the player, and it may, because of its pitch fluctuations, make the intonation appear to be better, although not all string teachers agree on this point. At least, vibrato will not harm pitch if the player is ready for it—that is, if he can place his fingers consistently and accurately on the proper notes.

Procedures for Instrumental Music Class

(1) Teach the students to tune their instruments. As elementary as this step may appear to be, it is surprising how many teenage musicians cannot do this properly. Allow sufficient time for the development of such a skill; it cannot be taught in one 15-minute lesson. Furthermore, the student himself must be given a chance to judge the tuning. The temptation is to say, "Dave, pull the slide out just a little," without giving Dave the opportunity to find out for himself. Call attention to the "beating" of out-of-tune notes, and the tonal characteristics that identify one tone as being sharper or flatter than another. Strings, of course, must learn to tune fifths (or fourths on bass). Not only is accurate tuning necessary for good intonation, but the process gives the students good experience in learning what is meant by being "in tune."

(2) Tune wind instruments to pitches other than the usual concert B flat. Because of the construction of many instruments in B flat, this particular pitch may sound good when played on several instruments, while a concert G or F sharp may be quite out of tune. Tuning on more than one pitch will give a more valid means of setting the overall pitch of the instrument.

(3) Take two identical instruments, perhaps clarinets. Have them tune perfectly on the usual third-space C. As they sound the C in unison and in tune, have one player transfer to the C an octave higher. Nine times out of ten this note is sharp on a clarinet, and the students can hear the "beating" caused by the out-of-tuneness. This technique works to some extent on wind instruments on almost all pitches one octave apart.

(4) Instruct two players to take the major third C–E and tune it up to everyone's satisfaction. Then have each player move up a semitone to C sharp–E sharp, or a whole step to D–F sharp. The new third will usually be out of tune and require adjustment. The players can progress to other thirds with similar results.

(5) Have the group play Bach chorales, unison scales and arpeggios, and chord studies—slowly and carefully. Pitches that are flat or sharp should be corrected on the spot.

(6) During practice on the regular repertoire, work out passages in which the intonation is faulty. Learning to play in tune should not be isolated from learning music.

(7) Use the tape recorder to analyze intonation. Individual performers, recorded one at a time, can hear themselves more clearly and objectively than is possible when the whole group plays together. Also, two performances of the same passage can be compared.

Choral Intonation

Because of the characteristics of the human voice, and because singers do not have the benefit of preestablished pitches, certain factors of intonation relate primarily to choral groups.

Range and Tessitura

The intonation of the human voice is affected by the range of the music and by the tessitura—the average or median pitch of the vocal line, excluding the occasional note at the extreme of the range. Whether strain is caused by attempting to sing a note in an extreme range or by singing too long in an uncomfortable tessitura, the effort breeds out-of-tune singing. When this occurs, it is not so much the fault of the singers as it is of the teacher, who selected music too difficult for their voices. Occasionally one or two notes, which might throw an entire phrase off pitch, can be altered or given to another part. For instance, a few tenors might help the basses with some high notes, or a few altos might help the tenors. This gives the line more support and helps retain pitch, while increasing the singers' confidence on the difficult passage.

Tempo

A piece of music in a slow tempo is more difficult to sing in tune than one in a rapid tempo. This statement does not mean that if a work such as Palestrina's "Adoramus Te, Christe" cannot be sung in tune at a slow tempo, then the tempo should be increased until the piece is in tune. The end—music—should never be sacrificed for the sake of a technical element such as intonation. It may help the singers if they think of continuous forward motion, or of tonal energy moving ahead. The notes are not static like big stagnant pools. On the first long tones in "Adoramus Te, Christe" the singers should mentally lean toward the next syllable of the word. This will help them maintain their pitch, without destroying the intent of the music.

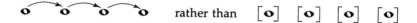

Modes

In present-day American culture, more music is in the major than any other mode. This cultural conditioning makes intonation somewhat more difficult in pieces that contain other tonalities. Before introducing music in a mode or minor key, the teacher may wish to have his students try various pentatonic, modal, and minor scales, drawing attention to the intervals and how they differ from those in major keys. In the minor mode, the melodic intervals particularly difficult to keep in tune are the minor third between steps 1 and 3, and the major second between steps 7 and 8 in the unaltered form.

Modulations

While modulation to a closely related key almost never causes a problem, an unusual modulation can present difficulties. The teacher must carefully accustom the students' ears to the musical logic of the harmonies. As the sounds become familiar, he can suggest ways to find the new notes. For example, in the "Coronation Scene" from *Boris Godunov*[3], the solo of Boris ends on a G chord and the chorus, with only the aid of a trilled G, must start singing an E flat chord.

The teaching steps, which should be repeated on several different days, consist first of hearing the last measure of the solo, then the trill, and then the chorus' chord. Next the teacher can point out that the first sopranos have the same note as the trill, the second sopranos have the root of the chord a major third below, the altos the fifth of the chord, and so on. If the students have had some practice at finding chord members, each section may quickly practice finding its note when given the E flat chord, then when given only the trilled note. Finally, the spot can be practiced as written with the piano accompaniment. Similar procedures can be used with less difficult changes of key, such as a sudden chromatic modulation to the key a semitone higher.

---

[3]Copyright, 1938, by E. C. Schirmer Music Co., Boston, Mass., and used by permission.

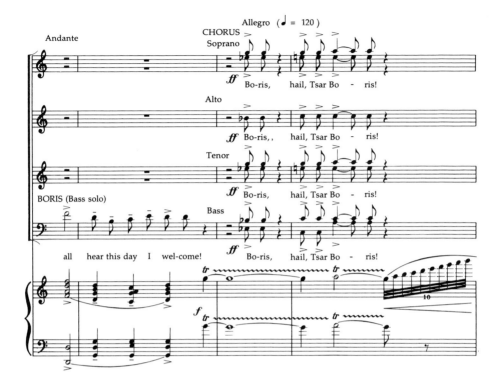

Intervals

When singers perform a series of ascending chromatics, their tendency is to miss just slightly getting all notes up to pitch. With descending chromatic passages, the inclination is to overshoot and end below pitch. There is often a tendency to undershoot all ascending wide intervals. The appearance of the interval—the way it is written enharmonically—also affects the accuracy of its performance. Although the good aural judgment of the students should prevail, with groups that are not particularly experienced it is advisable to say, "Lean a bit on the sharp side as you go up for that top note."

The other notes in the chord likewise affect intonation. For example, it is much more difficult to sing an accurate B natural against a C than against a D. One of the most taxing chores for a secondary school teacher is to teach a group to perform dissonant pitches in tune. A healthy dissonance sometimes becomes discord because of poor intonation. A dissonant work demands slow, careful practice, and thorough orientation to the new sounds.

Lack of Ensemble

A final reason for intonation problems is what might be termed "lack of ensemble." Sometimes, especially in choral groups, the musician feels like a man out in the middle of the ocean trying to keep his head above water. The group plays or sings along and the student can scarcely hear himself, least of all hear what the other sections are doing.

There are many reasons for this inability to hear other parts. The individual, or the people around him, may be too loud, and the other sections may be too weak, or located so that they are difficult to hear. It is important, however, that the students develop mental control of their music making. The "lost" sensation is most prevalent among teenage musicians when they participate on an instinctive, unthinking level.

If a choral group has been singing in a raucous, out-of-tune manner, a calming effect can be produced by directing each student to place his hand or finger over his ear when singing. This seems to center his attention on the mental control of his singing, and permits him to hear himself. As the student becomes aware of what to listen for in music, learns to fit his voice into the group, and stays on the alert for sagging pitch and other errors in singing, much of the "lost in the ocean" feeling will disappear.

Another cause of lack of ensemble in choral music is inability to hear the piano. If this occurs during public performance, the students are at a distinct disadvantage. The audience is likely to hear both piano and singers, and is thereby provided with a constant pitch comparison. The problem can usually be remedied if the position of the piano is changed, or its lid opened. The group can sing more softly and the accompanist can play more loudly. As the group advances, less and less dependence should be placed on the piano. After all, it is intended to accompany the singers, not supplant them. When the pianist gives the pitches for *a cappella* singing, the notes must be struck with sufficient volume to be heard by all the singers. Even if the audience hears the pitches, this is preferable to the hesitant, out-of-tune start that results when singers can't find their starting notes.

Procedures for Vocal Music

Here are some procedures to develop the students' listening powers in vocal music.

(1) Play a tone on the piano and ask someone to match it, singing a neutral syllable. When he has attempted to sing back the pitch, ask another person if the rendition was flat, sharp, or exactly on pitch.

(2) Encourage careful singing of major scales and chords. At first, the students should sing each note simultaneously with the piano or immedi-

ately after the piano has sounded the note. When they can sing accurately in this manner, play the entire chord or scale and let them repeat it un-accompanied. After several days, give them a pitch and tell them to sing a chord or scale from it. Initial work should be confined to major scales and chords. If minor is introduced before major is learned thoroughly, the result will be a hybrid of major and minor. This does not preclude singing songs in minor, however. If singing in major is accurate, the minor seems to take care of itself automatically when it appears in a song. Accuracy must be em-

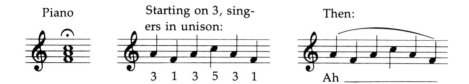

Piano   Starting on 3, sing- Then:
          ers in unison:

3 1 3 5 3 1   Ah _____

phasized to the students at all times during such exercises. Triads should be sung from the root, third, and fifth. Unless the students are used to the solfège syllables, it is best to use numbers or a neutral syllable for these drills. A section or an individual should sing these patterns alone once in a while.

(3) Assign a chord and let the singers trade parts. For example, the first time the basses can take the root or 1, tenors and altos 3, and sopranos 5. The next time the basses take 5, tenors 1, altos 5, and sopranos 3.

(4) Play a chord on the piano, call out "one," "three," or "five," and ask someone to sing back the proper chord member. This procedure can be made more elaborate by calling out a complete chord with correct doubling, so that there is one chord member for each section. The use of chord imagery not only makes the students more conscious of pitch; it also gives them a technique for finding the correct notes at the beginning of a phrase, a skill that is of the utmost value in choral music.

(5) Lead the group in a familiar melody, unaccompanied and on a neutral syllable. Start the singers with a conductor's beat, and at some point indicate by a prearranged signal that they are to stop singing aloud. They continue singing silently in their "mind's ear," following the conductor's beat, until they see the signal to resume singing aloud again. This gives them practice in thinking pitches accurately.

(6) Encourage the singers to try some harmonizing by ear outside the regular class. This makes them conscious of tuning their voices with others. Harmonizing by ear is not recommended on regular four part music, of course, but there are many familiar melodies that are well-adapted to impromptu harmonizing.

(7) When the group is singing a work of music, stop on any chord that is being sung out of tune, and rebuild it with the help of the piano. Don't let the singers become accustomed to poor intonation.

(8) Make use of the tape recorder. Students can be more objective about their ability to sing in tune when they hear a recording of their singing.

Questions

1. What reasons might a vocal music teacher give for having a group sing a piece with the piano in order to stay on pitch, rather than sing un-accompanied with poor intonation?

2. Which aspect of unaccompanied singing should the teacher empha-size: staying in tune within the group itself, or being able to finish the song exactly on the properly notated pitch?

3. What is wrong with each of these examples of teaching as it pertains to intonation?

(a) With a pained expression on his face, Ray Jones complains to his group, "You're out of tune! *Out of tune!* OUT OF TUNE!"

(b) Joyce Knapp says to her girls' glee club, "Now sopranos, we're going over this piece until you can sing it in tune."

(c) Jan Artz tells her string players, "Just play everything a little higher than you think you should. That will keep us from going flat."

(d) On a warm May afternoon Marilyn Carson has had her singers sitting for over half an hour. As they finish a song out of tune, she whines, "Now, there you are, flat again!"

Projects

1. Think of two analogies in addition to those mentioned on page 322 that a teacher can use to describe proper intonation.

2. Listen to a trumpet, cornet, French horn, trombone, and tuba each play middle C. Have the players tune to this pitch until the intonation satisfies you. Notice how the timbre of each affects the impression you get of the pitch of the instrument.

3. Talk to a specialist on a wind instrument that is comparatively un-familiar to you. Ask him which notes on the instrument are most difficult to play in tune, and what he does to compensate for these notes. Ask him how the dynamic level of the music and the weather affect the pitch of the

instrument. Request that he play the same pitch several times using a slightly different embouchure each time. As he does this, notice the effect on the pitch.

4. If you are a wind instrument player, take a trumpet and pull the tuning slide out at least two inches. Then tune the individual valve slides. (If you are not a wind player, observe someone do this.)

5. Have two classmates who play the same wind instrument bring their instruments to class. Listen to them as they tune notes an octave apart. Also listen to them tune major thirds as they raise the pitch level by a semitone.

6. Have the class sing without accompaniment two stanzas of "Silent Night" in C major, carefully checking the pitch with the piano at the end. Then have them sing it in C sharp major, again checking the pitch at the end. Notice which is easier to sing in tune.

7. Have the class sing in tempo a well-known song such as "Dixie," checking the pitch carefully at the end. Then request that they sing through the song at a much slower tempo, and again check the pitch at the end. Compare the accuracy of pitch of the two singings.

8. In a choral work, find a place that contains a sudden modulation to a foreign key. Plan how you would teach the passage to a school group. Determine what clues the music gives the singers to help them find the new notes.

9. Do some research into the acoustical basis of timbre. Determine why two identical pitches of different tone qualities might give the impression that they are not in tune.

Suggested Readings

Colwell, Richard J., *The Teaching of Instrumental Music.* New York: Appleton-Century-Crofts, 1969.

Pottle, Ralph R., *Tuning the School Band and Orchestra.* (Published by the author, Hammond, Louisiana, 1962).

Stauffer, Donald W., *Intonation Deficiencies of Wind Instruments in Ensemble.* Washington, D.C.: The Catholic University of America Press, 1954, Chapters III, VII.

14

Singing and Teenage Voices

Most teenagers have only a vague notion of the correct methods of singing. In fact, many are not aware that there are correct methods, or that methods make a difference in the musical results. These students think that a singer just opens his mouth and whatever sound comes out is the way it is, be it good or bad.

The choral music teacher faces conditions that differ from those prevailing in instrumental music. Students in vocal classes are sometimes of a less select quality than instrumentalists, who usually have survived the attrition of several years of study. Some students enter vocal classes after having had almost no contact with music making for a year or more, but this almost never happens in instrumental music. Teenagers know that techniques are required to play an instrument; but singing, which has been spontaneous since childhood, does not appear to demand a learned technique. Most singers of popular music — the only ones many students know about — are untrained, and their singing earns them a sizable income.

Vocal proficiency may not be required for the singer of folk songs or the recording star whose singing is manipulated by electronic amplification, reverberation, and spliced tape. But at the secondary school level, singing technique must be taught for students to sing well. In more sophisticated, serious music the singer needs an appropriate aural image to work toward, and a firm technical foundation. He cannot sustain tones and phrases, reach high pitches, or attain good tone quality without instruction in how to sing.

Since singing methods in a choral music class must be taught in a group situation, with a variety of student abilities and interests, and with a definite limitation on the time available, the teacher must use a technique that meets the following criteria:

(1) It must be usable in a group situation. There is little time for individual instruction, and few students have the time, money, opportunity, or inclination for private voice lessons outside of school hours.

(2) It must be simple, direct, and as natural as possible. Few teenage

choral groups can learn much from a singing lesson as it is generally taught in the private studio. Private instruction is often too advanced for them, and it requires for its success much personalized attention from the teacher. Techniques that call for a series of ho-ho-ho's or dangling the arms while bending the head and making noises like a propeller-driven airplane are not suitable for a class of 65 down-to-earth adolescents. A singing method for secondary school students must be stripped of all but basic learnings.

(3) It must be applicable to the music the group is singing. Young people need to see improvement in their singing of the repertoire, more than in their performance of isolated drills.

(4) It must present the fundamentals of proper singing.

What is Correct Singing?

There is little consensus among singers on proper methods for correct singing. Voice teachers differ on matters of tone, diction, boys' voice change, and range; they disagree further on whether or not the sinus cavities help resonate the tone, whether air is released or "blown out" while singing, what muscles should be used to produce the proper tone quality, and whether or not physical actions should be taught.[1] The differences of opinion cause confusion for the school choral director, who conscientiously wants to teach his students something about singing.

The lack of consensus derives partly from the differing views on what artistic singing should do. Some singers strive for brilliance and power in singing, others for expressiveness, and others for a kind of prettiness. The position a singer takes on this matter naturally affects his tone, volume, and diction, and determines to some extent the methods he advocates for singing. What is a "big tone" to one singer is "forcing" to another, and what is proper breath support to one voice teacher is muscular tension to another. A further reason for disagreement is the highly individualistic nature of singing. Two excellent singers may have been taught to sing in ways that are in contradiction to each other. Or the opposite may be true: two singers of apparently equal interest and ability are taught by the same teacher, one turning out to be an excellent singer and the other mediocre.

Although the differences of opinion leave the school music teacher in an uncomfortable position, because almost anything he tells his students can be disputed by some specialist, he cannot stand helplessly by while his students flounder through the music. He must act. Therefore, this chapter will present suggestions for giving teenage singers a proper vocal founda-

---

[1]For two writers who are diametrically opposed on this point, see: *Pro:* Kenneth N. Westerman, *Emergent Voice* (2nd Ed.) (Ann Arbor: Carol F. Westerman, 1955), p. 17. *Con:* Sergius Kagen, *On Studying Singing* (New York: Holt, Rinehart & Winston, 1950), p. 59.

tion. The suggestions are a synthesis of the different views on singing techniques that have proved to be workable and practical in secondary school choral classes. This synthesis is *one* method for helping teenagers to sing; it is not the *only* method. It represents one attempt to meet the criteria listed for successful class instruction.

Two approaches should be undertaken simultaneously. One is developing physical actions that result in proper singing. The other is that of "mind over matter" — instilling aural concepts and psychological attitudes to obtain good singing.

Physical Actions for Correct Singing

The drawings on this page show the position of the lungs, diaphragm, and abdominal wall after inhalation and exhalation.[2] Below the lungs is the muscular floor called the diaphragm, which is lowered when taking a breath, allowing air to enter and fill the lungs. The abdominal wall moves out somewhat to make room for this action. As breath is released, the diaphragm moves up and the abdominal wall moves in. The chest and shoulders do *not* move. Although some room for breath can be made by sharply expanding

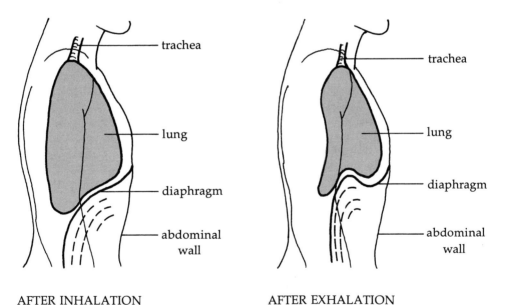

AFTER INHALATION   AFTER EXHALATION

---

[2]Westerman, p. 14. Reprinted by permission.

the rib cage (thorax) with each inhalation, it is difficult to control this breath and not as much air can be inhaled as when deeper breathing is employed. Deep, abdominal breathing is necessary for breath support.

Since the vocal cords remain silent until activated by breath, control of the breath becomes all-important. The diaphragm is responsible for this, and requires the singer's attention to his abdominal area. The vocal cords, on which experienced singers are so prone to center their attention, are merely a passage through which air moves. By slight and almost effortless adjustment, the vocal cords regulate pitch. Since they sound best when vibrating freely, any tension in the throat is detrimental to both intonation and tone quality. The only place where muscular tension should be present is in the large muscles associated with the diaphragm and abdominal area. The cavities of the sinuses, nose, and eyes serve as resonators.

This brief description of the processes involved in singing covers the essential points basic to a good singing technique. How can these basic physical actions be organized so that students in a class can master them? Basically, by formulating a simple routine of physical actions which, if followed strictly, will establish the correct bodily movements for singing. The following four steps have proved successful with teenage singing groups:

(1) Without taking a breath, straighten the spine, relax the shoulders, and hold the chest comfortably high.
(2) Inhale a full breath, as if the air is going directly into the abdomen.
(3) Keep an open and relaxed throat.
(4) Sing a full sound that "floats" out.

Correct Position

When introduced to the first step, the students must realize that to make room for the needed air, the bottom of the lungs and the diaphragm cannot be squeezed or cramped in any way. This is why they are instructed not to take a breath for the first step. Room should be made for the breath, rather than the breath having to make space for itself. The students also should know that lifting the shoulders is just that—lifting the shoulders, and it has little to do with expansion of the lungs. To help keep the chest up, the students can think of the top of the rib cage as the top of a barrel, the lid of which is extremely light and is trying to float away.

Initially, the students should stand when working on correct singing. The position should not be like a soldier standing at attention, stiff as a ramrod. Rather, it is a natural but alert bodily attitude. Many voice teachers suggest leaning slightly forward so that the weight of the body is on the balls of the feet. If the singers are sitting, they can be instructed to sit straight with their backs two inches away from the back of the chair. Good sitting posture is aided when a person places his feet back under the seat of his chair. It's much more difficult to slouch in such a position. Holding music in the palm of the left hand also encourages a good position, because if slouching occurs the music will drop.

The teacher should walk among the students from time to time to remind individuals who are not assuming good posture. Maintaining the right position is necessary because if the physical setup for singing collapses, so does the tone quality. Maintaining proper singing posture has another function: it gives the student something positive on which to concentrate while singing. If he focuses attention on the wrong muscles or on his feelings of inadequacy, tension will result and will affect the sound adversely. The more he concentrates on establishing the proper position, the more he transfers his attention from places that cause tension to areas that can absorb concentration and improve singing at the same time.

Deep Breath

For the second step, inhaling a deep breath, the student should place one hand lightly against the abdominal wall. Later he can place both hands, thumbs forward and fingers to the back, on each side of the waistline, and feel expansion under the hands at those points. If he takes a deep breath properly, the wall will expand somewhat around the beltline. The lungs are larger at the bottom than at the top, so most of the expansion and control comes from the muscles in and around the abdomen. The expansion should occur not only in front, but also at the sides. The students need to know that during inhalation the abdominal wall moves *out*, and during singing and expending air the wall moves *in*. To get the feel of this action, they should try a simple experiment at home: lie on the back with arms relaxed at the sides. Keeping the chest motionless, take a deep breath and notice the expansion of the abdomen. Release the breath slowly and there will be a gradual contraction. If one hand is rested lightly on the abdomen, the out-and-in motion will be more apparent. The exercise is recommended because in a supine position the deep breathing necessary for singing is natural and practically unavoidable. It then becomes relatively simple to duplicate the action while standing.

The diaphragm itself has almost no muscle feeling, although the results of its action can be felt,[3] particularly when clearing one's throat. Control of the diaphragm in singing depends on the correct action of muscles around the abdomen.

---

[3]Westerman, p. 18.

To convey the correct muscular tension in the abdominal muscles, the teacher may describe the process as follows: "Take in a full breath and hold it, using the *abdominal muscles only*. They should be just tense enough to hold back the breath. The sensation should be one of firm but flexible muscles, something like a light steel spring being gently pulled . . . Exhale.

"Now, this time when we repeat the deep breath, make sure there's no tension anywhere else—don't squeeze the throat shut or get a tight feeling in the chest. Just let the abdominal muscles do the work of holding back the air. Everything else is relaxed. Try it . . . Exhale.

"Now let's see what happens when you sing and use up air. As the abdominal wall moves in, you'll feel an increasing amount of muscle tension there. If you sing to the point where you have no breath left, the muscles begin to feel as though they're in a knot." The students can experience this by singing a long tone to the point of silence and noting how they feel when nearly out of air.

The teacher's words should suggest a balance between effortlessness, which is impossible to achieve, and tremendous tension, which inhibits action and causes tension at other places, such as the throat and neck. The teacher can say, "Look, when you walk, your leg muscles can't be completely relaxed because you would just drop to the floor. They can't be too tense, either, because then you would look like a stiff-legged clown. The same is true in singing—some tension is needed, but not too much." To give the students another analogy, the teacher might say, "Pretend that you're going to blow the seeds off a dandelion, but stop just before blowing out any air. The amount of tension in your abdominal wall is the amount you should have when you sing."

Relaxed Throat

The third step, maintaining an open throat, is necessary for a full, pleasant, and freely produced tone. The correct throat position is similar to a yawn. In fact, some teachers refer to the tone produced as "yawny." The tongue is low and relaxed, and the back of the mouth where one swallows is open and round. It may be helpful to vocalize on the sound "awe," which requires openness in the back of the throat. This sensation should be maintained even when the lips are closed.

The students should be told that the throat is a passageway, and once it is set up, it should not be disturbed. In singing, the throat is the sphere of calm through which the tone must be allowed to flow freely. The singer must sing *through* the throat and not *with* it. It should not produce the sensation of shifting, even for very high or very low notes. If the position of the throat changes, the swallowing muscles take over and upset the structure, which should remain stationary. Evidence of muscular interference is not hard to see. A high larynx is one symptom of tension, as are raised eyebrows and sluggish articulation. The most common indication, especially among boys, is the protruding, raised jaw, accompanied by a straining of the muscles under the chin. For some reason, boys will try sticking out their chins to sing what are for them high pitches. It never helps, but they do it anyway. The jaw should be relaxed and loose, as if it were suspended by rubber bands.

Action of Breath in Singing

The fourth step emphasizes the term "float" in connection with tone production to indicate that the air is not rammed through the vocal cords but rises slowly through the throat. Students should learn that singing does not require large amounts of air. As Paul Roe says: "Ask a good singer who smokes (there are a few) to inhale and then sing a tune. It will be noticeable that no smoke will appear until the smoker stops singing; then smoke will come in a gush. In other words, there is so little air used in good singing that no smoke is visible during the act of singing."[4] When singers push the tone or expel air carelessly, they achieve a forced, fuzzy quality that lacks resonance, intensity, and solidity. It has no "center."

To be efficient, the singer must achieve a maximum amount of vocal cord vibration with a minimum amount of air. The teacher can say, "The breath coming out as you sing should move as slowly as if you were warming your hands with it." Another way to achieve intensity is to imagine that the air is "spiraling" or "spinning" as it comes from the back of the throat and moves out of the mouth. Boys know that a football must be spiraled for a good pass. This analogy is often helpful in improving the intensity of their singing tone.

An excellent exercise that combines the four actions required for good singing is to have the singers practice long hisses. The hiss requires little air and no effort in the throat. The extended hiss—at first 20 seconds, but working over a period of time up to 40 or more seconds—calls for correct breath action, smooth and sustained, as in singing. After the students have learned the correct routine, the hiss can be alternated with singing on a vowel: "Hissss-Aaaah-Hissss-Aaaah" executed without a break.

Resonance

If the students are progressing well in their comprehension of correct tone production, the teacher should start to develop resonance in the voices.

---

[4]Paul R. Roe, *Choral Music Education* (Englewood Cliffs, New Jersey: Prentice-Hall, 1970), p. 80.

Although advanced work is best undertaken in private lessons, the school music teacher can begin the initial steps. First the singers should be shown what resonance is. They can experience it by feeling vibration in the head. To do this, they should place the fingers of one hand lightly on the nose and sing "ping." After experimenting to discover the tone placement that encourages the greatest vibration and resonance, they should work to achieve the same vibrant sensation on sounds other than "ng." The object is to encourage resonation by sending the tone through the head and face.

Teaching Suggestions

Whether the four steps for good singing should be taught together or independently is a matter of judgment. One step makes sense only as it is related to the others, and yet some attention needs to be given each step by itself, so a process of alternation between whole and parts is called for. The level of development of the singers should be assessed by the teacher. A musically immature group may not be ready to tackle these techniques for some time. *Interest and motivation also must be present to some degree before the steps will bring forth positive musical results.* By way of further preparation, the students should have memorized some songs that can be sung while learning the routine. Memorization lets the students devote their attention to the newly presented steps. To be meaningful to the singers, the routine for correct singing should always be presented in association with actual music. As soon as possible, the steps should be applied, even though imperfectly, to their current repertoire.

The teacher must be persistent in presenting these singing steps. They involve a complex of skills and understandings, and these cannot be mastered in a period or two. They need to be worked on day after day in many ways, through imaginative warm-up and careful attention to the music. The singer should see the necessity for building good habits and letting proper actions become so ingrained that they will see him through whatever distractions may occur during public performance.

Aural–Psychological Approach

Since the advent of the phonograph, there have been several cases of young singers who, without any private instruction, have demonstrated rare ability, to the astonishment of auditioning committees from conservatories and opera companies. How is it possible for a totally untrained person to sing a difficult Verdi or Puccini aria so well? By listening to a recording of a renowned artist. It has happened several times.[5] These cases illustrate again the shaping power of a singer's tonal concept. It is no accident that Italian operatic tenors have a similar sound, and Irish tenors, to say nothing of Wagnerian sopranos and French *chanteuses*. They sound alike because they have similar concepts of tone and singing.

Since singing involves so many muscles and bodily parts, and since it is impossible for any teacher to describe adequately all the muscular sensations, no physical routine in itself is sufficient to teach correct singing. Physical steps are needed to get the student started in the right direction and to avoid developing habits that hinder singing. But complementary to that effort, the teacher must also convey an aural concept of singing, and then have the students strive for that vocal quality. The human voice is so involved with feeling and thought that what the singer thinks is certain to affect how he sounds. In a very real sense it is the ear (or more accurately, the mind) that controls the throat position, the action of the diaphragm, and the position of the tongue. At times, the vocal teacher feels as much like a psychologist as he does a music teacher, and perhaps this is as it should be.

Style and Tone

As a first step toward developing a concept of good singing, the teacher must disabuse the students of the notion that currently popular styles in singing represent the acme of vocal performance. Popular song style is fine for popular music, but for art music it is badly out of place. When students realize that there are distinct styles of singing, they begin to develop a concept of a legitimate, serious style. Basically, they learn good singing by hearing it, be it from other students, recordings, or the teacher.

Students learn more from one another than a teacher likes to admit. One good bass or alto can do much without realizing it to teach the other singers in the section. If the members of a section, say the tenors, get the idea that a certain tenor is a good singer, they will imitate him.

When selecting recordings for models of tone, the teacher must be particular about the choice of singer. A mature performer may have a highly developed tone that no teenager can or should emulate. Recordings of good collegiate singers are often suitable.

A choral music teacher who is himself a good singer has an advantage. Pianists and other instrumental majors should take heart and notice that the word "singer" is used, not "soloist." A highly trained voice is fine, but it is

---

[5]In fairness it should be pointed out that no doubt some very promising young singers have ruined their voices trying without proper singing technique to imitate recordings of great artists. These young singers are never heard from again.

not necessary. What is needed is a voice with pleasing quality and sufficient flexibility to illustrate various aspects of phrasing, style, and tone. To make their illustrations as effective as possible, some teachers practice singing with a breathy tone, pointed chin, constricted throat, or other handicap. Then they can say to the class, "Look, here's what you're doing—notice what it does to the tone. Now I'll do it right . . . see what a difference it makes?" This helps the student to hear himself as others hear him.

The teacher can strengthen the concept of proper singing by word as well as example. "Hey, that's too rough and blatant. Smooth it up. Be gentler." "Men, that sounds sick. Come on, let's hear some muscle in your tone." Or with word and example together: "Now, the rest of you girls listen to the altos at letter G. This is what I mean by a beautiful tone. Notice that it's warm and flowing, with body to it."

One style, encountered often among boys, especially in junior high school, is what might be called "piano-like" singing. The boys do not sing through their tones, and the result is a combination of speaking and singing. Each note is a short spurt of sound, usually with a pushed tone of debatable pitch, followed by a rest. Probably this is caused by a lack of self-confidence in singing. The cure may involve singing the songs on a neutral syllable, allowing breaks in sound only at breathing points. Other suggestions for legato singing are offered in Chapter 12.

Range

The ease with which a singer adapts to range is affected by his mental outlook. For instance, if a person is asked to walk along a line on the floor, he has no trouble doing so. But if that line were along the roof edge of a ten story building, he would find this feat nearly impossible. The way in which a singer thinks about a tone, especially a pitch at the top of the range, will determine in most cases whether or not he can sing it. Some teachers with the best intentions talk this way: "Now, I know that high A is a difficult note to reach. Why, even professional singers have trouble with it! I hope you can get it, or else we'll have to move it down an octave." The result is, of course, that the students are talked out of singing the note. The teacher should say, "Space suits on. Let's get that A, with a good tone. Sing the line using the technique we worked on—deep breath, open throat." The students should be encouraged to try, but they should not be "whipped" into further effort: "Listen, we're going to get that A or else!"

Girls will gain more freedom in the top part of their range by vocalizing on patterns such as these:

With each singing, the pitch should be raised a half step. Altos may sing, as long as they are able, in unison with the sopranos. Perhaps the girls can be held on the high pitch, then cut off and told, "You know, that note is a whole step higher than the highest note in the 'Hallelujah Chorus,' which we're singing." In this way the exercises are made functional. The vocalization should be continued on a somewhat regular basis until the "high-note phobia" has been overcome. Boys' voice range is discussed later in this chapter.

Diction

Singing has been defined as sustained speech. Making the words intelligible is one of the singer's more significant responsibilities. Unless the words are understandable, the listener is receiving only half of what the composer intended. Furthermore, the singer must produce the words understandably without allowing them to detract from the tone quality and musical effect. Some singers vocalize beautifully, but when they add words the singing loses quality. The words interfere with the singing.

To make words understandable, singers should be made conscious of the need to pronounce words clearly as they sing. In speaking, sloppy pronunciation is more easily covered up because the sounds are relatively short, but in the sustained tones of singing, such concealment is hardly possible. To some degree pronunciation should even be exaggerated during singing. One simple device that helps here is to whisper the words, since whispering requires extreme clarity to be intelligible. A common fault in singing is negligence regarding final consonants, especially *d* and *t* before

[6] Harry R. Wilson, *Artistic Choral Singing* (New York: G. Schirmer, Inc., 1959), p. 204.

[7] Lisa Roma, *The Science and Art of Singing* (New York: G. Schirmer, Inc., 1956), p. 73.

a rest or breath. The students may be careless, or they may be uncertain about when the tone should end. If this is the case, the teacher when conducting can close the thumb and second finger of his right hand precisely at the end of a word, and this will help the singers to execute the final consonant together.

A difficult task for inexperienced singers is to keep the proper throat and mouth position while forming words. There must be freedom from tension in the jaw, tongue, and lips, and consistent application of good methods of singing. Both conditions are helped if jaw movement is kept to a minimum. As Walter Ehret states, "In *legato* singing, particular attention must be paid to the jaw, which should move very *little* if a legato flow is to be preserved. Actually the jaw has to move only for six letters (B, F, M, P, V, and W), and even in these instances the motions are small."[8] Excessive jaw movement creates tension and often leads to less accurate pronunciation. To correct this, the students can practice singing while touching their fingers lightly on their chins. They will be surprised to discover that they can sing and enunciate just as clearly with more economy of movement.

Some teachers and singers want the different vowels to be sung with almost no change of mouth and throat, but others along with Harry R. Wilson[9] feel that such rigidity drains the singing of color and variety. In either case, the students must put first things first. Never should they allow their setup for singing to collapse because they wish to sing a certain sound. They should concentrate on the proper method of tone production and especially on the open throat, so that changes from one vowel to another will cause as little disruption as possible.

Because vowels are the vehicles for sustained tone, which is the essence of singing, they deserve attention. When singers sing the same vowel but do not all sing it alike, they create an illusion of faulty intonation and they blur the words. People who speak the same language in generally the same way are sometimes inconsistent when singing it. They speak a word one way and sing it another. Thus the terms "cleaning up vowels" or "working on vowels" are frequently heard in choral music discussions.

In some cases, good intentions have led teachers into long and complex discussions of palate position, nasalization, and diacritical marks, accompanied by tedious sessions on how to sing the 30-plus vowel sounds of the English language in conjunction with a labial, aspirate, or lingua-palatal consonant. This approach bewilders the students because for years they have been saying words without being conscious of shaping the palate or moving the uvula. Also, such manipulative efforts sidetrack their attention into areas removed from the qualities of the music itself.

---

[8] Walter Ehret, *The Choral Conductor's Handbook* (New York: Edward B. Marks Music Corporation, 1959), p. 36.

[9] Wilson, p. 179.

One remedy for the varied phonation of a vowel is to practice singing it uniformly from a model sound in a familiar word. Traditionally, voice teachers have confined their efforts to the five Italian vowels *i, e, a, o, u,* (*ē, ā, ä, ō, ōō*). English is not Italian, however, and these vowels account for only 12 percent of the sounds on a written page of English.[10] Just the English short *ĭ* as in *sit* accounts for over 12 percent. Westerman in his book *Emergent Voice* lists 15 vowel sounds, which he says represent more than 90 percent of the sounds and 95 percent of the muscular movements involved in singing English.[11]

vē	as in *veal*
sĭ	as in *sit*
tā	as in *take*
thĕ	as in *them*
shă	as in *shall*
lä	as in *large*
gô	as in *gone*
dŭ	as in *dust*
nō	as in *note*
pû	as in *push*
rōō	as in *room*
mī	as in *might*
bou	as in *bounce*
few	as in *few*
coi	as in *coin*

A chart of vowel sounds can be posted on the wall of the classroom. If a word in a song is not being sung consistently, the teacher can point out the sound for the students to practice.

Some vowel sounds are diphthongs, or compounded sounds. Perhaps the most common is the pronoun "I." When singers "chew" its execution as

Ah - a - ay - ee,

the effect is unpleasant and unclear. For a more satisfying result, the singers should hold the initial vowel sound and then at the last moment move to the second or "vanish" sound. Thus "I" is sung:

Ah - - - - ee.

---

[10] Westerman, p. 61.
[11] Westerman, p. 63. Reprinted by permission.

Some choral directors feel it is their "deeyooty" to teach a special version of the English language for singing—a version that is aesthetically superior to spoken English. The value of such a project is questionable. The English language needs little enhancement to be an artistic means of communication.

Because singing exaggerates the unpleasant as well as pleasant sounds of the language, the music teacher might spend a few moments, but no more, to make the undesirable sounds less conspicuous. One is the sibilant *s*, which if sustained produces a hissing effect. The singers should execute it together and should never prolong it. The conductor can help by closing his fingers to indicate the end of the sound. Another troublesome consonant is the *r*. Instead of singing the word "father" as *fahtherrrr*, the singers should sustain *uh* and add the *r* at the very end: *fah-thuh-r*. To soften a vowel so that it will not be harsh, the singers should open the back of the throat and round the lips slightly.

Whether or not the last consonant of one word should be attached to the first of the next word in legato singing depends on the word and on the musical phrase. For example, the words "lost in the night" can be sung "law-sti-nthuh nah-it." In this case, clarity is improved. However, Mendelssohn's lovely "He Watching over Israel" becomes comic if this technique is stressed for the words "slumbers not."

Girls' Voices

The voice quality most often encountered among teenage girls, especially in middle/junior high school, is breathy, thin, or fluty. It is typical of many young girls in the process of physical and vocal growth. To an extent, the teacher has to live with the problem. It is a result of many factors—muscular immaturity, lack of control and coordination of the breathing muscles, and insufficient voice development. Precise and concentrated effort applied to the steps involved in proper singing will help to improve this condition.

In the high school there are few true altos with a rich quality in the low range around A and G below middle C, and there are almost none in middle school. Most teenage altos sound like second sopranos singing low. A word of warning is appropriate here for those teachers who assign a few altos to sing tenor in a mixed four part chorus. If this practice is followed extensively for any one alto, it will tend to strengthen and overuse the tones in her middle and lower range. In addition, she may develop a fear of singing high. Therefore, transferring altos regularly to tenor parts should be avoided.

High school sopranos should not sing much higher than top-space G, or perhaps an occasional A. Younger sopranos should stay about one step lower. The range will depend on the experience of the singers.

Boys' Voices

Boys' voices are usually less breathy than girls'. In the untrained high school boy singer there is often a decided difference between the quality of the low range and the high. As long as the bass voice does not develop signs of a raucous, hard tone quality, the teacher can be assured that there will be no strain if the basses are encouraged to sing out in the low part of their range. In baritones and tenors the quality will often be light and almost colorless in the upper range.

One cannot arbitrarily set up a neat chart of voice ranges, although many writers attempt to do so. The top note of the average high school tenor may be either F or F sharp, and of a baritone either D or E flat. The top note is that note which is fairly comfortable and which occurs occasionally in selections suitable for high school choruses.

High Notes for Boys

The topic of an extended high range for boys leads into a matter about which there is some confusion—the falsetto voice, variously referred to as the "head voice" or "half voice." Music teachers have never been quite sure about whether the falsetto voice is desirable or usable, and there is even some difference of opinion on what action of the vocal cords causes this sound. There is no doubt that boys can extend their singing range by the use of falsetto. True, the tone lacks power and healthy masculine sound, and for that reason boys are not eager to try it. However, as Wilson points out, "it is the normal production for changed male voices to use on high tones. It is both easy and natural."[12]

For years fine professional tenors have been mixing falsetto with the full voice without anyone's being quite sure which voice is being used. Trained solo tenors have demonstrated the closeness of the two voices. With adolescent boys the teacher can say, "Use falsetto to reach tones you can't get with your regular voice." But he should add, and this is most important, "After you've learned the part, try to sing those tones as much as you can with your regular voice. Approach the high tones easily and freely, if you're going to sing them falsetto, and in time you can probably sing them with regular voice." In a few weeks, most boys will be able to sing the high pitches in regular voice, because their apprehensions over high tones have been eliminated. The boys know that they can sing the note one way or another, so doubt is removed. Falsetto is a good model for singing high notes because it is unstrained and free.

---

[12]Wilson, p. 206.

Special attention to developing the falsetto will facilitate its use. The object is to effect a smooth transition from one voice to the other. The first step is for the boy to find his falsetto voice by singing with an *oo* sound on D, E flat, or E above middle C. After the voice has been found, slur down an octave. Wilson suggests moving from the light quality *down* into the regular voice.[13] The boys should not be taken beyond this point for a few days, although the slur can be slowed down with practice. The next step is to sing a descending scale, making the transfer from falsetto to regular voice as smooth and inconspicuous as possible. Finally, after some experience with the scale on the *oo* sound, other vowels may be tried. Until the boys are proficient in the use of falsetto, they should start the tone on an *oo* sound and then change to the desired vowel. Gradually the starting note of this pattern should move chromatically from D above middle C up to A. Basses should be included with the tenors in this work, because they also have occasional problems with high pitches.

Procedures for achieving falsetto must be presented with caution. The teacher cannot walk into class the first day and ask a healthy teenage boy who is proud of his new-found manhood to sing a tone that sounds like an owl hooting. The teacher must bide his time until the boys encounter difficulty with a particular note. Then he can say, "Here's a way for you to get that note." Another condition must be met: the boys must have confidence in the teacher. They need to feel that his directions can be trusted to help them sing better. Finally, the beginning work on falsetto should not be done in the presence of girls. The boys will be sensitive at best, so even if it means putting the girls in another room to study, it is advisable to separate the two groups. Let the girls hear the results of the work as the music is sung. They need not observe the process.

Voice Change

Miss Miller, vocal music teacher at Thornton Middle School, looks dejected as she meets the instrumental teacher in the hall. "I'm losing my wonderful boy soprano, Tom Jenkins," she says. "His voice is starting to change. Too bad." Too bad? Tom Jenkins is growing up. What's so bad about that? Besides, what happens now? Must he go into musical oblivion, as so many other boys have done when their voices change? Is there something for her to do besides shake her head and say, "Too bad"?

For the sake of music education there had better be something more. Tom Jenkins represents every normal boy who goes through school. Most

---

[13] Wilson, p. 207.

boys at some time or another during the period of voice change are involved in music, often in compulsory classes. What happens to Tom and his male peers during the voice change not only shapes their present attitude toward music, but also influences what they will do with singing during the rest of their lives. For these reasons, the topic of the changing voice cannot be treated as a passing curiosity. It deserves serious study and thought.

There is almost no subject in the field of music education that is more fascinating, frustrating, and fraught with differences of opinion than what happens to a boy's voice at puberty and what should be done about it. To begin with, there is the question of whether or not the boy should sing during the period of change. The first published work on the topic appeared in England in 1885 under the intriguing title, *The Child's Voice: Its Treatment with Regards to After-Development*.[14] It concluded that singing during voice change was injurious and ruinous. This theory found little acceptance in America, nor is it held in present-day England.[15]

The big question is, what pitches and parts should the boys sing? Competent music educators have reported interesting findings as a result of their work with countless numbers of boys. The writings of three authorities in the field will be cited. For the sake of accuracy and clarity, each will be presented as an entity in itself, without being synthesized with the others. Because there are no standard definitions for "singing tone," "body in the tone," "straining the voice," or "voice change," some of the differences of opinion cited here may be due to the writers' particular definitions of words.

Essentially, Frederick Swanson advocates keeping the boys singing in a range that is easy for them, even if it means rearranging parts. About the bass range, he states:[16]

> Basses who can sing to a low G' (first line of the bass clef) are quite common in the junior high school. These very "new" basses frequently find middle-c or even B and A quite uncomfortable and must strain to produce these tones. Their "bread and butter" notes are from A' to G. Boys who can produce an audible low E' without strain are not at all rare. . . . In the 13–14-year-old brackets we have found from 30 to 40 of these low basses out of every 100 enrolled in general music classes.

---

[14] Emil Behnke and Lennox Browne (London: Sampson Low, 1885).

[15] Duncan McKenzie, *Training the Boy's Changing Voice* (New Brunswick, N.J.: Rutgers University Press, 1956), pp. 11, 14.

[16] Frederick Swanson, "The Proper Care and Feeding of Changing Voices," *Music Educators Journal*, XLVIII, No. 2 (November–December 1961), 63. Reprinted by permission.

Swanson's footnote explains: "Pitches in the bass clef are indicated by capital letters, in treble clef by small letters. Capitals followed by the prime (') are in the second octave *below* middle-c, while the single capital letter indicates a pitch in the octave immediately below middle-c. The prime after a small letter indicates the second octave *above* middle-c."

Regarding tenors, Swanson says:

> Yes, there are tenors in grades eight and nine. There are boys who have matured physically rather early who find the range D to e quite comfortable for singing. These boys display the typical "break" at about f, and the lowest notes, D and E, tend to thin out and lose resonance. These boys maintain this singing range, adding only a few tones during several school years, indicating that this is not a transition period but a final "settling" of the voice into its approximate adult range.[17]

Swanson urges homogeneous classes for boys, and further segregation into basses and tenors for a year if possible.[18] The music sung should be extremely simple at first.

The most complete work currently available on the changing voice is by Duncan McKenzie, author of *Training the Boy's Changing Voice*. He believes that the boy's voice gradually moves down in pitch through second soprano, to alto, to what he calls a "youth" stage—a stage that is neither changed nor unchanged in quality.[19] He also states that some boys descend into a bass range, only to ascend eventually back to a tenor range.
As for bass range, he writes:

> Considerable differences are found in the comfortable ranges of boy basses during the junior high school period, but by the time the boy gets to high school the voice is nearing the settled stage. This is likely to occur in the eleventh or twelfth year of school.[20]

He then lists bass range as:

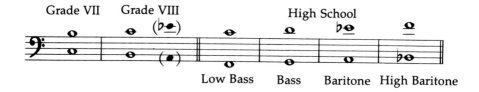

Grade VII   Grade VIII   High School

Low Bass   Bass   Baritone   High Baritone

---

[17] Swanson, "The Proper Care . . . " p. 64. Reprinted by permission.

[18] Frederick Swanson, "When Voices Change," *Music Educators Journal*, XLVI, No. 4 (February 1960), 50.

[19] McKenzie, p. 28. Reprinted by permission.

[20] McKenzie, p. 32. Reprinted by permission.

The alto-tenor range he considers to be from G below middle C to G above. The change from alto-tenor to tenor is an almost imperceptible change of quality and an extension of the lower part of the range to C below middle C.

McKenzie advocates flexibility in assigning boys' voices to a particular part.

> The foundation of any successful plan to preserve the boy's singing voice during adolescence is the "comfortable range" policy. As the alto-tenor plan, for example, is carried out in the junior high school, a boy is transferred to the next lower classification as soon as he begins to have difficulty with the highest notes of the one he is in. Thus the lowest notes have an opportunity to develop, while the highest notes, being unused, gradually disappear. Success with the alto-tenor plan lies in encouraging the voice to lower, for that is what nature intends it to do. Accordingly when there is any doubt about the classification of a voice during the adolescent period, it is best to put the boy in the lower one with the proviso that he must never force the lowest notes.[21]

A third view of the changing voice is presented by Irvin Cooper, who has successfully demonstrated his theories at many meetings of music educators. He offers the following ranges:[22]

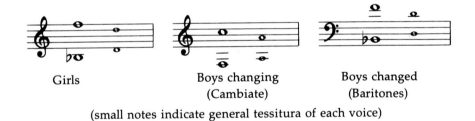

Girls   Boys changing   Boys changed
                 (Cambiate)   (Baritones)

(small notes indicate general tessitura of each voice)

To indicate a departure from the traditional alto-tenor, Cooper adopts the term *cambiata* (plural *cambiate*), from the Italian for "changing." He maintains that vocal teachers for years have been victims of an aural illusion: the changing voice often appears to sound one octave lower than its true pitch. To date, there is no research to support this view, and there is some evidence that refutes it. Cooper says that the cambiata voice cannot be located through individual testing. His procedure is:[23]

---

[21]McKenzie, p. 34. Reprinted by permission.

[22]Irvin Cooper, and Karl O. Kuersteiner, *Teaching Junior High School Music* (2nd Ed.) (Boston: Allyn and Bacon, 1970), pp. 59–60.

[23]Cooper and Kuersteiner, pp. 34–36.

Pitch the key of D major, give the starting note F♯, beat one measure of silence to establish a desirable tempo, then lead them in. Immediately it will become obvious that the boys are singing in octave unison.

Determine which boys are *definitely* singing in the lower octave, tapping on the shoulder each boy who will be a baritone. Any voice about which you are uncertain leave alone for further checking later.

The boys still remaining in front are either sopranos or boys whose voices are passing through the first phase of change (cambiate).

Tell the boys now remaining in front that they will sing the chorus of "Jingle Bells" again, but this time you will give them a different starting note (C in the key of A♭). You will tap all boys who are singing soprano. . . .

Pitch the key of A♭ major, give the starting note C, beat one measure of silence to establish a desirable tempo, then lead them in. As was the case in the first phase of classification, it will become obvious the boys are singing in octave unison:

Repeat the procedure employed in diagnosing baritones, only this time tap all obvious sopranos. Do not waste time trying to diagnose *wanderers*; tap only those who are without doubt sopranos.

Very soon all sopranos will be silent, and the rest will for the time being be classified as cambiate who have been discovered by a simple process of elimination.

The differences among the writers are evident regarding the range of voices and what parts the boys should sing. McKenzie favors the alto-tenor plan of accommodating and anticipating a gradual dropping of the voice. In a critique of the cambiata plan, he raises questions about how the transition of range should be handled.[24] Swanson appears to be more concerned with helping the boys as soon as they have a significant change of voice, a drop into tenor at least.

In view of the differences of opinion about the changing voice, what should Lorene Miller and other middle junior high school vocal music teachers do about it? What should be Tom Jenkins' fate in music? Here are some specific suggestions for Tom's teacher.

(1) Take a positive approach to boys with changing voices. Help them understand what is happening to their voices. More important, let them know that this change can add new tones and color to the music sung. Talk of progress. "Doug, let's see, according to my records you could sing from C up to G two weeks ago. Today you got up to A, and with good quality, too, so you're improving. Keep it up."

(2) *Never* allow a class to ridicule or laugh at the singing efforts of a boy in the throes of change. Although they may pretend to be unconcerned, boys at this age are extremely sensitive about the status of their masculinity, and one bad experience can cause permanent withdrawal from further efforts at singing. More positively, an effort must be made to build a feeling of mutual assistance, understanding, and encouragement in the class. This point is directly related to the first, since to some extent the students reflect the teacher's attitude.

(3) Try assigning parts in performing groups according to each of the different views presented in this chapter. It is not necessary now to make a hard and fast decision about which method is best. Teachers for whom this problem is especially pertinent will have over a period of a year or two more than one group containing changing voices. Try to identify the cambiate in one class, the alto-tenors in another. Only experience can tell what will work in a particular school situation. It's possible that one approach will work better with ninth grade boys than with seventh-graders. The boys' previous musical training, the amount of time for class meetings, whether or not the students are selected—all of these considerations affect what the boys can and should sing. Try segregating boys from girls for a semester or a year, if the school schedule will permit.

(4) Check the range and quality of the boys' voices at least three or four times each year during the period of change. Encourage each boy to ask for an immediate voice check when he feels his range has changed to the point that he is having trouble reaching the notes of his part. The rate and extent of change are highly individual matters, and there is as much variation in voice development as there is in any area of physical maturation. Nor is change consistent within the individual. There may be plateaus, sudden changes, and inexplicable regressions.

By checking and observing the development of each boy's voice, a

---

[24]McKenzie, p. 83.

young teacher can learn firsthand what voice change sounds like and how it progresses. With experience it is possible to judge range by the boy's speaking voice and physical appearance. A short conversation with the boy will indicate the general pitch level of his voice. Heavier facial features, stature, and enlarged larynx usually indicate a maturing voice.

(5) Attempt to meet boys' vocal needs in general music classes. Too often, teachers in a general music class of 30 teach as if the three boys with changing voices weren't there. Begin by seating them together, in the front row near the piano. Add to the section as other boys join in the change. Then on easy unison songs help the changing voices sing an octave lower by playing their notes on the piano, especially the starting pitch. If the teacher is a man, he should by all means sing some of the time with these boys. Select songs with parts for the changing voices, especially lines that are *easy*. When none is included with a song, try writing a simple part — perhaps the chord roots to a song such as "Down in the Valley," or a short ostinato figure. True, it is hard to do much for the first boy whose voice changes, unless he is a capable musician who can hold a part on his own. But what happens to a boy's voice during the change is so important that special efforts should be made to ease the transition.

(6) Be especially careful in selecting music. Vocal numbers should not consistently violate the pitch limits revealed through checking the boys' voices. Again, choose simple music, at least until the voices are stabilized. If a number doesn't fully fit the needs of the group, don't use it.

(7) Stress correct singing, with proper breathing and freedom from tension. The voice is never helped by forcing or straining to reach certain tones, or by singing with a blatant quality in an attempt to sound like a male ten years older. Occasionally, a boy may be asked not to sing certain notes, but as a regular practice this kills interest and should be avoided.

Classifying Voices in High School

Testing voices has two purposes: to serve as a means of selecting singers, and to place the singer in the right part. Initially the teacher should screen would-be members of a performing group to see that they possess the minimum requirements to profit from choral experience. After hearing the voice and reviewing the information presented on the student information sheet (suggested on page 82), he must judge whether or not the rewards of study *for the student* justify the student's expenditure of time and interest.

The best time for auditions is in the spring, so that the class can start right to work in the fall, without delays to wait for testing voices.

Voices are generally grouped according to two criteria — range and quality. In high school the customary ranges for the various classifications are:

Soprano   Alto   Tenor   Bass

Many students cannot sing all the notes in any one classification. Such singers are assigned to the sections that most nearly represent their ranges.

Although the prospective teacher may be familiar with the timbre of the various voice classifications of professional or collegiate singers, the quality of adolescent voices is noticeably less mature. The quality of a typical adolescent bass or alto can be recognized only after experience in working with teenage singers. There are a few good recordings of high school choirs, including some numbers in the albums prepared for the *Performing Music with Understanding* books.

For several reasons it is almost impossible to classify adolescent voices with certainty.

(1) Adolescent voices, especially boys' voices, are not stable.

(2) Psychological factors enter into the student's performance. Under one set of conditions he may capably sing passages that under other circumstances he can't even approximate. Usually the conditions in an audition are about as unfavorable for the adolescent as they can be.

(3) Many students who audition at the beginning of the year do not know how to sing correctly. Developing correct singing habits makes a noticeable difference in a student's range and tone quality.

(4) The voices of teenagers, especially girls in early adolescence, are, like their actions, remarkably homogeneous. What is frequently encountered is an SATB chorus largely composed of second sopranos and baritones with a limited range.

Balance within the group should be considered in classifying voices. If a girls' glee club consists of 100 voices, clearly there cannot be 50 second sopranos and only 15 altos. Some adjustments must be made. This does not mean that a teacher can or should get an additional alto merely by moving a soprano into the alto section. But classifications within the group should be considered, to maintain a reasonable balance of parts. If good balance is impossible, the teacher will have to do the best he can with the available apportionment of voices.

For these reasons, extensive discussion of the "break," color in the voices, and elaborate tonal patterns to aid in classifying does not seem warranted for the school vocal teacher. Some singing teachers even decry the idea of registers in the voice, because they feel the voice is derived from one pair of vocal cords and should have a continuous compass.[25]

---

[25] Roma, p. 36.

Since some classification is necessary for part singing, however, the teacher must make judgments on range and quality, imperfect as these judgments may be. If possible, students should be heard privately.

Place the singer where he cannot see the keyboard, because a student with musical training may have preconceived ideas about the notes he can sing. Then have him sing a five note ascending and descending scale pattern:

Begin girls on middle C and boys an octave lower, and move up stepwise until the top notes of the pattern show strain. Then shift to this pattern, starting at what appears to be the student's middle range and moving down:

Next, have each student sing a familiar song such as "America." Transpose the song into three different keys about a fourth apart, possibly into C for a low range, F for a middle range, and A or B flat for a high range. Listen for intonation as well as for range and quality. Other simple testing procedures may be included if time permits. The range, general tone quality, and other pertinent facts about each voice should be written down, dated, and filed for future reference.

Occasionally a teacher wants to identify the better students for a select choir or ensemble. In such a case, the procedures can be expanded in the following manner:

(1) Check the student's ability to match pitch quickly and accurately. Play a series of three or four pitches in the singer's range on the piano and see how rapidly and exactly they are sung back.

(2) Listen for a highly individualistic tone quality that may not blend well with other voices.

(3) Present the singer with a line of music to sing at sight.

If individual auditions are not possible, group methods will have to suffice, such as those recommended by Cooper for finding cambiate. The patterns recommended for individual testing can also be used for group testing in which changing voices are not involved. Work the boys up to D above middle C. Then arbitrarily place in the tenor section all boys who can sing the D comfortably; the remainder of the boys will make up the bass section. The same technique can be followed with the girls — all who can sing F on the top line comfortably are placed in the soprano section. An individual audition should follow later in the semester.

What's in a Name?

Students at the junior high/middle school level are sometimes concerned about the name of the part they sing. Boys are sensitive about being called "soprano" or "alto" — names associated with girls. To eliminate any problem here, some teachers call boy sopranos "first tenors." Cooper has proposed the term "cambiata" partly because he feels it inspires greater pride among the boys.

Caution must be exercised in designating certain parts as "first" and "second." No one wants to be second in anything in modern-day America, so the term "high" can identify the girls' or treble part, and "low" the boys' or bass clef part. Because girls' voices are so much alike in early adolescence, some teachers regularly have girls trade parts, one section learning the high part for one song and the low part for another.

Whether an organization is called choir, chorus, glee club, troubadors, sextet, or ensemble is not a serious matter to the teacher. As long as the terms are used conventionally — a sextet contains six singers, and glee clubs are either boys or girls — almost any name is acceptable. But students, especially in early adolescent years, place considerable importance on the name of a group. In some schools the "choir" is for the talented and the "glee club" is for anyone else. The teacher should discuss with the group the possibility of another name. In some schools it has been the making of a new attitude, and the students can contribute their own ideas.

Group Size and Seating

Generally, the larger a student group, the better it will sound. Teenagers whose voices are not yet fully developed need the support of a number of singers on their part. This gives them confidence and makes their efforts more satisfying. Happily, a group of average voices can, when put together properly, sound quite beautiful. The individual voice timbres apparently combine to make a rich tone, and minor pitch deviations are no longer noticeable. If two performers are five vibrations apart, the "beats" are easily heard. But when other voices are added, some of them being one, two, or three vibrations different, the "beats" are no longer distinguishable. A tone with such pitch variation may lack brilliance and clarity, but it can still be pleasing.

Optimum group size depends on the ability and age of the singers, the demands of the music, and the acoustics of the place of performance, so no ideal size can be recommended. Probably student choral groups sound best with 45 to 90 voices; beyond this number the size becomes unwieldy for the teacher to handle in the regular manner. Nor can the proper distribution of singers on each part be stated with much certainty. Since the lower pitches of a singer's vocal range do not have the carrying power of high pitches, and since the lower parts in a choral group are more easily overbalanced, the low voice parts generally need more singers.

In assigning seats in a section, two strong singers should be placed side by side, so that they can support each other. Then less mature singers can be placed on either side of the more able students. In this way, the weaker singers can learn from the better ones. The seating should be changed from time to time so that the singers learn to sing with different persons and have a chance to hear the group from other locations.

Selecting an Accompanist

A poor accompanist can virtually break a choral group by slowing the class pace and confusing the singers by playing the music incorrectly. The teacher must select the accompanist carefully, and then train him to follow and even anticipate the teacher's directions.

If possible, several accompanists should be selected for the organization. One can substitute for another, and an entire rehearsal will not be disrupted because an accompanist is absent. Most teachers must choose their accompanists from within the choral group. In such situations, the rotation of several accompanists gives more students the experience of accompanying, and also gives them a chance to sing.

Unfortunately, a distinction often must be made between accompanists and pianists. Because of the pedagogical practices of some piano teachers, it is possible for a player to perform a few concertos and etudes extremely well, and still not be able to read the simplest of music. These "rote" performers usually make poor accompanists because they have to commit to memory almost every piece they play, and sometimes there isn't time to memorize the accompaniment. This type of pianist also tends to be inflexible in following a conductor.

In selecting accompanists, three simple tests can be given.

(1) Have the applicants sight-read the accompaniment to a piece of octavo music that is not too difficult. Rate them on their ability to keep

going without stopping, and of course on their general accuracy in playing the music.

(2) Have the applicants sight-read only the voice parts of a choral number. Do not select a contrapuntal work for this purpose, because music of this type is too difficult for most high school students to sight-read. Some applicants will have trouble reading the voice parts in SATB music.

(3) Choose a simple octavo selection and have the applicants learn the accompaniment before the audition. At the tryout, have each pianist play the piece while you conduct. To see how well he can follow, go through the piece and alter the tempo several times. Then ask him to play a certain passage—for example, the tenor part on page four, second score, fourth bar. This will reveal his alertness in following verbal directions. If the accompanist can transpose and modulate, this is an added boon to the class.

Few teachers are fortunate enough to have accompanists who can play fluently through the three tests just mentioned, so some training is in order. Learning to play the notes on the page and to read the voice parts is simply a matter of individual practice. If an accompanist studies privately, his teacher is often willing to give him special assistance. At the beginning of the year, it is wise to hear the accompanists play their music privately *before* the piece is practiced with the singers. The most common cause of trouble for inexperienced accompanists is the clef sign used for the tenor part. It is usually necessary to explain this phenomenon to a pianist. When seen on a tenor part, any of the first four clefs (shown below) indicate that the notes do not sound as written, but rather one octave lower. The fifth sign is the tenor clef, on which the pitches sound as written, with middle C on the fourth line.

The main task in training an accompanist is to teach him to anticipate tempos and verbal instructions. The development of this ability will be hastened if the teacher is consistent in his approach to the music. An accompanist should also learn to think by phrases and sections rather than note by note. This helps him to play more musically and to envisage possible starting and stopping places.

Use of the Piano

The piano is of limited help in teaching vocal music. Aside from the initial playing of parts in the rote learning process, the piano should be avoided for demonstration purposes because its tone is so unlike the tone of the voice. Once a tone is struck on the piano, it immediately begins to fade away. In vocal music the objective is a continuous, full sound.

A beginning choral teacher who was not a voice major in college may be self-conscious about singing in front of a large group of students, and consequently he may be tempted to rely on the piano for all demonstrations. To correct this habit, he should at first sing short and easy passages for the group to gain confidence in his ability to demonstrate musical ideas.

The proper amount of accompaniment depends on the ability of the singers. Musically advanced groups can and should sing frequently without the piano, even on works that will be accompanied in performance. Inexperienced musicians, too, should do some singing without the piano in almost every class meeting. Care must be taken so that the piano does not cover up faults in the singing. Also, the singers must develop a degree of independence from the piano, because in the unfamiliar circumstances of a performance they may find it more difficult to hear the accompaniment.

Memorizing Music

Choral groups almost always memorize the music that they perform before an audience, while instrumental groups never do, except for one or two standard numbers played on the marching field. There are good reasons for choral groups to memorize:

(1) There are no distractions caused by holding music or turning pages. All the singers' attention can be centered on singing and watching the director.

(2) The appearance of the group is improved because there is no chance for a singer to bury his head in the music.

(3) Many annoyances are eliminated — loose pages fluttering to the floor, and music brushing the back of a singer's neck.

(4) Memorized pieces are usually thoroughly learned.

Memorization is aided by applying the psychological principles described in Chapter 9. The principle of distributed effort means that memorization is most easy and thoroughly accomplished in many short periods, rather than in one or two long ones. Recognizing patterns and relationships in music is also directly applicable to memorization, because most works of music have an overall pattern or form. The music can be scanned for accents, holds, solos, and tempo changes, because these features often show a pattern in themselves. Noting the phrase endings that rhyme is helpful in recalling both words and music.

There are several teaching devices to help the students memorize. They can be asked to write the words to the songs, as a test that will influence their grades. A group memorization technique can be operated in this manner: Select a logical section of from two to four lines, and let each student study it by himself for about 20 to 30 seconds. Then ask the entire group to recite the words together without music. If this goes well, call on two or three individuals to recite the phrases. Move on to another portion of the text, and after it has been memorized, ask the group to recite both segments. Move the process along as quickly as possible, and do not keep it up too long at one time.

To vary the procedure, words can be passed back and forth between teacher and singers. For example, Now let EVERY TONGUE ADORE THEE; or, now LET every TONGUE adore THEE. Another variation is to recite a line and ask for the first word of the next line. Chorus: NOW LET EVERY TONGUE ADORE THEE. Teacher: "George?" George: "Let." Chorus: LET MEN WITH, etc.

The teacher can facilitate memorization by asking the students to sing the piece from memory at an early stage of preparation. Singers can become so accustomed to the "crutch" of looking at music that it is difficult for them to break away from it. Memorization should not be urged too soon, however, because it may encourage faking.

The teacher should impress on the singers the necessity of thinking ahead when singing. Foresight is necessary to prevent such serious mishaps as singing through a break, or starting out on the wrong section of the music. Lines are less likely to be forgotten when the singers think ahead.

Calamity can also be averted by good spot practice. In a piece of music there are frequently a few crucial places at which the music is most likely to break down—change of section, change of key, and so on. The singers should be made to feel especially confident at these points.

Some teachers, in an effort to build the confidence of their singers, unconsciously develop habits which increase the students' dependence. One of these is the habit of singing along with the group. Generally this should be done only to help a part that is weak, or to encourage the singers in a strategic place such as the beginning of a new section. The danger is that the singers begin to rely on the teacher's help. Since he cannot sing along in a concert, the students should learn to do well without his support. Another disadvantage is that the teacher's singing tends to make the music sound better to him than it actually is. He should be listening carefully to the group, not to his own voice—even though the latter may sound better.

The teacher should also avoid mouthing the words. This technique is of only limited help to the singers. If all the parts do not have the same words at the same time, the help is negligible; and even if the words are synchronized, it is doubtful whether the singers are able to lip read. They should have the words learned well enough to get along without this assistance.

All music memorized by the singers should also be memorized by the director. He makes a poor impression when he conducts from the printed page while his singers perform from memory. The teacher should maintain eye contact with the singers at all times during performance, and this precludes looking at a copy of the music.

Questions

1. How would you explain to a choral class of high school freshmen and sophomores why it is important for them to learn how to sing correctly?

2. How would you explain to a ninth-grader that the style of singing used by the latest teenage group is not appropriate for art music?

3. Should a choral teacher attempt to develop an adult-like singing tone in a high school choir? in a junior high school choir? Why, or why not?

4. What analogies can be used to give the students the idea of the open throat?

5. Ronald Clark can sing from C below middle C up to D above middle C. According to Cooper, which part should he sing? According to McKenzie?

6. Suppose that several boys in chorus show a marked tendency to force tones, producing a strained, unpleasant quality. What can be done to reduce this problem? Which step in the singing routine should be emphasized?

Projects

1. Find three choral pieces that contain long tones suitable for work on proper breathing. They should be simple, yet musically worthy of study. Handel's "Thanks Be to Thee" is an example.

2. Review three collections of part songs for boys' changing voices. Note the range and tessitura of the parts in each of the three books.

3. Listen to recordings of solos by sopranos, altos, tenors, and basses. Select one of each voice type that is suitable as a model for teenage singers to emulate.

4. With your college music methods class, work out a consistent vowel pronunciation on the following phrases: "I'm going away," "Still are your thoughts." Then practice singing these words together:

chance   o - ver

5. Using members of your methods class, give several an audition for a choral music group. Classify their voices and assign them to an appropriate part.

Suggested Readings

Appelman, D. Ralph, *The Science of Vocal Pedagogy.* Bloomington, Indiana: Indiana University Press, 1967.

Baker, George, *The Common Sense of Singing.* New York: The Macmillan Company, 1963.

Cooper, Irvin, and Karl O. Kuersteiner, *Teaching Junior High School Music* (2nd Ed.). Boston: Allyn and Bacon, 1970, Chapter 3.

Garretson, Robert L., *Conducting Choral Music* (3rd Ed.). Boston: Allyn and Bacon, 1970.

Huls, H. S., *The Adolescent Voice: A Study.* New York: Vantage Press, 1957.

Kagen, Sergius, *On Studying Singing.* New York: Holt, Rinehart & Winston, Inc., 1950.

McKenzie, Duncan, *Training the Boy's Changing Voice.* New Brunswick, New Jersey: Rutgers University Press, 1956.

Roma, Lisa, *The Science and Art of Singing.* New York: G. Schirmer, Inc., 1956.

Rosewall, Richard B., *Handbook of Singing.* Evanston, Illinois: Summy-Birchard Company, 1961.

Westerman, Kenneth, *Emergent Voice* (2nd Ed.). Ann Arbor, Michigan: Carol F. Westerman, 1955.

Wilson, Harry R., *Artistic Choral Singing.* New York: G. Schirmer, Inc., 1959.

15

Teaching
Instrumental Music

The instrumental teacher faces conditions different from those encountered by the choral music director. The most significant difference is the degree of specialization. Instrumental music involves a conglomeration of fingerings, embouchures, bowings, and other specialized techniques and knowledge. Scraping a bassoon reed, stopping notes on the French horn, spiccato bowing on the violin, the several fingerings for high G on the clarinet—these are all highly technical bits of skill and learning.[1] The teacher of singing faces many challenges, but at least all human voices produce sound in the same way.

Beginning Instrument Instruction

In most school systems instrumental music is begun in the fourth or fifth grade. But in a few districts such instruction is not offered until junior or even senior high school. Even in systems that begin instruction in the elementary grades, beginning classes should be offered in middle/junior high school for students who are new in the district or who are just now becoming interested in music study. This makes some beginning instrument teaching a distinct possibility for the instrumental music teacher in the secondary school.

Pre-Band Instruments?

In some instrumental music programs much emphasis is placed on pre-band instrument classes. These inexpensive and easy-to-play instruments

---

[1] An aid to the teacher in recalling instrumental fingerings, trills, rolls, positions, and transpositions is *Fingering Charts for Instrumentalists* by Clarence V. Hendrickson (New York: Carl Fischer, Inc., 1957). The book is a convenient pocket size.

are like modern-day recorders, although they lack the range and gentle tone of the recorder. They are included in the instrumental program to weed out the less talented and less interested students, and to provide training in reading notation.

The involvement of the instrumental teacher with special classes of pre-band instruments is questionable on several counts. One: it is a pre-*band* program. What is being done to encourage and train string players during this experience? Two: these simple instruments have little carry-over to real band instruments. There is no transfer of embouchure and very little of fingering. Three: the validity of pre-band instruments as prognosticators of success in instrumental music has not been established. Four: if training in music reading is valuable, it should be carried on as a part of the regular elementary basic music program, the benefits of which will accrue to all students.

In the elementary music program, work with keyboard and recorders, or an exploratory program including strings, is a more valid way to encourage the child's continuing participation in music. Teaching legitimate instruments is, after all, the surest way to build a successful instrumental music program.

Pupil Guidance

Since the instrumental program is part of the music curriculum, its goals and practices must be consistent with those of music education in general. Instrumental music sometimes deviates from other music courses in its selection of students. Because the school music program exists to educate all students as fully as their interest and ability allow, the idea of selecting only those young people who are most likely to succeed is objectionable. As in learning any valid skill, all except the clearly incapable should be allowed a fair trial. If after a year Donald decides the trumpet is not for him, at least he has had that educational experience and hopefully has learned from it. It would have been fine if he had shown the interest and ability to continue the trumpet or attempt another instrument, but no one has suffered because he was offered the experience.

Furthermore, no one could really have predetermined whether or not Donald would be a success in instrumental music. Sometimes a student who shows little promise or motivation turns out to be a fine instrumentalist a few years later.

In the 1920s, the school board in one city informed a local professional musician that they would be glad to start a band in the schools *if* he could present a "playing band" in three weeks! With such a deadline, he gave all interested students a hastily created test before they were allowed to become members of the pilot band. The students were asked to march around the school gymnasium to the beat of a drum. All who fell out of step were eliminated. The director freely admitted years later, "I don't suppose that test was worth a thing. But I had to do something to cut the numbers down so that there'd be enough instruments to go around." Such a procedure was understandable in those years and under those conditions.

But now instrumental music has been well established in the schools for over four decades, and expedient actions should be retired. Today's decisions affecting the lives of youngsters should be made with care and knowledge, and not on the basis of homemade tests by the teacher. The topic of talent testing was discussed in Chapter 6, and the limitations of carefully constructed, scientific efforts were pointed out at that time. How much less valid, then, must be a test that a teacher concocts for his own use?

Furthermore, through rental instrument plans with music merchants, the rental of school owned instruments, and the cooperation of an informed board of education, all but the most financially depressed districts can now make it possible for sincerely interested students to try instrumental music.

Only general guides can be offered regarding what instruments should be assigned to individual students. If a youngster faces a lengthy session with braces on his teeth, or if he has an underbite (lower teeth in front of upper) or crooked teeth, he should be guided away from brasses. Generally, small students should not try large instruments. Boys who have thick fingers should be encouraged to try instruments other than violin, because notes in the higher positions are too close together to allow for thick fingers without some kind of compensatory movement, which is difficult. Students whose pitch sense is below average should especially avoid strings, French horn, and trombone.

The most important point to consider in assigning an instrument is the student's desire. A teenager can accomplish wonders—when he wants to. He can become proficient on an instrument while appearing to defy all the physical qualifications. The teacher should guide students in instrument selection, but he should not require that they take a particular instrument or none at all. There is a higher-than-normal incidence of dropping out among students who begin on an instrument other than their first choice.

Although instrumental music is offered for the values that accrue to the student, the teacher should attempt to maintain some balance in instrumentation, both for playing music in the near future and in high school. To achieve this balance, he will have to exercise tact and judgment in guiding students in their selection of instruments. Even then he has no guarantee that three years hence he will not have a half-dozen drummers and no baritones. The number of students encouraged to begin on each instrument should be in proportion to instrumentation needs listed on pages 390 and

391, with consideration given the fact that a few clarinet players, for instance, will transfer to oboe and bassoon. It is helpful if the school owns the instruments, so that the inventory available to beginners is balanced.

Many schools own instruments that are rented to beginning students for a nominal charge. If the school system does not provide instruments, or if its supply cannot meet the demand, students may rent from local merchants. Some school systems closely integrate their activities with a certain merchant, in which case ethics must be closely observed as to bids and equal opportunity for all merchants. If at all possible, the student should not be required to purchase an instrument before study is undertaken, because this entails a financial risk for the parent. Instruments that are relatively expensive, uncommon, or difficult to play (oboe, viola, tuba, bass clarinet) should not be offered beginners, if for no other reason than to cut down on the variety of instruments in the class. Generally, beginning instruction is offered on the following instruments: flute, clarinet, trumpet, horn, trombone, baritone, percussion, violin, and cello.

Organizing the Beginning Class

Class lessons are necessary in school, because few schools can support the prohibitively high cost of individual instruction. Besides, in many communities competent private teachers are not available on all orchestral instruments. Class lessons, then, are an expedient, but they are a good expedient in several ways. There is a unity in what is taught and in the rate of progress, so that within a year or two the students can be combined to form a band or orchestra. There is also motivation when students work together and learn that other people have difficulty in playing their instruments, too. Finally, as the teacher becomes experienced in class techniques, he finds that he can accomplish during the first year or two of the students' study almost as much as he could in private lessons. Naturally, as students advance and playing problems become more individualized, private lessons become more valuable.

Beginning classes should meet a minimum of two times a week for 30 to 45 minutes, and each group should not exceed 12 members, unless larger numbers cannot be avoided. If class sizes are consistently too large, the teacher should work to secure additional teaching help. With strings, for instance, it takes some time just to tune 12 instruments, and the larger the number, the less time there is in which to teach and give attention to each student.

The class should be as homogeneous as possible, although this will depend primarily on the schedule of the school and teacher. Mixing strings and winds should be avoided. Sharp keys are better for strings and flat keys for winds, and the two do not mix well until the intermediate level. Even families of instruments in the same class present problems to the teacher. Just as he gets ready to call out a note to the clarinets he remembers that the note will be different for the flute; when he mentions one fingering to the violins he must be ready to suggest another to the cellos. Range problems occur when the instruments are mixed. Concert F is easy for the trumpet, but either somewhat high or low for a young French horn player.

Beginning Instruction Books

Many publishing companies offer inexpensive instruction books for beginning instrumentalists. The books contain simple pieces that can be played by a complete ensemble at a remarkably early stage. Though generally well-written, many of them reveal distressing similarities. There seems to be an attempt in 32 pages to give the player all the signs and notes that might conceivably appear on the printed page, even symbols that are seldom encountered in beginning literature. Too often "the introduction of technical problems is dry and unimaginative . . . and [yet] does not present enough material to master the problems. . . ."[2] Wolfgang Kuhn suggests the following criteria for selecting a methods book:

> (1) Are there general instructions on the care and use of the instrument?
> (2) Are there correct illustrations of fundamental posture, positions, embouchure?
> (3) Is there a complete fingering chart?
> (4) What is the value of the musical content?
> (5) Are technical problems introduced logically and functionally?
> (6) Are directions given simply and clearly?
> (7) Is the music edited well?
> (8) Is ensemble music included?
> (9) Is there a list of musical terms?
> (10) Is the physical makeup and appearance of the book appropriate?
> (11) Is there a score and teacher's manual provided?[3]

Because so many instruction books contain limited material, supplementary music of a simple nature will be needed, especially if within the year the beginners attempt to play for an audience, which it is desirable to

---

[2]Wolfgang E. Kuhn, *Instrumental Music: Principles and Methods of Instruction* (Boston: Allyn and Bacon, 1962), p. 112.

[3]Kuhn, *Instrumental Music* (2nd Ed.), 1970, pp. 28–30.

have them do. Simple, solid arrangements of folk songs and well-known melodies are appropriate for such performances.

Teaching the Beginning Class

The teaching principles presented in Chapter 9 are of course applicable to teaching beginning instrumental music. The most challenging problem for the teacher is to clarify the complex nature of playing an instrument, as was illustrated on page 193 in the multiplicity of instructions given the young violinist. The beginner can't do everything at once. Therefore the teacher must settle for concentrating on one thing at a time, and by alternate emphasis on wholes and parts he slowly builds the complex action involved in playing an instrument.

Because kinesthetic learning is so basic to instrumental playing, the teacher's efforts should also be directed toward building good habit patterns. For example, developing an embouchure is largely a matter of muscle movement and strength. A teacher cannot hope to establish proper embouchure if he presents it once and then proceeds to other things. Embouchure must be reinforced over a long period of time, through a variety of approaches and frequent short reminders.

Mastery of an instrument is a complex amalgamation of many simple habits. The teacher must carefully combine different phases of the learning activity. He might ask the clarinet players to play long tones on open G, checking with their left hand to see that they are "keeping their chins down" as they play. When they are successful at this, he can point to a line of music that has been studied previously, and say, "Now that you have the position of your lower lip and chin right, let's see if you can play this line *while at the same time* keeping your good lip and chin position." If the students have worked enough on their embouchures and notes and rhythms, they will be able to put together the two aspects of good playing. If they fail, they should again concentrate on one thing.

Two procedures are helpful in the beginning class. One is to have the students sing the line of music *in rhythm* at proper concert pitch, singing the note names while fingering the notes on their instruments. Sharps, flats, and naturals can also be sung, using only the note names while the students think and finger the accidentals. Attention should be drawn to the key signature and accidentals before going through the line. A variation is to have the students say "tah" or "lah" for each note. Singing while fingering is especially helpful in the first semester of study. Another practical step is silent fingering, which is helpful to students at any level. There is no need for players to sit idly by in an instrumental music class. While one section is playing, the others can be fingering a new line, or one on which they need practice.

Rote Procedures

Rote teaching is useful in the early stages of study since beginning students find it difficult to coordinate the mechanics of instrument playing with reading notation. Rote procedures allow the proper mechanics of playing to be assimilated without distraction. When there are no music stands the teacher can move about freely to help with fingering or playing positions. There is no reason for him to remain in front of the group, because formal conducting isn't meaningful to students at this stage. The class is started by verbal cues instead of hand motions. Usually the teacher should count out a complete measure, inserting "ready, begin" or "ready, play" in tempo on the final two counts.

Sometimes difficult problems, such as crossing the break between registers on the clarinet, are best introduced by rote. A portion of "Three Blind Mice" (B-A-G, B-A-G) can help the player get across more easily, and it makes the relationship between the two registers more clear to him. "Three Blind Mice" is also a very helpful pattern for trumpeters who cannot get low C easily (E-D-C, E-D-C), and for trombonists who need to practice slide positions (D-C-B flat, D-C-B flat, or A-G-F, A-G-F). On violin it provides practice in crossing strings (B-A-G, B-A-G).

Rote procedures are especially valuable in strings classes because all string instruments are in concert pitch, all produce tone in the same manner (whether plucked or bowed), and all have most of their open strings in common. The teacher can say, "Pluck the notes D and E–open D then first finger. Let's play it this fast (*said in tempo using quarter notes*): D-E-D-E-rest rest, D-E-D-E-rest rest. Instruments in position . . . (*in tempo*) Ready, play." The class plays the pitches and says the notes and rests aloud. Many variations are possible to enliven the class. For one, the teacher may turn his back to the students, pick up his violin and play a simple pattern (D-E-F sharp-E-D) and ask, "I started on D. What other notes did I play?" If the students are quick to tell the proper note names, he can try this step: "I started on D. Don't tell me what I played. Just play it back to me . . . (*in tempo*) Ready, begin."

On another occasion, he may show the students the notation for the patterns presented in the rote experience. Three approaches can be used. For the five note pattern D-E-F sharp-E-D, the teacher can write the notes on the board and say, "Here's a picture of the notes we played. This is what they look like when they're written down." Another approach is for him to write the pattern on the board before the rote instruction, and have the students read it, which is of course the normal reading process. A variation of this is for the teacher to say, "Follow the notes on the board. I may or may not play what's there. Check me to see if I do." The third approach, and in some ways the most educational, is to ask a student to think up a five note pattern and sing it to the class, being sure to get an accurate starting pitch. Then he can play it on his instrument, and write it on the board. The singing is more likely to be an accurate representation of the pattern he thought up, so it serves as a check on the accuracy of his writing and playing.

Rhythm and bowing on string instruments are closely integrated. Rote work is excellent for getting the bow arm to move properly in rhythm, and such training should be introduced early in the study of the instrument. "Now we've played on the four open strings G, D, A, and E. Let's play one note down bow and one up bow, rest two counts, then go to the next string. Do G first, then D, A, and E. After that, we'll come back down E, A, D, and G." The students then play the pattern:

Other patterns can be approached in the same manner so that the players simultaneously gain freedom of bow movement and comprehension of rhythm.

Because time is at a premium in every beginning class, instruction should be as efficient as possible. One way to hear individual students quickly and still keep everyone learning is for the class to play a line together. Then, in rhythm, the teacher calls out, "Ralph, play," and Ralph plays the line alone, as the rest of the students finger along. Then the teacher calls for the entire group again or for another student. Thus there is no break in the music until the teacher requests it. Another way to save class time is to hear individual students play their assigned lesson on an informal rotation basis. Only two or three students selected at random need play a line of music alone. In this way, all students prepare because they may be called on.

Stress the Musical Qualities

The teacher of the beginning instrumental class should make a special effort to keep the activities musical. Because so much attention must be placed on moving a finger and counting a note, musical expression seems to get lost. After all, when a student knows only three or four notes, and whole notes at that, it is difficult to perform with much expression. A certain amount of technical facility must precede making music on an instrument. But the teacher should not give up teaching music. Again, rote and memorization are real helps here. Because of the effort required to learn a piece from the written page, many students will have nearly memorized the piece anyway, so not much additional effort is required to have the class play it from memory. When the distractions of reading music are eliminated, it's easier to introduce the concepts of musicianship.

When the class learns its first melody, be it "Lightly Row" or "Twinkle, Twinkle, Little Star," the teacher should work further to bring out its musical qualities. What is the high point of the melody? What groups of notes belong together? Should the piece be smooth or choppy? Books of simply arranged solos and duets are available to supplement the method book. Whatever the materials selected, instrumental classes should make music.

Rhythm

An instrumentalist who gets lost and can't perform the notes with the rest of the players is a hindrance to any group effort. One of the first requirements of music instruction is that it teach the execution of rhythm. Beginning students can be permitted to tap the foot lightly on each beat. Unless they have considerable previous musical experience, the students during the first year may continue to maintain the beat with the foot.

If students have trouble performing a rhythm correctly, they can set aside their instruments and clap out the pattern. If they have trouble maintaining a steady beat, they should practice standing up, marking time, and playing the music as they march in place. A frequent problem among young students is lack of distinction between the beat which they tap and the rhythmic figure which they play. Many times they will do this:

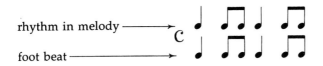

Marching helps to cure this tendency.

In addition to feeling a steady beat, students must know a system of counting. Suggestions for rhythmic syllables are given in Chapter 11. Students should count out lines of music in vigorous singsong fashion before playing them. Singsong counting accentuates the rhythmic swing or pulse, and helps prevent a dry, mechanical recitation of beats.

Practicing

Strange as it may seem, a teacher must teach his instrumentalists how to practice. Telling the young student, "Practice 30 minutes every day" is comparable to the physical education instructor saying, "Spend 30 minutes a day building up your muscles." How? Doing what? A portion of each lesson must be devoted to giving specific directions on what is to be done outside of class. The beginning student needs to know how fast to play the line of music, and he must know how to check his embouchure or position. Above all, he should realize that practicing is not a matter of "putting in time." The emphasis should be on practicing *correctly*. Shorter practice periods with a high level of concentration are more productive for the beginning instrumentalist.

If possible, the student should establish a daily practice time that is respected by his family and friends. Some teachers ask each student to fill in a card that parents initial to indicate the amount of time spent practicing. Such efforts are fine, as long as they do not stress time rather than results. There is so much to learn about playing a new instrument that the student's attention might better be focused on remembering the musical, rather than the clerical, aspects of his instruction.

Need for Teaching Fundamental Skills

Teaching fundamental techniques should not end when the students have completed a year or two of study. The teacher cannot assume that such fundamentals as breath support and tonguing have been learned adequately in one year of class lessons. If only it were that easy! Fundamentals must be taught over a span of time, from beginning classes into the bands and orchestras of the secondary schools. Fortunately, as in the case of singing, if students grasp the fundamentals of producing the sound properly, they have come a long way in their study of music.

Almost all prospective instrumental music teachers are required in college to take instruction on instruments other than their major instrument. These "techniques" classes provide the future teacher with a basic knowledge of tone production, fingerings, playing position, and the like. Because the presentation of the first lessons is usually covered in such classes, this chapter will stress the basic points that need to be taught in some degree to all secondary school students regardless of their level of proficiency.

The preceding chapter devoted considerable attention to the topic of a correct method of singing. The concern was, as it is in this chapter, for techniques that can be taught successfully in a group situation. This book does not cover all the worthwhile points that a singer or instrumentalist should learn. Indeed, entire books have been written on just the techniques of playing the clarinet or violin. So the information here is merely introductory.

Through reading, conversation, and firsthand experimentation, the instrumental teacher should gain as much specialized information as he can about instruments other than his own. It will all be useful in his work.

Fundamentals of Wind
Instrument Performance

All wind players should learn to play with adequate breath support, to form the correct embouchure, and to start and stop tones with the tongue. Each of these three basic skills can be furthered in a group situation.

Breath Support

Rafael Mendez considers breath support alone to be 40 percent of playing a brass instrument,[4] and wind players agree almost unanimously with his sentiment, if not with his precise percentage. Instrumental breath support is similar to the breath support required for singing. The same organs and muscles are used and their function is the same. The differences are in the degree of abdominal muscle action demanded, and in the natural resistance offered the air stream by reeds and brass mouthpieces.

The player should first place his free hand lightly on his abdominal wall to see that the wall moves out as he inhales, and moves slowly and steadily in as the tone is played. In instrumental playing the *depth* of breath should be emphasized. Mendez says to the student, "Think DOWN . . . DOWN . . . DOWN . . . against the belt. Now fill the middle part of the lungs. Think . . . OUT . . . side-to-side . . . front-to-back."[5] Keith Stein tells his students to imagine, if they can, filling only the top half of a pitcher, the point being that the deep part of the lungs must fill first.[6] Students should try this exercise:

> Stand. Place hand against abdominal wall. Inhale, filling the lungs *deeply*. Then, with the teacher and/or students timing the action, blow out the smallest possible stream of air between the lips, and note the slow inward movement of the abdominal wall. If ten seconds is achieved, repeat the exercise, increasing the time to 15 seconds, then to 20, and so on over a period of days until at least 60 or even 90 seconds is reached.

To strengthen muscles for breath support, both Stein and Mendez suggest this simple exercise which can be done at home.[7]

> Lying on the back, feet together, toes pointed away from the body, SLOWLY raise stiffened legs to a ninety-degree angle with body, then SLOWLY lower again.

---

[4]Rafael Mendez, *Prelude to Brass Playing* (New York: Carl Fischer, Inc., 1961), p. 10.

[5]Mendez, p. 12. Reprinted by permission.

[6]Keith Stein, *The Art of Clarinet Playing* (Evanston, Ill.: Summy-Birchard Publishing Company, 1958), p. 18.

[7]Stein, p. 20; and Mendez, p. 15.

Other home exercises are:

> (1) Inhale a deep breath, hold it *with throat open,* and place a mirror close to open mouth. Mirror will get cloudy if breath escapes.
> (2) Inhale, counting to four, then exhale while slowly counting to eight, again keeping throat open.[8]

As in singing, playing a tone requires a relaxed and open throat and a slow, controlled air stream. Tension should be maintained in the abdominal muscles as the sound is produced. An advanced player may not require a great amount of abdominal muscle tension, because he knows precisely which muscles to use and how much to use them. But for almost all wind players in secondary school, the abdominal wall should be kept as firm as possible at all times when playing.

It is more difficult to maintain breath support when the player's attention is diverted to fingerings or rhythmic figures. Breath support, therefore, must become a habit. When the students forget about breath support because their attention is on notes, the teacher can refer to the passage and say, "Now, the last time at letter L you got the right notes, but the tone was weak. Do it again, and this time *at all costs* I want you to keep up your support, even if it means a wrong note." Strangely, instead of bringing forth many wrong notes, such a direction usually leads to better playing from the standpoint of both tone and technique.

To convince students of the need to support tones, the teacher can demonstrate, if he is a brass or woodwind player. He can play an unsupported, and then a supported tone, so that the students hear the difference. He can demonstrate the effect of proper control when playing at the extremes of the range of dynamics. The upper range on brasses demands much support, unless these notes are obtained by pinched lips which produce crude sounds or by "squealer" mouthpieces with shallow cups and narrow bores.

Basic Embouchure

The subtleties of embouchure are best taught in private lessons, but by close observation and reminders, the teacher in a group situation can prevent many grievous embouchures from developing.

Single-Reed Instruments.   The embouchure for both clarinet and saxophone is set in this way: Without pulling the corners of the mouth back,

---

[8]Stein, p. 20.

tighten the muscles in the corners of the mouth. Then, with the lips just barely touching, try vigorously to pull them apart in an up-down separation. This will stretch out or thin out the muscleless areas around the mouth, especially just below the center of the lower lip. The result should be a pointed or "Dick Tracy" chin. The reason for the pointed chin may be explained to the students in this manner: "Your car can't go far on a flat tire; the wheel on the road needs to be firm. The lower lip needs to be firm, too, so that the reed can vibrate without being soaked up in a flabby lip." The lower lip in single-reed playing should be the consistency of a pencil eraser. The teacher should be on the lookout for lower lips incorrectly "rolled up" underneath reeds. Correct embouchure is needed at all times, particularly on high notes. When playing correctly, most students will show muscle action along a line running two inches down from each corner of the mouth. Clarinet and saxophone embouchures differ in the amount of lip tension or "grip"; the saxophone requires less.

The clarinet should form a 45-degree angle with the chin and teeth. Some students hold it straight out like a cigar, and then try to achieve the proper appearance by tipping the head down until the chin is almost to the collarbone. A 45-degree angle means that the upper teeth touch the mouthpiece at a point about one-eighth of an inch from the tip of the mouthpiece, while the lower lip touches the reed halfway up the vamp or cut of the reed. The lower lip should rest on top of the lower teeth, with half of it going over the teeth and half remaining in front. Unless a student has thin lips, some of the lower lip should show when he plays. One suggestion that usually helps single-reed embouchure is for the player to stick out his chin a little bit, just enough so that the teeth would meet if the mouth were closed.

The embouchure for clarinet is:

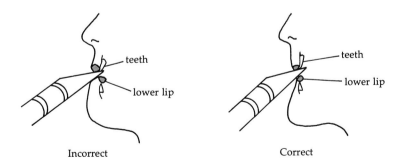

Incorrect   Correct

Double-Reed Instruments.   The embouchure for oboe and bassoon is similar to that used for clarinet. The upper lip is brought more into play because like the lower lip it goes between the reed and the teeth. A little more side-to-side stretch between the corners of the mouth may be required, so that there is a pulling away of the broad outer circle of muscles below the eyes, in the cheeks, and on the chin, and a squeezing in of the inner circle of muscles around the lips.

Much of a player's success on a double-reed instrument depends on the quality of his reed. Commercial reeds are made to one major specification: they must produce a tone easily, even for the immature player. As a result, they are usually too soft, with the raspy sound characteristic of a soft reed. A good player makes his own reeds, but it is an unusual secondary school student who learns to do this. So the teacher should try to make arrangements with a professional double-reed player, who can then make suitable reeds for the students. By the way, when a willing professional is found, he should be treated with deference. It takes time to make reeds, and seldom is the effort financially worthwhile for the maker.

Flute.   The aspect of the embouchure to watch is the angle between flute and lips and the degree of tilt at the blowhole. The flute should be held parallel to the lip line, with the edge of the blowhole at the lower edge of the lower lip. The flute should tip neither high nor low on the right side of the mouth.

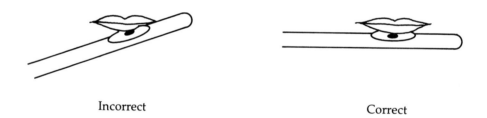

Incorrect   Correct

The blowhole should tilt just slightly toward the player's lips. The precise angle can be determined only after carefully listening to the tone quality.

The flute achieves its change of register by the speed and angle of air going into the blowhole. Many students attempt to play high notes not by making the opening in their lips smaller and by pushing the chin slightly forward, but by blasting out more air. The result is a breathy tone and frequent inability to reach high pitches, to say nothing of the unnecessary effort expended by the player. For high notes, the opening of the lips should be made "as small as the eye of a needle." This results in a smaller but faster air stream.

Brass Instruments.   The basic formation for the vibration or buzzing of the lips is the same for all brass instruments. The corners of the mouth should be tightened, and the center of the lips slightly puckered, as for a kiss. The mouthpiece is set lightly, *not pressed,* on the lips, in the center of the mouth, with an equal portion of the mouthpiece on each lip (French horn excepted). Slight variations or off-center positions caused by individual differences in facial and dental structure are of no concern as long as the tone is free and clear. French horn players should be taught to rest the rim of the mouthpiece on the rim of the lower lip, thus placing one-third of the mouthpiece over the lower lip and two-thirds over the upper.[9] The adaptation of the embouchure required for trombone, baritone, and bass depends mainly on lip tension and the degree to which the lips are pursed out.

Pushing the mouthpiece against the lips is a poor technique that is too often used as an emergency measure. It achieves temporary improvement, especially in reaching high notes. But the sacrifices are great: feeling is lost in the lips, notes crack or fail to speak, the low register is weak, intonation suffers, slurring is uneven, and permanent damage can be done to the lips.[10] This quick solution is to be avoided at all costs. The player should pretend that the instrument is suspended from the ceiling on strings, and that without touching it with his hands he can move up to it and play it. Some teachers actually hold the instrument lightly for the student so that he can experience the sensation of playing without pressure. The muscles in the corners of the mouth, plus support from the diaphragm and abdomen, should do the work in reaching correct pitches. For this reason, the teacher should select music that does not move brass players into high notes before sufficient facial muscles or "lip" have developed. One practical remedy to too much pressure on the lip on trumpet or cornet is to encourage the player to try a hand vibrato in private practice. To achieve this, he must withdraw pressure, and the process helps wean him away from a dependence on pressure.[11]

Brass players should not be seduced into quick and easy playing of high notes by relying on extreme mouthpieces. For whatever is gained in one phase of playing, something is lost in another. Mouthpieces with medium cups, rims, and bores are preferable.

Tonguing

A third fundamental of wind instrument playing that can be taught in the group rehearsal is correct tongue action. This is more than merely a technique for executing staccato runs in eighths and sixteenths. It is a fundamental action necessary to articulate any note regardless of speed or rhyth-

---

[9]Phillip Farkas, *The Art of French Horn Playing* (Evanston, Ill.: Summy-Birchard Publishing Company, 1956), pp. 21–25.

[10]Mendez, pp. 22–24.

[11]Robert D. Weast, *Brass Performance* (New York: McGinnis & Marx, 1961), p. 34.

mic pattern. To play "America" requires the same basic tonguing action as a difficult solo.

In a way, "tonguing" is the wrong word, because making a tone depends on air and a vibrating mechanism. So the first requirement for proper articulation on wind instruments is breath support. A student sometimes complains that he cannot get his tongue to work properly, when the real problem is a lack of breath support.

Instruction in tonguing should start as soon as students can support their tone. It might be better for them to wait a year, but this is not a realistic expectation. They see music that calls for tonguing, and even slurred phrases need to have the initial note articulated. Besides, students experiment with tonguing whether the teacher likes it or not, although they may not do it in his presence.

Tonguing is based on the *release* of air, not the *pushing out* of air, as the uninitiated student often thinks. First, the tongue acts as a dam to hold back the air. Air pressure resulting from continuing breath support builds up behind it. Then the tongue is quickly pulled away from the reed or teeth. At that exact moment the sound starts distinctly. This is referred to as the attack (in many ways a misleading word for the tongue-breath action it describes). The process is like turning on a garden hose at low pressure and attempting to hold back the water with the thumb. When the thumb is removed from the opening, the initial forceful squirt is comparable to the "spring" or "kick" of a good attack on a wind instrument. With the hose, it does no good to turn the water on harder after the flow starts, because the initial spurt is unaffected by later increases in pressure. The same is true of the tongued attack. Once the air has started, additional air will merely give a pushing effect that is musically undesirable. Because of this, the attention in tonguing is on the *beginning* of the note. In fact, in rapid tonguing the player can think only about the start of each tone.

Unnecessary movement complicates the tonguing process. Too often students move the jaw, lips, and throat in an attempt to improve on an action that should involve only continued breath and coordination of the tongue. Since it is difficult for the player to work at just holding still, he can be directed to concentrate his attention on breath support and the quick action of the tongue in pulling away to start the tone. He should work harder on active breath support when no sound is heard than when it is, illogical as that may seem. To emphasize the build-up of pressure before the note is sounded, the students can be told to feel a "ping-pong ball" of air pressure between the tongue and the roof of the mouth just before the tone starts.

As Chapter 12 pointed out in discussing interpretation, the style of attack differs with the demands of the music. The difference in attack is determined by the amount of air pressure built up (with greater pressure bringing a harder attack) and by the speed with which the tongue is pulled away (the faster movement causing a more distinct start).

On brasses and flute the tip of the tongue is placed behind the upper teeth at or near the point where the gum meets the teeth. On lower brasses some fine players tongue at the edge of the teeth with no audible difference in the quality of tonguing. On reeds the tip of the tongue is placed lightly, not pressed, against the tip of the reed (the lower reed on oboe and bassoon). Clarity is improved if the tip of the tongue is made firm and pointed. On all winds, the movement of the tongue to start the tone is mainly down, not backwards, and only the tip of the tongue moves. The tongue is rather large, and if all of it moves, speed and clarity are impossible.

Students who have trouble feeling the tongue movement might try this: rough the tip of the tongue on the edge of the upper teeth by rubbing it back and forth. Then practice flicking the tip against the edge of the teeth.

On brasses the best syllable for tonguing is determined by the pitch level of the note. "Tah" is good for the middle range, "toh" for low notes, and "tee" for high notes. "Tah" is used on woodwinds.

Closing off a staccato tone is too often hindered by unnecessary effort. On a reed instrument it is not easily noticeable if the tone is stopped with the tongue, but on a brass instrument this action causes an undesirable "ut" sound at the end of the tone. The player needs to focus his attention on the start of tones of moderate or long duration, and avoid using the tongue to end them. The closing operation will then be taken over by a holding-back action of the abdominal muscles.

Fundamentals of String Instrument Performance

In a majority of schools, the strings work by themselves several times a week, while the winds are brought in for only one or two periods to form a complete orchestra. Because string instruments are difficult to play well, and string parts are often more demanding than wind parts, the extra time is needed to learn the music. Furthermore, string players who are not advanced benefit from the additional work on basic skills.

Bowing

Young string players tend to place their entire attention on the left hand when playing. Advanced players know that the skill of the bow arm is at least as important as the dexterity of the left hand. Because the right arm is generally neglected, special work on bowing is urged.

Students should understand the factors that affect bowing: pressure on the bow, length of bow stroke, and speed of bow stroke. Each one affects the quality and volume of sound. A slow bow with much pressure produces one timbre, while a fast bow with light pressure produces another. Several books on bowing are available, or the teacher may create his own bowing routines.

Common bow patterns should be learned so well that they become second nature. The first patterns should be very simple so that the players' attention can be centered on drawing the bow properly, and they should be patterns that are common in the repertoire of the group, such as the following:

WB UH UH WB LH LH   WB UH UH WB LH LH

WB   UH UH WB

(WB indicates whole bow, UH upper half, and LH lower half))

Slurred notes of equal value should receive nearly equal portions of the bow so that none of the tones sound cramped or squeezed:

L⅓ Mid⅓ U⅓   U⅓ Mid⅓ L⅓   L½ UM¼ U¼ WB

Dotted figures in one bow are more difficult, especially if a change of bow occurs immediately after a short, detached note. In such a situation, beginners are likely to become confused over bow direction. Slow and rhythmic practice will establish the feel of the proper bow motion.

Many styles of bowing are best taught in the private lesson, but even in a group situation the students can work on two of the most common styles. *Legato* bowing requires smooth change of bow direction and a generally consistent bow speed. Beginning students should strive first of all to develop a fine legato style, like the singing tone of the human voice. This style is the essence of string performance. A second style of string playing often encountered in orchestral literature is the *détaché*, or full, detached stroke. The secret of détaché is the "catch" at the start of the tone, indicating an abrupt, precise beginning. A slight bit of extra weight on the bow, plus a sudden and fast initial movement, will produce this effect. It is imperative that the student be able to draw a straight bow parallel to the bridge. Any lack of bow control will show up when détaché is attempted, because the bow will either skid out of control or move at a crooked angle.

No orchestral string part contains complete bow markings, so the students have a fine opportunity to figure out bowings in an actual work of music. The teacher can give the players an unmarked page of photocopied music and request that they mark in bowings as homework. These can be examined in class, compared, and discussed. The string players should be asked questions such as, "Why did you start with another down bow? What's the musical effect of this bowing? What style of bowing does the music suggest here? Could it be bowed another way? Would it be simpler?" This helps the players to understand the mechanical and musical factors involved in bowing a string part.

Left Hand

Intermediate string methods move the left hand into higher positions, and this entails work on shifting. For a few moments the attention of the players should be concentrated on the two pitches involved in the shift. At first, the players can practice the shift silently, using a light pizzicato occasionally to check the accuracy of pitch. The quickness and precision of the left hand should be emphasized. Then the two notes involved in the shift can be played, followed by a playing of the entire phrase.

The real beauty of string tone is brought to life with vibrato. Without it, the quality remains thin and colorless, especially when the players are performing on instruments that are far from the best. Some successful string teachers begin vibrato in the second year of study, although others prefer to wait a little longer. In any event, it is started when the teacher feels that the basic playing fundamentals are well established.

A practical method is suggested by Charles Righter:

> The following steps may be helpful, either in first learning to execute the vibrato or in correcting faulty habits: (a) start with the second finger on

the second or third string (C sharp or F sharp on violin—F sharp or B on viola); (b) lift all other fingers from the string, but hold them near their normal playing positions; (c) draw the thumb slightly more UNDER the neck of the instrument than would be normal, to provide better support; (d) withdraw the base joint of the first finger from direct contact with the neck of the instrument (these steps will reduce the contact points from three or more to only two—the second finger and the thumb); (e) ROLL the second finger alternately as far forward and as far backward as possible, utilizing the flexibility of the wrist and of all the finger joints; (f) do this very slowly and very evenly at first, gradually introducing rhythmic groupings (twos, threes, fours, sixes) and increasing the speed of the roll slightly; (g) repeat the entire process using the third finger, and eventually the fourth and the first fingers, and also practice the exercise on the first and the fourth strings. These basic exercises will seem cumbersome and difficult at first and they may appear to have little relation to the production of a free and natural-sounding vibrato. Gradually, however, the skill will establish itself and, when this occurs, the rhythmic treatment can be abandoned except as a corrective device. The amplitude of the roll will diminish and its speed will increase with practice. The same general approach will apply to the cello and the string bass, on both of which instruments the hand is in a better natural position to start the rolling process.[12]

The teacher may also wish to examine the approach of Waller, which is more specific and detailed.[13] Some teachers feel that it is best not to become too technical with the students, preferring the original advice of Monteverdi to "shake" the hand. Too much technical talk, they feel, may inhibit the proper muscle action. At any rate, teaching vibrato requires persistence, because the process may take up to two years with some pupils. The goal should be to increase the speed and narrow the amplitude of the vibrato to the extent that the change of pitch is not perceived as such by the ear. Of course it is essential that the students have a chance to see and hear good vibrato, either from the teacher or from an advanced student.

Percussion

Percussion playing requires a variety of techniques, most of which are not as complex as those involved in playing winds or strings. Many teenage drummers do well on the stroke-bounce technique for the roll; the trouble is they cannot put it in the right place in the music. There are occasions—in dance bands and marching bands—when drummers have little need for

---

[12]Charles B. Righter, *Teaching Instrumental Music* (New York: Carl Fischer, Inc., 1959), pp. 45–46. Reprinted by permission.

[13]Gilbert R. Waller, *Waller Vibrato Method* (Chicago: Neil A. Kjos Music Co., 1951).

reading music. Apparently the habit of nonreading carries over to concert playing, with unfortunate results. The students have trouble producing the correct rendition of the printed music and fitting the percussion part into the ensemble. It is hard for percussionists to integrate the part they play with the group in phrasing, dynamics, and style. The problem is not usually one of technique but rather of musicianship. By asking the right question at the right time, the teacher can encourage percussionists to think more musically. "Which snare should you use at letter A, the five-inch or the six-and-a-half-inch? Why? Which stick are you going to use on the timpani at letter G? How important to the music is the roll at the repeat of the melody?"

Instrumentation

Any suggestions for instrumentation must be considered in light of the quality of the players. One alto saxophone is sufficient for a band of 50 players, if he is a creditable performer. If he is weak, an additional alto saxophone is needed. Directors have differing tastes, some wanting more mellowness, others more bass sound, and others more brilliance, all of which require somewhat different instrumentations. Although orchestral instrumentation has been fairly well standardized over the past 150 years, band instrumentation has changed frequently and is still in the process of being modified, often on the specifications of the composer or arranger.

In an orchestra, the difference between a large or small group is mainly accounted for in the strings, because in the winds only one player is normally used on a part. Therefore the teacher of a small orchestra finds it more difficult to achieve proper balance. Table I gives suggested numbers of players for three sizes of orchestra.

Table II represents one concept of balanced band instrumentation. Unless players of outstanding ability are available, instruments such as bass saxophone and E flat soprano clarinet should be avoided, because they can do more harm than good.[14] If these instruments are vital to a particular piece, it is best to have a good clarinetist double on the E flat clarinet for that number. The numerical balance of first, second, and third parts in the clarinets, and the proportion of trumpets and/or cornets, can be determined only by the sound of the particular group. Because low notes apparently do not "carry" as well as higher pitches, and because less advanced students usually play the lower parts, these parts may require a greater number of players for a balanced sound. The choice between trumpets and cornets is a matter of taste for each band director. Traditionally two cornets were recommended for one trumpet, but in smaller groups trumpets are more effective. Double B

---

[14]John Phillip Sousa reportedly said that the E flat soprano clarinet should be used only on February 29, and then played very softly.

Table I

Instrument	Small	Full	Complete symphonic
Flute and piccolo	2	2	3
Oboe and English horn	1	2	3
Clarinet	2	3	3
Bassoon	1	2	3
French horn	2	4	6
Trumpet	3	3	3
Trombone	3	3	3
Tuba	1	1	1
Percussion and piano	2	3	4
Harp	0	0	1
Violin	12	24	30
Viola	4	7	10
Violoncello	4	7	10
String bass	3	4	6
	40	65	86

flat upright tubas are suggested in a ratio of three to one over E flat tubas (if the latter are used at all), because of their bigger tone quality, stronger low notes, and better intonation. A report by a committee of the College Band Directors National Association recommends only BB flat tubas.[15] Generally the E flat tuba doubles the BB flat tuba one octave higher, but since these notes are well within the range of trombones and baritones, this function of the E flat tuba is of limited value.

Seating

Traditionally, players in a section have been seated in order of ability. If all the players are highly competent, as in a professional symphony orchestra, this system works well. In a school group where the level of capability may vary greatly from first to last in a section, it is better to assign places by putting the best player in first chair, the next best at the second stand (or at the first stand of the second section), and so on. This arrangement puts stronger players on all parts and stands, not just the first. In the violin sections, it puts the better player on the outside where he is most

[15] Richard Franko Goldman, *The Wind Band: Its Literature and Technique* (Boston: Allyn and Bacon, 1961), pp. 167, 169.

Table II

Instrument	Small	Average	Large
Flute and piccolo	2	5	7
Oboe	1	2	3
B flat clarinet	12	20	25
Alto clarinet	1	2	4
Bass clarinet	1	2	4
Bassoon	1	2	4
Alto saxophone	1	2	2
Tenor saxophone	1	1	2
Baritone saxophone	0	1	1
Cornet and trumpet	6	9	12
French horn	3	4	8
Baritone	2	3	4
Trombone	3	4	6
Tuba	2	3	6
String bass	1	1	2
Percussion	3	4	5
	40	65	95

easily heard and seen, and where he can keep playing when a page of music is turned. A minor variation of this plan is to place the best three or four players in the first chairs, and then seat players according to ability, moving back a stand or part with each one. These seating systems help to remove the stigma of playing a part other than the first.

In instrumental music, especially band, some teachers encourage competition for the best chairs. While this motivates some students, it should not be the primary spur to improvement. The work in band and orchestra should be sufficiently interesting and pleasurable to motivate the players without the teacher's hanging the carrot of a better chair in front of them. Students can study and learn no matter what chair they are sitting in, and a sour note detracts from the group's performance regardless of its source in the section, so the chair in which a person sits is not an important matter.

The most educationally valid method of seating is for the teacher to rotate either students or music so that all members of a section get to play first, second, or third parts. Rotation gives the students a greater knowledge of all the parts and more experience in reading music, besides diminishing the emphasis on seating. For performance, the teacher without much ado should seat players according to ability and seniority. If and when chair tryouts are held, the teacher might have another music teacher in the system hear them also, so that he cannot be accused of personal bias. To avoid confusing musical ability with personal popularity, students should not be involved in evaluating other students.

Transferring Students to Other Instruments

Students in elementary school are seldom started on several of the instruments listed in the instrumentation tables for band and orchestra. Either the instruments are too large, too delicate, or too difficult for beginners. For this reason, the middle/junior high school teacher must be prepared to transfer some youngsters from one instrument to another. Transfers should be planned well ahead of the time they are made, and they must take into full consideration the student's desires, parents' wishes, and the student's musical potential. Sometimes a student begins clarinet with the intention of switching to oboe after a year or two of study. The clarinet training gives him a good musical foundation, and contributes to his success as an oboist, whereas starting on oboe might have ended in frustration. Some changes will seem advisable after study is begun, as in the case of a trumpeter who lacks sufficient lip strength and is therefore transferred to tuba. The following list suggests the most logical transfers:

B flat clarinet to any saxophone
> Upper octave of clarinet is almost identical with saxophone; player must learn to relax embouchure for low notes.

B flat clarinet to oboe
> Upper octave of clarinet is similar to oboe; player will require a little time to get used to smaller reed and use of both lips in playing.

B flat clarinet to bassoon
> Fingering of open holes is similar but keys are different; reed change is not quite as difficult as with oboe; player must learn bass clef.

B flat clarinet to alto or bass clarinet
> Fingerings are identical; player needs only a short time to become accustomed to larger reed, mouthpiece, and instrument.

Flute to saxophone
> Fingerings are similar; embouchure on saxophone is not too demanding.

Saxophone to all other saxophones
> Fingerings and notes are identical; very short time is needed to get used to new size of reed, mouthpiece, and instrument.

Trumpet to low brasses
> Basic fingerings are identical; time is needed to learn bass clef and become accustomed to large instrument; change to trombone is more difficult, although slide positions are related to valve combinations.

Trumpet to French horn
> Fingerings present only a minor problem; main difference is in concept of tone; some change of embouchure is necessary, which requires careful attention.

Low brass to trumpet
> Treble clef must be learned; fingerings present no problem, but change

from an instrument requiring less embouchure tension to one requiring more is difficult.

Violin to viola

Time is needed to learn alto clef. Some authorities believe that all violinists should have at least a semester of experience on viola.[16]

Piano to string bass

Pianists know bass clef and have an understanding of how bass part is organized in music.

Piano to percussion instruments with definite pitch

Pianists read music and know keyboard; timpani roll can be learned without great difficulty.

Students who transfer will need special help at first, the amount depending on the difficulty of the change, and the talent and diligence of the student. It is helpful if he can have access to a practice room during study period, with the teacher stopping by occasionally. Perhaps the teacher can work with him after school. Progress will be most rapid, however, if the student can study privately with a specialist teacher. As soon as he can play the parts on his new instrument, he should be moved back into the band or orchestra.

A special word should be said about French horn. Because the horn uses primarily the partials in the harmonic series which are one octave higher than partials on other brass instruments, the pitches are much closer together in the harmonic series and are more difficult to play accurately. For this reason, there has been a persistent problem about how best to start young players. At one time the E flat mellophone was thought to be the answer, a solution from which a true lover of the French horn recoils in horror. The argument then centered on the virtues of the F and B flat horns, with the former having the proper timbre and the latter being easier to play. Double horns are ideal, but few school systems can afford to provide them for beginners. More and more horn teachers now advocate starting the student on a single B flat horn. (He reads F horn music, but is taught B flat fingerings.) After about three years, he is transferred to double horn and taught to use the F horn for the lower pitches, gradually increasing its use for notes in other ranges.

Substitution of Instruments

Sometimes an instrument called for in the score is not available. Rather than deny the rest of the players a chance to play the music, the teacher as an expedient can assign another instrument to substitute. Although there

---

[16]Righter, p. 21.

are no "good" substitutions, some are more satisfying than others. Following is a list of common and passingly successful substitutions. An asterisk indicates that transposition is required in making the substitution. The E flat instruments indicated by the double asterisks may read bass clef by adding three sharps to the signature and reading the notes as if they were in the treble clef.

> Oboe: muted trumpet*, viola
> English horn: alto saxophone*, oboe*
> E flat clarinet: flute*
> Alto clarinet: alto saxophone
> Bass clarinet: tenor saxophone
> Bassoon: tenor saxophone*, bass clarinet*, cello
> Tenor saxophone: bass clarinet
> Baritone saxophone: bass clarinet*
> French horn: alto saxophone*, clarinet*, cello*
> Flügelhorn: cornet
> Baritone: trombone
> Tuba: string bass, baritone saxophone**
> Viola: violin (Many publishers sell a Violin III part, which is the viola part
>   put in treble clef with the lowest notes moved up an octave.)
> Cello: tenor saxophone*, alto saxophone**
> String bass: tuba, piano
> Harp: piano

Equipment and Supplies

The physical needs of the instrumental music program are clearly more extensive than in other phases of the music curriculum. In addition to the administrative suggestions for the entire program mentioned in Chapter 5, the instrumental teacher must deal with unique matters of equipment and supply.

Supplies—items such as reeds, strings, rosin, valve and slide oil—can be sold at cost through a student supply store operated by the school or the music department. Some dealers will provide and stock a reed-vending machine that eliminates the need for handling. When the school makes supplies available, the students don't lose time waiting to get to the music store for a reed or string.

Repair on privately owned instruments is facilitated if they are sent in with school owned instruments to the repairman. The school pays the repairman for all work done, the teacher keeps a record of the cost of repair on the privately owned instrument, and the student reimburses the school.

If the student should prove forgetful or balky about payment of his bill, his report card can be held up in the school office, as is done for unpaid library fines and other delinquencies.

In the purchase of school owned instruments, the teacher should inform the administration of the need for two grades of instruments. One is the rugged, adequate instrument for the beginner. The other is the good instrument (not artist model) for the high school player. Since most schools limit the amount of time during which one student has an instrument as a beginner, well-built plastic clarinets and similar "student-line" instruments are appropriate. But for advanced work in the high school band and orchestra, better instruments are needed. A cheap instrument at this level is poor economy. Many secondary schools provide these instruments for competent players: alto and bass clarinet, piccolo, oboe, bassoon, baritone saxophone, French horn, baritone, tuba and sousaphone, harp, cello, string bass, and percussion equipment. Most schools provide all beginners with instruments.

Some specifications for particular instruments can be suggested. The mouthpiece and reed have much to do with clarinet tone. A good medium to medium-wide lay mouthpiece and a reed not softer than $2\frac{1}{2}$ in strength work best for most high school players. All hard rubber mouthpieces warp over a period of two or three years. Refacing is not expensive and often improves the mouthpiece. Good quality clarinets should be wood, as should the piccolo, which should be pitched in C, not D flat. Oboes and bassoons should be checked by a specialist on the instrument before a purchase is made. The good French horns should be double horns. If the school can afford both sousaphones and tubas, upright bell BB flat tubas are favored, with either a fourth valve or a compensating mechanism to improve the intonation.

Cases and stands or chairs are needed for tubas or sousaphones. Percussion equipment of high quality gives a noticeably better sound. There is something musically disappointing about hearing a group build to a beautiful climax followed by a cymbal crash on a cheap, small pair of cymbals with handles. The advice of a professional symphony percussion player can be valuable when deciding on brands and equipment. A movable cabinet helps to preserve the percussion equipment and prevent the loss of small items such as maracas, triangle beaters, and brushes. The cabinet should have a lock to prevent unauthorized use of equipment. Violins, violas, and cellos with Caspari pegs are somewhat easier for beginners to tune. It's also desirable to have fine-tuners on the two highest strings (string basses excepted).

When the time comes for the student to purchase a trumpet or clarinet, some parents hurry off to the nearest discount house. Often the "buy" they get is a cheap instrument that is out of tune and carelessly made. To combat this, the teacher should try to establish the point in a letter or other communication with the parents that a cheap instrument may be the poorest buy of all. Next, he should urge parents to have a trained person inspect the instrument they plan to purchase, and he may announce his availability to consult with them about instruments. He should recommend all music merchants in the area who sell good quality instruments and follow ethical business practices. He might also list good used instruments that families in the area have told him they would like to sell. Not only does this make it possible for prospective purchasers to buy a good instrument at less cost; it also lets them know that a share of their investment in an instrument is redeemable. In listing used instruments, the teacher makes no contacts and suggests no price. The listing is only a service to interested parties.

Preparation on the Score

An instrumental music teacher must understand the transpositions and technical problems in a score containing as many as 20 lines occurring simultaneously. In addition, he must decide on the correct tempos, phrasing, and methods for teaching the music.

More often than not, secondary school conductors face an additional obstacle: the condensed score. Since complete scores are expensive to publish, and many school music teachers do not buy them even when they are available, music publishers are reluctant to prepare complete scores. So the instrumental teacher must learn to do the best he can with the condensed score. When the music is simple, like a chorale, a condensed score is usually sufficient. The more complex the music, the more inadequate a condensation becomes. Its most limiting feature is that it does not indicate exactly what each part is playing, and some parts, such as the E flat alto clarinet, are ignored. The condensed score is similar to a piano reduction of an orchestral score, and is in concert pitch. In fact, not too many years ago the part for the director was called "Piano-Conductor," probably as an outgrowth of the performance custom of the old theater-pit orchestra.

Before directing from a condensed score, the teacher should compare it with the instrument parts. Pencil in hand, he should look through the condensed score and stop at the first place where the instrumentation is not clearly indicated. Then he can examine the parts at that point, writing in the conductor's score more indications of what is happening. For marches written on the small march-size sheet, the teacher can take one first clarinet, first cornet, baritone, French horn, trombone, and percussion part, tape them together to form one large sheet, and make a score of sorts.

A rehearsal can deteriorate fast when the teacher is not thoroughly familiar with the disposition of notes.

Bill Morgan stops the band and says to the second alto saxophone, "Mary Ann, we missed your F sharp in the first chord at letter H." "I don't have F sharp there," Mary Ann answers; "I have a D."

"Well, who has a concert A besides the second flutes? . . . *(no answer)* . . . Good grief! Tenor sax, what do you have?" "D natural," comes the reply.

"Bass clarinet, according to my score somebody has a concert A. Do you?" "No, I have a D."

"Are you sure? Well, let's begin at letter G again and see if we can figure it out this time."

Stage or Dance Band

In schools where players of sufficient ability are available, a dance band or stage band is a valuable component of the music program. The case for the school stage band is this. Students interested in playing popular music are going to play it someplace, so it is best that they have the experience in a situation properly supervised for selection of music, hours and location of playing, and type of personnel. The stage band also helps bridge the gulf between popular and serious music. A strong case can be made for some popular forms as valid musical experiences, ones which the school should not ignore.

There are disadvantages to the stage band. It can encroach on the main effort at music education. To prevent this, rehearsals of the group should be held outside of the regular rehearsal period, and should not make unreasonable time demands on the students or teacher. The music should be performed well, however. Sometimes the student attracted by the stage band is not the careful, hard working type, and too often such a player is content to skim through the music in a sloppy manner. Therefore it should be the *best* members of the concert band who are selected for the stage band, not the weaker ones. Hard work is necessary for the music to sound acceptable and for bad playing habits to be avoided.

The business affairs of the stage band must be managed so as not to violate the Code of Ethics with the American Federation of Musicians (see Appendix A). Appearances of the group should be limited to school events.

The past few years have brought forth many stage band arrangements written specifically for high school musicians. In general, the tunes are well arranged, without the technical demands and the *ad lib* solos of the commercial "stock" arrangements. The simpler arrangements can also be played with a more varied instrumentation. The band may not be able to learn enough pieces to consume three hours of playing time without some repetition of music. Repetition is preferable, however, to playing music that is inadequately rehearsed.

Although stage band music is written with the conventional nomenclature, it should not be performed in a strictly conventional way. The subtleties of the style are too numerous to explore here, and they change with the times. A firsthand acquaintance with the style is the best preparation for teaching it. Some music publishers provide recordings of their arrangements, and these also convey the proper style.

The following materials and books are available as aids in developing a stage band:

Baker, Dave, *Developing Improvisational Technique.* Libertyville, Illinois: National Education Services.

———, *Developing Improvisational Facility.* Libertyville, Illinois: National Education Services.

Bower, Bugs, *Chords and Progressions* (2 vols.). New York: Charles Colin Publisher.

Coker, Jerry, *Improvising Jazz.* Englewood Cliffs, New Jersey: Prentice-Hall.

Fenno, Dick, *How to Play a Good Jazz Chorus.* Beverly Hills, California: Gordon Music.

Hall, M. E. "Gene", *Stage Band Techniques.* San Antonio, Texas: Southern Music.

Hermann, Rudy, *Contemporary Scales and Chords.* New York: Henry Adler.

La Porta, John, *Developing the School Stage Band.* Boston: Berklee Press.

Niehaus, Lennie, *Basic Jazz Conception for Sax.* Hollywood, California: Swinghouse.

Polhamus, Dedrick, *How the Dance Band Swings.* Delevan, New York: Kendor Music Publishing.

Ralph, Alan, *Dance Band Reading and Interpretation.* New York: Sam Fox Publishing.

Rizzo, Phil, *Modern Music School Theory Text.* Manhattan, Kansas: Jazz Education Press.

———, *Modern Music School Workbook.* Manhattan, Kansas: Jazz Education Press.

———, *Scale Variations.* Cleveland: Modern Music School.

———, *Spread Chord Voicings.* Cleveland: Modern Music School.

Wiskirchen, George, *Developmental Techniques — Stage Band.* Boston: Berklee Press.

———, *A Guide to Improvisation.* Boston: Berklee Press.

Marching Band Techniques

The training and administration of a marching band is a specialized area of music education. Several books are available on the subject, and the person who desires information on marching bands should consult one of these sources:

Hjelmervick, Kenneth, and Richard Berg, *Marching Bands—How to Organize and Develop Them*. New York: A. S. Barnes, 1952.

Lee, Jack, *Modern Marching Band Techniques*. Winona, Minnesota: Hal Leonard Music, 1955.

Loken, Newt, and Otis Dypwick, *Cheerleading and Marching Bands*. New York: Ronald Press, 1956.

Marcouiller, Don R., *Marching for Marching Bands*. Dubuque, Iowa: William C. Brown, 1958.

Spohn, Charles H. and Richard W. Heine, *The Marching Band*. Boston: Allyn and Bacon, 1969.

Wright, Al G., *The Show Band*. Evanston, Illinois: The Instrumentalist, 1957.

Musical Instrument Repair

A second specialized topic beyond the scope of this book is the repair of musical instruments. A reader who is interested in the subject may refer to the following books:

Brand, Erick D., *Selmer Band Instrument Repairing Manual* (Rev. Ed.). E. C. Schirmer, 1946.

Springer, George H., *Maintenance and Repair of Band Instruments*.

Sur, William R., and Charles F. Schuller, *Music Education for Teen-Agers*. New York: Harper & Brothers, 1958. Chapter V.

Tiede, Clayton H., *Practical Band Instrument Repair Manual*. Dubuque, Iowa: William C. Brown, 1962.

Questions

1. Suppose a boy has his heart set on playing the trumpet. The teacher already has more trumpets than he can use in a balanced group. Should the boy be allowed to start on trumpet, or should he be told to take something else or not be in instrumental music? Why, or why not?

2. Suppose a student is studying privately with a teacher who suggests that he withdraw from school instrumental music organizations "so that he

won't get any bad habits." What arguments could you offer to persuade the parents of the student that he should also participate in the school group?

3. On page 374 the combination of singing-fingering is suggested. Why should the singing be done on the correct pitch level? From what was said in the chapter on principles of music teaching, why is it logical that this teaching technique is a good one?

4. Why is it a good practice from the standpoint of music education to utilize the procedure suggested on page 376, in which the student thinks of a note pattern, sings it, and then writes it down or plays it?

Projects

1. Using the criteria for evaluating beginning instrumental instruction books mentioned on page 373, make a study of all such books that you can secure for examination. Report your findings to the class. Compare evaluations with other class members.

2. Study the beginning instrumental program in a school system near your college. Find out at what grade level instruction is first offered, whether it is offered in subsequent years, how large the classes are, how homogeneous they are, whether the instruments are rented through the school or a dealer, what instruction books are used, how much time is devoted to class sessions, and what instruments are offered beginners. Report to your class. Compare reports with other class members.

3. Study the complete instrumental music program in a secondary school near your college. Find out how much variety it offers, whether there are "second" groups for the less talented students, whether there is an orchestra, what credit is given for private instruction, whether technical instruction is included in group rehearsals, and whether there are small ensembles. Report your findings to the class. Compare evaluations with other class members.

4. Take a very simple melody, such as "Twinkle, Twinkle, Little Star," from an elementary instrumental instruction book. Look it over and decide, seriously, what you could teach the students about its *musical* qualities — important notes, phrasing, style of articulation, and repeated melodic patterns.

5. Practice the breathing exercises described on page 379 and see if they seem applicable to the wind instrument you may be studying privately or in class.

6. Think of analogies other than the one mentioned on page 384 that might be useful in helping teenage students understand the proper action of tongue and breath in starting a tone on a wind instrument.

7. Study the embouchures of fine wind players. On single reeds notice the appearance of the muscles of the chin, the appearance of the lower lip, and the angle of the instrument in the mouth. On brasses, notice the placement of the mouthpiece and ask the player to pull the mouthpiece away as he plays a tone so that the position of the lips can be observed. Watch the embouchure of a flutist as he slurs up an octave, and of a brass player as he slurs to a higher tone with the same fingering.

8. Take a simple community-type song, such as "America the Beautiful" and mark in all the bowings a violinist might use in playing it. Compare your bowings with those of others in your class.

9. From a condensed score, select eight consecutive measures that are fairly complex. Then refer to the individual parts, find the same eight measures and copy the parts in full score on manuscript paper. Compare and contrast the two scores, and evaluate the adequacy of the condensed score in giving an accurate picture of what the instruments are to play.

10. Visit several instrument dealers and look over the "student" quality instruments. If you are an instrumentalist, check your major instrument for intonation and tone quality, quality of construction, and case. Compare them with instruments of the next higher level in quality and cost. Report your findings to the class.

11. Write a letter to parents regarding the purchase of an instrument for their son or daughter. Explain the need for buying a good quality instrument and offer your services in making a selection.

Suggested Readings

General

Colwell, Richard J., *The Teaching of Instrumental Music*. New York: Appleton-Century-Crofts, 1969.

House, Robert W., *Instrumental Music for Today's Schools*. Englewood Cliffs, New Jersey: Prentice-Hall, 1965.

Kuhn, Wolfgang, *Instrumental Music: Principles and Methods of Instruction* (2nd Ed.). Boston: Allyn and Bacon, 1970.

Neidig, Kenneth I., *The Band Director's Guide*. Englewood Cliffs, New Jersey: Prentice-Hall, 1964.

Righter, Charles Boardman, *Teaching Instrumental Music*. New York: Carl Fischer, 1959.

Winds

Holz, Emil, and Roger Jacobi, *Teaching Band Instruments to Beginners.* Englewood Cliffs, New Jersey: Prentice-Hall, 1966.

Mendez, Rafael, *Prelude To Brass Playing.* New York: Carl Fischer, 1961.

Percussion

Blades, James, *Orchestral Percussion Technique.* London: Oxford University Press, 1961.

Spohn, Charles, *The Percussion: Performance and Instructional Techniques.* Boston: Allyn and Bacon, 1967.

Strings

Galamian, Ivan, *Principles of Violin Playing and Teaching.* Englewood Cliffs, New Jersey: Prentice-Hall, 1962.

Green, Elizabeth, *Teaching Stringed Instruments in Classes.* Englewood Cliffs, New Jersey: Prentice-Hall, 1966.

Kuhn, Wolfgang, *Principles of String Class Teaching.* Rockville Centre, New York: Belwin, 1957.

16

Music Appreciation, Fine Arts, and Theory Courses

Courses in music appreciation, the fine arts, and theory generally emphasize studying music rather than making music. Seldom do these classes present public programs. Often the students who enroll are not members of a performing organization; this fact is even true of some of the students in theory classes.

Music appreciation, fine arts, and theory courses are similar in other ways. Nationwide their enrollment is only one-twentieth the enrollment of instrumental and choral groups in grades 9–12.[1] But in recent years each of the three courses has received more attention and modest increases in enrollment. A concern for the "other 80 percent"—the students not in any music class (the actual figure for public high schools is 76.4 percent)—has been expressed more frequently, as in the Tanglewood Symposium of 1967.[2]

Another point in common among the three courses—one that is disappointing—is that often the persons promoting them are *not* music teachers. Instead, the initiative has been taken by principals and curriculum directors, by social studies and English teachers, or by committees of parents and students. Too often music teachers have shown little interest in such courses and the students who usually take them. The teachers may feel pressured by the confining six-period day in many schools, a pattern that seems to be slowly changing. They believe, with some justification, that crowded teaching schedules eliminate the possibility of additional courses. Other teachers fear that such classes may draw students out of their performing groups, a fear that has proved to be largely groundless. Still others, recognizing the lack of precedent, feel inadequate to plan course content in new areas.

Special courses in theory, appreciation, and fine arts are needed in the high school curriculum, even if teachers of performing groups decide to give more time to such matters in their rehearsals. There are three reasons

---

[1] "Subject Offerings and Enrollments in Public Secondary Schools" (OE–2401 5–61) (Washington, D.C.: U.S. Government Printing Office, 1965).

[2] "The Tanglewood Symposium: Music in American Society," *Music Educators Journal*, LVI, No. 3 (November, 1967).

for this. One: most students do not have the time, interest, or ability for a performance course, and provision should be made for them. Two: even if the teacher of a performing group is very interested in enriching rehearsals, he can never devote as much time to theory or literature as a specialized class can. Three: if well taught, these classes involve the intense, serious learning that justifies a place in the school day and granting credit. Unless the general music course is altered considerably from the broad and varied activities discussed in Chapter 10, it hardly deserves full status in the senior high school. If the course is changed significantly, then a new name would seem appropriate.

Should all high school students be required to take at least one course in music or fine arts? As implied in Chapter 4, the answer is "Yes." Many students take their last music or art course in seventh grade, and they probably won't take another unless someone requires them to do so. This means that 12-year-olds are receiving their last instruction in a broad and challenging area of their culture. Nearly all other curricular areas are required in high school: three or four years of English, courses in science, language, mathematics, physical education, and social science. The omission of a requirement in the arts suggests that the arts aren't important enough to merit study by the average student. Some music teachers shy away from requiring music because a few uninterested students will be in the class. But if education is to provide students with new understanding and appreciation, then it is the uninterested teenagers who most of all should be enrolled.

To Combine or Not to Combine?

Can music appreciation and theory be combined into one course to reinforce the learnings of each? Probably not in the high school, although taken at face value it appears to be a good idea. The general student in the music appreciation course usually is not interested in theory, nor can he profit from it. Moreover, at the high school level the study in each area becomes too sophisticated and specialized to allow for an easy combination of learnings. With an autoharp and vocal chording, a class can examine the harmonization of a folk melody, but the autoharp and voices are inadequate to study the harmonic intricacies of César Franck. Finally, although the integration of music theory and music literature has been explored by many colleges, it has been attempted only occasionally, with infrequent cases of success.

What about the combined arts course? There is much to be said for it from both a theoretical and a practical point of view. A practical advantage is the fact that in a single course the student learns about several different arts. Because the high school day is crowded, the idea of bringing several subjects together in one course is a tempting one. Theoretically, the arts reinforce one another. A student who gains a concept of Neoclassicism in painting will often more easily grasp the idea of Neoclassicism in music. The fine arts do have in common an aesthetic value, and a similar mental process is required to understand them.

As good as the idea of a combined arts course is, there are three practical pitfalls that must be avoided for such a course to be successful. One pitfall concerns time. A one semester course meeting daily meets about 90 periods. If painting, sculpture, music, drama, literature, dance, and some philosophy are squeezed into 90 periods, one doesn't need to be much of a mathematician to figure out that no subject is going to be covered adequately. Perhaps a little study is better than none at all. But if the existence of the fine arts course lulls the school and community into a sense of complacency about its educational effort in the arts, then the limited understandings gained by the students may be too high a price to pay. The first pitfall can be avoided by allocating enough time for music, which is probably most easily accomplished by lengthening the course to one year, and by not permitting the fine arts course to substitute for other courses in the arts.

The high school student, unlike the college music major, is usually not familiar with any of the arts. Some curriculum theorists maintain that a combination of intellectual disciplines should be attempted only after one of the areas to be combined is rather well understood. Otherwise the students wind up with virtually no understanding; $0 + 0 = 0$. There is much logic in the advice to avoid combining bits of knowledge from several different areas. Adequate time must be allocated to each art presented in the course.

The second pitfall concerns selecting faculty for such courses. Few teachers are competent enough in several arts to teach a combined course. It takes more than a couple of courses in music to teach the subject well, and it's the same with painting, dance, and the other arts. Team teaching is sometimes the answer, but it isn't easy to create a compatible team of a musician, an artist, a dancer, and a drama teacher. And even if they work well together, team teaching is "teaching by committee." The committee must find plenty of time to meet. Actually, many team teaching arrangements fall into a pattern of "let's-each-take-a-turn," in which the students receive several "mini" courses instead of one integrated course. Either a competent teacher must be employed, or a genuine team must be formed, with sufficient time for planning.

A third pitfall is the tendency to draw false relationships among the arts, to force parallels that simply do not exist. One cannot hear the stained glass windows of a cathedral in a Bach organ work; the chords that accompany a melody do not support the melodic line as the pillars on a Greek temple support its roof; the artist and the musician mean different things when they use the word "rhythm." Now, the arts do have some points in common:

similar reasons for being, similar degrees of worth, and similar outlook. But direct parallels are as impossible and false as attempting to draw a picture of three minutes of time.

This discussion is not intended to imply that the combined arts approach should be avoided. Not at all. A combined arts course can be very good when handled properly. But it can also be very bad when not taught well.

Music Appreciation

Courses of this type appear under many different titles: "music appreciation," "music literature," "music understanding," "introduction to music," and so on. Course titles containing the words "history" or "literature" imply specialized courses that are more appropriate for the music major at the college level. The term "music appreciation" has been abused and misunderstood in recent years, and now seems to connote superficial and unmusical little lessons. The title "music understanding" is preferred because it connotes knowing in the fullest sense of the word, as well as enjoying and appreciating. This chapter will utilize the more common term, "appreciation."

Purpose and Problems

The music appreciation course has three goals. First, it should give the student some basic information about music. He should become familiar with the literature of music, its styles, forms, vocabulary, and other aspects that contribute to a basic knowledge of the art. Second, he should learn to listen to music intelligently and sensitively so that he can hear what is happening in the music itself. Third, he should learn to like music. The struggle is lost if the course causes him to turn against music and to avoid it after the course is completed.

Each of these goals is vital. If attention is focused on only one aspect of the course, it will be only partially successful. Just as a violinist needs more than one string on a violin to perform the Beethoven Violin Concerto, the student listener needs more than one aspect of a music course if he is going to listen to Beethoven's Violin Concerto intelligently.

Content

What constitutes "basic knowledge" in music? This is a difficult question on which no two musicians will agree completely. Each textbook written for the course provides a partial answer to the question. Although the teacher may disagree with some of the authors' judgments, the books do provide a starting place for decisions regarding content.

Whether or not a book is used, the course content should follow the criteria recommended in Chapter 4 for all music courses: the material should be representative of the world of music, learnable by the students, up-to-date, and fundamental to the subject.

A persistent problem is organization of the content. Some teachers favor a chronological approach; others prefer to develop the course around mediums or compositional techniques; others like to start with popular or folk music. No plan is without its strengths and weaknesses. The chronological approach is a natural organization because it's the way music developed. Starting with familiar music — whether pop or folk or show tunes — also has merit because it begins where the students are. Therefore, some combination of a "familiar music" and a chronological approach seems best. After getting the students involved in the course, the teacher can follow music more or less as it developed.

Listening

Certainly listening is fundamental to the art of music. A person can't appreciate what he doesn't hear. But he must have more than aural skills. The sounds he hears are transmitted to the brain, which organizes, interprets, and (one hopes) appreciates them.

Suppose that an art appreciation course devotes its attention to developing visual perception skills. Through studying fragments of paintings and pieces of sculpture, the students are drilled in recognizing aerial and linear perspective, chiaroscuro, negative space, color value and hue, and axis. Assume further that most of the students actually do learn to see such aspects of art works, and that their interest in the course does not wane during the tedious visual drills. How valuable is it for them to recognize chiaroscuro if they have no clear idea how it fits into the world of painting, which painters use it, what its effect is, how it relates to other factors such as perspective, and indeed, what the fine arts are all about? The art appreciation student should be able to observe all the aspects of a piece of art, but he also needs the knowledge to make what he sees meaningful to him.

Unfortunately, hearing all that happens in a piece of music is not as easy as seeing all that is present in visual art work. The parallel between visual and aural study is not a perfect analogy. One can take his time to study perspective in a painting. But music moves, and the motion of the harmony, the appearance of a countermelody, and the sound of a different timbre can occur almost simultaneously. So training in listening, *if handled in a meaningful way,* is a valuable part of a music appreciation course.

Methods of Teaching Listening

Teaching nonmusicians to listen carefully is no easy job.[3] The student must be sufficiently motivated to put forth a minimum effort, and he must possess the intellectual capacity to retain and make sense of the musical ideas his ear transmits to his brain. The teacher must persistently encourage and prod students to listen selectively. Besides asking, "Did you hear that?" or directing, "Listen for the melody in the clarinet," he can ask them to verbalize about a specific portion of the music.

As a beginning, students can be asked to render some judgments about aspects of the music they just heard. For example, is the tempo fast or slow? Is the melody in a high or low range? Is there much dynamic change? Is the beat steady? At first the students may not be able to hear details, so the obvious characteristics of the music are especially suitable for consideration at this point. General observations can lead to more precise listening ability as their study progresses.

Early in the course, students often grope for the right words in discussing music. Certainly it's important that they have the correct idea, even if they can't phrase it properly. But correct terminology should be encouraged so that confusion is held to a minimum. Quick reminders are helpful: "What's the musical term? Not 'rate of the music,' but _____."

In discussing music, students should not be asked to tell how they react to a piece. Their reactions are personal property. Besides, any discussion involving feelings soon reaches the dead-end of opinion and personal taste. Instead, insofar as words permit, the students should analyze what they hear in the selections, not their own feelings about the music.

More sophisticated judgments can be expected as the class gains listening experience. They should learn to recognize canonic treatment, for example, as in the introductory part of Berlioz' *Roman Carnival Overture*. Exactly when the imitation starts, the teacher can say to the class "NOW —what's happening?" After the section is done and the record or tape stopped, the class can attempt to answer the question. The teacher should generally ask several students in the class before he indicates whether an answer is right or wrong. If only a few students get the right answer, the section should be played again, with the same procedure. A third playing may even be necessary. Of course, before students are asked to identify canonic treatment aurally, they must understand what the word "canon" means.

A second way to draw out the students is to take a work such as the last movement of Brahms' Symphony No. 4, the movement containing the

---

[3]The author recalls that until it was necessary to listen carefully to pass dictation tests in freshman music theory, he had never really listened before.

chaconne. After becoming familiar with the chaconne theme, the students listen to the first five or six variations, with the teacher indicating each new portion as it appears. The students are told to write in their own words what happens to the original melody in each section. They should put down specifically what they hear in each particular variation. An answer is not acceptable if it merely says that the violins are playing in the fourth section; the description must be specific. Exactly what are the violins doing? Are they playing in a rough, masculine style? Are they playing the very high notes in legato style? Are they playing the variation on the melody, or a contrasting line? If two students disagree on what is happening in a particular portion, the matter should be settled by hearing the music again, not by the teacher telling the class.

A third technique is simply to count the number of times a melody appears in a work such as a fugue. The class can be asked not only to keep track of the number of appearances, but also to write down how the subject or melody is treated. Does it come back in a low voice, or in a high part? Is it complete? Is it played in the same style as the first statement? Is the countersubject played with the subject?

A fourth technique is to ask the students what happens in the development section of a symphony. Assuming that they have heard the themes often enough to remember them, they are asked to indicate which theme is stressed in the development, and what is done with it.

A fifth practice is to have the students follow the theme in one movement. This works well with Mozart, since he presents themes in a straightforward manner with well-marked cadences and transitions, and most movements are not long. Students need not write anything in this case. The teacher merely stops the recording and asks what is being done with the theme, and what this indicates about the form of the movement.

A sixth means of aiding listening is to give some simple ear training, but not necessarily of the type given to music majors in college. The teacher can play two brief patterns of pitches, chords, or rhythms, changing one note in the second version. The students are asked to tell whether the two examples were the same or different, and if different, to locate what was changed. The class can also sing back a short phrase. Music memory is developed in this way. To involve both ear training and notation, a simple example can be written on the chalkboard, overhead projector, or individual sheets. The instructor plays the example, but with one error for the students to locate.

A seventh technique is the "doodle map." The idea is for the students to listen to a section of a work and make a "map" of what they hear. These maps can take many forms. One person may chart the dynamics and textural thickness, another the pitch level, a third person the instrumentation, and so on. Most students will come up with unique maps that validly picture something about the music. One example of what a map might look like is this picture of the first portion of the third or "Chester" movement of William Schuman's *New England Triptych*:

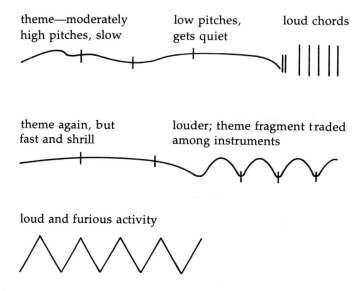

theme—moderately high pitches, slow

low pitches, gets quiet

loud chords

theme again, but fast and shrill

louder; theme fragment traded among instruments

loud and furious activity

The "doodling" aspect of the maps allows the student's mind to operate freely without the encumbrance imposed by words or standard notation. Many students find this freedom helpful.

After the maps have been created, they can be compared and a "master map" drawn on the chalkboard. The master chart is a synthesis of the students' maps. Mapping need not wait until the students know formal schemes such as sonata form. Such schemes are only one way of analyzing what is heard in music. Informal techniques can be valid too.

An eighth way to aid listening is for the students to follow notation. Most people can comprehend something from following notation, even if they can't read it. Themes can be placed on the chalkboard, projected, or followed in the textbook. A collection of simple line scores is helpful. Two such books are:

Bockman, Guy Alan and William J. Starr, *Scored for Listening*. New York: Harcourt, Brace, and World, 1959.

Hoffer, Charles R. and Marjorie L. Hoffer, *Scored for the Understanding of Music*—Supplemented Edition. Belmont, California: Wadsworth Publishing Company, 1971.

A line score has several advantages: (1) it keeps the student's attention from wandering while he listens; (2) it helps him remember the music by providing visual support for his aural impressions; (3) it helps him learn instrumental timbres because the most prominent instrument at a given moment is indicated in the score; and (4) the formal structure is marked in the score so that a nonmusician can follow the overall design of the music. Students with a strong background in music can follow conventional scores while listening.

A ninth technique is the "call chart" or "blueprint." The teacher makes a chart listing the significant points in the music — changes of meter, instrumentation, tempo, texture, themes, and the like. The first important point is numbered "1," the second "2," and so on. Then, as the work is played, the teacher can call or point out the numbers at the appropriate places in the music. If the students use the chart at times without the teacher present, the running time in seconds can be placed beside the call numbers. In this way the listener knows, for example, that "number 2" occurs 27 seconds after the music starts. All he need do is follow a clock or watch with a second hand. Another use for the call chart is to list two types of texture or other musical aspect at a particular number. As that spot comes up in the music, the student marks his selection of which aspect he thought he heard. This use of the chart is closely related to the blueprint. It is similar to the call chart, but is a more graphic representation. A number of blueprints are available commercially.[4]

A tenth means of improving aural skill is to give listening assignments. For example, "Listen to the third and fourth movements of Tchaikovsky's Sixth Symphony and determine which movement has the faster tempo, which is generally louder, and which has the more clearly defined form." After a few weeks, rather than ask for a conventional term paper, the teacher can assign a listening project by suggesting a list of specific works to hear, or specific composers, or simply a certain number of major compositions from each stylistic period. The students are required to listen to the music outside of class and prepare a report on it. In one way or another they must commit themselves on each piece heard, by commenting on the form, style, unusual musical factors, or the expressive quality of the music. This eliminates the possibility of circumventing the assignment, and encourages the students to listen carefully, rather than just put in time hearing some records.

An eleventh way to aid listening is to urge the students to listen to the same work several times. Only in this way will they become sufficiently familiar with it, so that they can remember what they have heard. When one thinks how many times teenagers hear the latest pop tunes — pieces that are usually much shorter and less complex — it's easy to understand the need for repeated hearings of a piece of art music. For this reason, recordings of the music studied should be easily accessible to the students.

The role of memory in understanding is a vital one. When a person hears

---

[4]Saul Feinberg, *Blueprints for Musical Understanding* (New York: Warner Bros. Publications, Inc.).

music, he actually experiences only an instant of sound at any given moment. This exact instant of sound can have meaning only if the hearer remembers what he has heard prior to that instant and anticipates what he will hear in subsequent instants. Listening to music is like trying to view a picture that is entirely covered by a sheet of paper, with a small slit extending from the top to the bottom of the picture. The picture is seen only as the slit is moved across it. All that is in the picture on either side of the slit must exist in the viewer's mind in the form of memory or anticipation. In other words, the customary spatial comprehension of the picture is now changed to comprehension in time.

Memory and anticipation also exist in relation to style. If a trained musician listens to a new work composed in a style familiar to him, he finds it easier to remember what he has actually heard, and to anticipate more fully what is about to occur. It is as though a slit were moved across pictures of similar subjects painted in a similar style.

A twelfth technique to promote listening is to discourage using music as a springboard for personal fantasizing. Sometimes students enter a music appreciation class with the notion that they must visualize something concrete as they listen—ships sailing, sunsets, horses galloping. This is usually a carry-over from some misguided instruction in the past. While some pieces are written to express feelings aroused by specific incidents, the attention should be focused on what is happening musically. If students need to be persuaded on the inability of music to express specific stories or pictures, the teacher can try one of two devices. One: make up a new and different story to fit a programmatic piece of music. Tell it to the class and ask them to judge as they listen to the record whether the story is the one the composer intended to describe. Play the record, and after hearing the students' opinions, tell the traditional story. Two: without mentioning its title, play a short programmatic work such as "The Great Gate of Kiev" from *Pictures at an Exhibition*, or "Pines of the Appian Way" from *The Pines of Rome*, and ask the class to imagine a movie scene that would fit the music. Invite each student individually to describe the scene which the music suggests to him. Although the ideas may bear some resemblance to one another, the details will vary sufficiently to impress the students with the fact that music is not equipped to give an accurate description of pictorial or nonmusical observations.

Aesthetic Sensitivity and Understanding

Besides gaining skill as a listener, the student should understand the nature and value of the fine arts. Unless he senses their purpose—at least intuitively even if he can't verbalize it—he misses much of the reason for music as an art.

When students first enter a music appreciation course, they carry with them all their old patterns of thinking about subjects they study. They naturally expect music to be like the familiar academic disciplines, and do not realize that if they are going to get the point, the *raison d'être* of listening to Bach or Brahms, they will have to reorient their manner of thinking for the course. They should realize that the arts provide experiences, not "answers." They should learn to look for quality, not size or quantity, in a work of art. The student who claims that a certain pianist is best because he can play more notes per minute than anyone else, is missing the point and applying a faulty, quantitative standard. A work of art is its own reason for being. It invites contemplation as an end in itself.

The teacher can encourage contemplation of musical sounds by playing a short example, sometimes only a few notes, from a recording or on the piano. A few seconds of silence should follow the example to allow the students to think about the musical excerpt. They should not be required to verbalize about each example they hear, however. If they are asked to express themselves about every musical fragment, they may spend the time thinking up what they will say if called on, rather than contemplating the sound itself.

To stimulate the students to think about aesthetic questions, the teacher can ask them to pair off paintings and musical compositions on the basis of mood or aesthetic impact, not subject matter. Sometimes they should be asked to explain their pairings. Another technique is to discuss or debate such questions as "Is photography an art?" "Does a ballet have more aesthetic quality than a square dance? Why, or why not?" "Are aesthetic experiences limited to an intellectual elite?" "Are knowledge and intelligence necessary to appreciate works of art?"

Most students bring to the course habits and outlooks that must be overcome if they are to gain an understanding of music as an art. One condition is the "protective coating" most of us acquire to protect ourselves from the sounds that are around us everyday. We learn not to notice sounds — traffic noise, Muzak, airplanes, talking that doesn't include us, and so on. This lifelong habit of not noticing must be reversed if listening to subtle and complex music is to be appreciated.

A second predisposition is the time sense that the student has about music. In popular music, nearly all the musical ideas are presented in the first 30 or 40 measures; subsequent music is a reworking of the opening material. Art music involves the manipulation of musical ideas over much longer time periods. So, for art music the teenager must greatly expand his comprehension and tolerance of musical time.

A third condition involves dynamic levels. After hearing popular tunes booming in his ears at loud dynamic levels, the adolescent is likely to find the gentle sounds of Debussy or Palestrina pale and ineffective. So another readjustment is called for, one in the sense of musical dynamics.

A fourth outlook is the students' attitude toward the manipulation of sound. Few popular works contain much thematic development or large formal schemes. Sometimes teenagers become impatient when listening to a portion of a symphony or concerto in which they can't hear the melody. The composer's skillful manipulation of musical ideas seems to them to be "busy work" without any real value.

Correcting each of these conditions involves careful, persistent effort by the teacher.

Recognition of Styles

Sometimes students are asked to memorize a list of characteristics of a musical style before hearing the music, or without ever hearing the piece at all. Such a procedure is like taking an art course and being required to memorize phrases such as "form through color," "distortion of depth dimension," and "informal design," without seeing representative paintings. A much better approach is to see the painting or hear the music, and then deduce what its features are. This procedure conforms to the guidelines for teaching music suggested in Chapter 9.

In most cases, it is better for the teacher to do a thorough job on a limited number of musical works than it is to scatter the emphasis. He should use a "post hole" approach by which he helps the students remember a particular work and composer. Between the post holes he will need to "string lines," so that one area of concentrated attention can be logically connected to the next. This means leaving out some good composers and music—and how painful that is to a teacher! But it's better to do this than to inundate the student in a flood of information and music.

For the students to form concepts about music—and this is vital if they are to remember what they have learned—they must gain an understanding of musical styles. A study of styles places the emphasis on musical qualities and adapts well to the post hole approach. Stylistic periods represent a solid element of musical experience and knowledge for the students to hang on to—an element to which other aspects of music, and other fine arts, can be related. Although the classification of periods is by no means perfect, there is a Romantic movement in painting, sculpture, and literature, as well as in music, and the student's understanding of one will contribute to his understanding of the others.

The study of musical style helps him approach works that are unfamiliar to him. When he says he doesn't like this or that music, often the problem is that he is missing something that is there, or he is looking for something that is not there. A course in understanding music should lead the student to look at a musical work through the proper pair of glasses, so to speak. He must not expect to be overwhelmed in a bath of sound when hearing Mozart, for example, because Mozart represents an age that proclaimed reason, good taste, and the universal nature of truth and beauty.

Introducing a New Work

New music need not always be presented in the same way. There are times when a record may be played with no preparation by the teacher; then he can ask the class to describe the expressive quality of the music. He may simply wish to set a mood. For example, during the playing of a Grieg number, the class might be shown color slides of fjords and other Norwegian scenery. Certain portions of the music can be played as "teasers" for the entire work. On other occasions the class can learn the theme and sing it before hearing it in context. This is especially helpful in enabling the students to follow sonata form more easily. Sometimes the themes can be placed on the board or on large pieces of paper around the walls of the room, and the teacher can point to them when they occur in the music. Before an opera is presented, the libretto might be presented as a play, with acting. This works well with Menotti's *The Telephone*, for example. Perhaps the class can sing the first 16 or so measures of three or four of the solos. In any case, the methods of presentation should be as imaginative and varied as the works of music. The teacher must be more than a disc-jockey who announces the next selection to be played.

Testing

In addition to the traditional cognitive tests, which were discussed in Chapter 6, the student in a music appreciation course should also be evaluated on his skill in listening to music. Some teachers allot up to half of the examination score to listening items. In view of the importance of listening, such a proportion does not seem excessive.

Because the students are nonmusicians, general questions are preferable to exacting, specific items. For example, several minutes of an unfamilar work can be played, and the students can be asked to classify it according to stylistic period. Other general listening questions about a selection might be: "Listen to this concerto; is it of the solo type, or is it a concerto grosso? Is there a cadenza? Is the form *A B A*, or theme and variations? What instrument or type of voice is featured?"

In preparing the listening section of a test, the teacher must select works that are typical of the period they are intended to represent. Also, if he stresses the organ only during the presentation of Baroque music, he will have to prepare the class especially for Romantic organ music if he expects them to identify the period of a César Franck organ work correctly.

At some point in a formal pattern, the recording can be stopped and the students asked to identify where the music stopped in the form. Or, after the exposition of a fugue, the class can respond by telling how many voices the fugue has.

Listening questions adapt easily to a multiple-choice format. Example:

> The music will stop during the performance of a movement in sonata form. Determine where the music stops.
> (a) introduction
> (b) first theme of exposition
> (c) second theme of exposition
> (d) development
> (e) beginning of recapitulation

Usually about two minutes of a selection is sufficient. Shorter passages don't allow the student enough time to consider the work, and longer examples consume too much test time. If a student wants to hear an example again, and if time permits, it should be repeated before going on to the next item. Jumping back and forth between items can be confusing to the students. Listening examples can be dubbed on tape prior to the examination to ensure against incorrect needle placement and related problems.

Textbooks

Most music appreciation textbooks are written for college, rather than high school, students. There are of course wide differences among such classes, so an able class of high school juniors and seniors can benefit from a book written for college freshmen. The following books are generally appropriate for high school classes.

Hoffer, Charles R., *The Understanding of Music* (2nd Ed.). Belmont, California: Wadsworth Publishing Company, Inc., 1971.

Machlis, Joseph, *Adventures in Listening.* New York: Grosset & Dunlap, 1968.

———, *The Enjoyment of Music* (Shorter Edition, 3rd Ed.). New York: W. W. Norton and Co., Inc., 1970.

McKinney, Howard D., *Music and Man.* New York: American Book Co., 1962.

Rossi, Nick and Sadie Rafferty, *Music through the Centuries.* Boston: Bruce Humphries, Publishers, 1963.

Fine Arts Courses

There are nearly as many types of arts courses as there are schools offering them. Basically, the courses can be divided into two categories. One category emphasizes the role of the arts in human thought. Often they carry the title "humanities." The other category is more confined to the arts as disciplines in themselves (painting, music, dance, etc.). Such courses are known as "fine arts," "allied arts," and "related arts."

Because lack of time is a problem in combined arts courses, the fewer areas a course attempts to cover, the better it will be able to educate students in those areas. For this reason, humanities courses are usually more difficult to teach well. When philosophy, sociology, and similar disciplines are included, music almost gets squeezed out. For example, a state humanities guide once suggested that the instructor "play a Beethoven symphony here." This was the extent of its treatment of music in one of its chapters.

In the interest of a balanced overall program for the high school student, the music teacher should promote the idea of omitting English and American literature from the combined course. All students receive instruction in literature in their English classes, so no deprivation is involved. Duplication is avoided, and more time is left for art and music, which most students do not cover in other classes.

As in the case of music appreciation, there are several approaches to course content, and each has advantages and disadvantages. The chronological plan shows the development of the arts and emphasizes styles, but it starts in ancient Egypt and Greece, not where the students' interests are, and it may unduly emphasize historical relationships. The aesthetic principles approach focuses on the basic characteristics of art, but it tends to overlook the influence of time and place, and is inclined to make sweeping generalizations. The theme approach (for example, "Man and Nature" or "Society and the Artist") coordinates well with the experiences of the students, but there is a temptation to bend the subject to fit the chosen theme. The conceptual approach (line, texture, rhythm, and so on) is appropriate for dealing directly with art media because it aids perception, but it encourages false analogies among the arts and neglects style.

Teaching music in a combined arts course is much like teaching it in a music appreciation course, except for the limitation of time. Both situations can answer the need for basic information, for development of listening skills, and for building positive attitudes. In addition, the aesthetic aspects may receive greater emphasis in the arts course. Basic concepts such as tension and release, repetition, and variation become even more important.

Many fine-arts teachers believe that no textbook should be used for such a course. Also, because of the wide diversity in the organization and content of the courses, only a few textbooks have been published. Included among them are:

Cross, Neal M., Robert C. Lamm, and Rudy H. Turk, *The Search for Personal Freedom*. (4th Ed.). Dubuque, Iowa: William C. Brown, 1972.

Janson, H. W., and Joseph Kerman, *A History of Art and Music*. Englewood Cliffs, New Jersey: Prentice-Hall, 1970.

Van de Bogart, Doris, *Introduction to the Humanities*. New York: Barnes & Noble, 1968.

Wilson, A. Verne, *Design for Musical Understanding*. Evanston, Illinois: Summy-Birchard Company, 1966.

Wold, Milo, and Edmund Cykler, *An Introduction to Art and Music in the Western World* (4th Ed.). Dubuque, Iowa: William C. Brown, 1972.

Music Theory

Music theory, like music appreciation, enjoys a variety of names such as "basic music" or "fundamental musicianship." As with music appreciation, it is difficult for high school students to work a full year theory course into their schedules. Many schools must settle for a one semester course, while others can offer the class only in alternate years.

At this point, the similarity between theory and appreciation (or fine arts) ends. The theory course is not for the general student; it is for the person with at least a minimal musical background.

Except in a few specialized high schools, there is insufficient enrollment to permit courses in several areas of theory. As a practical measure, the high school theory course must be an integrated one, or else significant topics will be left out. Besides, the unified approach to theory is more musically and educationally valid. Melody and harmony are interrelated, and are necessary components of keyboard and guitar experience. Similarly, successful arranging of music depends on ear training and aural experience. For both practical and pedagogical reasons, then, the high school theory course should be integrated.

Teaching theory in the secondary schools differs in three respects from teaching it at the collegiate level. One: the high school class may be more limited in time, often being only one semester long. Two: the students are not as facile in music notation, so they require more time to write out music. Three: the high school class is not as highly selected and able as a college class. For these reasons, efficiency is of paramount importance in teaching the secondary school theory class.

The high school theory course should be both functional and versatile. The approach to harmony, for example, should be of sufficient scope to embrace the nineteenth-century as well as the eighteenth-century style. This will lead quickly into seventh chords, augmented sixth chords, and more drastic and frequent modulations. Harmonic analysis should encompass many forms: the chorale and hymn, the song accompaniment. A class should not become so involved with a certain style or approach to music that it never learns about other styles and approaches. Nor should it confine its study to highly specialized techniques and problems that pertain to only a small portion of the world of music. Sometimes attention has become centered on intricate rules. Not only does this teaching procedure violate the students' need to experiment with actual music, but many of the rules themselves are more complex than they need be, and some are applicable only infrequently.

Theory instruction should be functional, enabling students to write and arrange music for their school stage bands, combos, and student musicals. Writing or arranging is both motivating and educational for students, and it makes the class more relevant.

Two criticisms have sometimes been leveled against theory courses as they have been taught in many high schools. One is that they deal mostly with the traditional style and music of the common practice period. The course should not be confined only to this music, but the critics might be reminded that even today most music—popular songs, Broadway musicals, hymns, film scores, and much art music—still contains tonality and tertian chords. Serialism, quartal and secundal harmonies, pandiatonicism and the like should be studied, but the basis for the theory course should be the past three centuries of music.

The other criticism contains much truth: The theory course has often been unmusical. Students have learned to spell scales and chords, name intervals, avoid parallel fifths and octaves, and figure out correct meter signatures, with little idea of what these intellectual tasks mean in relation to musical sounds. The content of such a course is oriented toward the "head" rather than the "ear." Keyboard work, singing, ear training, and composing have largely been ignored.

Content

Even though a minimum musical knowledge is a prerequisite for the course, the first efforts should concentrate on fundamentals of musical nomenclature, with the symbols experienced through listening and singing or playing. Although some members of the class are in many respects good musicians, their knowledge of theory may be spotty and not cohesive. Few students are completely at ease with the double-dotted note, the 12/8 meter signature, or the three forms of the minor scale. The work on fundamentals in the high school class should proceed rapidly, consuming not more than about eight weeks of daily class meetings to cover this content:

Note names, including bass clef
Rhythm—note and rest values, meter signatures, borrowed units
Major scales, constructed by interval and key signature
Minor scales, constructed by key signature—natural, harmonic, and melodic forms
Intervals, including inversions
Chord types, including inversions—major, minor, augmented, diminished, seventh
Chord functions, identified by name and Roman numeral

Much of this information can be taught quickly with the aid of one of the many programed or semi-programed books available. Some of them are:

Ashford, Theodore, *A Programmed Introduction to the Fundamentals of Music*. Dubuque, Iowa: William C. Brown, 1969.

Clough, John, *Scales, Intervals, Keys, and Triads*. New York: W. W. Norton, 1964.

Dallin, Leon, *Foundations in Music Theory* (2nd Ed.). Belmont, California: Wadsworth Publishing Company, 1967.

Harder, Paul, *Basic Material in Music Theory*. Boston: Allyn and Bacon, 1970.

Howard, Bertrand, *Fundamentals of Music Theory*. New York: Harcourt, Brace and World, 1966.

Martin, Gary, *Basic Concepts in Music*. Belmont, California: Wadsworth Publishing Company, 1966.

Winold, Allen, and John Rehm, *An Introduction to Music Theory*. Englewood Cliffs, New Jersey: Prentice-Hall, 1970.

Henry Lasker, who for years has taught theory at Newton High School outside Boston, offers this listing of content for a one semester theory course.[5]

> In Theory I, all the major and minor scales and the modes are taught with a great deal of emphasis on the singing experience, with or without the syllable methods, as well as the application of scales and modes to the piano keyboard. The principle that the written note symbolizes a sound, and must be heard and felt, is stressed continually. In this way, the singing experience helps considerably in developing the sensitivity of the ear. The primary chords—tonic, dominant, dominant 7th, and sub-dominant—in root position and inversions, form the vocabulary in Theory I. Here again,

---

[5]Lasker, Henry, *Teaching Creative Music in Secondary Schools* (Boston: Allyn and Bacon, 1971), pp. 50, 52.

the singing experience is constantly used. The chords are sung in arpeggio form in unison and then concerted with the class divided into the necessary parts.

Knowledge of the ranges of soprano, alto, tenor, and bass is required for the voicing of these chords in four parts in open and closed positions. This is followed by the progression of chords in cadences according to accepted procedures. All progressions are sung and played at the piano.

As the students do their work, they are urged to do it independently of the piano at first, in order to help them develop a sense of hearing mentally before they perform their work. "See with your ears; hear with your eyes."

The Color-Basic principle, actually first species counterpoint, is then taught; a soprano is harmonized with an economically, well-disciplined bass line using root positions and inversions. Again, they must be sung and then played.

With all the above as a foundation, the students proceed to the harmonization of 4- and 8-measure sopranos to be sung and played with an understanding of the following functions: section; phrase; sentence; half- and authentic cadences; harmonic rhythm; use of inversions and root positions, with the economy of the primary chord vocabulary to create bass line interest; proper doubling, spacing, and voice leading, employing principles of stagnation and activity in relation to tempos; the three principal motions; and avoidance of the traditional errors of cross parts, tritones, consecutive fifths and eighths.

Analysis of intervals and construction of intervals above and below a given note, significance of consonance and dissonance in relation to intervals and chord construction are gradually taught. Ear training, melodic, rhythmic, and harmonic dictation are an important part of the course too. Figured bass in relation to the primary chords is presented, as well as elementary analysis of materials within the vocabulary.

Keyboard Experience

Limited work at the keyboard should accompany the study of fundamentals. The word "keyboard" as used here does not encompass the complex activities required of college music majors. In the early stages, keyboard experience in the high school class involves simply playing the right notes on the piano. This is a necessary preliminary step because some students entering the course have only a sketchy acquaintance with the piano.

As major and minor scales are studied, they should be played at the keyboard, and the same is true for intervals and chords. Then as students progress into creative work, they will be more free and musical in their approach to the piano, especially in writing and playing simple accompaniments.

Ear Training

One of the most important and continuing phases of the theory class is ear training. Although the ability to listen carefully and selectively is not easily taught, a "good ear" is a necessity for any musical effort, be it composing, teaching, or performing. Music is an aural art, and never should this fact be forgotten, least of all in the theory class.

In melodic dictation the use of numbers can save class time. By writing scale step numbers without a staff, the students get the essential experience of taking down what they hear without spending time putting it into musical notation. The number system is of course limited to tonal music and phrases that do not modulate. The technique is this: the teacher simply tells the class the number of the starting note. (Later, when the class is able to isolate a particular note in a chord, the teacher can play the tonic triad and let the students find the first number from it.) For example, the teacher plays the figure below twice, and the students write and/or sing back "1–3–4–2–7–1"

from memory. As the phrases become longer, the numbers will need to be written down. To help the students see the relationship between numbers and musical notation, a melody that has been taken down correctly with numbers should occasionally be transcribed into musical notation.

Another practical way to relate musical sound with notation is for the students to recall a familiar melody, perhaps a popular song, and write it on the staff. This saves time normally spent in dictating the melody.

Whether the response involves numbers or notes, all melodic dictation should follow essentially the same procedure. First, the students should be told the starting pitch, or should be given a clue about how to find it. Then the teacher should play the phrase *twice*. Long melodies should be dictated phrase by phrase. During the first two hearings, the class should *not* attempt to write anything; they should just listen. The no-writing policy trains the students to listen more closely and develops their musical memory. After the second hearing, the class can sing back the melody to gain a concrete experience with it. Then and only then should they attempt to write down the melody. The teacher should play the melody two more times, pausing after each playing to allow for checking of work.

Rhythmic dictation is helpful, especially early in the course, if melodic dictation is confined to numbers instead of the complete notation with its rhythmic symbols. The procedure for rhythmic dictation is similar to melodic, in that the students should listen carefully to the pattern the first two times it is tapped or played on the piano. As use of notation is increased, rhythmic dictation becomes less necessary because rhythm is present in melody.

In addition to melodic and rhythmic dictation, the students should learn how to identify aurally the soprano and bass members of a chord. Before actual identification is attempted, the class should have experience in singing major triads with numbers. The first singing should be from the root; later the starting tone can be the third or fifth. As soon as the triad pattern is established in the students' ears, these steps are recommended for dictation of chord members:

(1) Play a triad in root position, or inversion, with one note doubled. Arrange the tones so that the bass note is a distance of a fifth or more from the others, and play it more loudly. Hold the triad until the sound fades away. After a short pause, ask the class to sing back the bass note.

(2) Play the chord once more, and again sustain it. Ask the class to experiment by assuming that the note sung is 1 and singing 1–3–5–3–1. If the starting pitch was not 1, this will be obvious to the class. Proceed then to 3, and to 5 if necessary.

(3) When the class becomes proficient at singing patterns starting from the bass member of the chord, drop the singing and have the students merely identify the tone as 1, 3, or 5.

(4) When the bass can be heard fairly well, follow the same procedure to find the soprano member of the triad.

A fourth phase of ear training in the secondary school theory class is identifying chord types. The initial attempt should be confined to a choice between major or minor chords in root position. Then the work can progress to inverted positions as well. This is followed by introducing the diminished triad, and finally the augmented triad. For the first several weeks, practice in chord identification should involve hearing only two of the four types during one session. This avoids overwhelming the uninitiated ears of the students with too many types at once.

Ear training can be promoted with especially designed tapes and books. They provide exercises that have been carefully developed and graded. The teacher may play them for the class to vary his performance at the piano, or the students can listen on their own in study carrels in a language laboratory or at listening tables in the library. Some of the ear training programs available are:

Benward, Bruce, *Teacher's Dictation Manual in Ear Training* (also *Student's Manual*), Dubuque, Iowa: William C. Brown, 1961.

Carlsen, James, *Melodic Perception*. New York: McGraw-Hill Book Company, Inc., 1965.

Horacek, Leo, and Gerald Lefkoff, *Programmed Ear Training*. New York: Harcourt, Brace, and World. Four Volumes, 1971.

Kraft, Leo, *A New Approach to Ear Training*. New York: W. W. Norton and Company, Inc., 1967.

Olson, Robert C., *Music Dictation: A Stereo-Taped Series*. Belmont, California: Wadsworth Publishing Company, Inc., 1970.

Thomson, William, and Peter DeLone, *Introduction to Ear Training*. Belmont, California: Wadsworth Publishing Company, Inc., 1967.

Singing

In his theory course outline Lasker rightly emphasizes the importance of singing. Because singing seems to be the surest way to develop tonal imagery — the ability to hear tones "in the mind's ear" — it should be a component of other learnings. For example, scales and chords should be sung as well as written. Melodic dictation should be sung back. Sight singing should be undertaken. A variety of material is available for this: folksongs, octavo music, and books especially written for sight singing.

Creative Work

Lasker continues his course outline, "From the first day of school in September, students in Theory I are encouraged to create." Creative exercises stimulate students to think musically, motivate them to feel a personal involvement with what they have written, and encourage them as creators of music. Even if not particularly successful, those students who have attempted to write some music will have a greater understanding and appreciation of what composers do.

The term "creative work" brings to mind an original musical composition of some magnitude. In the high school theory class, however, the time available and the abilities of the students do not usually permit efforts at major compositions. At this level, creativity is best nurtured through limited works, often not more than 16 or 32 measures in length. Of equal importance with the brevity of the work is the degree to which the teacher structures the assignment. Never should the neophyte composer be told, "Go home and write a song." Although it may appear to be an inconsistency, creative work for most high school students is better fostered at the start if they are given a precise set of specifications for their work. What they need at first is a sense of how to go about writing music, and a successful experience in doing so.

There are several ways to approach creative exercises. The more successful ones are usually based on song style. The teacher selects a jingle or couplet with a definite meter for the students to set to music. Even the familiar "Roses are red" is a possibility. The advantage of a jingle is its definite meter, which makes it easier for the student to come up with a strong, logical, rhythmic structure. After the words are metered out with accents and bar lines, the note values can be written in. Next come the pitches. For early creative efforts, the teacher should restrict their use by suggesting a particular key and a range, perhaps one octave. The student should be encouraged to give his melody as much coherence and logic as he can, at the same time maintaining some novelty and interest.

Another approach is to select a stanza of poetry with a definite mood. In this exercise the students attempt to achieve in the music the mood that prevails in the poem. Depending on the ability and experience of the class, the teacher may wish to suggest note values.

There are other ways for a teacher to introduce composing experience. He can create a tone row for the students to manipulate, or list the serial techniques they should follow after writing their own rows. He can offer a rhythmic pattern — either an overall plan like the jingle, or an ostinato figure. He can suggest a harmonic pattern from which they derive a melody — an approach similar to conventional jazz, except that the result is composed rather than improvised.

At first the student should be instructed to write the melody only. At the next class session, the teacher plays the melodies and discusses them, determining how well they meet the criteria of unity, variety, and appropriateness with the text (if one was given). If the melody is a good one, the student can add a simple block-chord accompaniment. If the melody is not so good, another try is called for. At this point in the course, writing a good melody and proper chords is a sufficiently ambitious undertaking. One or two more melodies can be attempted, with the teacher withdrawing some of his specifications each time. How long the structuring is continued depends on the success the students achieve with their compositions.

After several block-chord accompaniments have been written, the teacher should devote some time to showing the class how to embellish the chords and make them more interesting. Pianists find this rather easy, but nonpianists may need extra help. The class should hear many song accompaniments. This makes them aware of the countless ways of sounding the essential harmonic structure without resorting to thumping out block chords.

Before the end of the course the students should have an opportunity to write a melody for one instrument, accompanied by two or three others. Whenever possible, the teacher should specify that compositions be written for the instruments played by class members so that there can be live performances of the music. Composing for instruments will probably entail teaching transposition. Under the condition of limited time, the problem of range and orchestration is best handled by having the teacher specify the easy and practical ranges of the instruments for which the student plans to write.

Some teenagers who enroll in the theory course may be interested almost exclusively in electronic or tape recorder music. Should they be allowed to pursue only their limited area of interest? Probably not. The young composer ought to become acquainted with a broad spectrum of music and should learn how to compose in conventional media as well. As soon as he's acquired some skill at handling compositional problems, he can branch into the manipulation of tape and work with a tone synthesizer.

The theory class should be a musical learning laboratory in which works are presented for examination and evaluation. A most desirable outcome of the class, and one that does much to stimulate interest in music theory and composition, is performance of a student work by one of the school's performing organizations. Possibly the best student composition in each theory class can be arranged with the help of the teacher for performance. The composition need not be pretentious. A march, a simply arranged melody, or a song is adequate to impress the student body, and to provide educational benefits for the student composer.

Given time and student ability, there is no limit to the possibilities for work in theory. Whatever the extent of its content, the theory course should be functional, versatile, creative, and above all, musical.

Questions

1. Why is a music appreciation course more appropriate at the high school level than a course in advanced general music?

2. Suppose the high school principal asks the music teacher: "Why is a music appreciation course so important for the high school students who aren't in band or chorus? After all, they had music all through school up to the eighth grade. Why do they need more? If they were really interested in music, they'd be in band or chorus right now." How would you answer?

3. What are the advantages and disadvantages to beginning the music appreciation course with folk music? with Gregorian chant? with acoustics? with a Broadway musical? with a standard, easily accepted symphonic work? What could be the procedures for beginning with each?

4. Why is the music theory course not for the general student? Could some of its value be given to the general student in some other way? If so, how?

5. What are the advantages of the combined arts course? What are some of the practical problems associated with such a course?

Projects

1. Look over textbooks in music appreciation and evaluate their appropriateness for a high school class. Consider the writing style, amount of material covered, degree of emphasis on musical qualities, and presentation of material that is significant *for the listener.*

2. Look over textbooks in music theory and evaluate them for use in a high school class. Consider to what degree each book presents the learnings functionally, encourages creativity, and is versatile. Consider also whether the book would be appropriate in an integrated theory course.

3. Listen to these recordings and decide what feature of the music could be suggested as a focus for the students' listening. Mention any particular teaching procedure that would contribute to the value of the listening experience.

Aaron Copland	*A Lincoln Portrait*
César Franck	Violin Sonata, fourth movement
J. S. Bach	Brandenburg Concerto No. 5, first movement

4. Practice giving a melodic, rhythmic, chord member, and chord dictation exercise to one of the persons in your class.

5. Select a musical work and develop a "call chart" or "blueprint" for it.

6. Develop a short test to give students in a music appreciation course. Make about half the test consist of listening questions.

7. Prepare a set of directions and specifications to give the students in a theory class for their first attempt at composing.

Suggested Readings

DeLone, Richard P., *Music: Patterns and Style.* Reading, Massachusetts; Addison-Wesley, 1971.

Instructor's manuals for the Hoffer and Machlis music appreciation textbooks cited on page 416.

Lasker, Henry, *Teaching Creative Music in Secondary Schools.* Boston: Allyn and Bacon, 1971.

$$17$$

School
Music Performances

Janet Grissom has just started her new job at Westport High School. As she goes to her mailbox in the office, the principal says to her, "Oh, Miss Grissom, better get your concert dates set on the school calendar by a week from Friday, because we want to get the thing handed out by then." Janet checks last year's school calendar and sets dates for programs at approximately the same time for the coming school year. But as she makes plans for her next day's classes, she wonders, "Just how will the material I'm teaching now be related to the concert I've set in May, or in December, for that matter? I haven't even decided what to do—I've merely set a date for a program." After another moment she thinks, "Really now, why am I having programs in the first place? Why particularly in December and May? Why should I have these programs? Should I have more? What kind of programs should I present?"

Rationale for Performances

To begin to answer Janet Grissom, one must return to the question raised in Chapter 3: Why is music included in the curriculum of the school? The goals of music education are crucial to determining why there are performances and what they should be like. Certainly they should not be the "be-all" and "end-all" of school music, although sometimes they have been so regarded in many schools. Performances do contribute to the music education of students. But the teacher should keep his priorities straight. Students give performances because they have learned; they should not learn simply to give performances.

Some teachers think of school programs as being much the same as professional concerts or recitals. They regard the school program as a diminutive version of a professional performance. Such thinking is not logical. Professional musicians perform because that is their chosen work, and because they get paid for it. Any educational or psychological values accruing to them are largely irrelevant. It's the opposite with school musicians. Their pay is an occasional free meal. The educational benefits, which will be mentioned shortly, are paramount. Both school and professional musicians wish to give musically creditable performances, of course. This goal is the sole objective of the professional musician, but it is only one of several desirable outcomes for the school group.

"Performance" means both making music and performing music for an audience. The performance of music is vital to the art. Songs are meant to be sung, symphonies played, and compositions performed. Music is not the marks and dots on a sheet of paper; it is sounds, which are often re-created from what appears on sheets of paper.

Performances for an audience are not common outside of Western civilization, but in our culture they are accepted almost casually. And they are definitely of value to a school group, *if done properly.*

Value of Performances

Performances can benefit school musicians in a number of ways. For one, they provide a definite goal toward which to work. Learning is satisfying for most students, but they are more strongly motivated when they have something concrete to work for. The second benefit (student motivation) is an outgrowth of the first (definite goals). It's only human to work harder at something you know will be observed. A third value of public performance in school music is the education it offers the audience about music and the school curriculum. The program is in a sense a report about what is going on in the music class. Programs and concerts can also inform people about music. A fourth benefit is seen in the social and psychological values that accrue to the students. Teenagers achieve recognition for their accomplishments as performers, and they gain poise and self-confidence from appearing before an audience. A fifth value is the group consciousness performances help build, something that adolescents need. Sixth, there is a benefit to the school and community. The pep rally is peppier when a band is present, and the civic ceremony is more impressive when young people are making music.

Guidelines for Performance

A careless or poorly managed performance can negate the benefits just mentioned; no doubt about it. What can be done to achieve quality performances, without detracting from the music education of the students?

First, *performances should be an outgrowth of actual school work.* Education should not be interrupted to prepare something for a performance, something that's unrelated to current learning.

Second, *performances should present music of the best quality appropriate for the occasion.* The marching band and concert choir perform under very different circumstances. The type of music suitable for one is not necessarily suitable for the other. Each, however, should present the best music that is suitable for the occasion.

Third, *performances should receive proper preparation.* It is impossible to spell out specifically how much time is required to prepare a program. There are too many variables—the ability of the group, the length of the program, the difficulty and newness of the music, the degree of perfection demanded by the teacher, and his efficiency. Fortunately, if the performance is an outgrowth of class activity, time for preparation and time for learning the subject are no longer distinct and separate. For this reason, except when special circumstances prevail, all preparation should take place in the regular class periods for curricular groups. Preparation also includes routine matters such as publicity, tickets, and equipment.

Fourth, *performances by any one group should not be so numerous that they interfere with the total education of the students.* The precise number cannot be indicated for the reasons discussed under preparation time. But when the curriculum of a choral or instrumental group becomes merely preparation for one performance after another, the number is excessive. Time must be allowed to study music, as well as to perform it. Without such learning a band or choral group ceases to be an educational organization.

Fifth, *performances should adhere to acceptable moral and ethical standards.* The vast amount of music available makes it easy for the school music teacher to reject musical productions that cast students in morally undesirable roles, or in situations that are inappropriate to their age and experience. As an influential social institution, the school must promote the best aspects of civilization and personal conduct. With so much to teach and so little time to teach it, the schools cannot afford to do less.

Sixth, *performances should include all students who study music in performing classes.* The temptation, of course, is to concentrate on the most talented students because they present a more favorable picture of what is being done in music. This occurs when a chorus of 75 presents a musical built around two or three principals and five or six minor roles. The other 65 students sing a few simple chorus parts, make scenery, assist with makeup, and pull the curtain. The principal performers sometimes get an inflated view of their abilities and contributions. This is not to say that talented students should not be given additional opportunities, but they should never be given special attention to the detriment of the others. For example, teaching a solo number should take place in private sessions, not during class while the rest of the students sit as onlookers.

Seventh, *performances should be planned to receive optimum responses from the audience.* Unless the audience generally feels good about the program they have heard, little social or psychological value will be gained by the student musicians. The success of the performance affects future students as well as present members of the group. When the program is well received, not only are more students motivated to enroll in music courses, which in turn increases the effectiveness of performing classes, but there is also better support and understanding on the part of the school administration and public.

Eighth, *performances should be viewed in proper perspective by students and teacher.* If a concert is an outgrowth of classwork, then it should be treated as such. Some teachers think that by whipping up fervor in the name of the almighty performance, they will achieve the optimum effort from the students. Unfortunately, they usually achieve the optimum effort plus tension, fear, and stiffness. Certainly this is a misuse of performance. A month's work is not ruined because of a missed entrance in a concert; a month's work can only be lost in the classroom. The teacher should not get the cart before the horse here. His primary purpose is the musical education of teenagers, not the presentation of flawless performances.

Planning for Successful Performances

The education of the students and the interest of the audience are not necessarily contradictory propositions. In fact, a teacher with ability and imagination can combine the two. It is the less successful teacher who sees good music education and a high degree of audience enjoyment as irreconcilable, and proceeds either to ignore the listeners or to forget about music education for the sake of audience amusement.

If performances by school groups are to achieve their goal of being both educationally valid and successful in the eyes of the audience, then the teacher must keep in mind two points. One is the need for informality. Secondary school students are not collegiate or professional musicians, and music teachers should not present concerts that pretend they are. Teenagers have personality, imagination, and genuine audience appeal, if these attributes are not snuffed out in an oppressive, stiff atmosphere. There is no reason why the teacher cannot offer a few comments about the music during the program; no reason why there cannot be informative notes in the printed program, and no reason why a class activity other than performance cannot be shown to the audience. Music teachers sometimes overlook the fact that people are curious about the simplest things: how a French horn player who has been resting for several measures knows when to come in, how the singers know which note of a chord to start on, and what a conductor does to indicate loud and soft.

The second point is the age of the students. Younger students should be presented with greater informality. A seventh grade class can present a number or two using water glasses it has tuned to study the intervals of the scale and tuning, or it may sing a simple unison folk song with autoharp accompaniment. A senior high school group, however, should present more polished performances and more sophisticated music, simply because that is the level at which it studies music.

The School Assembly

Most school groups, with the exception of the marching band, perform almost entirely at school assemblies and public programs at school in the evening. The two situations, school assemblies and adult programs, are by no means the same. The school assembly involves a homogeneous audience, volatile and responsive, and composed of peers and friends of the performers. A stiff, formal assembly will not easily draw a favorable response from a student audience. Much of the audience at evening school concerts consists of friends and relatives of the participants. Success is more easily achieved under these less demanding circumstances.

The rapport that the teacher establishes is crucial to the success of a performance. Basically, he should let the assembled students feel that he understands how they view the program they are about to hear and see. He does this by the manner in which he informs them about various facets of the music and gives them something to listen for in each number. For more serious works, he might give the audience a breakdown of the major themes, with the group demonstrating them. He conveys enthusiasm for the program and respect for the listeners.

This rapport is delicate and easily lost. One music teacher during an assembly reprimanded some students in the audience who were inattentive. A few days after the performance, some members of the music group politely suggested that he not do that again. Apparently they realized that his action would only alienate the student body, probably not cure the misbehavior, and put the performers in the uncomfortable position of having a teacher, representing them, publicly drive a wedge between them and their peers.

For many nonmusic students, the assembly is their only opportunity to hear and see the music organizations. This performance will influence their opinions about music, and may determine whether or not they enroll in a music course. Secondary school groups should also perform for other schools in the district, especially elementary schools. These are less formal occasions, the purpose of which is to educate the younger children about music and the school music curriculum.

Whatever the age level of the student listeners, the assembly is important to both the immediate and long-range objectives of the music department. Every effort should be put forth by the teacher to schedule such assemblies and to make certain they are well received.

Assembly Singing

Although it is not common in American secondary schools, singing in assemblies has much to commend it. In many schools inadequate auditoriums, student behavior problems, or large enrollments make successful singing in a large group difficult. If the prospects for successful group singing seem favorable, it merits a try.

The secret seems to be in *not* letting the assembled students know that a real singing effort is expected of them. If the director says, "Today we're going to have a singing assembly, and we want *you* to sing," he is in for trouble. A "sing-along" technique works better. On a number with a solid, easily sung, familiar refrain the director can say to the student body, "When I turn around waving my arms, join the choir in singing the refrain. Most of you know it, I think."

Another secret is to ask the students to sing only a few numbers in an assembly. Two or three are plenty at first.

A third secret is a good accompanist. He can keep things going when the singing gets shaky.

Words to the songs may be projected on a wall or screen, or members of the choral group can hold up large cardboard signs with the words painted on them.

Informal Programs

So far the discussion of music presentations has centered on the band, orchestra, or choral organization, each of which is a performance oriented class. These are not the only groups, however, that appear before the public. General music classes, frequently in combination with other sections of the same course, may perform once or twice a year. In addition, performing organizations make informal appearances, such as the "Parents' Night." On these occasions audience interest is achieved by showing the learning activities of the class. Students can play portions of recordings they have heard and offer explanatory comments; they can display the music notebooks they have compiled; they can describe current class projects. The autoharp can be used to accompany songs, and part-singing can demonstrate the use of changing voices.

With performances of this type, attempts at a formal, professional presentation are out of character. The appeal to the audience lies in the personalities of the students and their own unique responses to the music. Instead of entitling a performance "Spring Concert by West Junior High School," it might be called "Music at West" or "Invitation to Music at West Junior High School." People appreciate an unassuming program appropriate to the age and nature of the students.

Programs Outside of School

Schools groups are often invited to perform for community organizations. It may be necessary for the teacher to apportion the number of such appearances so that the educational purpose of the music group does not suffer. If refusals for performances around the community are necessary, this is usually best handled through a policy statement on out-of-school appearances drawn up by the teacher, student officers, and school administration. In this way the onus does not fall on the teacher individually, and the matter receives the attention of more than one person.

Two special considerations should be given to performances outside of school. First, they must not infringe on areas which properly belong to the professional musician. The Code of Ethics, reprinted in Appendix A, states that school music groups may perform at educational nonprofit, noncommercial functions, as well as at benefit performances for charitable organizations, nonprofit educational broadcasts and telecasts, and civic events that do not usurp the rights and privileges of the local professional musician. Performances by school groups at other civic programs are permissible if they are mutually agreed on by the school authorities and official representatives of the local musicians' union. Recordings are permitted if they are strictly for education or audition purposes and are not offered for general sale to the public. The professional musician has in his province such events as community concerts and community-centered activities and other nonschool activities, and functions furthering private or public enterprise, partisan or fraternal organizations. The Code says further:

> Statements that funds are not available for the employment of professional musicians, or that if the talents of the amateur musical organizations cannot be had, other musicians cannot or will not be employed, or that the amateur musicians are to play without remuneration of any kind, are all immaterial.[1]

---

[1] Code adopted September 22, 1947. Reviewed and reaffirmed in 1948 and again in 1955 by all participating organizations.

The second consideration is the place of performance. If it is impossible for the group to practice in the new location, the teacher should at least see the surroundings beforehand. Some teachers have had the unfortunate experience of agreeing to sing for the Rotary Club only to find that the Rotary meets in a hotel dining room that is too small to hold both the singers and the Rotarians. If a piano is to be used, the position and quality should be determined ahead of time.

Television and Radio Performance

Some school groups have the opportunity to be heard and seen on radio and television. The status such an appearance gives a group is great indeed. Because extensive preparation is necessary, the teacher should consult special publications on the subject, and confer with the technicians at the local station. If a television technician seems more concerned with the visual aspects than the aural, the music teacher will need to check carefully to see that the sound is of good quality.

Adjusting to Performance Conditions

There are several ways a teacher can facilitate the adjustment of the performers to the place of performance and expedite the mechanics of presentation. If at all possible, the group should practice at least once in the place of performance. The shift from rehearsal room to stage can be difficult for teenage musicians. A new location sometimes gives a performer the unsettling feeling that he is performing alone. The seating or standing arrangement will probably be different, at least to the extent that the distances are altered among musicians and between the conductor and musicians.

During the practice the teacher should check to see whether the students can hear one another, and whether the choral groups can hear the piano. Then he should check the sound from the back of the room. If there are hearing or balance problems, some adjustment of the stage arrangement is called for. Draperies around the back and sides of the stage can be drawn together or apart. The piano can be moved, and its top raised or lowered. In instrumental groups, instruments with less volume can be moved forward, and louder instruments can be moved to the back of the stage, where more of the sound is absorbed in the curtains and lost in the gaping ceiling. If seated instrumental risers are available, their use can improve balance and ensemble. The performers should also be forewarned about the effect the audience will have on the acoustics of the room; the sound may be noticeably more "dead."

When a stage absorbs too much sound, making the tone appear weak to the audience, the possibility of a shell should be investigated. Manufacturing concerns produce shells that are quite adaptable and portable. If a commercial shell is too expensive, regular stage flats can be made and painted with several coats to give them a hard surface. Most important are the overhead panels that keep sound from rising up between the lights and becoming lost. If no other means of support are available, the panels may be suspended.

The choral teacher often finds it feasible to have two seating plans, one for the rehearsal room and one for performance. The rows on the risers may be a different length from the rows of chairs in the rehearsal room. Furthermore, in performance the students are arranged somewhat according to height to prevent unevenness in the appearance of rows, and to prevent tall singers from blocking out the shorter people standing behind them. When a mixed chorus is arranged by height, the boys, who are generally taller than the girls, are often placed in the back and center of the group.

Although a few outstanding collegiate and professional choirs scatter the sections, this technique is too difficult for most school groups. An inexperienced singer needs the confidence and help derived from others on his part who are located near him.

The exact arrangement of the vocal or instrumental group is not a vital matter. Traditional seating patterns and placement of sections are based as much on appearance as they are on musical results. Generally the larger and louder instruments are put in the back rows. Considerable experimentation is going on, especially in the case of band,[2] and many unique and valid placement patterns are observed in both choral and instrumental organizations. The teacher should feel free to vary the arrangement according to his personal desires, the size and instrumentation of his group, and the characteristics of the stage, so that the arrangement will produce the optimum in appearance and musical results.

The movements of a group must be carefully planned. Time and energy can be conserved by having the performers in place when the curtain is opened. Watching one person after another walk onto the stage is not an aesthetically satisfying experience. The footsteps make a distracting noise, and some of the group are obviously ill at ease. A row of singers may overshoot its place on the risers and someone from the wings has to signal them all to move back a bit. Why not save valuable class and concert time? Get in place, open the curtain, and start making music.

Occasionally, the group may perform where there is no curtain, and the musicians will have to get in place in full view of the audience. With choral groups the simplest way to handle this is to have the front row come out first, then the other rows, starting with the last and working down to the

---

[2]Richard Franko Goldman, *The Wind Band: Its Literature and Technique* (Boston: Allyn and Bacon, 1961), p. 250.

second row. In this way, the first row can somewhat shield the others as they line up. Military marching maneuvers, including the about-face used by some music groups, are out of character. If the students walk in a dignified manner, nothing further is needed to improve their entrance.

If a soloist is to step forward from his place in the group, a way must be cleared for him, unless he is in the first row. If a music stand must be moved into position, someone should be assigned this chore. The soloist must know how to acknowledge applause. If he performs from his position in the group, he should be invited to step forward or to stand afterward to receive recognition for his efforts.

The teacher, too, should plan to acknowledge the applause of the audience graciously, with dignity and humility. By stepping to one side of stage center and making a modest bow, he acknowledges the fact that the applause is for the students as well as for himself.

Proper deportment before an audience is such an obvious necessity that a teacher may forget to mention it, only to look up at the concert and see a singer chewing gum or a violinist chatting with his desk partner. Each student should be impressed with the fact that his total attention must be on his performance, and that his eyes should be fixed on the director. The students must be strongly admonished about behavior in the event of a mistake. They should not look around, giggle, look startled, or in any other manner show knowledge of an error. Such behavior makes the group look disorganized and childish. They need to be reminded that *someone* in the audience will be looking at each one of them every moment they are on stage.

When students wear robes, uniforms, or similar dress, they should not wear any article of clothing that focuses attention on an individual. Conspicuous appearance, like poor deportment, is distracting to an audience and therefore inappropriate, especially when singing sacred music.

Planning the Program

In selecting music and deciding on the manner of presentation, the teacher should keep these points in mind.

(1) Select an opening number that will give the students a good start. Choose something that is not very difficult, with a solid beginning and no undue demands for subtleties of intonation or phrasing. The opening number must set a mood of confidence for the performers.

(2) Arrange the numbers in meaningful sequence. Some directors like to put the heavy, serious numbers at the beginning or end of the concert, the light numbers first or last, and so on. Some go so far as to talk about building up a concert like a crescendo; others mention musical climaxes. Such con-

siderations seem unrealistic, because what is a high point for one listener may be a low point for another. The only aspect on which there seems to be general agreement is this: works should not be arranged helter-skelter, so that Palestrina winds up next to "De Camptown Races," or a popular song next to Bach. It is more cohesive for the audience and students if the numbers are grouped into logical units such as religious, Baroque, or American music.

(3) Check the overall length of the program. Young teachers in their eagerness often give concerts that are too long. Professional concerts may last for two or more hours, but the patrons of school music programs differ considerably in their musical interests from the patrons of opera or the symphony. Furthermore, few school groups are of professional caliber. If any misjudgment of time is to be made, err on the side of having the concert too short. It has been said a thousand times — it's better to have the audience leave wishing to hear more, than it is to have them leave with a sense of relief that their ordeal is over at last. *One hour is plenty of time for most school programs*, and that one hour includes time for changing the stage, moving pianos and stands, tuning, and (one hopes) for some applause.

To estimate the length of a program, compute the duration of the music, the time for applause between numbers, the time needed to get groups on and off the stage and to move music stands, chairs, and pianos. If an intermission is scheduled, add that time, although an intermission is unnecessary when the length of the program is kept within bounds.

(4) Plan to keep the program from dragging. Let other teachers or student officers help manage the groups so that when one is through performing, the next is lined up ready to go on stage. Get the performers on and off the stage as quickly as possible. Assign separate rooms to each group so that the students have a place to leave their coats and cases, do a little warming up, and generally get organized. If the stage has a halfway curtain, small ensembles or soloists can perform from the front half of the stage while another group is quietly getting into place in the back half. If many organizations are participating, it isn't necessary to have all groups appear on the stage. A choral group may sing from the balcony of the auditorium, while the band and orchestra remain on stage. In many auditoriums the best place acoustically is immediately in front of the stage in the pit or on the floor. This area can be used just as effectively as the stage. In any case, plan carefully to keep the program moving.

Ways to Enhance the Program

How can teenage musicians capture the interest of an audience? What, if anything, is needed beyond the creditable performance of worthwhile music? One way to add interest is to tie the performance together through the use of a narrator, who may or may not be the teacher. Not only does the narrator integrate the program, he also eliminates "dead spots" between works of music and changes of groups. Another method is to feature several groups —ensembles, glee clubs, soloists, stage band, and others. In some cases ensembles can be included from both junior and senior high schools in the performance.

Methods for enhancing the appeal of performances must differ between instrumental and vocal music, for several reasons. The stage setup for a choral performance can be altered quickly, since it involves only risers and piano, but changes in an instrumental setup require moving stands, chairs, podium, music folders, and instruments. Vocal music with its words can suggest specific actions or props, while even programmatic instrumental music can seldom be treated so exactly. There are differences in length of pieces, with instrumental works usually being longer. Finally, vocal music is generally a more personal, direct experience between performer and listener than instrumental music.

Staging Vocal Music Programs

The day is passing, if indeed it is not already past, when a school group can just stand on the risers, sing its program, and thrill the audience. Only musicians of exceptional performing ability are able to do this. Motion pictures, television, marching band shows—all have contributed to the fact that audiences now want programs with some visual as well as aural appeal.

In many schools the concerts have been lifted out of the doldrums by "staging" some numbers. Staging includes props, backdrops, and dress, as well as activities such as dancing and pantomime. For example, in one school a glee club prepared three religious songs. To create the proper atmosphere, the students built a white altar rail to stand in front of the singers, and two artificial stained glass windows. At another concert, the chorus presented a group of folk songs, with a few students performing an appropriate folk dance to two of the numbers.

Through such techniques, the audience can be educated and interested at the same time. It's easy to forget that many listeners cannot fully appreciate what the group is doing. Their attention can be stimulated by a little action or a simple prop. It need not be much, as long as it helps break a seemingly long spell of watching the students perform from one unvarying position.

The impression should not be given that every number must be staged. Probably one in four is sufficient.

Does staging reflect good music education? Yes—if the visual elements are not emphasized to such an extent that they detract from the music. Staging is essentially a means of extending a song from an auditory experience into a visual one as well. The music maintains its proper position as the primary ingredient of the concert.

Staging is good music education because it involves all the students, not just the most talented. It presents music in an appealing way without spending time on the spoken lines and complex stage movements of a complete show. Most important, it allows the teacher to choose the music he wants, rather than accept some second-rate pieces because they are part of a musical.

Good staging has the advantages of a musical, without the cost. Musicals call for a large expenditure of time and money. Time is required to memorize spoken lines, stage directions, and dance steps—activities that are only distantly related to music. Money is required for royalties, costume rental, and scenery. Staging concerts eliminates these problems almost entirely.

There are many ways to develop ideas for visual effects in choral music. Student committees can be formed for each song or group of songs to be staged. The categories might include religious music, songs from other countries, or excerpts from Broadway musicals. The committees should meet outside of class time to discuss plans, and the teacher should meet with each committee at least once to exchange ideas with them. After each committee, with the teacher's help, comes to an agreement on an idea or two, the thoughts are presented briefly to the whole group, and further refinements are sought.

Next comes implementation of the idea, and another student committee is formed to do this. Membership on these committees is determined by the type of work involved. If a prop is to be built, boys enrolled in shop courses can do the job. If painting is required, students taking art courses can demonstrate their talents. Those who have a common study period can work together on a project, and no one will have to be removed from class—always a delicate operation in maintaining a friendly atmosphere in the school. The result is that most of the planning, purchasing, and actual work is done by the students. Their increased sense of responsibility is a desirable outgrowth of this experience.

Three precautions should be mentioned. The teacher should never attempt extensive staging without the assistance of the students. A little prop may not sound like much work, but when he has to build and paint it himself, in addition to his teaching load, it can be overwhelming.

Second, the teacher must *not* assume that he can turn the staging over to the students and go on about his other business. Teenagers need guidance and assistance in such an undertaking. The teacher will often have to tell the students where to find what they need, what to buy, when to work, and how to do the job.

Finally, no group should attempt too many projects, especially the first year. Until the students have had experience in working at such things, they are slow and require much assistance. In addition, the last weeks before a concert are busy enough without the burden of extra projects. Some props can be saved for another year, and this makes staging subsequent concerts easier.

Types of Staging Activities

Here are some staging techniques:

Dancing.   Since the whole group cannot sing and dance at the same time, a few individuals are selected to do the dancing. Folk and square dances are effective, as are tap or soft-shoe routines, if good dancers are available. There are many excellent source books for such dances,[3] and physical education instructors can be most helpful in teaching steps to the students. In addition, one or two couples can be selected to perform the latest teenage dance. This always draws a favorable response from a high school audience.

It is preferable to use dancers who are members of the choral organization. This may create a vacancy in the ranks for some numbers, but the gain in singer interest will make this procedure well worthwhile.

Change of Dress.   Variety can be achieved by simple changes of clothing. Because robes hide nearly everything worn underneath them, the singers can have one change of dress by simply removing the robe. Many choral teachers feel that it is inappropriate to sing secular and semipopular songs in robes, so dual costuming is advisable for presenting a mixed repertoire.

The teacher must allow enough time for a change of dress, designate a place to change clothes, and provide a room in which to keep the robes or clothing. Boys can usually make such changes faster than girls.

Lighting.   Lights can change the entire atmosphere of a scene. Campfire settings and night scenes with carolers can be suggested with appropriate lights. Sometimes the mood of a song will suggest a predominant color ("Joshua Fit de Battle of Jericho" might be red); and some song titles mention colors. If the stage has a rheostat, infinite variations of dim and bright light are possible. Lighting mixtures should be planned by the teacher with the help of a lighting expert, rather than by a nonmusician. While the lighting should fit the mood of the music, it must never be obtrusive.

---

[3]Especially good are: Anne Schley Duggan, Jeanette Schlottmann, and Abbie Rutledge, *The Folk Dance Library* (New York: A. S. Barnes and Co., 1948); Edward Durlacher, *Honor Your Partner* (New York: Devin-Adair Co., 1949); and J. Tilman Hall, *Dance!* (Belmont, Calif.: Wadsworth Publishing Co., 1963).

Props and Scenery.   Props and scenery should be more suggestive than literal. If the action takes place on a Pacific island, one palm tree is enough to lend atmosphere. If the boys are supposed to be sailors, sailor hats will convey this idea, along with a mop or two for scrubbing the deck, and a few naval flags strung on a rope.

Props and scenery must be kept simple; no waterwheels with real water running over them, please. The school may have pieces of scenery that the dramatics or art teachers have used, and these articles may be well suited to the purposes of the music department. Many stages have a landscape backdrop, which is ideal for an outdoor song. The teacher should check with the local fire authorities to be sure that props and scenery do not violate fire regulations.

The music teacher should supervise scenery building himself rather than turn it over to the art, shop, or dramatics teachers. It is unfair to burden other teachers with the hard work required by such building projects, when the program is not their responsibility. Also, an embarrassing situation can result if a fellow teacher is not clear on what is wanted. The finished product may not be what the music teacher had in mind. Thus he must either use something he does not like, or break the rules of propriety by not using the set at all. There are books available on building scenery, but most of them are for complex, literal pieces, unsuited to simple staging requirements.

Action.   A few simple pantomime actions can illustrate the words to humorous songs and those with compound repetition, such as "The Twelve Days of Christmas." There is one limitation to this device, however; literal pantomime can make the number look like a kindergarten rendition.

A music teacher sometimes becomes so accustomed to watching the smooth actions of professional singers that he expects the same enthusiasm and naturalness from his own students. In most cases, however, he will need to coach them on their actions. At least he should check them out before the performance. In one school the boys were to sing a humorous song from a current musical. Because it was their first experience with staged numbers, the boys were quite restrained. Their motions were inhibited and stiff, even though they were not practicing in the same room with the girls. They were told to exaggerate everything, but this didn't help much at the time. Then came a rehearsal performance for the girls' glee club. A success—the girls loved it! Next came a school assembly, and one could see more inhibitions being thrown aside with each performance. Another success. By the time of the evening program, the problem was no longer how to get the boys to act, but rather how to get them to stop overacting! They threw themselves into the performance and brought down the house.

Limitations to Consider in Staging

The type of prop and action is limited by the facilities available. These conditions will have to be taken into account:

Size of the Stage.   The amount of available space should be figured with the curtain closed, since the area in front of a curtain is generally not usable as part of the stage setting. Room must be allowed for the risers and piano. If the singers sit down, more space will be needed. The type of dancing, if any, may be seriously curtailed by the space. When action occurs in front of the singers, the teacher must remember that generally the farther back a choral group is on the stage, the more its tone will be absorbed by the overhead curtains, and the weaker it will sound to the audience.

Size of the Offstage Area.   This consideration determines the ease with which students and props can be moved on and off the stage. Unused props must be out of the line of traffic.

Amount and Quality of Stage Equipment.   Before planning extensive staging, the teacher should know what stage equipment is available, and if it is in working order. In some schools the lights and switches are handled carelessly by many students and teachers, and it is difficult to keep stage equipment in repair.

Height of Props or Scenery behind Risers.   It's easy to forget that six-foot boys standing on a two-foot riser block out much of the backdrop. In addition, the audience views the stage from a lower level, thereby making objects on the stage appear even higher than they are. As a result, the background space is no greater than from five feet above the floor to the bottom of the overhead curtains.

Practice Facilities.   The amount and type of staging that can be undertaken is influenced to some extent by how much practice the group can schedule on the stage. If the stage is in the gymnasium, the presence of other classes may hamper practice. If the rehearsal room is large enough, it is wise to chalk or paint on the floor the exact area of the stage so that the students can become accustomed to working in the available space.

Staging Instrumental Music

Although bands and orchestras cannot as easily add visual interest to their programs as vocal groups can, there are some steps that can be taken to increase the appeal of an instrumental concert. A few of these suggestions are similar to those outlined for vocal groups.

Dancing

Instrumentalists need not descend into the pit to play a number that includes dancing. They can leave enough room at the front of the stage for the dancers, or if the stage is too shallow, a few of the players can move to one side to give the dancers more space and hence more freedom.

Scenery and Stage Setting

Instrumental groups can use a backdrop as well as many of the props and flags mentioned for choral programs. Although instrumental music does not have a text to provide specific meanings, there are many descriptive works that suggest visual treatment. In the field of geographical description alone, the possibilities range from "The Great Gate of Kiev" to national anthems and folk tunes from around the world.

Instrumentalists need not always sit in the same arrangement. The use of seated instrumental risers enables all players to be seen more easily by the audience, so sections can be rearranged and emphasized according to the needs of a particular work of music.

Featuring Sections

Stage bands regularly feature sections and soloists. This technique adds interest to the program and permits individuals to be commended on their own merits. The featured section should be placed in a prominent spot. Separated placement is especially desirable for antiphonal music. While the following device has been encountered almost too frequently, it is a definite crowd pleaser: the piccolos stand, then all the brasses stand during the trio of "Stars and Stripes Forever." The same type of thing can be done occasionally with other music. In one school system the flutists from every school learned a lovely folk melody, then joined together to perform it with band accompaniment.

In addition to the small ensembles that should be a part of the instrumental music curriculum, the teacher may form a novel group such as a German band or a "Jug and Bottle" band. One or two numbers that are frankly presented just for fun, and that have not demanded a large amount of rehearsal time, may be worth including in the concert. The players may adorn themselves with appropriate hats, and in this way add a little more flavor to the musical rendition without a complete change of costume.

Musical Variety

Because much prosaic and even crass music is available under the heading "novelty," it is with trepidation that the author even mentions the term. But its connotation need not be all bad. The instrumental teacher should seek a few works that are skilfully written and musically interesting, but not serious or complex. Such pieces are hard to find. The *Toy* Symphony of Haydn, *Peter and the Wolf* by Prokofiev, and "The Typewriter" by Leroy Anderson are examples. Some of these works are educationally valuable because they demonstrate the qualities of instruments so well. Other pieces contain unusual actions, as in Haydn's *Farewell* Symphony, or Johann Strauss' "Clear Track Polka," in which the conductor can add extemporaneous holds and rubato.

Vocal Soloists and Choral Groups

Not only does a vocal soloist provide variety at an instrumental concert, but the combination of voice and instruments can be a musical experience of the highest order. Also effective are some finale numbers that involve a large chorus. As a further bonus, this type of presentation brings the vocal and instrumental departments together in a cooperative venture.

Business Aspects

Some musicians do not want to involve themselves in publicity, printed programs, and the sale of tickets; but these matters must be handled properly, or unnecessary complications will result.

A practice that has been successful in a few schools is the appointment by the principal of another teacher to take care of the business details for the music department. If this can be done, the music teacher can devote his attention to teaching. Even if a formal arrangement is not made, the music teacher may ask for assistance from other teachers when he feels their special training would be helpful.

Printed Programs

The printed program is a vital part of the concert because it is closely examined by the public. Before hearing the students, the audience looks at the program and gains an impression of their work. Other music teachers will see the program, even though they may not hear the concert. Programs are mailed to relatives of the students, pasted in scrapbooks, hung on bedroom walls, and looked at months and years after the actual performance.

Because the printed program is a permanent item, and has a way of getting around, it must include the names of all the students who participate in the concert. If the students are listed by the part they sing or the instrument they play, the lists appear shorter, and each individual seems more important. Above all, the teacher must *make certain that no name has been left out, and that all names have been spelled correctly.* If an error or omission is discovered after printing, the correction should be announced publicly at the concert.

Everyone who has assisted the music teacher in some way should be acknowledged on the printed program. This includes stores from which props have been borrowed, teachers and departments who have given assistance, administrators who have helped in scheduling, and the school custodians. Such acknowledgments go a long way toward maintaining good relations in the school. Soloists, accompanists, student officers, and members of student committees deserve special mention. This will make the program considerably more valuable for many students, and if they have made extra contributions, they should be recognized.

The printed program can help educate the audience. Although it is easy for the teacher to list only the name of a work and its composer or arranger, a mere list of names does little to enlighten the audience. They will derive more learning and enjoyment from a performance in which the music has been explained somewhat.

So it is good use of the teacher's time, limited as it is, to write brief but informative notes about each piece. Here are some samples:

Soon Ah Will Be Done   arr. William Dawson
The early blacks in America took refuge in Christianity, finding peace and sometimes exuberant joy. One of the most dramatic of all spirituals is

this one in which the slave looks forward to leaving the grief of this world and anticipates the joy of heaven.

First Movement, Symphony in B minor, the "Unfinished"   Franz Schubert

This composition is called "unfinished" because it contains two movements instead of the usual four. Schubert is best known for his ability to write beautiful songs and melodies. He was also one of the first Romantic composers—one who permitted his personal, subjective feelings to be revealed in the music. The movement does, however, follow the Classical sonata form with its exposition, development, and recapitulation. One of its most melodic themes is beautifully suited for the cellos.

O Domine Jesu Christe   Palestrina
(O Lord Jesus Christ)

The outstanding composer of music for the service of the Roman Catholic Church was Giovanni Pierluigi da Palestrina, who lived in sixteenth-century Italy. One of his best known compositions is the motet *O Domine Jesu Christe*. The text is a prayer to Jesus, with special recognition of his suffering on the cross. It concludes, "I pray that through your wounds my soul may be redeemed." The music is polyphonic, which means that all four parts are equal in melodic importance. The music is restrained and intellectual in character.

What do these program notes emphasize? In each case it is the essential quality or message of the music—the Romanticism of Schubert, the restrained quality of Palestrina's motet, and the ecstatic character of the spiritual. This is what the listener should understand. Other information about the music or composer is mentioned only as it might contribute to this understanding. The fact that Palestrina lived in the sixteenth century is significant in appreciating his music. Similarly, an explanation of polyphony is helpful to the listener who is oriented to homophonic music. Touches of humor may be injected occasionally into the program notes, although a little of this goes a long way.

Since understanding the music is a prerequisite to writing succinct and helpful program notes, a few exceptionally able students might be given an opportunity to prepare the written material. The purpose of this effort is not primarily to lighten the teacher's work load, but to help the students better comprehend the music they are performing.

A program printed commercially looks best, but it is usually expensive. Before placing an order, it is wise to distribute copies of the material to different printers and have them submit written bids for the job. This should be done before any printing is started,-because much of the expense occurs at the first step, which is setting up galley proof. If commercial printing is too expensive, the typing teacher can have his classes make up a mimeographed or multilithed program. Some large schools have print shops that can reproduce the material inexpensively.

Outside pages or covers for programs are available from various firms. There are color pictures from which to choose, and the rest of the folder is blank to accommodate the printing. Original designs by skilled art students also make attractive programs.

The teacher should start working on the program a month before the concert. It will take a week to get bids back and two weeks for printing or mimeographing. It is desirable to have the programs five days before the concert so that copies can be sent out as invitations and publicity.

Tickets

Tickets are not required when admission is free. They can still be made, however, and distributed for publicity. Making tickets is simple and relatively inexpensive. If there are different price levels, each should be represented by a different colored paper. The ticket should state the following information: name of event, presented by whom, where, on what date, at what time, and the price of the ticket. It is wise to print more tickets than the number likely to be sold.

The policy of reserving seats has good and bad points. It has advantages for the reserved-seat holders (they don't have to arrive early to have good seats) and advantages for the organization (a little more can be charged for the ticket). The disadvantages can be considerable. Each ticket must have two parts, one to be taken at the door and another to be kept by the holder as a receipt. Both the stub and the seat must be numbered. A problem arises when the concert is given in a gymnasium and temporary chairs are set up. Also, if there should be a mix-up on reserved seats (as often happens with student ushers), some people will take the incident rather testily.

Tickets to school programs should be sold by the students themselves. People will turn down an adult more easily than they will a youngster. Giving the students tickets to sell is also one of the best methods of publicizing the event. As an incentive, some teachers offer prizes to the two or three students who sell the most tickets. This is not always effective, because about the second day of the ticket sales someone, perhaps a boy with a newspaper route, walks into class and says, "Well, I've already sold 40 tickets, and I've got promises for 12 more." At that moment everyone else gives up. What seems better from the standpoint of motivating the students and filling the auditorium, is to offer the student one free ticket for every five that he sells. He can do whatever he wants with the ticket—give it away or sell it and keep the money. This method makes a small reward accessible to all. Tickets should always be available at the door on the night of the performance.

The bookkeeping of ticket sales is no small item. The easiest method is to give each student a fixed number of tickets, possibly three adult and two student tickets. Dispensing extra tickets can be recorded. Students should be told to account for all tickets given to them, and they must understand that they will have to pay for tickets that they don't return. When students are told this, they seldom lose tickets. All ticket collections should be suspended during class periods the final week before the concert. Financial activities consume valuable time, and most of these business matters can be handled outside of class.

Publicity

The best publicity for a concert is to include in the program as many students as possible. When a son or daughter comes home from school and announces, "We're having our concert in two weeks — can you come?" the parents are as motivated as they are ever going to be. It's a mistake for a school music teacher to set great store in formal publicity efforts. For the sake of experiment, a teacher with a well-established reputation for good programs decided not to have a single poster or sign made up to advertise the concert. He simply had the event announced in the town and school newspapers. When the night of the performance came, he had another packed house.

If posters are to be made, it is best to assign this project to students who are taking art classes. The public has grown so accustomed to printed signs stuck in store windows that another sign is seldom noticed. The creations of the students are more eye-catching than commercially printed signs. Besides, the signs made by the students usually cost only the price of the materials used.

In many communities, radio stations will broadcast announcements of school events such as music programs, as a public service.

Local newspapers should be provided with notices of the event. The willingness of newspapers to publish material about school concerts varies. Many small-town papers are hungry for news and will publish anything given them, including pictures. Larger papers are less likely to print complete write-ups. However, many metropolitan newspapers publish local editions, which contain news of interest to only one area of their circulation. Some newspapers run a school supplement once a week.

All copy prepared for a newspaper should be double spaced. Below is a sample story written in newspaper style:

The first concert of the season will be presented by the Centertown High School Orchestra at 8:15 P.M. Friday, October 28, in the school auditorium, 1201 Center Avenue. The concert is free to the public.

The 65 piece orchestra will be conducted by James G. Smith, supervisor of instrumental music in the Centertown schools for 20 years. Featured soloist will be senior Dina Eidelstein, concertmistress, who will be heard in the first movement of the Mendelssohn Violin Concerto.

Also on the program will be the first movement of Symphony No. 2 ("Romantic") by Howard Hanson, American composer and long-time director of the Eastman School of Music.

Completing the program will be Schubert's "Rosamunde" Overture, and the Prelude, Chorale and Fugue by Bach.

The story should contain any items of interest about the concert, director, or soloists, and should be given to the newspaper several days before publication is desired. It should be written in some detail, even though space limitations may require cutting by the editor.

The school newspaper is an important vehicle for publicity. Although it contains little that the students don't already know, it is significant because of the teenagers' need to be recognized.

One of the most effective means of publicizing the program to the student body is to present a preview or "teaser" assembly, from ten to 30 minutes in length. The idea is to show the students the best of the coming program so that they will attend the actual performance, and more important, talk favorably about the music organizations. The portions of the regular program with the greatest student appeal should be presented. If the students like what they see and hear, they will attend the complete concert. There need be no fear that a good preview assembly will lose audience for the main performance. Of course, if the preview assembly is *not* good, the consequences will be disastrous. In many respects the success or failure of the preview assembly for the school is more crucial than the success of an evening performance for an adult audience. Adolescent listeners never hide their feelings, and their responsiveness to a good program motivates the teenage performer.

Trips and Tours

The value of trips and tours for performing groups is controversial among educators. Much of the controversy has arisen because of the occasional misuse of trips. Some directors have received "kickbacks" from the expense fees charged students; this is especially true of European tours. In other cases, an "invitation" to a fair or a bowl-game parade (which is often sent *after* the school has expressed an interest in attending the event) has necessitated a tremendous effort to raise $25,000 or more to make the trip. In some states, such situations have precipitated the establishment of codes and regulations by school principals' organizations or by state extracurricular supervisory boards.

What are the characteristics of a properly handled trip by a school organization? They don't differ much from the points cited for worthy performances.

The trip must be an educational venture for the students. Performance should be only one aspect of the undertaking. The students may listen to other music groups, see a musical or a documentary film, or visit a television station.

The students should be impressed with the fact that the trip is an educational event, and not merely a vacation from school. Naturally students will engage in some conversation with their classmates about "getting out of school," but the amount of such talk should be limited. The students should be told that the more "vacation" talk there is, the harder it will be for them to get permission for future trips.

The performances should be primarily for school assemblies, and, in keeping with the Code of Ethics, no admission can be charged for any performance while on tour. Some schools present goodwill concerts in the evenings in churches or school auditoriums, and then take a collection. The results generally are not satisfying. Many goodwill concerts are poorly attended, and the collection may not cover even the small cost of publicity and other items. In such cases, the evening would be better spent by having the students hear or see something related to music. A school assembly, on the other hand, guarantees a full house and the probability of an interested audience.

The teacher should plan to have his group perform for schools of about the same size as his own. If an average chorus from a small high school sings before a larger student body that has a larger chorus, the small school's chorus would be hard pressed to do as well as the larger school's organization. It would be difficult for the smaller group to get a good response from the audience.

The trip must be well planned and managed. Arrangements must be made for every meal, every overnight stop. One teacher carefully planned each phase of the journey, but forgot to arrange for a place for the bus drivers to stay overnight.

Of more importance than meals and lodging is preparing the students for the trip. The vast majority of students behave splendidly, but there are a few who look upon trips as a chance for a little hell-raising. Nothing can ruin a trip and eliminate the possibility of future trips faster than misbehavior. Many teachers and schools have found themselves in trouble because students got lost from the group, committed petty shoplifting, damaged property, or threw objects out of bus windows.

What can be done to insure proper deportment? First, the students should be informed that the trip is a privilege — it's up to them to prove they deserve the privilege and can handle it. Then, with the school administration and student officers, the teacher must establish policies regarding behavior and penalties for misbehavior. These areas should be covered: staying with the group, smoking, hours for going to bed, behavior on the buses, and behavior in public places. Students should know that if they misbehave the penalties will be stiff, including failure in music and suspension from school. All warnings and regulations should be stated in writing and presented to the students and parents, in case of later challenges or misunderstandings.

A sufficient number of parents and teachers should accompany the group as chaperones.

The roll should be called or checked by monitors each time before the buses move on.

Limits should be put on the amount of baggage that each student may bring.

Financing the trip must be kept to a minimum and handled in a sensible manner. The trip should not require an agonizing financial effort. There should be no need for a year of activities such as tag days, collections, dances, sales of baked goods, candy, records, and so on. A trip that requires much of this sort of thing is out of place in the public schools. A modest money-raising effort should be sufficient to cover all expenses.

Money-raising projects must be considered carefully. Often they require arduous work, and after all the expenses have been paid, there is not much profit. It's true that magazines, candy, and greeting cards are items that do not require an effort to make, but the customer pays a lot for what he gets. If other school groups also sell goods to the community, the field can get crowded.

Caution should be exercised in any money-raising project. Because the classroom, equipment, and teachers' salaries are already being paid for by the public through taxation, school organizations must not be too bold in seeking money.[4] Discretion is needed to help maintain the good will of the community and to impose reasonable limits on the financial aspirations of the group seeking support.

One successful method of financing is outright solicitation. Surprisingly, many people prefer this to buying candy or magazines they don't want. In one school there was no charge for concerts. During the intermission of one program a collection was taken for the express purpose of financing a trip. Over half the necessary funds were collected at that one time. In this case the audience was composed of persons who were clearly interested in the musical organization, and the collection was made at a time when they were receiving something from the music program. Service clubs can also be solicited for funds for worthwhile causes.

Funds can be derived from selling tickets to music concerts. Except in the case of a musical requiring expensive costumes, scenery, and royalties,

---

[4]Andrews and Cockerille, pp. 171–72.

the outlay for a program seldom exceeds the income from tickets. This money can be applied to the cost of the trip, or at least held in reserve in case the actual expenses run over the estimate.

To keep expenses down while en route, it's best to eat in school cafeterias or in churches whenever possible. Commercial restaurants frequently cut corners in feeding large groups, and seldom can young people get as much food for their money as they can in schools or churches. For overnight trips, it is desirable to have the students stay in the homes of members of musical organizations from the school that is being visited. A small payment can be made for each student who is lodged for the night and given breakfast. This practice gives the students a valuable social experience, and is far less expensive than staying in a hotel. When the group is divided by going to different homes, there can be little general carousing, and therefore less chaperoning is required.

The schedule of the trip should disrupt the normal school routine as little as possible. The trip should not be so long and strenuous that the students come back exhausted. A trip of two days and one night is long enough. The number of performances should be limited to not more than three in any day — one in the morning, one in the afternoon, and one at night. Professional groups almost never perform more than one or two programs in a single day. Scheduling more than three performances involves the risk of falling behind schedule, hurried meals, and general tension.

When possible, trips should take place during a school vacation time, if the schools to be visited are not also on vacation. When students are removed from classes for trips, a sensitive situation is created. The other teachers are naturally a bit envious of the music teacher. He receives frequent public recognition for his work and here he is again taking time for a trip. In addition, the other teachers are inconvenienced by having students miss their classes.[5] This is another reason why trips should not consume more than two days. The best way for the teacher to approach the situation is to explain carefully in faculty meeting the purpose of the trip and the manner in which absences from class will be handled. The most successful procedure is to have the students get a signed statement from each teacher that their classwork is at least "C" quality and that all possible assignments have been completed in advance. Students who cannot meet these requirements in their classes should not be permitted to go on the trip.

If these conditions are met, a trip can be a wonderful experience for the students. Never do they have such singleness of purpose, or put so much into their performance, as on trips. The students feel as they never have before: "We're really doing things in music!" The social contact, the experience in planning, the musical events heard and seen, all of these can make a tour the high point of the year.

---

[5] Andrews and Cockerille, pp. 147–50.

There is only one disadvantage to a tour: the students will want one every year!

Checklist for Program Planning

The following time schedule is helpful in planning a major performance. Items concerning costumes and scenery can be ignored for the less extensive concert.

September

(1) Select and enter dates on master calendar of school activities. If school does not have a central calendar, clear dates with athletic and drama departments and with school administration.

Three to six months before performance

(1) Select music.
(2) Establish a budget for performance—music, costume rentals, programs, etc. Have approved by administration, if necessary.
(3) Secure performance rights on music. Procure music.
(4) Make arrangements for costumes.
(5) Try out soloists or leads.

Two to three months before performance

(1) Establish rehearsal schedule containing approximate dates for learning specific portions of the music.
(2) Begin study of the music.
(3) Schedule the learning of spoken lines by leads and understudies.
(4) Make decisions regarding scenery and props.

One to two months before performance

(1) Construct scenery and props.
(2) Prepare publicity and program materials.
(3) Arrange for tickets and ticket sales. Order tickets.

Two to four weeks before performance

(1) Have program printed or reproduced.
(2) Arrange for ushers, stage crew, and after-performance cleanup.
(3) Put scenery in place and rehearse with it.
(4) Arrange for warm-up and dressing rooms.
(5) Arrange for piano to be tuned on day of performance, if possible.

One week before performance

(1) Mail out complimentary programs and tickets.

(2) Plan rehearsals to consist of complete "run throughs."

(3) Set aside one rehearsal for looking over different music; let the students relax and rest.

(4) Check stage equipment and public address system.

(5) Check to see that all small props have been secured.

(6) Arrange for curtain calls and/or acknowledgment of applause.

Performance

(1) Hold a brief warm-up session in which the students perform the first few measures of each number in a thoughtful and careful manner. Check the tuning of instruments.

(2) Make sure everyone is in place and equipment is functioning before starting.

(3) Start on time.

(4) Relax and enjoy the program (as much as possible).

After the performance

(1) Return all rented or borrowed music, equipment, costumes.

(2) Thank custodians, secretaries, teachers, administrators, and merchants who contributed to the program.

(3) Finish collection of money from ticket sales.

(4) Initiate procedures with proper school personnel for payment of bills.

(5) Deposit with proper accounting the income from ticket sales.

Questions

1. What do these performance-related incidents reveal about the teacher's understanding of music education?

(a) Ruth Farnham has five sections of eighth grade general music. For a PTA program on music, she chooses the best 25 girls from the five classes to sing. "After all," she says, "there are a lot of kids in those classes who have precious little ability."

(b) Ted Pearlman is rehearsing his high school band. The first horn bobbles a note. "If you do that in the concert," Ted says sternly, "I'll clobber your grade, so help me. The audience cannot excuse mistakes."

(c) Lynne Hardesty wants the performance of the latest Broadway musical to be as nearly professional as possible. As a result, her singers rehearse only that music for three months in preparation for the performance.

2. Suppose you are asked to have your students provide 15 minutes of

after-dinner music at a service club luncheon. The performance is strictly for entertainment. Should you not accept the engagement? Why, or why not?

3. Which performances are acceptable under the Code of Ethics with the American Federation of Musicians?

(a) An appearance by the band at a Memorial Day observance.

(b) A performance in connection with the opening of a new shopping center.

(c) A performance at the swearing-in ceremony of county officials.

(d) An airport appearance by the band when the national vice-presidential candidate comes through town.

(e) A performance by the school stage band at a school dance.

(f) A performance by the school stage band at a dance held in a private club paid for by a group of families.

(g) A performance by the choir at a hospital benefit dinner.

4. Should the group learn different music for a school assembly, an evening concert, and a performance at noon for a service club? Why, or why not?

Projects

1. Plan a 30-minute performance demonstrating the various activities of a general music class. Balance the amounts of time allotted to each portion, and mention points you want the audience to learn from the presentation.

2. Plan a program using two choral groups, one instrumental group, one small vocal ensemble, and one small instrumental ensemble to go on one stage with no halfway curtain, but with a good orchestra pit. Arrange the appearances of the groups so that maximum efficiency can be achieved, and state how many numbers each will perform.

3. Think of a simple staging idea for each of the following:

(a) a group of songs from Latin America

(b) "Black Is the Color of My True Love's Hair"

(c) "Johnny Schmoker"

(d) "This Is My Country"

4. Write program notes for the following works:

(a) "How Lovely Are the Messengers" from *St. Paul* — Mendelssohn

(b) *Water Music Suite* — Handel

(c) "Simple Gifts" — arr. Copland

(d) "El Capitan" March — Sousa

5. Select three band numbers, one featuring the clarinets, another the trombones, and another the percussion.

6. Select five songs especially suitable for assembly singing.

7. Practice making a bow and acknowledging applause in front of your college class. Offer suggestions to one another to improve this action.

8. Plan a choral or instrumental concert and write up a four-paragraph publicity story about it which could be given to a newspaper.

9. Write a script for the narrator of a program that includes a series of six Christmas numbers. Write a similar script for a program consisting of six works based on American folk music.

10. Set up a sample budget for the presentation of a musical comedy. Include royalties; rental of orchestra parts, costumes, and scenery; and the cost of programs and tickets. Then, assuming a seating capacity of 500 in the audience, compute the minimum ticket cost for one performance, and then two performances.

Suggested Readings

Tumbusch, Tom, *Complete Production Guide to Modern Musical Theatre*. New York: Richards, Rosen Associates, 1969.

18

The Profession and Progress

A music teacher is never alone in his work, even though he may be the only music teacher in a particular school or district. He is identified as part of a profession, whether he likes it or not. The results of his work are affected by what others in the profession have done in the past and are doing now. This happens in several ways. To begin with, a teacher usually succeeds other music teachers, and so inherits a legacy from his predecessors. If the previous choral director devoted his main efforts to one big musical each year, it may be hard to wean the students and community away from the annual spring entertainment.

Another influence is that administrators and teachers are aware of what goes on in neighboring school districts, and they make frequent comparisons among schools in relation to credit, curriculum, number of class meetings, and the size and quality of the performing organizations. There is an unfortunate tendency on the part of some school boards and administrators to be guided more by what similar schools are doing than by what is best for their particular situation. More than once a music teacher has been asked: "Why should we start a string program when Duxbury and Westfield don't have one?"

A third way in which a teacher is affected by his profession is through the pronouncements of professional organizations and the statements of leaders in the profession. These statements are acquired, sometimes in abbreviated form, by the news media, and so they influence the public to some degree, as well as persons in the field of education.

These contacts represent what might be called "minimum professional involvement." As Chapter 2 pointed out, the interested teacher can gain much by participating in professional organizations and by being alert to happenings within the profession.

What are the notable features of the music education profession? First and foremost, the profession is alive and vital; it is evaluating its present practices and trying new ones to better itself in the future. To the first sentence in this book—"A person who chooses to teach music in the schools has selected a profession that is interesting, worthy, and challenging" — should be added the word "dynamic" or "vigorous." This vitality is a good sign, and it bodes well for the future of music education. Not only does it attract the type of person who seeks a continuing challenge in his vocation, but it ensures that music education will progress and keep pace with education and society as a whole. Music education cannot afford to rest on its laurels, and if the current scene is indicative of the future, the profession is in no danger of standing still.

An active and dynamic profession that is seeking to do an even better job produces differences of opinion. And so it is in music education. A kaleidoscope of opinions can be found on almost every aspect of music teaching. To the beginning teacher, the lack of agreement can be confusing. He may wonder why a committee of recognized music educators can't meet, perhaps under the auspices of the MENC, and write a comprehensive and detailed book on the best way to teach music in the secondary schools. The answer is that music education, because it is trying new practices and considering divergent views, can agree on only general statements. Experimentation and differing ideas are not necessarily bad. In fact, they generally indicate intellectual curiosity and professional vitality.

The Profession in the Past

There has been music in America since the first Indians migrated to this hemisphere thousands of years ago. European music came with the first settlers to Jamestown and Massachusetts. But it is not clear when professional instruction in music started. The first music instruction books were the product of John Tufts, a minister, who in the early eighteenth century wanted to teach the church-going colonists to sing psalms and hymns. He devised a tetrachord system of notation in which the octave is broken into two identical halves. But Tufts chose the tetrachords E F G A and B C D E, which he identified by the first letters of the syllables *mi, fa, sol,* and *la.*[1] His system was later adapted into "shape notes" in which each of the four shapes of notehead indicate a syllable. Shape notes are still seen occasionally in the notation of some hymnals, especially in the southern states.

Tufts' efforts were followed by the "singing school movement" in which a music teacher traveled from one town to another to give lessons for a few weeks. The singing school was primarily to teach church music. One of the leaders in this movement was Lowell Mason, who in 1837 was able to persuade the Boston Board of Education to initiate singing in the school cur-

---

[1]Irving Lowens, *Music and Musicians in Early America* (New York: W. W. Norton & Company, 1964), Chapter 3.

riculum. New York had instituted music in the common school program in 1829. Mason was a strong advocate of the ideas of the Swiss educator Johann Heinrich Pestalozzi (briefly mentioned in Chapter 9), as were other music educators of that era.

Prior to the twentieth century, education consisted mainly of a common elementary school for children, and high school education was essentially a preparation for college. Only a small percentage of teenagers attended school, and their education was limited and routine by today's standards. Teachers were poorly prepared and paid, and were generally treated as second-class citizens.[2] Along with most other subjects, music received only rudimentary treatment at best.

The first organization of music teachers, called the National Music Congress, assembled in 1869. This organization grew into the Music Teachers National Association, which created a committee on public school music in 1884. Shortly before the twentieth century the leadership in school music passed to the Music Section of the National Education Association (NEA). The present MENC began in 1907 in Keokuk, Iowa as a meeting of music supervisors. Two years later the group met again and adopted the name Music Supervisors National Conference, which was not changed to MENC until 1934. The first issue of the *Music Supervisors Bulletin* was published in 1914, and the name was changed to *Music Supervisors Journal* in 1919.

The first elementary basal series music books were published by Edwin Ginn in 1870. The emphasis in these books was on music reading, and it remained so for at least the next half-century. The first instrumental groups appeared early in the twentieth century in Winfield and Wichita, Kansas, and in Richmond, Indiana. They were orchestras, and were initially combined school-community efforts. Bands became significant in the 1920s, and the first group method books for winds were published in that decade.

As mentioned in Chapter 11, the great increase in school music at the secondary level occurred between 1920 and 1940. The main emphasis was on the performing organization, complete with director, uniform or robes, competition for chair placement, and a goal of winning at the contest or festival. The result was a high level of performance skill by a small minority of the student body. Music instruction for the nonperforming student usually received only cursory attention.

Current Issues and Opportunities

By the 1960s some music educators had begun to question the adequacy of it all. Was music education affecting enough students? Was it even teach-

---

[2]Myron Brenton, *What's Happened to Teacher?* (New York: Avon Books, 1970), Chapter 4.

ing music adequately to the minority already enrolled? Was music education relevant to the lives of the students? What started as quiet murmurs had by the 1970s become heatedly discussed issues. The most important issues merit a brief discussion here.

Relevancy

One significant issue is the balance in emphasis between the current human needs of the students and their long-range need for an education in the art of music—the struggle between the "humanists" and the "artists." Chapter 2 suggested that much of the conflict is unnecessary. Because of the aesthetic and human values of music (which were discussed in Chapter 3), *a music teacher helps students most when he aids them in learning music.* Music is a form of human behavior; it was created by humans for humans. To consider music (even a Beethoven symphony!) "up in the clouds," as something above, different from, or inimical to humankind is an error.

Why then does the idea of separation between music and human welfare persist? There are two reasons, in addition to the usual semantic problems in any dispute. Often the differences between discipline oriented and socially oriented educators boil down to *how* the subject is taught best. It is difficult for some people to conceive of a structured content and flexible, imaginative methods existing together. They think the combination is impossible, like mixing oil and water. Such a union has taken place in many situations, but it ought to happen in many more.

The other reason for the separation is the realization that music cannot feed the hungry, clear out blighted housing, or provide a neglected child with loving parents. This fact frustrates some idealistic music teachers who want their teaching to right the wrongs of society and rectify peoples' unhappy lives. Music classes won't do these things—but neither will any other one subject, activity, and social program. Serious problems cannot be cured by merely giving a child a new environment, adequate food, remedial reading courses, or group therapy sessions. If only it were that easy! Each effort may help, but almost never will a single activity be enough. And so it is with music. It helps people, for the reasons suggested early in this book, but it can't do everything.

There are two dangers if a music teacher—with all good intentions—attempts to provide psychological counseling in his music classes: the subject of music is apt to be poorly or inadequately taught, and the psychology is liable to be mishandled because the music teacher is dabbling in something for which he has virtually no training.

Reaching All Students

The music education profession is showing renewed vigor in attempting to reach all students—the blacks in city ghettos, the rural poor, the handicapped child enrolled in special education, and the pre-schooler, as well as the middle class "average" WASP child. Although most of the deprived groups represent a small percentage of the school population, they are youngsters who have not been reached adequately by existing music programs. The former slogan of the MENC, "Music for every child, every child for music," has never been realized. The question is not whether the profession will try harder to reach all students, because it is already trying harder. The question is whether music teachers should extend the conventional school music program (which has not proved easily transplantable in the past), or whether they should devise different programs until some "music for every child" is finally achieved.

Creativity

Music education is emphasizing individual creative expression to an unprecedented degree. Part of this increased attention is the result of a general tendency toward downgrading social institutions and established leadership. In addition, there is a swing back to the nineteenth-century ideas of the supremacy of the individual's feelings, and the purity of nature, in contrast to the tainted character of civilization.

Part of the new attention given individual creativity is a reaction to another nineteenth-century phenomenon: the master composer who seemed to "hand down" his works for less talented people to appreciate. Art music had gotten away from the "usable" music idea found before the Romantic era; forgotten was the fact that Bach, Mozart, and Beethoven all improvised as well as composed. A composition became a "monument," something nearly untouchable and inaccessible. This attitude is still found in some quarters today. Music teaching that trains students only to reproduce and listen to the works of others, great as they may be, has some limitations. Music is not only "out there," as something to be learned, but also "inside"—something that each person draws from within himself. Music education is more interested than ever before in the music each student can create. The finished products are seldom "monuments," but they are valid personal expressions, and the creative experience can be truly educational.

Individual Instruction

Closely related to the idea of interest in creative effort is the interest in individualizing instruction. Admittedly this idea, which has received wide attention in education generally, has limited application to music instruction. In a classroom, music making is often of necessity a group activity. One can hardly perform Handel's *Messiah* with everyone doing whatever he wants to do whenever he feels like doing it! But adapting instruction to meet individual needs is possible to some extent. Units of learning can be packaged so that the content can be mastered individually, with the aid of proper equipment and materials. And it is not really necessary that every member of a 90 piece band, regardless of his ability, be present for every minute of every rehearsal. Able students can work alone or in small groups on music projects of special value to them.

Broad Coverage

The music curriculum in many schools is showing greater breadth in the types of music studied. Most teachers have for years played or sung some popular music, but until recently they haven't talked much about it at professional meetings. Partly because some popular music has recently acquired more musical substance, some of it now merits attention in the curriculum. More attention is also being given folk and ethnic music, probably because interest in other cultures has increased markedly. The music currently studied in American schools is more cosmopolitan than ever before, and is much more so than in any other nation in the world.

Accountability

No recital of current trends in music education can be complete without some discussion of accountability and the measurement of learning. Accountability and measurement are not the same thing. A teacher can and should assess how well his students have learned. The results may be used in a system of accounting for the learning that students achieve, but the data don't need to be so treated. On the other hand, it is impossible to operate a system to account for learning without some means of measurement. Because the topic of evaluation in teaching was treated in Chapter 6, there is no need to dwell on it here, except to say that it is a matter of first-rate importance in education today, and it appears likely to remain so for years to come. It appears that music teachers will be called on more and more to state specifically what they are teaching in each class, and to make objective evaluations of how well the students are learning.

Fads and Improvements

How deeply ingrained are the characteristics of any educational trend? Were the majority of teachers in the 1930s and 1940s followers of the progressive education philosophy? What about the curriculum reform movement of the early 1960s, or the often-voiced concerns for "innovation," "relevancy," "observable behaviors," and other educational interests? Is most of the talk "at the top" — in professional journals and books, which are usually written by college professors — or is it found in the ranks of classroom teachers themselves?

No accurate answer is possible, but it is likely that many teachers are only slightly affected by current educational issues. Rightly or wrongly, they go about doing their job, letting the latest educational catchwords come and go. Probably about half of the music teachers in the United States do *not* belong to any association of music educators, so it is unlikely that they are affected significantly by current debates. Again, rightly or wrongly, in recent years the program and interests of the National Education Association have moved closer to the ideas of the American Federation of Teachers, reducing the attention given to matters of curriculum and instruction. And even if much attention were given to such topics by general teachers' groups, music would be only one area among many, and consequently the chances would be against an effective restructuring of present programs. A few educators are very much caught up in current issues, and a larger group is mildly involved, but probably half are affected only a little.

A far more important question than how many teachers are involved is, how and to what extent should teachers be affected? Should they embrace each new, or apparently new, idea that receives wide attention in educational circles, or should they try to insulate themselves against both fads and improvements? The answer is clear: they should assume a position somewhere between the two extremes. Certainly the teacher should be informed about what is going on in his profession. To be ignorant of current concerns is a sure way to become "fossilized" as a teacher. It is quite justifiable for a music teacher to hold any opinions he wishes about music teaching, *as long as he is informed and has rational reasons for his beliefs.* Ignorance is no excuse for rejecting new ideas, and there is no excuse for ignorance in a day of professional organizations and publications.

Of course, knowledge does not necessarily lead to belief. The fact that a teacher has impartially examined a new method or point of view and rejected it does not mean that he is out-of-date, ineffective, and no longer growing. It is incumbent on the teacher to look with care at his teaching, whether the ideas are his own or an adaptation of something he has read or heard about. Some current ideas should be rejected or modified in their application to a particular situation. *The real criterion is not the newness of a method or proposal, but rather the contribution it can make toward educating students in music.* If an idea will improve one's teaching, it should be adopted; if not, it should be rejected or adapted.

One can rather safely predict for the foreseeable future that new ideas, methods, and concerns will continue to be presented for music teachers' consideration. There will always be a bandwagon to jump on, if one is so inclined. In this regard, music teachers are no different from other members of the "intellectual community" in America. In the opinion of some scholars, the ease with which concerns come and go does have some virtue. As John Adkins Richardson points out:

> Modern nations, particularly Anglo-Saxon and Scandinavian ones, almost always manage to institutionalize radical movements and de-fuse them. . . . In the arts, leaders of the avant-garde seem always to be ending up as full professors or artists-in-residence. The system turns cultural threats into passing diversions. . . . The high-brow is led to such faddishness by the same route he took first to Bohemia and then to Jazz and Zen and, more recently, to Rock and Funkiness. It is all a question of finding models of behavior and taste to set up over and against Babbittry—which American intellectuals have got into the odd habit of calling "middle class."[3]

Although such mobility of interests and beliefs may act as a beneficial safety valve, it indicates a lack of conviction on the part of those who shift easily from one point of view to another. It reveals a shallowness of thinking and a lack of serious commitment. It behooves the music teacher, for the good of his students, to develop consistent and rational positions. He should be firm but flexible.

The Future

Education will continue to evolve in the years ahead. Twenty years from now it will not be what it is today. There may be diversions and even regressions, but if the first 70 years of the twentieth century are indicative, there will be continued growth. Generally the changes will be evolutionary, not revolutionary. Real progress in human affairs, education included, seems to come in small increments.

---

[3]"Dirty Pictures and Campus Comity," *Journal of Aesthetic Education*, Vol. 4, No. 3 (June 1970), pp. 90–91.

The prospects for the future contain some encouraging signs, and also one that may not be good news, depending on how you look at it. Because of the leveling-off in the size of the school population, employment prospects for music teachers in the 1970s are only moderately favorable. No longer is there a teacher shortage, so schools will be more selective in employing teachers. This fact contributes to uneasiness and uncertainty for the prospective teacher, but in the long run it should mean a better quality of education for the students.

Two major trends in American society are favorable for the future of music education. One of these is the increased emphasis on education in general, and the other is an increasing interest in the fine arts, especially music. Partly because of the vast sums of money it requires, but more because of society's need for it, education is receiving more public attention than ever before, and much of it is favorable. Not only are more people going to school, but they are staying in school longer, and many others are returning to school in adult education programs. The percentage of persons age 14–17 enrolled in school has increased from 11.4 in 1900, to 32.3 in 1920, to 73.3 in 1940, to 86.1 in 1960, and to 93.7 in 1969.[4] The federal government is taking more interest in education, and foundations such as Ford and Rockefeller have invested large sums of money in educational experiments. Although there has been some increase since 1968 in the defeat of local school tax proposals, a majority of the elections have supported the proposed funding.[5] The percentage of the gross national product spent on education has increased from 2.6 in 1941, to 3.4 in 1951, to 5.6 in 1961, and to 7.5 in 1969.[6]

As for the fine arts, greater leisure and economic affluence (both of which seem destined to increase) have enabled artistic interests to develop among all classes of the population. Radio, television, and electronic reproduction of music have contributed to the trend. Certainly the great American experiment in mass education can also claim some credit for the increasing interest in the fine arts. For the first time in man's long history, society has the means, the time, and the financial resources to make great music and other arts available to practically everyone. Evidence of this trend is seen in the number of community orchestras, the number of musical instruments purchased, the sales of recordings and sound-producing equipment, the money spent for musical events, and the establishment of fine arts centers and arts councils in many cities and almost every state. Probably equally indicative of the trend is the percentage of personal income spent on new musical instruments, sheet music, and musical accessories. Since 1941 the percentage of money, not only the gross amount, has increased slowly from

---

[4]*Digest of Educational Statistics,* Department of Health, Education, and Welfare (Washington, D.C.: U. S. Government Printing Office, 1970), p. 49.

[5]*Digest of Educational Statistics,* p. 49.

[6]*Digest,* p. 21.

0.11 to 0.163 percent in 1970.[7] (The figure excludes recordings and sound equipment.)

The future of music education is promising, and the profession is vital and eager to move ahead. To be more complete and accurate, the sentence that opened this book should now be further expanded to read: "A person who chooses to teach music in the schools has selected a profession that is interesting, worthy, challenging, and dynamic, and one with a promising future."

---

[7]"Report on Amateur Music in the United States — 1971" (Chicago: American Music Conference), p. 1.

Appendix A

Code of Ethics with Professional Musicians

A Code of Ethics jointly agreed to and authorized by executive actions of the Music Educators National Conference, American Federation of Musicians, and American Association of School Administrators:

The competition of school bands and orchestras in the past years has been a matter of grave concern and, at times, even hardship to the professional musicians.

Music educators and professional musicians alike are committed to the general acceptance of music as a desirable factor in the social and cultural growth of our country. The music educators contribute to this end by fostering the study of music among the children, and by developing an interest in better music among the masses. The professional musicians strive to improve musical taste by providing increasingly artistic performances of worth-while musical works.

This unanimity of purpose is further exemplified by the fact that a great many professional musicians are music educators, and a great many music educators are, or have been, actively engaged in the field of professional performance.

The members of high school symphonic orchestras and bands look to the professional organizations for example and inspiration; they become active patrons of music in later life. They are not content to listen to a twelve-piece ensemble when an orchestra of symphonic proportions is necessary to give adequate performance. These former music students, through their influence on sponsors, employers, and program makers in demanding adequate musical performances, have a beneficial effect upon the prestige and economic status of the professional musicians.

Since it is in the interest of the music educator to attract public attention to his attainments for the purpose of enhancing his prestige and subsequently his income, and since it is in the interest of the professional musician to create more opportunities for employment at increased remuneration, it is only natural that upon certain occasions some incidents might occur in which the interests of the members of one or the other group might be infringed upon, either from lack of forethought or lack of ethical standards among individuals.

In order to establish a clear understanding as to the limitations of the fields of professional music and music education in the United States, the following statement of policy, adopted by the Music Educators National Conference and the American Federation of Musicians, and approved by the American Association of School Administrators, is recommended to those serving in their respective fields:

I. Music Education

The field of music education, including the teaching of music and such demonstrations of music education as do not directly conflict with the interests of the professional musician, is the province of the music educator. It is the primary purpose of all the parties signatory hereto that the professional musician shall have the fullest protection in his efforts to earn his living from the rendition of music; to that end it is recognized and accepted that all music performances by school students under the "Code of Ethics" herein set forth shall be in connection with nonprofit, noncommercial enterprises. Under the heading of "Music Education" should be included the following:

(1) *School Functions* initiated by the schools as a part of a school program, whether in a school building or other building.

(2) *Community Functions* organized in the interest of the schools strictly for educational purposes, such as those that might be originated by the Parent-Teacher Association.

(3) *School Exhibits* prepared as a part of the school district's courtesies for educational organizations or educational conventions being entertained in the district.

(4) *Educational Broadcasts* which have the purpose of demonstrating or illustrating pupils' achievements in music study, or which represent the culmination of a period of study and rehearsal. Included in this category are local, state, regional, and national school music festivals and competitions held under the auspices of schools, colleges, and/or educational organizations on a nonprofit basis and broadcast to acquaint the public with the results of music instruction in the schools.

(5) *Civic Occasions* of local, state, or national patriotic interest, of sufficient breadth to enlist the sympathies and cooperation of all persons, such as those held by the GAR, American Legion, and Veterans of Foreign Wars in connection with their Memorial Day services in the cemeteries. It is understood that affairs of this kind may be participated in only when such participation does not in the least usurp the rights and privileges of local professional musicians.

(6) *Benefit Performances* for local charities, such as the Welfare Federations, Red Cross, hospitals, etc., when and where local professional musicians would likewise donate their services.

(7) *Educational or Civic Services* that might beforehand be mutually agreed upon by the school authorities and official representatives of the local professional musicians.

(8) *Audition Recordings* for study purposes made in the classroom or in connection with contest or festival performances by students, such recordings to be limited to exclusive use by the students and their teachers, and not offered for general sale or other public distribution. This definition pertains only to the purpose and utilization of audition recordings and not to matters concerned with copyright regulations. Compliance with copyright requirements applying to recording of compositions not in the public domain is the responsibility of the school, college, or educational organization under whose auspices the recordings are made.

II. Entertainment

The field of entertainment is the province of the professional musician. Under this heading are the following:

(1) *Civic parades, ceremonies, expositions, community concerts, and community-center activities* (see I, paragraph 2 for further definition); *regattas, nonscholastic contests, festivals, athletic games, activities or celebrations, and the like; national, state, and county fairs* (see I, paragraph 5 for further definition).

(2) *Functions for the furtherance, directly or indirectly, of any public or private enterprise; functions by chambers of commerce, boards of trade, and commercial clubs or associations.*

(3) *Any occasion that is partisan or sectarian in character or purpose.*

(4) *Functions of clubs, societies, civic or fraternal organizations.*

Statements that funds are not available for the employment of professional musicians, or that if the talents of amateur musical organizations cannot be had, other musicians cannot or will not be employed, or that the amateur musicians are to play without remuneration of any kind, are all immaterial.

Appendix B

Ohio Code of Ethics with Music Merchants

A Code of Ethics between the Ohio Music Education Association and the Music Merchants Association of Ohio:

Whereas, both organizations are primarily interested in the music education of the school children of Ohio, and in furthering the interest of these young people in the art of music; and

Whereas, in this common effort, harmony and understanding should prevail;

Now the following Code of Ethics is adopted and approved:

First.   The retail music merchant shall sell musical instruments and merchandise, of good quality at fair prices, to the public-school pupils of Ohio; and he shall, at all times, assist and help the community public-school music teacher in promoting an interest in the study of vocal and instrumental music.

Second.   The public-school music teacher shall confine his activities to the teaching of music, as required by the laws of the State under Section 7718 G. C., and the regulations of the Educational Department, to the public-school pupils of Ohio; and he shall not sell musical instruments or merchandise directly or indirectly, to the pupils, or accept commissions of any kind, in any manner whatsoever, from any manufacturer, jobber, or music merchant for recommending any kind, brand, or make of musical merchandise.

Third.   It shall be the prerogative of every public-school music teacher in Ohio, to examine and test the suitability of all musical instruments and merchandise purchased by pupils for use in school study, and, if found deficient, to communicate with the retail merchant selling the same, looking to the immediate adjustment of the difficulty, but the public-school music teacher in Ohio shall not recommend to his pupils or their parents any single make or brand of instrument exclusively.

Fourth.   If shall be the duty of every retail music merchant in Ohio, readily and quickly to assist all public-school music teachers in his community, to see that pupils have proper and suitable instruments, by exchange or otherwise; to stock such musical instruments and merchandise for sale to pupils as the teachers may request or recommend to the dealer; to arrange for the renting or loaning of instruments to talented pupils upon the recommendation of the teacher; and generally to cooperate with the public-school music teachers along these lines. In the event any local retail music merchant fails, neglects, or refuses so to cooperate with his public-school music teachers, then, and in that event, the teachers shall have the right and privilege, without violating this Code, to seek and find other retail sources for the musical instruments and merchandise necessary and required by the pupils in the proper study of music.

Appendix C

From "Some Remarks on Value and Greatness in Music" by Leonard B. Meyer

At first it seems that the problem is not really very difficult. After all there are certain technical criteria for excellence in a piece of music. A good piece of music must have consistency of style: that is, it must employ a unified system of expectations and probabilities; it should possess clarity of basic intent; it should have variety, unity, and all the other categories which are so easy to find after the fact. But these are, I think, only necessary causes. And while they may enable us to distinguish a good or satisfactory piece from a downright bad one, they will not help us very much when we try to discriminate between a pretty good work and a very good one, let alone distinguish the characteristics of greatness.

Indeed the tune, "Twinkle, twinkle little star" possesses style, unity, variety, and so forth. And if we then ask is Bach's B Minor Mass better than "Twinkle, twinkle"—using *only* these technical categories—we shall, I am afraid, be obliged to answer that they are equally good, adding perhaps, "each in its own way." I shall return to the "each in its own way" argument presently. But for now, it seems to me that, granting listeners who have learned to respond to and understand both works, the statement that these works are equally good is preposterous and false.

Nor are length, size, or complexity *as such* criteria of value, though, as we shall see, complexity does have something to do with excellence. Thus some of Brahms's smaller piano pieces are often considered better works than, for instance, his Fourth Symphony. And I am sure that each of us can cite instances of this for himself. Perhaps it would be well at this point to turn to particular musical examples to see what we can learn from them.

Because a relatively thorough examination of even two brief pieces would involve a complex and lengthy analysis, I have chosen to discuss, briefly, two fugue subjects: the first is from Geminiani's Concerto Grosso Op. 3 No. 3; the second is from Bach's Prelude and Fugue in G Minor for organ. Since only the themes will be

Reprinted by permission from *Music, the Arts, and Ideas:* Chicago: University of Chicago Press, 1967.

discussed, it should be pointed out that good themes do not necessarily give rise to good total works. And though it is difficult to write a good fugue on a really poor subject, an unprepossessing theme—such as that of Bach's Fugue in C-sharp Minor from the *Well-Tempered Clavier*, Volume I—may act as the basis for a very fine work.

Even though it goes against critical canon I intend to treat the themes as entities in their own right, but as themes, not as complete works. For considered in themselves they will serve to raise some of the basic considerations which are involved in value and ultimately in greatness. And these considerations apply with equal force to complete works, even those of the greatest magnitude. In short, reversing the procedure of Plato, who inquired as to the principles of justice in the individual by considering the nature of justice in the state, we shall try to learn something about the value of whole works by considering the nature of value in a small segment.

Here then are the two themes:

Example 1.   A: Geminiani, Op. 3 No. 3. B: Bach,
Prelude and Fugue for Organ

They are certainly not equally good. And at first glance we observe that the Bach theme has more rhythmic and motivic variety, that it covers a larger range, and so forth than Geminiani's theme. However, there are good themes which lack obvious variety. In any case, it seems safe to say that variety is a means to an end, not an end in itself.

Looking at these two themes more closely, we see that they are quite similar in their basic melodic structure. Both begin on the fifth degree of the scale, move to the tonic (in the Bach, through the third of the scale), and then skip an octave. This skip creates a structural gap, a sense of incompleteness. We expect that the empty space thus outlined will be filled in, made complete. This melodic incompleteness is complemented by the rhythmic instability of this first musical shape. That is, the first separable musical events in both themes are upbeats which are oriented toward the stability of downbeats.

In a sense the structural gap and the rhythmic upbeats have established musical goals to be reached. We expect the melodic line to descend and ultimately to come to rest on the tonic note, reaching a clear organizing accent in the course of this motion.

And so in fact they both do. *But* with crucial differences. The Bach theme moves down slowly with delays and temporary diversions through related harmonic areas. It establishes various levels of melodic activity with various potentials to be realized. Furthermore, these delays are rhythmic as well as melodic (see analysis under Example 1). The Geminiani theme, on the other hand, moves directly—or almost directly—to its goal. The second measure is chromatic and contains a potential for different modes of continuation. Of these the return to the B is certainly the most probable, but only slightly so. However, once the B is reached, the descent to E seems almost inevitable. And when the theme falls to this obvious consequent with neither delay nor diversion, it seems like a blatant platitude, a musical cliché. Nor are there any rhythmic resistances. The initial upbeat perpetuates itself without marked disturbance down to the final note which arrives on the obvious downbeat.

Thus it seems that, here at least, value has something to do with the activation of a musical impulse having tendencies toward a more or less definite goal and with the temporary resistance or inhibition of these tendencies. The importance of the element of resistance can be made even more apparent if we rewrite the Bach theme in such a way that this element is eliminated.

Example 2

The theme is now as banal as Geminiani's.

From these considerations it follows (1) that a melody or a work which establishes no tendencies, if such can be imagined, will from this point of view (and others are possible) be of no value. Of course, such tendencies need not be powerful at the outset, but may be developed during the course of musical progress. (2) If the most probable goal is reached in the most immediate and direct way, given the stylistic context, the musical event taken in itself will be of little value. And (3) if the goal is never reached or if the tendencies activated become dissipated in the press of over-elaborate or irrelevant diversions, then value will tend to be minimal.

The notion that the inhibition of goal-oriented tendencies is related to value is not a new one. Robert Penn Warren writes that "a poem, to be good, must earn itself. It is a motion toward a point of rest, but if it is not a resisted motion, it is a motion of no consequence. For example, a poem which depends upon stock materials and stock responses is simply a toboggan slide, or a fall through space."[1] John Dewey's position is quite similar. "Impulsion forever boosted on its forward way would run its course thoughtless, and dead to emotion. . . . The only way it can become aware of its nature and its goal is by obstacles surmounted and means employed."[2]

---

[1]Pure and Impure Poetry," p. 251.

[2]*Art as Experience,* p. 59.

More recently information theory has developed concepts in which the relationship between resistance and value seems to be implicit. In order to understand how information theory relates to these considerations, it is necessary to examine the nature of goal-tendency processes in more detail.

Musical events take place in a world of stylistic probability. If we hear only a single tone, a great number of different tones could follow it with equal probability. If a sequence of two tones is heard, the number of probable consequent tones is somewhat reduced—how much depends upon the tones chosen and the stylistic context—and hence the probability of the remaining alternatives is somewhat increased. As more tones are added and consequently more relationships between tones established, the probabilities of a particular goal become increased. Thus in Bach's theme the probability of any particular tone following the first D is very small, for the number of possible consequents is very large. As the line moves downward through the B-flat and the A, the probabilities of the G become very high and it is partly the satisfaction of this motion which closes out the first pattern as a musical event. This pattern, after the octave skip, now becomes the unit of motion and the basis for probability estimates on a higher architectonic level. Note that the variety of events in this theme, as well as the delays already noted, makes the particular sequence of events seem much less probable than the sequence of events in the Geminiani theme.

Here information theory becomes relevant. It tells us that if a situation is highly organized so that the possible consequents have a high degree of probability, then if the probable occurs, the information communicated by the message (what we have been calling a musical event) is minimal. If, on the other hand, the musical situation is less predictable so that the antecedent-consequent relationship does *not* have a high degree of probability, then the information contained in the musical message will be high. Norbert Wiener has put the matter succinctly: ". . . the more probable the message, the less information it gives. Clichés, for example, are less illuminating than great poems."[3]

Since resistances, or more generally deviations, are by definition disturbances in the goal-oriented tendencies of a musical impulse, they lower the probability not only of a particular consequent but of the musical event as a whole. In so doing they create or increase information. And it does not seem a rash step to conclude that what creates or increases the information contained in a piece of music increases its value.[4] . . .

To summarize what we have learned from this excursion into the relationship of information theory to music and to value: first of all, we have found that resistance, or more broadly deviation, is a correlative of information. And since infor-

---

[3] *The Human Use of Human Beings*, p. 21.

[4] It is sometimes objected that analysis can never do full justice to the unique, ineffable beauty of a work of art and that, because it necessarily involves the use of conceptual categories, analysis always misrepresents and does violence to the unmediated quality of pure aesthetic experience. These points must, I think, be granted. The peculiar quality of a particular object, event, or experience—whether in art or in nature—can never be explained fully and without distortion. . . .

While the achievement of analysis is no doubt imperfect and more debatable—precisely because it is open to public scrutiny and criticism—it is also potentially more fruitful and useful because it can be communicated and, at least modestly, documented.

mation is valuable—as tautology is not—our hypothesis as to the importance of deviation has received confirmation. Second, our inquiry has pointed to a relationship between information and deviation on the one hand, and uncertainty on the other. This implies that uncertainty is somehow related to value. This apparently paradoxical pairing will be considered presently.

Hypotheses gain in plausibility not only through the corroboration of other investigators and through correlation with other fields of inquiry but also by accounting for facts observed but hitherto unexplained theoretically. Our hypothesis can do this in explaining the difference between primitive music and art music. In so doing it is hoped that another aspect of the relationship between tendency inhibition and value will be revealed.

If we ask, "What is the fundamental difference between sophisticated art music and primitive music" (and I do not include under the term "primitive" the highly sophisticated music which so-called primitives often play), then we can point to the fact that primitive music generally employs a smaller repertory of tones, that the distance of these notes from the tonic is smaller, that there is a great deal of repetition, though often slightly varied repetition, and so forth. But these are the symptoms of primitivism in music, not its causes.

The differentia between art music and primitive music lies in speed of tendency gratification. The primitive seeks almost immediate gratification for his tendencies whether these be biological or musical. Nor can he tolerate uncertainty. And it is because distant departures from the certainty and repose of the tonic note and lengthy delays in gratification are insufferable to him that the tonal repertory of the primitive is limited, not because he cannot think of other tones. It is not his mentality that is limited, it is his maturity. Note, by the way, that popular music can be distinguished from real jazz on the same basis. For while "pop" music whether of the tin-pan alley or the Ethelbert Nevin variety makes use of a fairly large repertory of tones, it operates with such conventional clichés that gratification is almost immediate and uncertainty is minimized.

One aspect of maturity both of the individual and of the culture within which a style arises consists then in the willingness to forgo immediate, and perhaps lesser, gratification for the sake of future ultimate gratification. Understood generally, not with reference to any specific musical work, self-imposed tendency inhibition and the willingness to bear uncertainty are indications of maturity. They are signs, that is, that the animal is becoming a man. And this, I take it, is not without relevance to considerations of value.

Appendix D

Teacher Rating Form

You have all waited for such a chance! Now, here it is! This is your chance to criticize me. All year I have been quick to point out your errors, so now I am giving you the opportunity to correct me. Please notice that nowhere on this paper are you asked to write your name. I shall have no way of knowing who said what. So feel free to criticize me fairly and frankly.

All you have to do is circle the words that seem to be the best answer. The following is an example:

How tall would you say I am?

Very tall   (Medium)   Very short

All the other questions are to be answered in the same way. There are a few which ask for extra suggestions. If you have none, skip those questions.

1. In general, I use words that are

   Too complicated   About right   Too simple
   to understand

2. How much do I talk in rehearsal?

   Too much   About the   Too little
                               right amount

3. My speaking voice is usually

   Too loud; practi-   Just loud enough   Too soft
   cally a shout   to be understood
                               clearly

4. How effective am I in what I try to say?

   Very convincing   Moderately   Not at all
                               convincing   convincing

5. How clear am I in presenting my ideas?

Very clear	Sometimes hazy	Very difficult to understand

6. In rehearsal do I clearly state where we are starting in the music?

Usually	Only occasionally	Seldom

7. How often do I go over spots in the music that are hard for you?

Too many times	About the right number of times	Not enough times

8. When rehearsing various numbers, I tend to

Stay on one piece too long	Rehearse a piece about the right length of time	Skip around too much

9. Do I make it clear how I want the music to be performed?

Instructions are seldom clear	Part of the time such things as speed, loudness, are made known	Instructions are almost always clear

10. As a rule, my conducting is

Very hard to follow	Fairly easy to follow	Very easy to follow

11. How sensible is my conducting?

Looks like a madman	A little funny sometimes, but usually O.K.	Looks quite sane and sensible

12. How much do I seem to expect of you when it comes to learning and performing music?

Too much	About the right amount	Not enough

13. Do I have any annoying habits such as mouthing words, scratching my head, and so on?

Several such habits	One or two such habits	No bad habits

14. If I do have annoying mannerisms, what are they?

15. How much do I look at the music when conducting?

| Too much | About half the time | Very seldom |

16. "Clothes make the man," they say, so how about me?

| Too flashy | About right for a teacher | Too conserv- ative |

17. How often do I smile?

| Not nearly often enough | Enough to be con- sidered a pleasant person | Face just beams most of the time |

18. Do I tend to pick on certain students? This includes both favorable and un-favorable contacts.

| Very much so | A little bit | Everyone treated equally |

19. How much interest do I take in you personally?

| A great deal | Some interest | Very little |

20. How do you feel about making requests and asking questions of me?

| Afraid to re- quest anything | Willing to request something if necessary | Very much at ease in making a request |

21. How am I about letting you students "in" on what is going on?

| Plans are kept secret | Group gets in on some planning | Plans are re- viewed and discussed |

22. How about my sense of humor?

| Difficult to find | About average | A tremen- dous wit |

23. Do I inspire you to do your best in music?

| Very much so | Sometimes | Not at all |

24. How strict am I in disciplining you?

    Too easy   About right   Too strict

25. Do you think that next year I should "crack down" more, or less?

    Crack down more   Be about   Relax rules
                            the same   a bit

26. Are my demands reasonable on small details such as chewing gum, sitting up, and so forth?

    Too rigid   About right   Too easy

27. How patient am I?

    Very hot-tempered   Average   Very even-
                                                       tempered

28. How much time do I spend in bawling out the group for talking, etc?

    Too much   About average   Not enough

29. Have I ever humiliated anyone in front of the class?

    Never   Once or twice   Several times

30. How am I about giving out grades?

    Tough   About average   Easy

31. How about the number of tests?

    Not enough   About the right number   Too many

32. How fair is my system of grading (attendance, citizenship, musicianship, and tests)?

    Very fair   O.K.   Very unfair

33. In general, do you like the music we have studied this year?

    Very much   O.K.   Not much

34. Please check the following items that you feel are TRUE.
    This year we have done too many numbers that are:

    serious (classical) _____
    popular _____
    difficult _____
    easy _____

35. Do you have any suggestions as to the type of music we might do next year?

36. Do you have any other comments to make about the teacher or the class?

Class _____ M or F _____
       (fr., soph., jun., sen.)

Appendix E

Band

Order or time of appearance _____   Event No. _____   Class _____   Date _____ 19____

Name of Organization _____

School _____ Number of Players _____

City _____ State _____ District _____ School Enrollment _____

Selections _____
_____
_____

Adjudicator will grade principal items, A, B, C, D, or E, or numerals, in the respective squares. Comments must deal with fundamental principles and be constructive. Minor details may be marked on music furnished to adjudicator.

TONE (beauty, blend, control) _____ ☐
_____
_____

INTONATION (chords, melodic line, tutti) _____ ☐
_____
_____

TECHNIQUE (articulation, facility, precision, rhythm) _____ ☐
_____
_____

BALANCE (ensemble, sectional) _____ ☐
_____
_____

INTERPRETATION (expression, phrasing, style, tempo) _____ ☐
_____
_____

MUSICAL EFFECT (artistry, fluency) _____ ☐
_____
_____

OTHER FACTORS (choice of music, instrumentation, discipline, appearance) _____ ☐
_____
_____

*May be continued on other side.   Signature of Adjudicator _____

Adjudicator's private comments for _____, to be detached by *adjudicator*
                                          (Name of Director)
and sealed in attached envelope furnished by Festival Chairman.

Use reverse side for additional comments

Choral—Large Group

					RATING

Order or time
of appearance_____   Event
No._____   Class_____   Date_____19___

Use as plus or minus signs in final rating

Name of Organization _____

School_____ Number of Singers_____

City_____State_____District_____School Enrollment_____

Selections _____
_____
_____

Adjudicator will grade principal items, A, B, C, D, or E, or numerals, in the respective squares. Comments must deal with fundamental principles and be constructive. Minor details may be marked on music furnished to adjudicator.

TONE (beauty, blend, control) _____ □
_____

INTONATION_____ □
_____

DICTION (clarity of consonants, naturalness, purity of vowels)_____ □
_____

TECHNIQUE (breathing and posture, precision, rhythm)_____ □
_____

BALANCE_____ □
_____

INTERPRETATION (expression, phrasing, style, tempo)_____ □
_____

MUSICAL EFFECT (artistry, feeling of ensemble, fluency, vitality)_____ □
_____

OTHER FACTORS (choice of music, discipline, stage presence and appearance)_____ □
_____

*May be continued
on other side.   Signature of Adjudicator_____

Adjudicator's private comments for_____, to be detached by *adjudicator*
(Name of Director)
and sealed in attached envelope furnished by Festival Chairman.

Use reverse side for additional comments

V-7, Official Adjudication Form. Copyright 1958 by National Interscholastic Music Activities Commission, 1201 Sixteenth Street, Washington, D.C. 20036. Reprinted by permission.

V-7, Official Adjudication Form. Copyright 1958 by National Interscholastic Music Activities Commission, 1201 16th Street, Washington, D. C. Must not be reprinted without written permission.

Orchestra or String Orchestra

RATING

Use as plus or minus
sign in final rating

Order or time
of appearance_____   Event No._____   Class_____   Date_____19___

Name of Organization_____

School_____Number of Players_____

City_____State_____District_____School Enrollment_____

Selections _____
_____
_____

Adjudicator will grade principal items, A, B, C, D, or E, or numerals, in the respective squares. Comments must deal
with fundamental principles and be constructive.   Minor details may be marked on music furnished to adjudicator.

TONE (beauty, blend, control)_____ □
_____
_____

INTONATION (chords, melodic line, tutti)_____ □
_____
_____

TECHNIQUE (articulation-bowing, facility, precision, rhythm)_____ □
_____
_____

BALANCE (ensemble, sectional)_____ □
_____
_____

INTERPRETATION (expression, phrasing, style, tempo)_____ □
_____
_____

MUSICAL EFFECT (artistry, fluency)_____ □
_____
_____

OTHER FACTORS (choice of music, instrumentation, discipline, appearance)_____ □
_____
_____

*May be continued
on other side.   Signature of Adjudicator_____

Adjudicator's private comments for_____, to be detached by *adjudicator*
                                   (Name of Director)
and sealed in attached envelope furnished by Festival Chairman.

Use reverse side for additional comments

OSO-3, Official Adjudication Form. Copyright 1958 by National Interscholastic Music Activities Commission, 1201 Sixteenth Street, Washington, D.C. 20036. Reprinted by permission.

Index

Accompaniment, in selecting music, 278
Accompanist, selection of, 362–363
Accountability, 464–465
Achievement Tests in Music (William Knuth), 113–114
Acoustics:
  of performance location, 436–437
  unit on, 222–223
Adjective circle, 118–119
Adjudication forms, 487–489
Adolescents (*see also* Relevancy):
  adjustment conditions, 129–130
  disadvantaged, 130–132
  musical development, 135–136
  need for adult image, 132–134
  physical development, 134–135
  problem areas, 127–129
  use of desire for maturity, 211–212
Advanced Placement Program, 92–93
Aesthetic:
  experience, 36–39
  sensitivity, in appreciation course, 412–414
Affective domain (*see* Attitudes)
American Association of School Administrators, 20
American Federation of Musicians, 20
American Federation of Teachers, 465
Andrews, Frances M., 206–207
Anderson, Donald K., 73
Appreciation course, music, 406–417
  importance of stylistic periods in, 414–415
  listening in, 407–412
  testing in, 415–416
  textbooks, 416
"April Is in My Mistress' Face" (Morley), 270–273
Aptitude, musical:
  attitude toward, 121
  tests of, 83–86
Arrangements:
  choral, 279–282
  instrumental, 283–285
  stage band, 397–398
Arranging music, 288–289
Assembly, school, 433–434
  for publicity, 451
Attendance, student, 160

Attitudes, 59–60
  evaluation of, 117–118
  toward rehearsal enrichment, 74
Audiovisual aids, in teaching general music, 219–220
Audition, for choral membership, 360–361
Ausubel, David, 11

Band (*see* Instrumental music)
Balance:
  in classifying voices, 359
  in instrumental music, 371–372
  in interpretation, 303–304
Barbershop singing, 146
Basic Concepts in Music Education, 40
Blend, 300–303
Books:
  beginning instrumental, 373–374
  music appreciation, 416
  theory, 420, 423–424
Bowing, 385–387
  in beginning classes, 376
Boys:
  development of high pitches in singing, 351–352
  recruiting of, 148–149
Breath:
  in singing, 341–343
  in wind instrument playing, 379–380
Brenton, Myron, 11
Broudy, Harry, 60

Cambiata voice, 355–356
Class instruction (*see* Instrumental music)
Code of Ethics, 20, 435, 452, 469–471
College Band Directors National Association, 390
Concepts, musical, 57–58
  learning of, 185–186
Conducting, unit on, 230–231
Contest, adjudication, 114–115
Convocations (*see* Assembly, school)
Cooper, Irvin, 207, 355–356
Copyright law, 287–288
"Coronation Scene" (from *Boris Godunov*), 330–331

Creating music, 463
  in general music class, 218–219
  in theory, 424–426
Creativity, musical, value of, 58
Credit for music study, 90–92
Cuisenaire rods, 185
Curriculum, music:
  balance, 68–69
  completeness of, 77
  courses, 68
  criteria for, 61–65
  for non-middle class students, 61–62
  nonperforming courses, 69–70
  outcomes in music, 53–61
  performing groups, 70–72
  relevance of, 64
  selection of, 63
  student needs, 43–44
  subject matter validity, 62–63
  unity of, 66–67

Dance band (*see* Stage band)
Dancing, in performances, 442
Democratic procedures, characteristics of,
    157–159, 161–162
Dewey, John, 36, 180
Diction, 347–350
Discipline:
  a
  democratic procedures in, 155–159
  handling serious problems, 168–170
  inability to participate, 159–160
  need for, 153
  penalty vs. punishment, 163
  private conference, 167
  removal of student from class, 169–170
  self-discipline, 153–154
  talking, 159
  teacher actions in, 164–167
  on tours, 452
Discovery method, 183
Distributed effort, 191–192
Domains of learning, 110–111
"Domine Jesu Christe, O" (Palestrina),
    448
Drill, 2
du Noüy, Lecomte, 36
Dykema, Peter, 40
Dynamics, teaching of, 304–307

Ear training:
  in music appreciation course, 409
  in theory course, 422–424
Ebbinghaus, Hermann, 188–189
Embouchure:
  brass, 382–383
  clarinet, 381
  double reed, 381–382
  flute, 382
  and intonation, 322
Enrollments in high school music,
    70, 467
Ensembles, small, 90
Equipment:
  care of, 99
  insurance on, 99

Ethos, doctrine of, 39
Evaluation:
  of attitudes, 117–118
  feedback, 108–109
  importance of, 7
  need for, 107–108
  of performance, 114–115
Expression (*see* Interpretation)

Falsetto voice, 351–352
Fauré, Gabriel, 226
Filing of music, 96–97
Financing:
  basis of requests, 94–95
  of music curriculum, 94–95
  of tours, 453–454
Fine arts:
  conditions for combining subjects,
    404–406
  course, 417–418
  teaching styles in, 226–227
  value of, 35–36
Folk music:
  and dances, unit on, 236
  English, unit on, 234
  general music unit on, 224–225
Forgetting (*see* Memory)
French horn, 393
Functional music, unit on, 229

Gehrkens, Karl, 40
General music, 199–239
  audiovisual aids in, 219–220
  craft projects in, 219
  creating music in, 218–219
  equipment and books, 220–221
  evaluating singing in, 206–207
  goals of, 201–204
  listening in, 217–218
  planning for, 221–222, 237–239
  singing in, 213–217, 227
  suggested units for, 222–237
Gestalt psychology, 187
Ginn, Edwin, 461
Gounod, Charles, on Franck's Symphony,
    66
Grading, 118–122
Graduation requirements, 91–92, 404
Guidance in music, 81–83

Homework in listening, 411
Humanities course (*see* Fine arts course)
Humming, 314

Individual instruction, 464
Inner-city:
  community, 22–23
  schools, 10
Improvisation, teaching of, 225–226
Instrumental music:
  beginning instruction, 369–378
  development of band, 284
  equipment and supplies, 394–396
  fundamentals of playing wind
    instruments, 379–385
  instrument repair, 399

Instrumental music (continued)
   instrumentation, 389–391
   marching band, 398–399
   organization of beginning classes,
     372–373
   percussion, 388–389
   physical qualifications for, 371
   stage band, 397–398
   strings, 385–388
   substitution of instruments, 393–394
   transfer of students to another
     instrument, 392–393
   types of scores, 396–397
Instruments:
   simple, unit on, 234
   unit on, 232
Insurance, 99
Interpretation:
   authenticity in, 296
   balance, 303–304
   deciding on, 293–297
   feeling and technique, 316
   humming, 314
   in learning music, 248
   legato, 309–310
   performance practices, 294–296
   personal judgment in, 296–297
   phrasing, 310–312
   staccato, 308–309
   of sustained sounds, 307–308
   teaching of, 297–316
   text in, 313
   of vocal music, 312
   vocal timbre, 313–314, 345–346
Intervals, in vocal music, 279
Intonation:
   choral, 329–334
   effect of dynamics on, 323–324, 327
   effect of tone production on, 322–323
   and environment, 324–325
   illusions, 319–320
   intervals, 331
   psychological factors on, 323–324
   string, 327–328
   students' lack of concept of, 321–322
   wind instruments, 325–327

Jazz, unit on, 225–226
Junior high school, 199

Kinesthetic learning (*see* Learning,
   psychomotor
Knowledge, effect on attitudes, 60
Kuhn, Wolfgang, 373
Kyme, George, 118

Langer, Susanne, 36
Lasker, Henry, 420–421, 424
Learning:
   affective, 194–195
   applications of principles to, 195–196
   cognitive, 180–190
   concentration in, 192
   conceptual, 185–186
   levels of difficulty in, 193–194
   memory, 187–189

Learning (continued)
   multisensory, 185
   need for aural experience in, 182–183
   need for involvement of students in,
     183–184
   need for understanding of purpose in,
     184–185
   psychomotor, 190–194
   transfer of, 189–190
   validity in, 181–182
   whole and part, 186–187
Leeder, Joseph A., 206–207
Legato, 309–310
Lincoln Portrait (Copland), 206
Listening:
   in appreciation course, 407–412
   in general music course, 217–218
   habits of not listening, 320–321
   by students, 254–255
   by teacher, 255–256
Literature, music (definition), 55–57
   (*see also* Music, selection of)
Locke, John, 180
Long, Newell H., 118
Lopez, Raymond, 62
Luh, C. W., 188–189

McKenzie, Duncan, 354–355
Mad magazine, 133, 156
Marching band, 76–77, 398–399
Mason, Lowell, 39, 460–461
Memorization, of vocal music, 364–366
Memory, 187–189
   in understanding music, 411–412
Mendez, Rafael, 379–380
Menotti, Gian-Carlo (*Amahl and the Night
   Visitors*), 210
Methods (*see* Teaching procedures)
Meyer, Leonard, 66
   "Some Remarks on Value and Greatness
     in Music," 475–479
Middle schools, 199
"Minstrel Boy, The," 214–216
Modes, and intonation, 330
Morale, group, 141–142
Motivation, 136–142
   extrinsic vs. intrinsic, 137–139
   techniques of, 138–141
Mueller, Kate (Hevner), 118
Music:
   in adult life, unit on, 236–237
   avocational value, 43
   definition of, 1
   ethnic, 132
   nonmusical value, 60
   as personal expression, unit on, 224–225
   popular, 210
   psychological value, 42
   scope of, 2
Music Achievement Test (Richard Colwell),
   113–114
Music Buildings, Rooms, and Equipment, 100
Music contests, value of, 24
Music curriculum (*see* Curriculum, music)
Music education profession (*see* Profession, music)

Music Educators National Conference, 20
  23, 461, 463
  Teacher Education Commission, 12–13,
    14–15
Music, evaluation of, 65–66, 475–479
Music in General Education, 202–204
Music Industry Council, 19
Music library, 96–97
Music rooms, 99–100
Music, selection of, 55–56, 275–286
  instrumental music, 282–285
  listings and sources of, 286–287
  program requirements, 285–286
  variety in, 464
  vocal, 276–282
Music teacher (*see* Teacher, music)
Musical aptitude (*see* Aptitude, music)
Musical Aptitude Profile (Edwin Gordon), 85
Musical comedy, unit on, 234–236
Musicians, contemporary, unit on, 232–233
Mussorgsky, Modeste, 212

National Association of Schools of Music,
  14
National Education Association, 465
National Interscholastic Music Activities
    Commission, 114
  adjudication forms of, 298, 487–489
Nonperforming classes, 403–404

Observable behaviors, 7, 107, 109–110
Ohio Code of Ethics with Music Mer-
    chants, 473–474
Ohio Music Education Association, 21
Opera, unit on, 234–236
Orchestra (*see also* Instrumental music):
  arrangements for, 285
  need for, 75–76
  scheduling winds into, 88–90

Parent-teacher relationship, 21, 140, 395–
  396
Parents' organizations, 95–96
Percussion, 388–389
Performances:
  adjusting to conditions, 436–438
  behavior of performers, 438
  business aspects, 446–451
  Code of Ethics for, 435
  effect of audience reaction, 142
  enhancement of programs, 439–446
  guidelines for, 430–432
  informal, 434
  length of, 439
  outside of school, 435–436
  planning checklist, 455–456
  programs, 447–449
  publicity, 450–451
  reasons for, 429–430
  scenery in, 443
  staging instrumental programs, 445–446
  staging vocal programs, 440–445
  tickets, 449–450
  value of, 430
Performing organizations:
  group morale in, 141–142
  homework, 257–258

Performing organizations (continued)
  marching band, 76–77
  name of, 361
  need for orchestra, 75–76
  need for variety in, 70–72, 74–75
  rehearsal enrichment, 72–74
  seating of instrumental groups, 390–391
  size and seating, 361–362
  teaching musical understanding in,
    269–275
Performing Music with Understanding (Hof-
    fer and Anderson), 23, 253, 270, 359
Penfield, Wilder, 183
Personality (*see* Teacher, music)
Pestalozzi, Johann Heinrich, 182, 461
Phrasing, 310–312
Piano:
  in orchestra, 285
  in teaching songs, 213
  in vocal music, 363–364
Planning:
  of course content, 67–68
  individual lessons, 237–239
  for performances, 432–439
  in performing classes, 243–245
  for tour, 452–453
  unit plan, 221–222
Plato, 39
Popular music:
  compared with art music, 413–414
  Rock unit, 223–224
Posture, for singing, 340–341
Practice, individual, 377–378
Praise, effect of, 143
Pre-band instruments, 369–370
Private study, credit for, 92
Profession, music teaching:
  character of, 1, 459–460
  current issues, 461–465
  fads and improvements, 465–466
  future of, 466–468
  history of, 70–71, 460–461
  teacher supply and demand, 467
  teacher's involvement in, 459
Programs, printed, 447–449
Pronunciation of foreign languages, 315
Psychology, 187
Publicity, 46, 450–451

Range:
  for male singers, 351–352
  for changing voices, 354–355
  psychological factors of, 346–347
Reading, music, 262–269
  counting systems, 265–267
  functional, 264–265
  pitch, 267–269
  solfa syllables in, 268
  systems of, 263–264
  unit on, 229–230
  vocal contrasted with instrumental, 263
Recording:
  for evaluation, 116
  in hearing blend, 303
  as motivation, 141
  rehearsal playback, 26
Recordings, as aid to listening, 256

Recruiting, 145–149
Rehearsal procedures (*see* Teaching
    procedures)
Relevancy, 64, 209–210, 462
Reliability, test, 84
Religious music:
    handling objections to, 157–158
    unit on, 224
    use in public schools, 158
Renting equipment, 98
Repair of instruments, 399
Resonance in singing, 343–344
Rhythm:
    in beginning instrumental classes, 377
    counting systems, 265–267
    in interpretation, 298–300
    unit on, 228
Richardson, John Adkins, 466
Righter, Charles, 387–388
Rock music, unit on, 223–224
Roe, Paul, 343
Rote procedures:
    in beginning instrumental music, 375–
        376
    in teaching rhythm, 300–301

SAB arrangements, 280
Scheduling, 87–90
Scheduling Music Classes, 88
Schopenhauer, Arthur, 36
Scores, simplified for listening, 410–411
Seashore, Carl, 321
Seashore Measures of Musical Talents (Carl
    E. Seashore), 84–85
Seating, for performances, 437
"Semper Fidelis" (John Phillip Sousa),
    teaching of, 245–247
S.P.E.B.S.Q.S.A., Inc., 148
Singing, in school assembly, 434
Singing methods (*see* Teaching pro-
    cedures; *see also* Voice production)
Skills (*see* Learning, psychomotor)
Small ensembles, scheduling of, 90
"Soon Ah Will Be Done" (William
    Dawson), 447–448
Spaced practice, 191–192
Staccato, 308–309
Stage band, 397–398
Stanislavsky, Constantine, 316
Stein, Keith, 379
Strang, Ruth, 134
Student teaching, 17–18
Students:
    and/or subject, 43–44
    attitude toward new music, 211–212
    course load, 86–87
    and curriculum, 43–44
    effect on music selected, 276
    grading, 118–122
    guidance, 81–83
    guidance of in instrumental music, 370–
        372
    meeting individual needs of, 253
    personal development, 41–42
    reaching of minority students, 463
    roles in program preparation, 441
    self-evaluation, 122

Summer music study, 93–94
Supreme Court, 158
Swanson, Frederick, 353–354
Symphony in B Minor (Schubert), 448
Syntax, musical, 54

Talent (*see* Aptitude, musical)
Tape recording (*see* Recording)
*Taxonomy of Educational Goals, Handbook
    I: The Cognitive Domain* (Bloom, et al.),
    113
Transcriptions:
    in development of band, 284
    value of, 274
Teacher Education Commission (*see* Music
    Educators National Conference)
Teacher, music:
    attitude, 142–145
    attitude toward discipline, 163–164
    attitude toward performance, 432
    and community, 19–20
    and curriculum, 53
    and educational goals, 44–46
    of general music, 204–205
    growth of, 23–24
    knowledge of procedures, 17
    need for objective listening, 255–256
    need for philosophy, 3–4, 33–35
    need for realistic goals, 178–179
    and new ideas, 465–466
    personal efficiency, 19
    personality, 9–13
    preparation, 13–16
    preparation of score, 396–397
    and professional musicians, 20
    and public relations, 45–46
    qualities of, 1, 132–134
    relationship with colleagues, 19, 454
    relationship with disadvantaged stu-
        dents, 131
    relationship with music merchants,
        20–21
    relationship with private teachers, 21
    relationship with school administrators,
        46, 145
    relationship with students, 5, 22–23,
        143–144
    and research, 23–24
    role in adolescent adjustment, 132–134
    role of, 3
    self-evaluation, 24–26
    supplementary employment, 26–27
    teacher rating form, 25–26, 481–485
    understanding of students, 135–136
Teaching procedures:
    for aesthetic qualities, 38–39
    awareness of other parts, 255
    balance, 303–304
    beginning instrumental music, 374–
        377
    blend, 300–303
    boy's changing voice, 356–358
    breath support, 379–380
    choral intonation, 332–334
    choral music, 248–250
    choral tone, 345–346
    concept of intuneness, 321–322

Teaching procedures (continued)
  creating music, 218–219, 424–426
  drill, 2
  dynamics, 304–307
  ear training in theory course, 422–423
  efficiency in, 250, 258, 261–262
  entrances, 251
  guidelines for general music, 205–213
  handling discipline, 155
  harmony in general music course,
      208–209
  hearing individuals, 252
  high notes for boys, 351–352
  improvisation, 225–226
  individual attention, 257
  instrumental intonation, 328–329
  instrumental music, 245–248
  interpretation, 297–316
  intonation, 325–326
  introduction of new work in
      appreciation course, 415
  involvement of students, 211
  isolating difficulties, 251–252
  keeping students occupied, 252–253
  legato, 309–310
  listening in appreciation course,
      408–412
  memorization, 364–366
  motivation, 138–141
  music reading, 262–269
  for music understanding, 245
  for music understanding in performing
      group, 269–275
  musical qualities, 212
  musical styles, 414–415
  opera in general music course, 235
  phrasing, 310–312
  and relevancy, 462
  review, 253
  rehearsal procedures, 258–261
  rhythmic interpretation, 298–300
  role of, 6
  singing, 337–338, 344
  songs in general music course, 213–217
  staccato, 308–309
  string instruments, 385–388
  student listening groups, 254–255
  use of audiovisual aids, 219–220
  wind instrument embouchure, 380–383
Teaching process:
  aspects of, 3–8
  definition of, 2–3
  ingredients of, 3
  relationship of aspects, 8
Team teaching, in fine arts course, 405
Teenagers (*see* Adolescents)
Tempo, and intonation, 329–330
Tenor part:
  clefs for, 363
  developing upper range, 351–352
  in selecting music, 278
Tessitura, and intonation, 329
Test of Musicality (E. Thayer Gaston), 86
Testing:
  in music appreciation course, 415–416
  of musical performance, 487–489
  use of tape recorder in, 116

Tests:
  achievement, 113–114
  cognitive, 111–114
  musical aptitude, 83–86
  of performing skill, 115
  teacher-made aptitude, 371
Tetrachord method, 460
Text:
  and interpretation, 313
  in selecting music, 276–278
Theory course, 418–426
  content, 419–421
  creative work, 424–426
  ear training, 422–424
  keyboard, 421
Thinking, musical, 57–58
Throat, in singing, 342–343
Tickets, 449–450
Timbre:
  and intonation, 320
  vocal, 313–314
Tonguing, 383–385
Tours, 451–455
Tufts, John, 460
Tuning (*see* Intonation)

Uniforms, 97–98

Validity, test, 84
Vandre, Carl, 230
Vibrato:
  effect on intonation, 328
  on strings, 387–388
Virtuoso music, unit on, 227–228
Voice:
  changed, 216–217
  changing, 134–135, 353–358
  classifying, 358–361
  falsetto, 351–352
  unit on voice change, 227
Voice production:
  and diction, 348–350
  disagreement on, 338–339
  nonphysical aspects, 344–345
  physical actions for, 339–344
Voice quality:
  boys, 352
  girls, 350
Vocal techniques:
  humming, 314
  runs, 314–315
  "scooping," 323
  and tone color, 313–314
Vowels:
  and diction, 348–349
  and intonation, 323

Waller, Gilbert, 388
Warm-up, 244
Watkins-Farnum Performance Scale, 115
Whole and part learning, 186–187
Wilson, Harry R., 348
*Wing Standardized Test of Musical
    Intelligence* (H. D. Wing), 85–86

Young Audiences, Inc., 20